Buddhism for Today

Nikkyō Niwano

BUDDHISM

A MODERN INTERPRETATION

FOR TODAY

OF THE THREEFOLD LOTUS SUTRA

KOSEI PUBLISHING CO. • *Tokyo*

The many passages from the Threefold Lotus Sutra quoted or paraphrased in this book are from *The Threefold Lotus Sutra,* translated by Bunnō Katō, Yoshirō Tamura, and Kōjirō Miyasaka, with revisions by W. E. Soothill, Wilhelm Schiffer, and Pier P. Del Campana, © 1971, 1974, 1975 by Risshō Kōsei-kai and published in 1975 by John Weatherhill, Inc., New York and Tokyo, and Kōsei Publishing Company, Tokyo. With the permission of Risshō Kōsei-kai, for this book brackets have been removed and Sanskrit words have been italicized. Occasionally, some quotations have been slightly modified in order to increase their clarity. This book is set in Monotype Bembo, with handset Bernhard Modern for display.

Translation by Kōjirō Miyasaka.

The publisher would like to thank Suzanne Trumbull for editorial assistance, and Rebecca Davis for typography and book design.

First edition, 1976
Ninth printing, 2011

Published by Kōsei Publishing Co., Kōsei Building, 2-7-1 Wada, Suginami-ku, Tokyo 166-8535, Japan. Printed in Japan.

ISBN 978-4-333-00270-2 LCC Card No. 79-375603

Contents

PART THREE: THE SUTRA OF MEDITATION ON THE BODHISATTVA UNIVERSAL VIRTUE

Preface

THE TEACHINGS OF BUDDHISM are considered very difficult to understand. One of the main reasons for this may be that the Buddhist sutras are difficult to understand. This is only natural, because the sutras were first written in Indian languages, such as Sanskrit and Pāli, about two thousand years ago; after being introduced into China, they were translated into Chinese, and these Chinese versions of the sutras were transmitted from China to Japan.

It is the generally accepted opinion that of the many Buddhist sutras, the Sutra of the Lotus Flower of the Wonderful Law (*Saddharma-puṇḍarīka-sūtra*), commonly known as the Lotus Sutra, is the most excellent. But reading this and other sutras in translation, we are confronted with many unfamiliar or exotic words, which give the reader the impression of a stiff sobriety. Most commentaries on the sutras give us only interpretations that adhere narrowly to the literal meaning of the original.

The Lotus Sutra also seems mysterious and far removed from our real lives because it presents fantastic stories and scenes of visionary worlds, while it also includes a number of philosophical terms full of hidden meanings. For this reason, most people give up the sutra in despair as too deep for them to understand, while some dismiss it altogether because, they think, it discusses matters that are not appropriate to our lives today.

However, the Lotus Sutra was not so difficult at the time that Sakyamuni Buddha preached it. Through his divine inspiration he did not speak of matters so mysterious as to be incomprehensible to the general public, nor did he impose private, esoteric views upon others. For a long time he pondered the problems of this world, of man, of how man should live in this world, and of human relationships, and finally he attained the knowledge of the universal truth that is applicable to every time, every place, and every person. The truth that applies to every time, every place, and every person cannot be so difficult that people do not understand it. For example, it is easy for everybody to understand the fact that one divided by three gives one-third. This truth is quite different from such irrational and yet widely held beliefs as sure recovery from illness by worshiping a particular object.

However, we cannot realize the truth that one divided by three gives one-third until we are old enough to understand it. Dr. Yōichi Yoshida, professor of Rikkyō University in Tokyo and a famous mathematician, recalls in his book, a collection of essays on mathematics, that studying decimal arithmetic in the third or fourth year of primary school, he encountered indefinitely indivisible calculations, such as that one divided by three gives 0.3333. . . . However, he could fold a piece of paper into three exactly equal parts. But he did not know why this was so. As he wanted to be a mathematician, Yoshida seriously pondered why one could not be divided by three by calculation, but could be divided in practice. When he was in the fifth or sixth grade, he was taught fractions and realized that the fractional number "one-third" provided a new way of looking at this problem. Somehow he felt he was being tricked when he was taught that the fractional number "one-third" was an answer to the problem of dividing one by three by calculation. However, he was very interested in fractions and tried hard to consider "one-third" as a number. Eventually he was able to understand why it was no miracle to be able actually to fold a piece of paper into three equal parts.

We can say the same thing of the teachings of the Buddha. Although in principle these teachings should be understandable to everybody, one cannot understand them even partially until he attains a certain degree of spiritual maturity. In studying mathematics, it would appear to be a good idea to teach schoolchildren about fractions at an early age. But teachers first teach whole numbers—one, two, three, and so on—and then proceed to fractional numbers because children in the first or second grade cannot understand fractions without this foundation.

In practice, teachers also teach children fractions like one-third, for example, by folding a piece of paper into three instead of by trying to explain the theory of fractions.

So Sakyamuni preached in various ways to the people of his day according to their power and level of understanding. He discoursed with them by various methods of reasoning and in parables so that the people of his time might be able to understand his teachings. Some people notice only the surface appearance of the Lotus Sutra and what it seems to express, and they think that they cannot possibly believe in the sutra because it discusses fantastic worlds that do not actually exist. Such considerations are superficial indeed in the case of the Lotus Sutra. If people realized the true spirit of the sutra, they could not help realizing that the sutra is filled with modern, scientific, and humanistic truths.

The people of Sakyamuni's day found it easy to understand his teachings. Because of this the Buddha's teachings caused a wonderful change in peoples' lives. If this had not been true, so many people could not have devoted themselves to his teachings after his short active life of fifty years. Moreover, it is said that the community of Sakyamuni had such a free atmosphere that "those who came were welcome; those who went away were not regretted." As shown in the case of the five thousand monks who left the assembly, recounted in chapter 2 of the Lotus Sutra, "Tactfulness," Sakyamuni did not try to persuade the five thousand conceited monks to stay in the assembly when he was about to preach the Lotus Sutra and so they left, saying that since they had already attained enlightenment it was not necessary for them to listen to the sutra. In spite of the fact that he forced people neither to come to hear him preach nor to stay on, followers of Sakyamuni's teachings rapidly increased to tens of thousands of people. This was undoubtedly due to Sakyamuni's incomparable power of inspiration and persuasion. But this power in turn was due to the fact that his teachings themselves were both valuable and easily understood.

However, Sakyamuni's liberal attitudes caused his disciples to be troubled with difficulties for a time after his death. The reason was his last words to his disciples. To them he said only, "All phenomena are always changing. Endeavor to practice Buddhism without negligence." He told them nothing about who should manage his community of believers or how. His surviving disciples naturally formed regional groups and observed his teachings. However, since they did not exercise any doctrinal control over Sakyamuni's teachings, there were differences of understanding among the various groups and regions of the vast country of India.

The basic problem was that Sakyamuni's teachings were correctly interpreted in the areas that he had visited often in order to teach, but in districts where the people had had no chance to hear his preaching directly and his teachings were only transmitted secondhand, the teachings were considerably changed according to the personal ideas that the various preachers added to the Buddha's teachings. Similar additions to the Buddha's teachings took place as time passed following Sakyamuni's death. The history of Buddhism shows that Sakyamuni's teachings were useful and vital during his lifetime and for some time after his death. But as time went on, the true spirit of his teachings was lost and only their form was preserved.

It was mentioned above that Sakyamuni's liberal attitudes caused his disciples difficulties for a time after his death. This "time after his death" is not limited to the first century or two following Sakyamuni's death but includes the present time, some twenty-five hundred years later. From the standpoint of the history of the human race, two thousand five hundred years is only a short time. In Japan, Buddhism, which was introduced from China, had a strong power for a time whenever a learned or distinguished priest appeared. But after a short time this power declined quickly. The thirteenth-century priest Nichiren, the founder of the Nichiren sect, for example, is believed to have infused new life into Japanese Buddhism. However, following his death, the teachings diverged from his true intention and degenerated into formalism.

In India, soon after the death of Sakyamuni the interpretation of his teachings began to differ in each region and in each group of disciples. Buddhist monks tried to establish their authority by practicing and preaching a way of life that is impossible for Buddhist laymen. As we can see in the Lotus Sutra, while Sakyamuni lived *bhikshus* (monks), *bhikshuṇīs* (nuns), *upāsakas* (male lay devotees), and *upāsikās* (female lay devotees) listened to the Buddha's preaching, practiced his teachings, and endeavored to spread the Law in harmony with one another. However, after the Buddha's death a gulf opened between monks and lay devotees before either group was aware of it.

This continually widening gap came about because some monks attached much more importance to the formalities of keeping the precepts than to the fundamental spirit of why the precepts should be kept. There were also monks who intentionally made Sakyamuni's originally pragmatic teachings into a very difficult philosophy in order to oppose other teachings and philosophies existing in India at that time.

On the other hand, some people developed selfish ideas, insisting that despite what Sakyamuni had said, it was impossible for all people to attain the same degree of enlightenment as the Buddha. It is quite impossible for us to become as great as the Buddha, they maintained. We need only free ourselves from the bonds of illusion and suffering in this world.

Seeing that Buddhism was thus being diverted from its true spirit and losing its power, lay believers in particular had the ardent desire to restore Sakyamuni's true spirit to the teachings. Thus a new Buddhist group appeared. People of this group called their Buddhism *Mahāyāna,* that is, the "great vehicle" to convey us to the world of the Buddha, and deprecated the established Buddhism as *Hīnayāna,* the "lesser vehicle." Monks of the older groups retorted: "It is *your* Buddhism that is false." Consequently, a strong clash occurred between the new and the old.

The Lotus Sutra appeared under these circumstances, as an effort to unite Buddhism in one vehicle. This sutra stresses that in Buddhism there is only one vehicle (*ekayāna*), to be followed equally by all people, and that the ultimate object of Sakyamuni's teachings is to bring all people to this vehicle.

The Lotus Sutra is thought to have been recorded about seven hundred years after the death of Sakyamuni Buddha. I see a deep meaning in the fact that the changes in Buddhism during its first seven hundred years established a pattern of change that has been followed throughout its long history. In the twentieth century, when Buddhism has adhered too much to form and has lost the power to save people, a religious movement has again arisen among lay devotees to restore Buddhism to Sakyamuni's true teachings and by the efforts of these lay believers is now spreading throughout Japan.

This new movement to reevaluate the Buddha's teachings has been spreading throughout the world, not only in Japan. In Western countries, there are many people who are unsatisfied with monotheism, atheism, or materialism and finally seek the solution to their problems in Buddhism. I hear that Buddhism has been made the principle of a new system of ethics even in the People's Republic of China, a communist country.

This is a most important period. We face the danger of the sudden annihilation of mankind unless man now comes to a new appreciation of human dignity by realizing the Buddha's teachings and returning to a way of life that helps others as well as himself to live.

I regret greatly that the Lotus Sutra, which includes the supreme teachings of the Buddha, appears to be so difficult and that it is studied by only a limited number of people and by specialists in religion. The Lotus Sutra is neither truly appreciated nor understood by people in general, and therefore it does not penetrate people's daily lives. This is the first reason for my decision to write this book. My earnest desire is to explain the Lotus Sutra so that its spirit can be understood by modern people and gain their sympathy, although I have remained faithful to the original intent of the sutra to the last.

We cannot truly understand the Lotus Sutra by reading only part of it. It is both a profound teaching and a wonderful work of art, unfolding like a drama. Therefore, we cannot grasp its true meaning unless we read it through from beginning to end. However, it is not easy to read the sutra, with its difficult and unfamiliar terminology, from cover to cover, and to grasp its meaning. We need a commentary that will help us understand the sutra in the context of our lives today. This is the second reason for my decision to write this book.

At the same time, we must always honor the original intent of the Lotus Sutra, as it is a noble work of art. Even in translation we find in the sutra an indescribable power that permeates our hearts. I think that readers will be able to understand the Lotus Sutra all the more if they consult it while reading this book. I believe, too, that they will be able to sense something of the spirit of the Lotus Sutra from this book.

If readers who understand the spirit of the sutra recite key portions morning and evening, its spirit will become more and more strongly rooted in the depths of their minds, and will surely be manifested in the conduct of their daily lives so that a new life will open before them. In this hope and belief I have written this book.

Introduction

FORMATION AND PROPAGATION OF THE LOTUS SUTRA. In the Preface I have mentioned briefly how the Lotus Sutra came to be written, but I will now give a more detailed description of the process that eventually brought the sutra to Japan.

In Sakyamuni's time there was no widespread writing system in India. Therefore his sermons were memorized and spread by word of mouth. At that time, when people were obliged to learn by heart whatever they wished to remember, they had powers of memory beyond our imagining. People's daily lives were also less complicated and bustling than they are today. The great disciples of the Buddha, who had clear heads and pure minds, listened attentively so as to absorb every word spoken by Sakyamuni. Therefore, it is almost certain that they did not mishear Sakyamuni's sermons. Moreover, after the death of the Buddha, his disciples held frequent conferences in order to see whether their memories were mistaken or not. After verifying the Buddha's actual words and correcting each other's mistakes, they systematized their ideas. For this reason Sakyamuni's words have remained correct in spite of their being transmitted by word of mouth.

Sakyamuni preached many sermons during his frequent travels on foot in the vast area of northern India over a period of fifty years. He also preached in various ways, according to his audience's level of understanding. We must acknowledge the fact that the interpretation of the Buddha's teachings differed from place to place and from group to group of his disciples, and that as time passed there grew up differences in the understanding and preaching of his teachings. However, Sakyamuni's teachings themselves were accurately transmitted through the efforts of his disciples. There is no sutra that is not holy. The teachings of Sakyamuni have been recorded in the Āgama sutras, the Prajñāpāramitā sutra, the Amitābha sutras, and many others. But only in the Lotus Sutra was the fundamental spirit of all Sakyamuni's teachings during his active life clearly expressed for the first time; in this sutra the important spirit of all his teachings has been unified and described in easily understood terms. In other words, in the Lotus Sutra the essentials of Buddhism, the very core of Sakyamuni's teachings, are explained exhaustively in simple yet powerful words.

Some people argue over the relative merits of various sutras and even harbor the illusion that the comparative merits of the sutras stem from differences in Sakyamuni's teachings. This is a serious mistake. No sutra was compiled by Sakyamuni himself. The fact is that he preached his numerous sermons to countless people during the fifty years between his first sermon to the five monks at the Deer Park in Vārāṇasī (Benares) and his death at eighty years of age. From among these many sermons each group of disciples and their followers placed in their own sutras the sermons that they had heard directly or had been taught by others. Through whatever sutra we may study the teachings of Sakyamuni, Sakyamuni himself is the same honored one who casts the same light of wisdom on us. Therefore, although the Lotus Sutra is certainly the most excellent teaching among the many sutras, it reflects a basic misunderstanding to despise other sutras by excessively extolling the Lotus Sutra.

SYMBOLIC EXPRESSION IN THE LOTUS SUTRA. The Lotus Sutra was compiled in the form of a drama so that the general public at that time could easily understand it. The compilers of the sutra endeavored to help people grasp it by representing intangible ideas in tangible form. For example, in chapter 1 of the Lotus Sutra, "Introductory," it is said that when the ray sent forth from the Buddha's brow illuminated the eastern quarter of the eighteen thousand buddha-lands, all the buddhas and their disciples were seen to be existing everywhere. This expression means that the Buddha is in every heavenly body as well as on the earth, that is, he exists everywhere throughout the entire universe.

Such descriptions as the shaking of the earth and the raining down of flowers belong this type of expression. Today we often encounter expressions like "I was so scared that my blood ran cold" or "I was convulsed with laughter." Nobody takes such expressions literally. But even if they are not factually true, they serve to communicate graphically and effectively the true feeling of the speaker or writer. This point offers us a key to understanding the Lotus Sutra. The important point is not "fact" but "truth," the truth of the Buddha's teaching. Even if in the Lotus Sutra we encounter things that seem to be unreal, we must firmly grasp the truth behind the surface of the words.

KUMĀRAJĪVA'S TRANSLATION INTO CHINESE. A number of people took the Lotus Sutra to China and translated it into Chinese, but the version in common use in East Asia today is the translation made by Kumārajīva. His father, Kumārāyāna, who came of a noble family in India, went to Kucha, a country situated in Central Asia, between India and China, and married the sister of the king of that country. Their son, born in 344, was Kumārajīva. Buddhism was flourishing in Kucha, and Kumārajīva entered a monastery at the age of seven together with his mother, then was sent to India to study Mahāyāna Buddhism.

It is said that when he returned to his home country his teacher, Sūryasoma, who discerned Kumārajīva's ability and character, taught him the *Saddharma-puṇḍarīka-sūtra* (the Sutra of the Lotus Flower of the Wonderful Law), and then said to Kumārajīva, laying his right hand on Kumārajīva's head, "The sun of the Buddha has set in the west, and its remaining radiance is about to reach the east. This sutra has a connection with the northeast. Reverently propagate the sutra there."

Thinking back now to Sūryasoma's words, "This sutra has a connection with the northeast," we realize that his prophecy had a very profound meaning, and we cannot help being moved by the realization that in later times Buddhism reached its greatest florescence in Japan, a country located far to the northeast of India.

In obedience to his teacher's word, Kumārajīva determined to propagate the Lotus Sutra in China, to the northeast. But as wars were common in China at that time and boundaries and nations were constantly changing, his plan could not be realized as easily as he had hoped. However, his fame as a translator spread throughout China, and in 401 he went to live in Ch'ang-an, capital of the Latter Ch'in dynasty, on the invitation of the king. Kumārajīva, who was already sixty-two years old at that time, was named National Preceptor, and for eight years, until he died in 413 at the age of seventy, he translated many sutras into Chinese.

Needless to say, the Lotus Sutra was the most important among the many sutras he translated. As he had found many mistakes in the Chinese translations that he had seen, he took a very prudent attitude toward his own work of translation. Although he had a good command of both Sanskrit and Chinese, he did not attempt to render Buddhist sutras into Chinese alone but assembled many scholars who were proficient in both languages. Moreover, he lectured on the Lotus Sutra in the presence of the king and others. Based on the notes that the scholars made from his lectures, each made a Chinese translation of the Lotus Sutra. After each scholar had completed his own translation and all had rigorously examined and discussed it, they finally completed a standard translation of the sutra. It is said that as many as two thousand men were engaged in this work. Therefore we may safely conclude that in Kumārajīva's translation of the Lotus Sutra from Sanskrit into Chinese, the teachings of Sakyamuni were transmitted almost without error.

The following story has been told concerning Kumārajīva's translation. The king of Yao Ch'in, who deeply respected the personality and ability of Kumārajīva, very much wanted him to have a child. So the king forced him to marry. On his death bed Kumārajīva remarked, "I was compelled to break the precepts by taking a wife, but I believe that what I have stated in words has never gone against the intention of the Buddha. If I have been honest in what I have said, my tongue alone will remain unburned when my body is cremated." It is said that when his family cremated his body his tongue alone did indeed remain unconsumed, emitting a brilliant light.

The Lotus Sutra subsequently played a very important part in Chinese Buddhism. After Chih-i,[1] who was revered as the "Little Sakyamuni," had made an exhaustive study of all the sutras of Mahāyāna and Hīnayāna Buddhism, he concluded that the true intention of the Buddha was included in the Lotus Sutra, and he wrote the excellent commentaries on the Lotus Sutra *Hokke-gengi*,[2] *Hokke-mongu*,[3] and *Makashikan*.[4]

1. Chih-i (538–97) is the third patriarch in the lineage of the Chinese T'ien-t'ai (Japanese: Tendai) sect.

2. *Hokke-gengi* is a ten- or twenty-fascicle work, the full title of which is *Myōhō Renge-kyō Gengi*, composed by Chih-i and written down by Kuan-ting in the Sui dynasty (581–618). In this work the title of the Lotus Sutra is explained in detail and the profound teaching of the sutra is briefly explained through its title.

3. *Hokke-mongu* is a ten- or twenty-fascicle commentary on the Lotus Sutra, the full title of which is *Myōhō Renge-kyō Mongu*, composed by Chih-i and written down by Kuan-ting.

4. *Makashikan* is a twenty-fascicle work explaining the various aspects of meditation

Consequently the Lotus Sutra spread still more widely throughout China, and soon it was introduced into Japan through Korea.

THE LOTUS SUTRA IN JAPAN. It was in 577 that the Lotus Sutra as translated by Kumārajīva was taken to Naniwa (present-day Osaka) in Japan, and thirty-eight years later the *Hokke-gisho*,[5] the first Japanese commentary on the Lotus Sutra, was written by the prince-regent Shōtoku (574–622). This is said to be the oldest extant book written by a Japanese.

Prince Shōtoku promulgated the code known as the Seventeen-Article Constitution, based on the spirit of the Lotus Sutra, and through this constitution the prince established the first law code in Japan. It is highly significant that the dawn of civilization in Japan was realized through applying the spirit of the Lotus Sutra. For fourteen hundred years since then, this spirit has been continuously transmitted from generation to generation among the Japanese people.

Many famous Buddhist priests in Japan endeavored to propagate the teaching of the Lotus Sutra, among them Saichō,[6] Dōgen,[7] and Nichiren.[8] Nichiren, especially, infused new life into this sutra at the risk of his life and exerted himself to propagate the sutra among the common people.

Almost seven hundred years have passed since Nichiren's death in 1282. The teachings of Sakyamuni had gradually lost their power after

---

from the standpoint of the T'en-t'ai sect. It is considered one of the three major works of T'ien-t'ai Buddhism.

5. *Hokke-gisho* is a four-fascicle commentary on the Lotus Sutra. Though it is based on the *Hokke-giki* written by the Chinese Fa-yün, this work also contains many unique explanations and opinions. The manuscript written by the prince himself is extant.

6. Saichō (767–822) was the founder of the Japanese Tendai (T'ien-t'ai) sect. In 804 he was sent by imperial order to China, where he studied the T'en-t'ai doctrines. After returning to Japan, he applied for government recognition of the Tendai sect. In 806 he was given the honorary title Dengyō-daishi by the emperor. This was the first instance of the use of the title *daishi*, "great teacher," in Japan.

7. Dōgen (1200–1253) was the founder of the Sōtō sect of Zen Buddhism in Japan. After entering the priesthood on Mount Hiei, near Kyoto, he became a disciple of the Rinzai Zen master Eisai. He studied in China for seven years. After his return to Japan he lived for a time near Kyoto, later establishing the great Sōtō Zen monastery of Eihei-ji in what is now Fukui Prefecture. He wrote several important works on Zen, including the monumental *Shōbō-genzō*.

8. Nichiren (1222–82) was the founder of the Japanese sect that bears his name. In 1253 he proclaimed that one should invoke the title of the Lotus Sutra with the formula *Namu Myōhō Renge-kyō*. During his active propagation of the Lotus Sutra he suffered much persecution, including exile. His works include a very important commentary on the Lotus Sutra.

his death, but they regained their vigor through the appearance of the Lotus Sutra seven hundred years later. Interestingly enough, the same thing occurred during the seven hundred years between the death of Prince Shōtoku and Nichiren's appearance. However, during the seven hundred years following Nichiren's death, the true spirit of the Lotus Sutra was again forgotten. Some people in Japan even believe that they can be saved merely by beating hand drums and repeating over and over again the formula including the title of the Lotus Sutra, *Namu Myōhō Renge-kyō*—I take refuge in the Sutra of the Lotus Flower of the Wonderful Law—or that their prayers will be answered if they only worship the verbal mandala written by Nichiren, which centers on this formula.

The contents and spirit of the Lotus Sutra are very holy. The practice of its teaching is also holy. We lead ordinary everyday lives, but by understanding the teaching of the sutra, believing it, and practicing it, we try to approach a state of mind free from illusion and suffering. We realize that people should live in harmony and render service to each other. If one has such a feeling for even a few hours a day, his health and circumstances will naturally change for the better—this is his true salvation. That all the people in the world have such feelings and live happily—this is the ultimate idea and vow expressed in the Lotus Sutra.

Indeed, the Lotus Sutra is the teaching of human respect, self-perfection, and peace. In short, it is the teaching of humanism. Today, just seven hundred years after the death of Nichiren, we must restore the spirit of the Lotus Sutra and establish a better life for the sake of ourselves, our families, our societies, and the entire world.

ORGANIZATION OF THE THREEFOLD LOTUS SUTRA. The Threefold Lotus Sutra, or *Hokke Sambu-kyō*, consists of the Sutra of Innumerable Meanings (*Muryōgi-kyō*); the Sutra of the Lotus Flower of the Wonderful Law (*Myōhō Renge-kyō*), commonly known as the Lotus Sutra; and the Sutra of Meditation on the Bodhisattva Universal Virtue (*Kan-fugen-bōsatsu-gyōbō-kyō*, or simply *Kan-fugen-gyō*).

THE SUTRA OF INNUMERABLE MEANINGS. Of the three sutras mentioned above, the Sutra of Innumerable Meanings contains the sermon Sakyamuni delivered on the Vulture Peak (Mount Gṛdhrakūṭa) immediately before preaching the Lotus Sutra. The Sutra of Innumerable Meanings, which is inseparable from the Lotus Sutra, is regarded as the introduction to the latter. This is because in the Sutra of Innumerable Meanings Sakyamuni states the reasons for the aims and the order of his preaching during the past forty years and also says that he has not yet manifested the truth. This does not mean that so far he had preached untruth but that he had not yet revealed the final truth, although all of his previous sermons were true. In other words, he had not yet manifested the full profundity of his teaching, being afraid that people would not be able to grasp it because their understanding and faith were not sufficiently developed. Therefore he made an important promise concerning his next sermon: "I am now to reveal the real truth." His next sermon was the Lotus Sutra. For this reason, if we do not read the Sutra of Innumerable Meanings we cannot realize clearly either the position of the Lotus Sutra among all the sermons that Sakyamuni preached during his lifetime or the true sacredness of the Lotus Sutra.

The title of the sutra, "Innumerable Meanings," expresses the idea of a teaching having infinite meanings. It is said in this sutra that the innumerable meanings originate from one law. This one law is that of "nonform." But Sakyamuni did not explain this law in detail here, so its meaning cannot be understood clearly through this sutra. He expounded it thoroughly in the Lotus Sutra, which he preached next. There he made clear that the teaching of the infinite meanings was ultimately attributable to the truth preached in the Lotus Sutra, which was the most important of the sermons delivered during his lifetime.

In short, the Sutra of Innumerable Meanings was preached as the introduction of the Lotus Sutra and therefore has a close connection with the latter, being called the "opening sutra" (*kaikyō*) of the Lotus Sutra. The Sutra of Innumerable Meanings consists of three chapters: "Virtues" (*Tokugyō-hon*), "Preaching" (*Seppō-hon*), and "Ten Merits" (*Jūkudoku-hon*). Chapter 1 is called the "introductory part" (*jobun*), chapter 2 the "main part" (*shōshūbun*), and chapter 3 the "concluding part" (*ruzūbun*). This tripartite division is common to other sutras, as well. The introductory part of a sutra expounds when, where, and for what kind of people the sutra was preached and why it had to be preached or what meaning it contained. The main part is the section including the main subject of the sutra, and is thus the most important of the three parts. The concluding part expresses what merit one can obtain through understanding thoroughly what is preached in the main part and by believing and practicing it, and therefore what divine protection will be given to those who revere the sutra and endeavor to spread it.

THE LOTUS SUTRA. The Sutra of the Lotus Flower of the Wonderful Law, commonly known as the Lotus Sutra, consists of twenty-eight chapters: Chapter 1, "Introductory"; chapter 2, "Tactfulness"; chapter 3, "A Parable"; chapter 4, "Faith Discernment"; chapter 5, "The Parable of the Herbs"; chapter 6, "Prediction"; chapter 7, "The Parable of the Magic City"; chapter 8, "The Five Hundred Disciples Receive the Prediction of Their Destiny"; chapter 9, "Prediction of the Destiny of Arhats, Training and Trained"; chapter 10, "A Teacher of the Law"; chapter 11, "Beholding the Precious Stupa"; chapter 12, "Devadatta"; chapter 13, "Exhortation to Hold Firm"; chapter 14, "A Happy Life"; chapter 15, "Springing Up out of the Earth"; chapter 16, "Revelation of the [Eternal] Life of the Tathāgata"; chapter 17, "Discrimination of Merits"; chapter 18, "The Merits of Joyful Acceptance"; chapter 19, "The Merits of the Preacher"; chapter 20, "The Bodhisattva Never Despise"; chapter 21, "The Divine Power of the Tathāgata"; chapter 22, "The Final Commission"; chapter 23, "The Story of the Bodhisattva Medicine King"; chapter 24, "The Bodhisattva Wonder Sound"; chapter 25, "The All-Sidedness of the Bodhisattva Regarder of the Cries of the World"; chapter 26, "Dhāraṇīs"; chapter 27, "The Story of King Resplendent"; and chapter 28, "Encouragement of the Bodhisattva Universal Virtue." The title of each chapter indicates part or all of its contents.

From ancient times Buddhist scholars have divided the Lotus Sutra in various ways for the purpose of understanding it better. According to the division followed by most scholars, a line is drawn between chapters 14 and 15. The former half is defined as the "Law of Appearance" (*shakumon*) and the latter half as the "Law of Origin" (*hommon*); each of these two Laws is divided into introductory, main, and concluding parts. In the Law of Appearance, chapter 1 is defined as the introductory part; chapters 2 to 9 are the main part; and chapters 10 to 14 are the concluding part. In the Law of Origin, the former half of chapter 15 is the introductory part; the second half of chapter 15, chapter 16, and the first half of chapter 17 are the main part; and the latter half of chapter 17 and the remaining eleven chapters are the concluding part.

THE LAW OF APPEARANCE AND THE LAW OF ORIGIN. The Law of Appearance means the teaching of the Buddha appearing in history (*shakubutsu*). The "appearing Buddha" indicates the historical Sakyamuni, who was born in this world, attained Buddhahood after years of asceticism, and died at the age of eighty. Therefore the Law of Appearance includes the teachings of the organization of the universe, human life, and human relationships on the basis of the experience and enlightenment of Sakyamuni, who attained the ideal state of a human being. Sakyamuni also teaches us that wisdom is the most important attribute for maintaining correct human relationships. The essence of the Law of Appearance is the wisdom of the Buddha.

The Law of Origin, with chapter 16 as its core, declares that Sakyamuni has continually taught people throughout the universe since the infinite past. In other words, the Buddha is the truth of the universe, that is, the fundamental principle or the fundamental power causing all phenomena of the universe, including the sun, other stars, human beings, animals, plants, and so on, to live and move. Therefore the Buddha has existed everywhere in the universe since its beginning. This Buddha is called the Original Buddha (*hombutsu*).

The human form in which the Original Buddha appeared in this world is the historical Sakyamuni as the appearing Buddha. We can easily understand the relationship between the two when we consider the relationship between electric waves and television. The electric waves emitted by television transmitters fill our surroundings. We cannot see, hear, or touch them, but it is a fact that such electric waves fill the space around us. When we switch on our television sets and tune them to a particular channel, the same image appears and the same voice is heard through every set tuned to that wavelength. The Original Buddha is equivalent to the person who speaks from the television studio. He is manifest not only in the studio but also permeates our surroundings like electric waves. The appearing Buddha corresponds to the image of this person that appears on the television set and to the voice emanating from it. The appearing Buddha could not appear if the Original Buddha did not exist, just as no television image could appear and no voice be heard if electric waves did not exist. Conversely, we cannot see the Original Buddha except through the appearing Buddha, just as we cannot receive electric waves as images and voices except through the medium of a television set.

Thus, the Original Buddha is the Buddha who exists in every part of the universe from the infinite past to the infinite future, but only through the teachings of Sakyamuni, who appeared in this world in obedience to the truth of the Original Buddha, can we understand that truth. We cannot declare that either the Original Buddha or the appearing Buddha is the more holy or the more important: both are necessary.

Radio and television stations emit electric waves, in the hope that as many people as possible will receive them through their television sets and radios. In the same way, the Original Buddha exists in every part of the universe, ready to save all beings of the universe. He instructs men, animals, and plants; and salvation means the full manifestation and complete development of the life essential to each form of life according to its true nature.

The Original Buddha is one with the truth of the universe. We have only to tune the wavelength of our own lives to that of the truth of the universe, and the Buddha appears to us. At that time the dark cloud of illusion covering our minds and bodies vanishes completely and the brilliant light of our essential life begins to shine from within our minds. This state of mind is our real salvation, and the spiritual state that we should attain.

The Original Buddha exists permanently from the infinite past to the infinite future, that is, this Buddha is without beginning or end. This Buddha appears in various forms appropriate to the particular time and place for the salvation of all people by means suited to their capacity to understand his teachings. This is the concept of the Original Buddha.

The Law of Origin is the teaching expressing the relationship between the Buddha and man, that is, the salvation of man through the Original Buddha. This salvation depends on the benevolence of the Buddha, and this benevolence is the essence of the Law of Origin.

THE SUTRA OF MEDITATION ON THE BODHISATTVA UNIVERSAL VIRTUE. This sutra teaches the practice of the Bodhisattva Universal Virtue. It consists of the sermon that Sakyamuni preached at the Great Forest Monastery of Vaiśālī in central India after he had taught the Lotus Sutra, and establishes the way of repentance as the practice of the spirit of the Lotus Sutra.

We are greatly encouraged when we read the Lotus Sutra, grasp the true meaning of the sermons that Sakyamuni preached during his lifetime, and realize that we can attain the same state of mind as the Buddha through practicing his teachings. However, the fact is that in our daily lives we are continually troubled with suffering and distress, and we are continually seized by desires of one kind or another. For this reason, we are apt to become disheartened and forget the valuable lessons of the sutra.

Although we understand theoretically that we can become buddhas, we do not know how to rid ourselves of our illusions; our minds are liable to be covered with a dark cloud of illusion. Repentance means the sweeping away of such dark clouds, and the Sutra of Meditation on the Bodhisattva Universal Virtue teaches the way to do this. Therefore this sutra also has a close relationship to the Lotus Sutra, and, as the epilogue of the Lotus Sutra, is called the "closing sutra" (*kekkyō*) of the Lotus Sutra. Because of its content, it is also called the "Sutra of Repentance."

Part One: The Sutra of Innumerable Meanings

CHAPTER 1

Virtues

As already mentioned, this sutra is an introduction to the Lotus Sutra. It begins with the description of a number of bodhisattvas extolling the virtues and excellence of Sakyamuni Buddha. The chapter begins with the phrase, "Thus have I heard," and following this are stated in beautiful and dignified language the circumstances at the time that the Buddha was staying at a monastery on Mount Gṛdhrakūṭa, or Vulture Peak (so called because it resembled a vulture in shape), together with a large assemblage of great *bhikshus,* twelve thousand in all.

A *bhikshu* is a Buddhist monk, and the great *bhikshus* are the major disciples of the Buddha, such as Śāriputra and Kāśyapa. Though these *bhikshus* have not yet attained bodhisattvahood, they have already reached the stage of *arhat,* one who is free from all illusions, by means of the Hīnayāna teaching. One need not take literally the number of twelve thousand given for the great *bhikshus.* We often encounter large numbers in the sutras, but they may be taken generally to indicate merely "a great number."

In the great assemblage there were also many bodhisattva-*mahāsattvas.* A bodhisattva is one who practices the teaching of Mahāyāna Buddhism. *Mahā* means "great" and *sattva* means "person," so that *mahāsattva* indicates "great person," that is, one who has a great goal. The bodhisattvas are so called because all have the great goal of seeking supreme enlightenment and of finally attaining buddhahood by enlightening all people.

There were also gods, dragons, *yakshas,* spirits, and animals in the assemblage. Gods are beings living in the various heavens, while dragons are serpent-shaped demigods who live at the bottom of the sea. *Yakshas* are flying demons. Thus the beings at the great assemblage included demons, who are generally regarded as harmful to human beings, as well as animals. This kind of description is a characteristic of Buddhism that cannot be found in other religions. The Buddha did not try to lead only man to enlightenment but had such vast benevolence as to save all creatures of the universe from their sufferings and lead them to the shore of bliss. Therefore, even man-eating demons were permitted to attend the assemblage to hear the Buddha preach.

Besides these, there were people of all classes: *bhikshus* (monks), *bhikshuṇīs* (nuns), *upāsakas* (male lay devotees), *upāsikās* (female lay devotees), many virtuous kings, princes, ministers, and ordinary people, men and women alike, as well as very rich people. They showed their devotion to the Buddha by prostrating themselves at his feet and by making procession around him. After they had burned incense, scattered flowers, and worshiped him in various ways, they retired and sat to one side.

For Buddhists, worshiping the Buddha is an expression of gratitude. When we have a deep sense of gratitude, we must always be sure to express it in our conduct. Gratitude without worship cannot be said to be true gratitude. To venerate the Buddha, Japanese Buddhists worship at their family altars by presenting flowers, tea, and water and by burning incense and beating gongs.

All the bodhisattvas in the assemblage were great saints of the Law and had attained the precepts, meditation, wisdom, emancipation, and the knowledge of emancipation. They were continuously in meditation, their minds tranquil and undistracted, and they were content with any environment and indifferent to worldly gain. They were immune to all delusion and distraction. They always possessed profound and infinite consideration through their calm and clear minds. Having maintained this state of mind for a long time, they could remember all the innumerable teachings of the Buddha. Moreover, having obtained the great wisdom, they had the ability to penetrate all things.

Wisdom is the ability both to discern the differences among all things and to see the truth common to them. In short, wisdom is the ability to realize that anybody can become a buddha. The Buddha's teachings stress that we cannot discern all things in the world correctly until we are completely endowed with the ability to know both distinction and equality.

These virtuous bodhisattvas spread the Buddha's teachings, just as all the buddhas roll the Law-wheel. The order in which bodhisattvas are to propagate the teachings is plainly stated in this chapter. First, just as a dewdrop lays the dust on the parched earth, the bodhisattvas dip the dust of men's desires in a drop of the teachings. This is most valuable in opening the gate to nirvana. Then they preach the way of emancipation and remove all the sufferings and illusions with which people are faced. They also make people feel great joy and refreshment, as if their minds had been washed by listening to the Law. Next they teach the doctrine of the Twelve Causes to those who suffer from ignorance, old age, illness, and death, and thus help these people free themselves from their sufferings, just as a rain shower cools those who are suffering from the summer heat. Up to this point the bodhisattvas have been preaching the Hīnayāna teaching.

The Law of the Twelve Causes, also called the doctrine of the twelve-link chain of dependent origination, is one of the principal Hīnayāna teachings. In this important doctrine, Sakyamuni explains the process a person goes through from birth to death and how this process is repeated in his transmigration in the three temporal states of existence—the past, the present, and the future. In connection with this, he also shows that, as all human sufferings stem from fundamental ignorance (illusion), people can rid themselves of suffering by removing ignorance and can gain happiness by transcending the three temporal states of existence. A detailed explanation of this doctrine is given in chapter 7 of the Lotus Sutra, "The Parable of the Magic City."

The bodhisattvas enlighten the general populace through the order of teachings mentioned above, and make all people put forth the sprout of buddhahood. They also adopt tactful means to promote the Mahāyāna and to try to make all accomplish Perfect Enlightenment speedily. The phrase "to make all accomplish Perfect Enlightenment speedily," found often in the sutras, is very important. The word "speedily" includes the meaning of "straight, making no detour," as well as that of "quickly or rapidly."

Next, these bodhisattvas are extolled in the highest terms for their various virtues and for their importance to all people. Many *bhikshus* are also lauded as being excellent *arhats,* unrestricted by any bonds of faults, free from attachment, and truly emancipated.

This admiration of the bodhisattvas and *bhikshus* is not mere empty praise. It indicates the pattern of how these people have practiced the teachings of the Buddha. We cannot attain the same state of mind as the Buddha in a single leap. In the first place, we must study the practice of the bodhisattvas and the *bhikshus*. Some people consider our inability to follow the same kind of practice as due to its being far removed from the realities of everyday life. It is natural that they should think this, but that is no reason not to try to follow the pattern of the bodhisattvas and *bhikshus*. There is a key or a chance of opening the gate of enlightenment in following even only one of the many virtuous practices of the bodhisattvas that are expressed in the sutras.

Seeing that all the groups were seated with settled mind and were fully prepared to hear the Buddha's teachings, the Bodhisattva Great Adornment rose from his seat together with many other bodhisattvas and paid homage to the Buddha with various offerings. Making obeisance at the feet of the Buddha, the Bodhisattva Great Adornment praised him in verse. Verse is frequently used in the sutras to restate succinctly the major points that have been previously stated in prose or to praise the Buddha and the bodhisattvas.

All the beings, including the Bodhisattva Great Adornment, praised the holy mind of the Buddha who had realized all, had transcended all, and had led all creatures of the universe as he wished. They also admired the beauty of the Buddha's face, body, and voice, which were naturally manifested by his virtue, and the wonder of his enlightening all living beings through his teachings. They also praised the fact that the Buddha thought nothing of himself during his long striving and that he devoted himself to saving all living beings by enduring all kinds of distress and renouncing all, as the result of which he attained the great wisdom that enables all living beings to be led to enlightenment. The final verse portion of this chapter, which praises the Buddha's having become the Great Enlightened One, the Great Holy Lord, expresses the admiration of the bodhisattvas, who are on the way to attaining this state, of the exertion that the Buddha made over a long period. They concluded their praise with the words, "We submit ourselves to the One / Who has completed all hard things."

Praise of the Buddha serves to implant our ideal of the Buddha deep in our memory. It sets forth the eternal goal of buddhahood by constructing a picture of the Buddha's figure and power as the one who receives the greatest honor and is absolutely perfect.

CHAPTER 2

Preaching

IN THIS CHAPTER, the main part of the Sutra of Innumerable Meanings, Sakyamuni teaches us that since his enlightenment, the Buddha had preached the Law with a certain aim and in a certain order. Although the Law was preached in various ways, the fundamental truth was always that one Law, or truth, is the origin of the infinite laws, or teachings.

Together with the many bodhisattva-*mahāsattvas,* the Bodhisattva Great Adornment said to the Buddha: "We wish to ask you about the Buddha's Law. We earnestly hope you will listen to us."

The Buddha addressed them: "Excellent! Excellent! You have asked me this question at just the right time. You might have missed your opportunity had you not asked me now. I will enter *parinirvāṇa* before long. I am afraid lest any question should be left after my death. Ask me what you like. I will answer any question you wish."

Thereupon the Bodhisattva Great Adornment with the many other bodhisattvas said to the Buddha in unison: "If the bodhisattva-*mahāsattvas,* who have practiced the Mahāyāna teaching, want to accomplish Perfect Enlightenment quickly, what doctrine should they practice?"

The Buddha addressed them: "There is here one holy doctrine, which is called Innumerable Meanings. If a bodhisattva studies this doctrine, then he will accomplish Perfect Enlightenment. A bodhisattva, if he wants to study the doctrine of Innumerable Meanings, should observe that all laws, or phenomena, seem to be different and to change constantly, but actually their foundation is a great unchanging power that is manifested in various ways. You should realize that at the basis of all laws there is one truth that transcends discrimination and is eternally unchangeable. Because of their ignorance of this truth, living beings discriminate selfishly, 'It is advantageous' or 'It is disadvantageous.' Therefore they entertain evil thoughts, give rise to various evil karmas, and transmigrate within the six realms of existence."

The six realms of existence (*rokushu* or *rokudō* in Japanese) are the six worlds in which living beings transmigrate: hell (*jigoku*), hungry spirits (*gaki*), animals (*chikushō*), demons (*shura*), human beings (*ningen*), and heaven (*tenjō*). This doctrine teaches us the mental states of man as well as the construction of the world with man as its center.

"Hell" is the mental state in which our minds are consumed by anger. Everyone and everything seems to be an enemy when we burn with anger. For example, when a man has quarreled with his wife, he hates even the dishes, which have nothing at all to do with the quarrel, and may even smash them. But by smashing dishes or striking an opponent, he cannot really destroy the dishes or the opponent. The one who suffers most is the person who is angry.

"Hungry spirits" is the mental state in which a host of desires arises in our minds. Desire is not confined to money and material things but includes the craving for honor or for another's affection. Because of our greed, we do not know how to be satisfied even when we attain our desire of the moment. The more desires we have, the more attached to them we become, in a vicious circle.

"Animals" expresses the mental state that lacks wisdom and is unreasoning. A person who does not reason acts from instinct alone and does whatever he wishes without reflecting on the consequences.

"Demons" means the mental state of being self-centered in everything, having only one's own interests at heart. It is this kind of mentality that leads to conflict, quarrels, disputes, and wars among men. This is the spiritual state in which selfishness leads to dispute.

"Human beings" expresses the mental state of trying to check the four evil mentalities mentioned above by means of conscience so that we do not go to extremes, although we all possess these four mental states. This state of mind is that of ordinary man.

"Heaven" indicates the world of joy. However, this is not the unchanging joy gained through the Buddha's enlightenment. It is the pleasures of the senses and feelings, that is, the pleasures caused by illusion, so it is a temporary joy that may lapse into the worlds of hell, hungry spirits, or demons as soon as anything unpleasant occurs. Rapture is typical of such a mental state. In this case, "heaven" indicates a place whose inhabitants have no sufferings or troubles; but so long as we cannot attain true enlightenment, even if we should reach the state of "heaven" we would be unsatisfied with it. Ordinarily one supposes that he would be free from all cares if he should become a millionaire, living in a mansion and having many servants. However, practically speaking, matters never turn out as he thinks. If there were a so-called paradise where people could lead idle lives doing nothing the whole day, they would become bored and generate the desire to do something. "Heaven" is such a stagnant mental state.

The six worlds continually occur in man's mind and shift from one to another. This state of mind is called "transmigration within the six worlds" (*rokudō rinne*). If we have no good teaching and no way of practice, we permanently transmigrate within the six worlds, and our distresses and sufferings will never disappear. Anyone will realize this as soon as he reflects on himself.

The Buddha taught the bodhisattvas as follows: "When you, bodhisattva-*mahāsattvas,* observe all the living beings who are transmigrating within the six realms of existence, you should raise the mind of compassion and display great mercy so as to relieve them from such realms. First, you must penetrate deeply into all the laws. If you understand them deeply, you can realize naturally what may emerge from them in the future. You can also realize that they remain settled, without changing, for a time. You can also realize that they change. Moreover, you can realize that they eventually vanish. Thus you can observe and know the reasons that good and evil laws emerge. Having finished observing and knowing all four aspects of the laws from beginning to end, next you should observe that none of the laws remains settled for even a moment, but emerges and vanishes anew every moment. After such observations, you can know the capacity, the nature, and the desires that each living being possesses as if you had penetrated each of their minds.

"As they have innumerable natures and desires, your preaching to them should be immeasurable, and as your preaching is immeasurable, its meanings should be innumerable. This is because the teaching with innumerable meanings originates from one Law. What is this one Law? It is the truth. What is the truth? It is nonform, which transcends the discrimination of all things. Things are equal in having the buddha-nature. This fact is the truth and the real aspect of all things. Bodhisattva-*mahāsattvas!* The mercy that you can display spontaneously after realizing this true aspect is virtuous and not futile. With this mercy you excellently relieve living beings from suffering and, furthermore, allow all of them to obtain pleasure. Therefore a bodhisattva, if he practices completely the doctrine of the Innumerable Meanings, will soon be able to accomplish Perfect Enlightenment without fail."

Then the Bodhisattva Great Adornment asked the Buddha another question: "Though we have no doubts about the laws preached by the Buddha, we repeatedly ask you for fear that all living beings should be perplexed and unable to understand the laws. You have continuously preached to living beings all laws, especially the four laws, during the more than forty years since the Tathāgata attained enlightenment. The four laws are suffering, voidness, transience, and selflessness. Suffering means that human life is filled with all sorts of sufferings. Voidness indicates that all things seem to be different from one another, but we must discern the aspect of equality that is beyond such differences. Transience expresses the fact that in this world there is nothing existing in a permanently fixed form, but all things are always changing. Selflessness reveals that nothing in the universe has an isolated existence without any relation to other things, and we must not be attached to our own self. Further, you have taught us the real aspects of all things in various ways. Those who have heard these laws have attained merits in varying degrees, have aspired to enlightenment, and lastly have attained the highest stage of the bodhisattva-way.

"Thus it seems that the Tathāgata has preached the same laws all these forty years, but we know that during this period you have preached them more and more deeply. However, we are afraid that all the living beings may not discriminate the differences between your past and present preaching on the laws. World-honored One! Be pleased to expound it for all living beings."

Hereupon the Buddha said to the Bodhisattva Great Adornment: "Excellent! Excellent! Great good sons; you have well questioned the Tathāgata about this. It truly shows your great benevolence that you have asked me about the wonderful meaning of the profound and supreme Great-vehicle preached by the Buddha, not for the sake of your own enlightenment but for the sake of all living beings. Good sons! I was able to accomplish Perfect Enlightenment after six years' right sitting under the Bodhi tree. When I saw all the laws with the Buddha's eye, they had such various appearances as to be inexpressible. I knew that the natures and desires of all living beings were not equal. For this reason, I preached the Law variously with tactful power for more than forty years. But during that period, I have not yet revealed the truth. Living beings' powers of understanding the law are too different to enable them to accomplish supreme buddhahood quickly.

"Good sons! The Law is like water that washes off dirt. The nature of water is one, but a stream, a river, a well, a pond, a valley stream, a ditch, and a great sea are different from one another. The nature of the Law is like this. Though each cleanses equally well as water, a well is not a pond, a pond is not a stream or a river, nor is a valley stream or a ditch a sea. All the laws preached by the Tathāgata are like this. Though the preaching at the beginning, in the middle, and at the end all alike effectively wash away the delusions of living beings, the beginning is not the middle, and the middle is not the end. The preaching at the beginning, in the middle, and at the end are the same in expression but different from one another in meaning.

"Good sons! When I first rolled the Law-wheel of the Four Noble Truths for the five monks at the Deer Park in Vārāṇasī, I preached that the laws are naturally vacant, ceaselessly transformed, and instantly born and destroyed. I also preached the same thing when I discoursed explaining the Twelve Causes and the Six *Pāramitās* for all the *bhikshus* and bodhisattvas in various places during the middle period. Now in explaining the Sutra of Innumerable Meanings, this Great-vehicle, at this time, I also preach the same thing.

"Good sons! Therefore the preaching at the beginning, in the middle, and at the end are the same in expression but different from one another in meaning. As meaning varies, the understanding of living beings varies. As understanding varies, the attainment of the Law, the merit, and the way also varies. This is well known by the result of my enlightening those who listened to my preaching in each period—when at the beginning I preached the Four Noble Truths at the Deer Park; when in the middle I preached in various places the profound Twelve Causes; and when next I preached the twelve types of sutras of Great Extent and other sutras.

"Good sons! In other words, I have preached only one truth from the beginning. This is not limited to me; all the buddhas have done the same thing. Because the fundamental truth is only one, the buddhas extensively answer all voices with one word; though having one body, they reveal clearly innumerable and numberless bodies, in each body displaying various and countless forms, and in each form showing countless shapes.

"Good sons! This is the incomprehensible and profound world of buddhas. Men of the two vehicles[1] cannot apprehend it, and even the bodhisattvas who have attained the highest stage cannot realize it.

"Only a buddha together with a buddha can fathom it well. Therefore, you must endeavor to attain the same stage as the Buddha through the Sutra of Innumerable Meanings that I am now preaching. This wonderful, profound, and supreme sutra is reasonable in its logic, unsurpassed in its worth, and protected by all the buddhas of the three worlds. No kind of demon or heretic can break into it, nor can any wrong view or life and death destroy it.

"Therefore bodhisattva-*mahāsattvas* who want to accomplish supreme buddhahood quickly should learn and master the Sutra of Innumerable Meanings, this profound and supreme Great-vehicle."

At the close of the Buddha's preaching, heaven and earth were shaken in various ways and presented varied spectacles of unearthly beauty; celestial flowers, perfumes, robes, garlands, and treasures of priceless value rained and came rolling down from the sky, and celestial music was played in praise of the Buddha, all the bodhisattvas, the *śrāvakas,* and the great assembly.

Thereupon many bodhisattva-*mahāsattvas* in the assembly attained the contemplation of Innumerable Meanings and many other bodhisattva-*mahāsattvas* obtained the numberless and infinite realms of *dhāraṇī.*[2] All the *bhikshus, bhikshuṇīs, upāsakas, upāsikās,* and others in attendance, hearing the Tathāgata preaching this sutra, acquired the enlightenment suitable to each one's spiritual state. Moreover, all came to have the aspiration to want to attain the same stage as the Buddha by following his teachings and spreading them earnestly.

1. *Śrāvaka* and *pratyekabuddha*. The former means a person who listens to the Buddha's teachings and exerts himself to attain the stage of *arhat* by practicing the Buddha's teachings. The latter indicates a self-enlightened person who obtains emancipation for himself without any teacher through recognizing the twelve links of causation (the Law of the Twelve Causes).

2. Formulas of mystic syllables that sustain the religious life of the reciter. The formulas very often do not make sense as words.

CHAPTER 3

Ten Merits

THIS CHAPTER EXPOUNDS the merit one can gain, the virtuous deeds he can accomplish, and the service he can render to society if he understands the teachings preached in this sutra. Some people say that religion should not bring merit to its believers, but this is a specious argument. It would be, rather, a wonder if one did not gain merit when he truly understood a correct religion, believed in it deeply, and practiced it. Needless to say, there are varying degrees of merit according to one's degree of understanding and the speed of the actual manifestation of merit. In any case, it is natural for one to gain merit through his religion when he has faith in it.

As mentioned earlier, the teachings of the Buddha are the truth of the universe, which of course includes human beings. It is no wonder, and certainly no miracle, that if one lives according to the truth, his life works out well. This is like the fact that if we switch on the television set and tune in exactly to the wavelength beamed from a particular television station, a vivid image appears on the screen and a clear voice is heard.

If no image appears on the television screen, however often we try to tune in the channel, the television set is useless. It will be put away in some storeroom, where it will be covered with dust. Numerous religions have sprung up throughout history, but some of them have gradually lost their power and finally have become distant from the people. This is because they have forgotten the merit to be gained by believers, or because they have preached only the merit to be gained after death—that one will go to heaven or be reborn in paradise.

The true teachings of the Buddha, however, do not preach an intangible merit that one cannot realize until after death. The merit preached by the Buddha appears clearly in our lives in this world. In addition to ourselves, it is a merit that exerts an influence upon all of society and upon all people. If we disregard this merit and make light of it, it is as if we deliberately shut out the light of the Buddha's teachings with a black curtain. Such an attitude is due to the shallow understanding peculiar to people today.

We should abandon such shallow thinking and bathe ourselves in the light of the Buddha by drawing aside the curtain. This is the true hope of the Buddha and the sole purpose of his appearance in this world.

The Bodhisattva-Mahāsattva Great Adornment, who was deeply moved by the Sutra of Innumerable Meanings, said to the Buddha that he could understand that this sutra was wonderful, profound, and great in its power. The bodhisattva-*mahāsattva* then asked the Buddha: "World-honored One! This sutra is inconceivable. World-honored One! Be pleased to explain the profound and inconceivable matter of this sutra out of benevolence for all the people. World-honored One! From what place does this sutra come? For what place does it leave? At what place does it stay?"

The Buddha addressed the Bodhisattva-Mahāsattva Great Adornment: "Good sons! This sutra originally comes from the abode of all the buddhas, leaves for the aspiration of all the living to buddhahood, and stays at the place where all the bodhisattvas practice."

These words are very important. The expression "This sutra originally comes from the abode of all the buddhas" means that it flows naturally from the Buddha's mind. The Buddha emphasizes here that this sutra, as a Great-vehicle, is truly a profound teaching that comes spontaneously from the Buddha's benevolent mind, so that he cannot help preaching it. The place for which it leaves, namely, its purpose, is to make all living beings aspire to buddhahood. The place at which it stays is the practice of the bodhisattvas, the many and varied practices leading to the Buddha's enlightenment. It is also stated that everybody can gain such great merit as to be able to attain the enlightenment of the Buddha if he practices this sutra.

The Buddha then expounded in detail the ten merit-powers of the sutra. Here we will concentrate on the first merit-power, which is regarded as the most fundamental one.

The Buddha said: "Good sons! First, this sutra has the following merits: it makes the unawakened bodhisattva aspire to buddhahood and makes a merciless one who has no concern for making others happy raise the mind of mercy. It also makes one who likes to bully others or to kill creatures raise the mind of great compassion. It makes a jealous one raise the mind of joy. If those who are apt to be envious of others and to feel superior to them should read this sutra and come to recognize gratefully the Buddha's teachings, they can understand that a person who seemed to be not at all equal to them is the same as them before the Buddha, and they are filled with the mind of joy and want to be as excellent as the Buddha. As a result, envy and jealousy of others vanishes.

"It is natural that man feels attached to things around him—his property, status, honor, family, and so on. However, if he clings to these things, he has various mental sufferings. If he should attain such a state of mind as to be able to renounce them at any time, his mind becomes free from them. Because of not being attached to anything, he can lead a peaceful life with his family, can use his property usefully, and can make the best of his station in life. This sutra has the merit of making an attached one raise the mind of detachment.

"This sutra makes a miserly one raise the mind of donation. If those who are stingy with their own things and covet things that belong to others can realize the Buddha's mind, motivated only for the sake of living beings, they come spontaneously to have the mind of donation and of being kind to others. They come to be useful to others.

"This sutra makes an arrogant one raise the mind of keeping the commandments. If those who are proud of their superiority, of their intelligence, or of their conduct should recite this sutra and realize the existence of the Buddha, they become aware of their mistaken thinking and conduct, and they raise the mind of keeping firmly the various precepts that the Buddha has established.

"This sutra makes an irascible one raise the mind of perseverance. If those who are apt to become angry over trifles should pattern themselves after the Buddha's mind, they no longer have anger and hatred for what others may say or may do. On the contrary, they feel sympathetic toward others and wish compassionately to correct their deluded thinking. This is the mind of perseverance, which can bear what is ordinarily unbearable and make the intolerable tolerable.

"This sutra makes an indolent one raise the mind of assiduity. An indolent person is one who cannot direct his course for the future, who neglects his duty and becomes caught up in trivial matters. However, he cannot help endeavoring to guide his life if he understands the Buddha's teaching that all lives can be lived rightly, each in its own way, and that this is the way that makes the whole world work for what is right. Commit no evil, do all that is good, purify your mind.'

"This sutra makes a distracted one raise the mind of meditation. Even those who are swayed and distracted by every change in their circumstances can continuously maintain quiet, peaceful minds when they realize that there is a permanent truth beneath all changeable phenomena.

"This sutra makes an ignorant one raise the mind of wisdom. An ignorant one is a person who thinks only of the present and cannot reflect on the consequences of his actions. Therefore he is apt to be distracted by immediate circumstances and often becomes angry or worried about such things. If he studies the teaching of the Great-vehicle and has the mind of wisdom, he gradually comes to see things in context and not to feel displeased about everything, and his mind becomes clearer.

"This sutra makes one who lacks concern for saving others raise the mind of saving others. If such a person realizes that others as well as himself should be saved, because he does not live in this world alone in isolation from others, he spontaneously raises the mind of helping others.

"This sutra makes one who commits the ten evils raise the mind of the ten virtues. The ten evils are killing, stealing, committing adultery, lying, improper language, a double tongue, ill speaking, covetousness, anger, and ignorance. When a person acquires the true teaching of the Great-vehicle, he gradually comes not to entertain such evils.

"This sutra makes one who wishes for existence aspire to the mind of nonexistence. Even those who are strongly self-centered in everything they do naturally come to raise the mind of unselfishness when, through this sutra, they approach the Buddha's mind, which regards all living beings as equal.

"This sutra makes one who is inclined toward apostasy raise the mind of nonregression. Those who are apt to backslide in their spiritual progress come to have courage, so that they aim at attaining buddhahood and persevere in the discipline of their practice, never sliding back an inch, when they have realized the teaching of the Great-vehicle through this sutra. This is quite natural, because they can see their path shining and open before them, and they cannot but be inspired by it.

"This sutra also makes one who commits defiled acts caused by illusion raise the mind of undefilement free from illusion, and makes one who suffers from delusions raise the mind of detachment."

Having expounded this, the Buddha said: "Good sons! This is called the first inconceivable merit-power of this sutra."

The merit-powers mentioned above are immense. Even if we accomplished only one of them, it would be a wonderful achievement for us as people living in this modern age. When we read of the many merits mentioned here, we must not be daunted by thinking that they are beyond our powers, because if we can accomplish only one merit, we can accomplish others. Let us accomplish just one merit—it is very important that we think this way in order to study eagerly and to persevere in such discipline.

Secondly, the Buddha states that if a living being can hear this sutra but once, or even only one verse or phrase, he will penetrate countless meanings because this sutra contains innumerable meanings. Of the second inconceivable merit-power of this sutra, the following is said: From one seed a hundred thousand myriad seeds grow, from each of a hundred thousand myriad seeds another hundred thousand myriad seeds grow, and by such a process seeds increase infinitely. This sutra is like this. From one law a hundred thousand meanings grow, from each of a hundred thousand meanings a hundred thousand myriad meanings grow, and through such a process meanings increase boundlessly.

The third inconceivable merit-power of this sutra is as follows: If a living being can hear this sutra but once, or only one verse or phrase, he will penetrate countless meanings. After that his delusions, even though existent, will become as if nonexistent; he will not be seized by fear, though he moves between birth and death; and he will raise the mind of compassion for all living beings, and obtain the courage to obey all the laws. Just as a ferryman, though he stays on this shore owing to a serious illness, can be enabled to cross to the other shore by means of a good solid boat that can carry anyone without fail, so also is it with the keeper of this sutra. Though he stays on this shore of ignorance, old age, and death owing to the hundred and eight kinds of serious illness with which his body in the five states is afflicted, he can be delivered from birth and death through practicing this strong Mahāyāna sutra of Innumerable Meanings, which realizes the deliverance of living beings.

The fourth inconceivable merit-power of this sutra is as follows: If a living being can hear this sutra but once, or only one verse or phrase, he will obtain the spirit of courage, and will succor others, even though he cannot yet save himself. He will become the attendant of the buddhas together with all the bodhisattvas, and all the buddha-*tathāgatas* will always preach the Law to him. The words "all the buddha-*tathāgatas* will always preach the Law to him" have a very deep meaning, indicating that although up to now he had ignored or deliberately shunned the Buddha, he now turns to face the Buddha directly. Whether he likes it or not, he is exposed directly to the light of the Buddha. This is a very important merit that he can obtain from the Buddha. The oftener he comes to receive the teachings of the Buddha, the more people he can spread the teachings to, according to the methods best suited to different people.

The fourth inconceivable merit-power teaches that if a bodhisattva can hear one phrase or verse of this sutra once, twice, ten times, a hundred times, a thousand times, a myriad times, or innumerable times, he will be able to enter deeply into the secret Law of the buddhas and will interpret it without error and fault, even though he himself cannot yet realize the ultimate truth. He will always be protected by all the buddhas, and treated with special affection, because he is a beginner in learning.

The fifth and sixth inconceivable merit-powers of this sutra are the following: If there are good sons or good daughters who keep, recite, and copy this sutra either during the Buddha's lifetime or after his extinction, even though bound by delusions, their speech and conduct will be useful to society. They will deliver living beings from the life and death of delusions and make them overcome all sufferings by preaching the Law to them. This is a most important practice of the bodhisattvas and indicates that one can preach the teaching to others even if one has not accomplished it thoroughly; one must share one's own knowledge, however small it may be, in order to proceed further oneself. The following parable illustrates the sixth merit-power: Suppose that a king, in journeying or falling ill, leaves the management of national affairs to the crown prince, though he is only an infant. The prince, by the order of the great king, leads all the government officials according to the law, and propagates right policies, so that every citizen of the country follows his orders exactly as if the king himself were ruling. Good sons or good daughters who keep the sutra are like this prince.

The seventh, eighth, ninth, and tenth merit-powers of the sutra express a very difficult mental stage that proceeds further at every step. To summarize these merit-powers briefly: as one understands this sutra more deeply, practices it, and transmits it to others, one can accomplish it himself and at the same time can save others; and finally, one can attain the same state of mind as the Buddha.

At the close of the Buddha's teaching of the ten inconceivable merit-powers of this sutra, the earth shook and celestial flowers, perfumes, robes, garlands, and priceless treasures rained down from the sky, and these things were offered to the Buddha, all the bodhisattvas, the *śrāvakas,* and the great assembly. At this time, together with many other bodhisattva-*mahāsattvas,* the Bodhisattva-Mahāsattva Great Adornment vowed to the Buddha that they would widely propagate this sutra after the Tathāgata's extinction, in obedience to the Buddha's command, and have all keep, read, recite, copy, and adore it without fail.

The Buddha was very glad to hear their vows and said in praise: "Excellent! Excellent! All good sons; you are truly the Buddha's sons. You are those who save all living beings from their sufferings. Always bestow the benefits of the Law extensively on all."

The Sutra of Innumerable Meanings ends with the following words: "At that time all in the great assembly, greatly rejoicing together, made salutation to the Buddha, and taking possession of the sutra, withdrew." To sum up briefly the essential point of this sutra, it is that all the laws originate from one Law, namely, the real state of all things. All phenomena of the universe, including human life, manifest themselves in myriad different ways, and appear, disappear, move, and change. Man's mind is apt to be led astray in suffering from and worrying about discrimination and change. If we pay no attention to such visible discrimination and change, and if we are able to see in depth the true state of things transcending surface discrimination, the true state that is unchangeable forever, we will be able to attain the mental state of being free of all things while leading ordinary everyday lives.

However, the Sutra of Innumerable Meanings does not explain in detail what the "real state of all things" is and what we should do to discern it. This important point is elucidated in the Lotus Sutra, which follows.

Part Two: The Sutra of the Lotus Flower of the Wonderful Law

CHAPTER 1

Introductory

THE MEANING OF THE TITLE. Before discussing the Sutra of the Lotus Flower of the Wonderful Law itself, I wish to comment on the title of the sutra, which expresses in brief the form and content of the sutra. I believe that this title is unique in its succinct expression of the profound meaning of the entire sutra.

The original of the Sutra of the Lotus Flower of the Wonderful Law, written in Sanskrit, is called *Saddharma-puṇḍarīka-sūtra*. The title as translated into Chinese by Kumārajīva is *Miao-fa-lien-hua-ching* (Japanese, *Myōhō Renge-kyō*). In the Sutra of the Lotus Flower of the Wonderful Law the absolute truth realized by Sakyamuni Buddha is presented. This truth is called the "Wonderful Law" (*saddharma, miao-fa, myōhō*) because of its profound meaning, as shown in the discussion of the Sutra of Innumerable Meanings. First, as shown by the words "real state of all things," "Law" means all things that exist in the universe and all events that occur in the world. Secondly, it means the one truth that penetrates all things. Thirdly, it means the Law as an established rule when the truth appears as a phenomenon that we can see with our eyes and hear with our ears. Fourthly, it means the teaching of the truth.

The truth that expresses the original idea of these four meanings of "Wonderful Law" is the Buddha. Accordingly, the Law that rules the relationships of all things, including man, is also the Buddha; and the teaching, explaining how one should live on the basis of the truth, is the Buddha too. In short, the Law and the Buddha are one and the same. In other words, the Buddha and all the functions of the Buddha can be expressed with the word "Law." Because the Law has such a supreme, profound, and inexpressible meaning, it is modified by the adjective "Wonderful."

"Lotus" (*puṇḍarīka, lien-hua, renge*) means the lotus flower. In India this flower was regarded as the most beautiful in the world, for a lotus is rooted in mud but opens as a pure and beautiful flower unsoiled by the mud. This is an allegorical expression of the fundamental idea of the Lotus Sutra, that though man lives in this corrupt world, he is not tainted by it nor swayed by it, and he can live a beautiful life with perfect freedom of mind.

"Sutra" literally means a string or the warp threads in weaving. The people of ancient India had a custom of decorating their hair with beautiful flowers threaded on a string. In the same way, the holy teachings of the Buddha were gathered into compositions called sutras. All together, the title "Sutra of the Lotus Flower of the Wonderful Law" means "the supreme teaching that man can lead a correct life, without being swayed by illusions, while living in this corrupt world."

This chapter is called "Introductory" because it forms the introduction of the Lotus Sutra. The circumstances of its preaching are explained first: when Sakyamuni Buddha finished preaching the Sutra of Innumerable Meanings on Mount Gṛdhrakūṭa (Vulture Peak) for the sake of all the bodhisattvas, he sat cross-legged and entered contemplation, in which his body and mind were motionless.

This is a very important description. The Buddha always entered contemplation in this way before and after preaching. During his contemplation, he considered how he should preach in order to make his teaching sink deeply into the minds of his audience, and he also prayed that the teaching preached by him might be rightly received and spread by the hearers. It is said that Sakyamuni Buddha was lost in such contemplation for five hours a day. Following the example of the Buddha, it is desirable for us to close our eyes for a few minutes before and after listening to the Buddha's teaching so as to keep it constantly in our minds, to purify our minds with it, and to pray to be united with the Buddha.

At this time, when the Buddha entered contemplation, heaven and earth were moved by his teaching. Beautiful flowers rained from the sky, and the earth shook in six ways. Then all of the assembly obtained that which they had never experienced before, and they looked up to the Buddha with joy, with folded hands and of one mind.

Then the Buddha sent forth from the circle of white hair between his eyebrows a ray of light, which illuminated eighteen thousand worlds in the eastern quarter. In every part of this quarter were seen all the living beings in the six realms; likewise the causes of their present situations were seen. In every part of this quarter the buddhas were seen, and the people who had listened to the preaching of those buddhas and had practiced the Way could also be seen. Further, the bodhisattvas who walked the bodhisattva-way and the stupas of the precious seven substances, made to house the relics of the buddhas after they had entered final nirvana, were also seen.

At that time Maitreya Bodhisattva wondered at the inconceivable and unprecedented appearance of the Buddha, and he wished to ask the Buddha why he had displayed such a marvel. But he could not ask the reason because the Buddha had entered into contemplation. Maitreya Bodhisattva then reflected that Mañjuśrī Bodhisattva had been in close contact with and paid homage to innumerable former buddhas and should be able to answer his question concerning these unprecedented signs. So Maitreya Bodhisattva, desiring to resolve his own doubts and observing the perplexity arising in all the assembly, inquired of Mañjuśrī: "What is the cause and reason for this inconceivable thing, that a ray of light was sent forth from the circle of white hair between the Buddha's eyebrows? Why did this luminous ray light up the eighteen thousand eastern buddha-lands and reveal in detail the splendor of those buddha-realms?" Thereupon Maitreya Bodhisattva, desiring to repeat what he had said, inquired the same thing in verse.

Then Mañjuśrī said to Maitreya Bodhisattva and all the other leaders: "According to my judgment, the Buddha, the World-honored One, is preparing to preach a very important Law. This is because whenever any of the former buddhas displayed such an inconceivable appearance and emitted a ray of light, they thereupon preached this very important Law.

"Infinite, boundless, countless years ago, there was a buddha called Sun Moon Light Tathāgata, who was endowed with perfect virtues. He proclaimed the right Law, which is good at its beginning, good in its middle, and good at its end. His teaching was always based on one truth. It was profound in its meaning, subtle in its terms, pure and unadulterated, perfect, flawless, and noble in practice. For those who sought to be *śrāvakas* he preached the Law of the Four Noble Truths for the overcoming of birth, old age, disease, and death, and finally leading to nirvana; for those who sought to be *pratyekabuddhas* he preached the Law of the Twelve Causes;[1] for the bodhisattvas he preached the Six Perfections[2] to cause them to attain Perfect Enlightenment and to achieve perfect knowledge."

The doctrines of the Four Noble Truths and the Six Perfections, or *Pāramitās*, teach us how we can fundamentally solve the problem of the suffering and distress that we are faced with in our daily lives and how we can obtain a mental state of peace and quietude. As these doctrines form the core of the Buddha's teachings, we will explain them here.

THE FOUR NOBLE TRUTHS. The Four Noble Truths (*shitai*) are the Truth of Suffering (*kutai*), the Truth of Cause (*jittai*), the Truth of Extinction (*mettai*), and the Truth of the Path (*dōtai*).

The first of the Four Noble Truths is the Truth of Suffering. This means that all things in this world are comprised of suffering for those who do not listen to the Buddha's teachings. Human life is filled with spiritual, physical, economic, and other forms of suffering. To acknowledge the real condition of suffering and see it through, without avoiding it or meeting it only halfway—this is the Truth of Suffering.

The Truth of Cause means that we must reflect on what causes have produced these human sufferings, and we must investigate them and understand them clearly. The investigation of the cause of suffering is shown clearly in the doctrines of the Reality of All Existence (*shohō-jissō*) and of the Law of the Twelve Causes (*jūni-innen*) explained in chapter 7 of the Lotus Sutra, "The Parable of the Magic City."

The Truth of Extinction is the state of absolute quietude wherein all the sufferings in human life are extinguished. It is the state in which we cut off spiritual, physical, economic, and all other forms of suffering, and realize in this world the Land of the Eternally Tranquil Light (referred to in the Sutra of Meditation on the Bodhisattva Universal Virtue as the land of the Buddha Vairocana). This is a state attained only by awakening to the three great truths that Sakyamuni has taught us: "All things are impermanent" (*shogyō mujō*), "Nothing has an ego" (*shohō muga*), and "Nirvana is quiescence" (*nehan jakujō*). These three great

1. The Twelve Causes are ignorance, actions, consciousness, name and form (mental functions and matter), the six entrances (the six senses), contact, sensation, desire, clinging, existence, birth, and old age and death.

2. The Six Perfections (or *Pāramitās*) are donation, keeping the precepts, perseverance, assiduity, meditation, and wisdom. *Pāramitā* literally means "arriving at the other shore."

truths are also called the Seal of the Three Laws (*sambō-in*). They are so important that they are said to be the three fundamental principles of Buddhism.

However, an ordinary person cannot easily realize these three great truths. In order to do so, it is necessary for him to practice them and endeavor to achieve them in his daily life: he must practice the bodhisattva-way with his mind, his body, and his actions. This means that he must devote himself to the practice of the doctrines of the Eightfold Path

TRUTH OF SUFFERING spiritual, physical, economic, other — sufferings	TRUTH OF CAUSE Investigation of the cause of suffering based on the principles of the Reality of All Existence and the Law of the Twelve Causes
TRUTH OF EXTINCTION The tranquil state without — spiritual, physical, economic, other — sufferings	TRUTH OF THE PATH Method of practice for extinguishing sufferings: the Eightfold Path and the Six Perfections of the bodhisattva-way

The Four Noble Truths

(*hasshō-dō*) and the Six Perfections (*roku-haramitsu*). The Truth of the Path shows the way to absolute peace and the state of quietude that we can attain by practicing these two doctrines.

The Law of the Four Noble Truths teaches us to face the reality of human suffering (the Truth of Suffering), to grasp its real cause (the Truth of Cause), to practice daily the bodhisattva-way (the Truth of the Path), and thereby to extinguish various sufferings (the Truth of Extinction). The diagram of the Four Noble Truths above illustrates this progress.

Following is a brief explanation of the three great truths known as the Seal of the Three Laws to help the reader gain a fuller understanding of true Buddhism and thus the ability to lead a better daily life.

ALL THINGS ARE IMPERMANENT. The true meaning of the words "All things are impermanent" has gradually come to be misunderstood in Japan and is now generally interpreted as "Life is fleeting." This is probably because the term has been often used with such a connotation in classical Japanese literature. This has been one of the great causes of misunderstanding Buddhism in Japan. It has given the general public the idea that Buddhism teaches us only to pray earnestly for rebirth in a better world because life is fleeting.

In order to correct this basic misinterpretation, we must understand clearly the meaning of the words "All things are impermanent" (*shogyō mujō*). *Shogyō* means "all phenomena that appear in this world" and *mujō* means "impermanent," that is, "nothing existing in a fixed form" —in short, "All things change." Therefore, the teaching of *shogyō mujō* is that all phenomena of this world are always changing.

Modern science has proved that the sun, which seems to shine in the sky without changing, is actually changing every moment. We think that there is no change between ourselves of yesterday and ourselves of today, but the fact is that the cells of the human body are constantly dying and being born, so that all the cells of the body are replaced every seven years. Each cell of our body is changing continuously, though we are not aware of it. And everyone knows from experience how the suffering, sorrow, joy, or pleasure that we feel can change in an instant.

Simply because such a state of constant change bears witness to the teaching that all things are impermanent, however, it would be a fundamental error to think that the Buddha's teaching suggests that we take things as they are in this transient and unreliable existence. The law that all things are impermanent is the teaching that we should be aware of the changing nature of all things and so not be surprised at or shaken by trifling changes in phenomena or circumstances.

When we understand in this positive way the law that all things are impermanent, we realize how great is our power as human beings; and finally, we clearly understand why man must live in such a way as steadily to grow and improve. We also become keenly aware of the necessity to express gratitude to one another and to live together in harmony, with equal love for others and with a feeling of unity.

Billions of years ago, the earth contained no life; volcanos poured forth torrents of lava, and poisonous vapor and gas filled the air. However, when the earth had cooled sufficiently, about two billion years ago, living creatures evolved. These first creatures were simple unicellular microscopic organisms. Although these tiny life forms were exposed to great floods, tremendous earthquakes, volcanic eruptions, and extremes of heat and cold, they were not destroyed. Far from disappearing, they increased in number and gradually evolved into more complex life forms. It is the established theory today that life developed from amoeba-like organisms to insects, fish, reptiles, amphibians, birds, mammals, and finally man.

We should consider anew the strength of life. In doing so, we can regain confidence in our own lives and thus gain the courage to have faith in the basic strength of life and its power to withstand temporary sufferings and setbacks. In the process of his evolution man has overcome many trials and difficulties. This life-power dwells in our own bodies. When we consider the evolutionary process from the amoeba to man and then look back on human history, we realize that when all is said and done, man has advanced upward step by step. At the same time, we become aware that to advance upward is the most fitting human way of life and that to stagnate in a particular stage, much less regress to a wrong course of life, is to deviate from the proper path of man's life. If we can grasp this, we can come to understand that we must advance continuously toward the ideal state of man—indeed, that to do so is most natural.

Needless to say, the ideal state of man is buddhahood. Therefore, when we have the desire to become buddhas and practice the Buddha's teachings continuously, we are following the natural direction of human life. This is nothing extraordinary, but rather a matter of course. It is also natural that our health and our home life will become more balanced when we return to the natural way from which we have deviated.

When we look back upon the evolutionary process that gave birth to life on the earth, which was originally filled only with melted lava, metals, gas, and vapor, and how life forms divided into plants and animals, the latter evolving gradually through insects, fish, amphibians, birds, and mammals, and finally into man, we realize also that wood, stone, metal, and all other substances in the world have the same ultimate ancestors as ourselves. We can regard all plants, birds, and beasts as our kin. We then feel a natural gratitude to plants, insects, fish, birds, and beasts. If we feel grateful to these creatures, how much more deeply thankful should we be for our parents and grandparents, our nearest kin, and for the spirits of other ancestors! We come to understand this clearly and feel it deeply.

Truly all things in the universe are related; what can we say when human beings in this world are not brothers to one another? They oppose each other, hate each other, attack each other, even kill each other. This is not what man's life was intended to be. The reason that we do not realize this truth is because we are overwhelmed by the changes that impinge on us directly and are blinded by considerations of immediate gain and loss. If all men could see clearly the Buddha's teaching that all things are impermanent, they would be awakened from such illusion and could realize a peaceful and correct way of life in this world.

NOTHING HAS AN EGO. The law that nothing has an ego is the teaching that all things in this world, without exception, are related to one another. There is nothing that leads an isolated existence, that is wholly separated from other things. When we consider that even tiny insects, birds flying high in the sky, and pine trees growing on a distant hill were part of the same matter at the beginning of time on earth billions of years ago, we realize that these creatures are permeated by the same life-energy that gives us life. The same applies to earth, stone, clouds, and air.

When we turn our attention to the present and consider our own existence, we know that we are given life by earth and stone, and that we are obligated even to insects and birds. For example, if there were no clouds in the sky, we would have no rain; no plants would grow, and we would have no food. If there were no air, we could not live even a few minutes. Without exception, we have some invisible relationship even with those things that seem externally to have no connection with us.

To take a familiar example, even if our human bodies and minerals, such as iron, seem to be quite different, actually most of the body consists of water containing minerals; we live by the grace of such minerals as salt, calcium, iron, and copper. This fact demonstrates how things exist in connection with one another and are interdependent. It goes without saying that we have a much closer and stronger relationship to other human beings.

The late Dr. Albert Schweitzer, winner of the Nobel Peace Prize, who worked as a medical missionary among the Africans for over forty years at Lambarene, Gabon, was one of the greatest men of the twentieth century. It is said that Dr. Schweitzer firmly resolved to succor the African people when one day, listening to a Bach organ composition, he felt a sudden strong conviction. Reflecting on this story about Dr. Schweitzer, we cannot help being deeply impressed by the hidden linkings of cause and effect. Bach, who had died long before Dr. Schweitzer heard his music, could never have dreamed of this connection between himself and the people of Africa. However, a beautiful piece of music composed by Bach provided the catalyst that led to the great resolution of the young scholar of Alsace, Albert Schweitzer.

This is only one example of how invisible human relationships extend widely and deeply, like the meshes of a net. We can easily realize how much more closely the people of the same country are linked to one another. Economics provides an example of how relationships that appear superficial are actually much more deeply interwoven. For whom are the taxes that we pay used? Who benefits by the health-insurance premiums that healthy people pay? Who pays the unemployment-insurance premiums that the unemployed receive? Such invisible and unrealized connections are more numerous than we can imagine. We are inseparably bound up with one another, and we all exist through being permeated by the same life-energy. In spite of this, opposition, dispute, struggle, and killing cause each of us to be swayed by his own ego and to live selfishly for his personal profit alone. This is the important reason why we must realize the truth that nothing has an ego. When we have a deeper view of things, we realize that, as mentioned above, stagnating in a particular state or returning to a wrong course of life is sinful and evil because it goes against the historical inevitability and the natural course of human life that man advance upward step by step.

The Buddha's teachings instruct us that sin and evil did not originally exist in this world. They are due to the cessation of the proper progress of human life or the return to a wrong course. Therefore, the moment we abandon such negative uses of energy, that is, as soon as we are free from illusion, evil disappears and the world of the light of the brilliant rays of the Buddha is revealed before us. Our "non-advance," our "non-approach" to the Buddha, is sin and evil because such action is contrary to the proper course of human life.

From the selfish point of view of ego, we think that we can do as we like so long as we are prepared to accept the consequences of our actions, and ask only to be left alone and not interfered with by others. However, such an attitude is a fundamental error because our lives are related in some way to the lives of all others, so that the evil produced by one person inevitably exerts an influence upon other people somewhere, and the negligence of one person is sure to prevent others from advancing. If we understand this, we can be spiritually awakened to the fact that our own stagnation or retrogression hinders others, so that we determine to advance upward bit by bit. This is the true spirit of the law that nothing has an ego, and this is the reason why the true spirit of Buddhism consists in constant endeavor.

NIRVANA IS QUIESCENCE. The law that nirvana is quiescence is the third of the three major fundamental principles of Buddhism. This law has been misunderstood because of misconstruing the word "nirvana." Many people think nirvana is synonymous with death. The words "Sakyamuni Buddha entered nirvana" are ordinarily used to refer to the death of the Buddha. For this reason the law "Nirvana is quiescence" has been understood to refer to a paradise like the Pure Land of Amitābha Buddha, which in Pure Land Buddhism is believed to be our ideal destination after death.

The Sanskṛit word *nirvāṇa* has the negative meaning of "extinction" or "annihilation." Therefore this word also means the state in which one's body dies or disappears. At the same time, nirvana means the state reached by extinguishing all illusions, and this is the sense in which it is used in the teachings of the Buddha. In the true sense of the word, nirvana means the state attained by completely destroying all illusions and of never being tempted by them in the future. Therefore the words "Sakyamuni Buddha entered nirvana" mean not his death but the enlightenment attained by him.

The law "Nirvana is quiescence" teaches us that we can completely extinguish all the sufferings of human life and obtain peace and quietude when we destroy all illusions. How can we reach this state? The only way is to realize the two laws "All things are impermanent" and "Nothing has an ego."

The reason we worry about various kinds of sufferings is that we forget that all phenomena in this world are impermanent, that all things continuously change according to the law of cause and effect; we are deluded by phenomena and influenced by considerations of immediate gain or loss. If we study the way to buddhahood and by practicing it realize the truth of the impermanence of all things, we become able to attain a state of peace and quietude in which we can never be swayed by shifting circumstances. This is the state of "Nirvana is quiescence."

We sometimes feel troubled by shortages of goods, setbacks in business, or personal conflicts and disputes. This is because we lack harmony between ourselves and inanimate things and with other people. Why are we not in harmony with one another? This is because either we do not realize the truth that nothing has an ego or we have forgotten this truth.

We can attain harmony with others spontaneously when we remember the truth that all things and all men are permeated by one great life-energy and that all things are invisibly interconnected, and when we make the best use of this interconnection by abandoning the idea of ego, that is, by enhancing this interconnection to benefit both ourselves and others. When in harmony with others, we can give up excess and deficiency, struggle and friction, and can maintain peaceful minds. This is the state expressed in the law "Nirvana is quiescence." It is an ideal state that can be only attained by realizing the other two laws, "All things are impermanent" and "Nothing has an ego."

The doctrines of the Eightfold Path and the Six Perfections teach us how to live in order to reach the state of "Nirvana is quiescence" and how we should practice the Buddha's teachings in order to do so. As these two doctrines have a close connection with the doctrine of the Four Noble Truths, a brief explanation of them follows.

THE EIGHTFOLD PATH. The Eightfold Path consists in right view (*shō-ken*), right thinking (*shō-shi*), right speech (*shō-go*), right action (*shō-gyō*), right living (*shō-myō*), right endeavor (*shō-shōjin*), right memory (*shō-nen*), and right meditation (*shō-jō*). Many precepts and teachings containing numbers—such as the Eightfold Path—appear in Buddhist scriptures. This is because people could not record the teachings in writing at the time that Sakyamuni Buddha was preaching the Law but were obliged to memorize what they heard. Therefore Sakyamuni Buddha used numbers in preaching various doctrines so that people might easily remember them. However, it is not necessary for us to be too literal about such numbers.

Those who find it difficult to remember the doctrine of the Eightfold Path because of its eight divisions may find it easier to understand it by dividing it into four parts. The first is its fundamental purpose, to establish correct faith in a religion based on the wisdom of the Buddha, which discerns and understands the principle of the Reality of All Existence. The second is to have a right attitude in our daily lives; the third, to have right daily conduct; and the fourth, to follow the right way of practicing the Buddha's teachings.

"Right view" means to abandon a self-centered way of looking at things and to have a right view of the Buddha. In other words, it is to take refuge in the Buddha.

"Right thinking" means not to incline toward a self-centered attitude toward things but to think of things rightly, from a higher standpoint. This teaches us to abandon the "three evils of the mind," covetousness, resentment, and evil-mindedness, and to think of things rightly, with as generous a mind as the Buddha. More precisely, these three evils are the greedy mind (covetousness) that thinks only of one's own gain; the angry mind (resentment) that does not like it when things do not turn out as one wishes; and the evil mind (evil-mindedness) that wants to have its own way in everything.

RIGHT VIEW	To see all things rightly, based on the Buddha's wisdom, which discerns and understands the principle of the Reality of All Existence
RIGHT THINKING	To think rightly, avoiding the three evils of the mind
RIGHT SPEECH	To speak right words, avoiding the four evils of the mouth
RIGHT ACTION	To act rightly, avoiding the three evils of the body
RIGHT LIVING	To gain food, clothing, shelter, and other daily necessities in a right way
RIGHT ENDEAVOR	Never to do evil and always to do good
RIGHT MEMORY	To have a continuous right mind toward both oneself and others
RIGHT MEDITATION	To strive constantly for the true Law and to be fixed and settled in it

The Eightfold Path

"Right speech" teaches us to use right words in our daily lives and to avoid the "four evils of the mouth": lying (false language), a double tongue, ill speaking (slander), and improper language (careless language).

"Right action" means daily conduct in accordance with the precepts of the Buddha. For this purpose it is important to refrain from the "three evils of the body" that hinder right actions: needless killing, stealing, and committing adultery or other sexual misconduct.

"Right living" means to gain food, clothing, shelter, and the other necessities of life in a right way. This teaches us not to earn our livelihood through work that makes trouble for others or through a vocation useless to society but to live on a justifiable income that we can obtain through right work, a vocation useful to others.

"Right endeavor" means to engage constantly in right conduct without being idle or deviating from the right way, avoiding such wrongs as the three evils of the mind, the four evils of the mouth, and the three evils of the body mentioned above.

"Right memory" means to practice with a right mind as the Buddha did. It cannot be truly said that we have the same mind as the Buddha unless we have a right mind not only toward ourselves but also toward others, and still further, toward all things. If we hope that only we ourselves may be right, we will become stubborn and self-satisfied people who are alienated from the world. We cannot say we have the same mind as the Buddha unless we address ourselves to all things in the universe with a fair and right mind.

"Right meditation" means always to determine to believe in the teachings of the Buddha and not to be agitated by any change of circumstances. This teaches us to practice consistently the right teaching of the Buddha.

Taken altogether, the doctrine of the Eightfold Path is the teaching that shows us the right way to live our daily lives.

THE SIX PERFECTIONS. This doctrine teaches us the six kinds of practice that bodhisattvas should follow to attain enlightenment. The Six Perfections are donation (*fuse*), keeping the precepts (*jikai*), perseverance (*ninniku*), assiduity (*shōjin*), meditation (*zenjō*), and wisdom (*chie*).

A bodhisattva is a person who, unlike the *śrāvaka* and *pratyekabuddha,* wishes not only to extinguish his own illusions but to save others, as well. Therefore, the doctrine of the Six Perfections has the salvation of all living beings as its aim.

The practice of donation comes first in this doctrine. There are three kinds of donation: donating material goods, donating the Law, and donating fearlessness (the body). The first means to give others money or goods. The second refers to teaching others rightly. And the third means to remove the anxieties or sufferings of others through one's own effort. There is no one who is unable to perform some form of donation. No matter how impoverished one is, he should be able to give alms to those who are worse off than he or to support a public work with however small a donation, if he has the will to do so. Even if there is someone who absolutely cannot afford to do so, he can be useful to others and to society by offering his services. A person who has knowledge or wisdom in some field should be able to teach others or guide them even if he has no money or is physically handicapped. Even a person of humble circumstances can perform donation of the Law. To speak of his own experiences to others can be his donation of the Law. Even to teach others a recipe or how to knit, for example, can be a way to donate the Law.

It is essential that we be useful to others by practicing these three kinds of donation within the limits of our ability. Needless to say, nothing can be better for us than to practice all three. The fact that donation is the first of the practices of the bodhisattva is highly significant.

The practice of keeping the precepts is the second of the Six Perfections. This teaches us that we cannot truly save others unless we remove our own illusions through the precepts given by the Buddha, and that we should perfect ourselves by living an upright life. However, we must not think that we cannot guide others just because we are not perfect ourselves. We cannot improve ourselves if we shut ourselves off from others in our efforts to live correctly. A major point of keeping the precepts is to render service to others. The more we do for others, the more we can elevate ourselves, and the more we elevate ourselves, the more we can render service to others. Each reinforces the other.

The third of the Six Perfections is perseverance, a quality that is especially important for people today. Sakyamuni Buddha was endowed with all the virtues and became the Buddha through his constant practice. Although it is a sin against him to emphasize only one of his virtues, the greatest virtue of the Buddha as a man seems to have been his generosity. No matter what biography of Sakyamuni Buddha we read or which of the sutras, we find that nowhere is it recorded that the Buddha ever became angry. However severely he was persecuted and however coldly his disciples turned against him and departed from him, he was always sympathetic and compassionate.

If I were asked to explain with a single phrase the character of Sakyamuni Buddha as a man, I would answer without hesitation, "A person of perfect generosity." Therefore, I think that there is no action that makes Sakyamuni Buddha more sorrowful than when we become angry about something and reproach others or when we blame others for our own wrongs. Above all else, we should refrain from such actions toward each other. Perseverance is, in short, generosity. As we persevere in the practice of the bodhisattvas, we cease to become angry or reproachful toward others, or toward anything in the universe. We are apt to complain about the weather when it rains and to grumble about the dust when we have a spell of fine weather. However, when through perseverance we attain a calm and untroubled mind, we become thankful for both the rain and the sun. Then our minds become free from changes in our circumstances.

When we advance further, we come not only to have no feeling of anger and hatred toward those who hurt, insult, or betray us but even to wish actively to help them. On the other hand, we should not be swayed by flattery or praise of the good we may do but should quietly reflect on our conduct. We should not feel superior to others but should maintain a modest attitude when everything goes smoothly. All these attitudes

Donation	"Makes a miserly one raise the mind of donation": to serve sincerely the community and other people
Keeping the precepts	"Makes an arrogant one raise the mind of keeping the commandments": to remove the mind of arrogance and to admonish and discipline oneself
Perseverance	"Makes an irascible one raise the mind of perseverance": to remove anger and to endure
Assiduity	"Makes an indolent one raise the mind of assiduity": to endeavor constantly
Meditation	"Makes a distracted one raise the mind of meditation": to calm one's mind and not be agitated
Wisdom	"Makes an ignorant one raise the mind of wisdom": to remove prejudice and evil thinking through correct judgment

The Six Perfections

come from perseverance. This mental state is the highest point of the practice of perseverance. Even though we cannot attain such a state of mind immediately, we can attain an attitude of compassion toward those who cause difficulties for us sooner than we expect. We ought to advance at least to this level. If this kind of perseverance were practiced by people throughout the world, this alone would establish peace and make mankind immeasurably happier.

The fourth of the Six Perfections is assiduity. This means to proceed straight toward an important target without being distracted by trivial things. We cannot say we are assiduous when our ideas and conduct are impure, even if we devote ourselves to the study and practice of the Buddha's teachings. Even when we devote ourselves to study and practice, we sometimes do not meet with good results or may even obtain adverse effects, or we may be hindered in our religious practice by others. But such matters are like waves rippling on the surface of the ocean; they are only phantoms, which will disappear when the wind dies down. Therefore, once we have determined to practice the bodhisattva-way, we should advance single-mindedly toward our destination without turning aside. This is assiduity.

The fifth of the Six Perfections is meditation, *dhyāna* in Sanskrit and *zenjō* in Japanese. *Zen* means "a quiet mind" or "an unbending spirit," and *jō* indicates the state of having a calm, unagitated mind. It is important for us not only to devote ourselves to the practice of the Buddha's teachings but also to view things thoroughly with a calm mind and to think them over well. Then we can see the true aspect of all things and discover the right way to cope with them.

The right way of seeing things and the power of discerning the true aspect of all things is wisdom—the last of the Six Perfections. The meaning of this word is not explained here because it has already been discussed on page 4. We cannot save others without having wisdom. Let us suppose that there is an impoverished young man lying by the road. And suppose that we feel pity for him and give him some money without reflecting on the consequences. What if he is mildly addicted to some drug? He will grab the money given to him and use it to buy drugs. In this way he may become seriously, even hopelessly, addicted. If we had handed him over to the police instead of giving him money, he would have been sent to a hospital and could start life over again. This is the kind of error we may commit in performing donation without wisdom. Though this is an extreme case, similar cases on a smaller scale occur all the time. Thus, even though we may do something useful for others or practice good conduct in order to save them, none of our mercy or kindness is effective unless we have true wisdom. Far from being effective, our mercy may have a harmful effect. Therefore wisdom is an absolutely indispensable condition in practicing the bodhisattva-way.

Now to return to chapter 1 of the Lotus Sutra. Mañjuśrī continued to speak to Maitreya Bodhisattva-Mahāsattva and all the other leaders: "All ye good sons! Thus Sun Moon Light Tathāgata preached a proper Law for those who sought to be *śrāvakas* and *pratyekabuddhas,* and he also preached a suitable Law for the bodhisattvas. He made them attain Perfect Enlightenment and achieve perfect knowledge. Again there was a *tathāgata,* also named Sun Moon Light, who preached the same Law, and again a *tathāgata,* also named Sun Moon Light, who did the same; and in like manner there were twenty thousand *tathāgatas* all bearing the same name, Sun Moon Light.

"Before the last of these *tathāgatas* left home, he was a king and had eight royal sons. All these princes, hearing that their father had left home and attained Perfect Enlightenment, renounced their royal position and, following him, left home, and they planted roots of goodness under thousands of myriads of buddhas.

"At that time the Buddha Sun Moon Light preached the Great-vehicle sutra called the Innumerable Meanings, the Law by which bodhisattvas are instructed and which the buddhas watch over and keep in mind. Having preached this sutra, he at once, amidst the great assembly, sat cross-legged and entered meditation. At this moment the sky rained beautiful flowers over the buddhas and all the great assembly. As soon as the universal buddha-world shook in various ways, the Buddha Sun Moon Light sent forth from the circle of white hair between his eyebrows a ray of light, which illuminated eighteen thousand buddha-lands in the eastern quarter, just like those that now are seen.

"Know, Maitreya! At that time in the assembly there were a great many bodhisattvas who joyfully desired to hear the Law. All these bodhisattvas, beholding this ray of wonderful light, desired to know the causes and the reasons for that ray. Then there was a bodhisattva named Mystic Light, who had eight hundred disciples. When the Buddha Sun Moon Light arose from contemplation, he preached by means of the Bodhisattva Mystic Light the Great-vehicle sutra called the Lotus Flower of the Wonderful Law, by which bodhisattvas are instructed and which the buddhas watch over and keep in mind. For six hundred thousand years he rose not from his seat, and during all these long years his hearers in that assembly remained seated in their places, motionless in body and mind, listening to the buddha's preaching and deeming it but the length of a meal."

The above passage tells us that there were twenty thousands *tathāgatas* in succession, all bearing the same name and performing the same function. (*Tathāgata* means "one who has come from the truth" and is one of the epithets of a buddha.) The last of these buddhas preached the Great-vehicle sutra called the Lotus Flower of the Wonderful Law. His preaching continued for six hundred thousand years, but his hearers in the assembly deemed it only the short length of a meal. A full explanation of the true meaning of this story will be given in the discussion of chapter 16, "Revelation of the [Eternal] Life of the Tathāgata." Briefly, however, this mysterious story demonstrates clearly that true enlightenment is an eternal truth everywhere and is not affected by time and space.

Mañjuśrī continued: "Having preached this sutra, the Buddha Sun Moon Light proclaimed to all in the assembly: 'Today, at midnight, will the Tathāgata enter the nirvana of no remains.' After the buddha's extinction, the Bodhisattva Mystic Light, having retained in memory the Sutra of the Lotus Flower of the Wonderful Law, expounded it continuously for men.

"The Bodhisattva Mystic Light had a disciple whose name was Fame Seeker. This disciple was greedily attached to gain, and though he read and recited many sutras repeatedly, none of them penetrated and stuck; he forgot and lost almost all. So he was named Fame Seeker. This man also, because he had planted many roots of goodness, was able to meet innumerable buddhas, whom he worshiped, revered, honored, and extolled. Know, Maitreya! The Bodhisattva Mystic Light of that time was I myself, while the Bodhisattva Fame Seeker was you yourself.

"Now I see that this auspice is no different from the former one. Therefore, I consider that the present Tathāgata will preach the Great-vehicle sutra called the Lotus Flower of the Wonderful Law. All ye good sons! Wait for his preaching with folded hands and with one mind. He will be sure to preach the truth thoroughly to us and to give the seeker of the way satisfaction."

Mañjuśrī concluded his speech thus and then repeated the substance of his discourse in verse. With this, chapter 1 ends.

What is most impressive in this chapter is the immeasurable value of the Buddha's mental powers. Vividly expressed in the story of the last Buddha Sun Moon Light is the fact that Sakyamuni Buddha, who knew that the time of his entering nirvana was approaching, was determined to leave the most important experience of his enlightenment to posterity. However, we know that at that time his body had grown very weak from illness and old age. In spite of this fact, he began to preach the vast and profound Law of the Lotus Sutra, the strongest, most positive, and most affirmative teaching of his life. We must bow down before the greatness of his mental power and the depth of his enlightenment. And we must not forget that his mental power came from his great compassion for the yet unborn people of later times.

CHAPTER 2

Tactfulness

CALLED THE CORE of the Law of Appearance, this important chapter is the pivot of the Buddha's preaching in the first half of the Lotus Sutra. The Japanese title of this chapter, *"Hōben,"* is a compound word consisting of two characters, *hō* and *ben. Hō* originally means "a square" but sometimes means "right." *Ben* means "method" or "means." Therefore *hōben* means "a right method" or "a right means." As seen in the Japanese proverb *Uso mo hōben* (A lie can be expedient), it is regrettable to see how far the understanding of this word has deviated from its true meaning. The word *hōben* originally indicated the idea, "an enlightening method appropriately applied to the person and the occasion." Unless we keep in mind this original meaning, we cannot correctly understand this chapter.

When Mañjuśrī foretold, "As his last teaching, the Buddha will certainly preach the highest enlightenment that he obtained," all in the assembly waited expectantly for the Buddha to begin to preach. At that time the World-honored One, rising quietly and clearly from contemplation, addressed Śāriputra: "As buddhas can penetrate the real state of all things, their wisdom is very profound and infinite. Their wisdom-school is difficult to understand and difficult to enter, so that the *śrāvakas* and *pratyekabuddhas* cannot apprehend it. Wherefore? Because the buddhas have been in fellowship with countless numbers of buddhas, perfectly practicing the infinite Law of all buddhas, boldly and zealously advancing and making their fame universally known.

"As the buddhas have perfected the very profound, unprecedented

Law, those who do not practice it deeply cannot understand its meaning. The buddhas also have preached it in various ways as opportunity served; it is very difficult for hearers to understand the buddhas' real intention and for what purpose they have preached thus.

"Śāriputra! Ever since I became Buddha, with various reasonings and various parables I have widely discoursed and taught, and by countless tactful methods have led living beings, causing them to leave their selfish ideas [all attachments]. Wherefore? Because the Tathāgata is altogether perfect in his method of leading living beings in his tactfulness and his power to discern the real state of all things [*pāramitā*, or perfection of wisdom].

"Śāriputra! The wisdom of the Tathāgata is broad and great, profound and far-reaching; the Tathāgata can discern all from the infinite past to the infinite future. He possesses the following great minds [the four infinite virtues], which ordinary men cannot imagine: the infinite virtue of benevolence [the desire that one's own life make others happy]; that of compassion [the desire that one's conduct remove others' pain]; that of joy [the enjoyment of the sight of those who have obtained happiness]; and that of impartiality [the mind that has abandoned both the idea of revenge for injury inflicted by others and attachment to recompense for one's good deeds]. His expositions are unimpeded; his powers, his fearlessness, his meditations, his emancipations, and his contemplations have enabled him to enter into the boundless realms and to accomplish all the unprecedented Law.

"Śāriputra! The Tathāgata is able to discriminate each of the hearers, to preach laws skillfully to each of them, to use gentle words and cheer the hearts of all. Śāriputra! Essentially speaking, the Buddha has altogether fulfilled the infinite, boundless, unprecedented Law."

THREE REQUESTS AND THREE REFUSALS. At this point the World-honored One suddenly fell silent. After a short time he began to speak again: "Enough, Śāriputra, there is no need to say more. Wherefore? Because the Law that the Buddha has perfected is the chief unprecedented Law, and difficult to understand. Only a buddha together with a buddha can fathom the Reality of All Existence, that is to say, all existence has such a form, such a nature, such an embodiment, such a potency, such a function, such a primary cause, such a secondary cause, such an effect, such a recompense, and such a complete fundamental whole."

These ten categories are termed the doctrine of the Ten Suchnesses (*jū-nyoze*), since they consist of ten terms preceded by "such." The doctrine of the Ten Suchnesses is the truth that applies to all things in the universe; and the concept of "Three Thousand (Worlds) in One Thought" (*ichinen sanzen*), arising from this doctrine, is itself the truth preached by the Buddha. But just as Sakyamuni Buddha hesitated to expound this doctrine, for us to give a full explanation of this teaching at this point would be likely to confuse rather than enlighten readers. Therefore this doctrine will be fully explained later (pages 110–13).

Then the World-honored One, desiring to proclaim this teaching over again, spoke in verse to the following effect: "The Buddha's wisdom is immeasurable. It is not a wisdom that I obtained easily after quick study but the wisdom that I finally attained after having followed countless buddhas in former times and having perfectly walked the right ways. In other words, it is the supreme wisdom, which I have been able to attain by cultivating my mind continuously.

"The Buddha's wisdom cannot be fathomed by following anyone—those who have been called the greatest wise men among many other people, *pratyekabuddhas* who have obtained enlightenment by their own experience, bodhisattvas who have newly vowed to attain the same enlightenment as the Buddha together with the mass of the people, and bodhisattvas who are so advanced in their practice that they are free from falling back.

"I now have wholly attained this profound and mysterious Law, as have all the buddhas of the universe. Though these buddhas preach various teachings, the foundation of all their teachings is the same. The buddhas' teachings always include only one fundamental truth, even though the words of the buddhas differ from one another. You must know this fact. The various ways to manifest this fundamental truth, that is, the tactful powers of the Buddha, are very important and valuable. In order to free beginners who seek enlightenment from illusions and sufferings in their daily lives, I have employed the three-vehicle teaching: the *śrāvaka*-vehicle, the *pratyekabuddha*-vehicle, and the bodhisattva-vehicle. This was for the purpose of showing the greatness of the Buddha's tactful powers."

Listening to the Buddha preaching thus, all present in the great assembly wondered why the World-honored One now extolled the tactful way so repeatedly. All reflected thus: "So far the Buddha has taught us to be free through the fact that all phenomena in this world are always changing, and at last we have reached such a mental state after earnest practice. But now the Buddha says that those who are in such a mental state cannot understand the Buddha's wisdom. We cannot grasp what his words really mean." Thus all of them felt confused.

At that time Śāriputra, apprehending the doubt in the minds of all present in the great assembly and also himself not having mastered the meaning of the Buddha's preaching, spoke to the Buddha: "World-honored One! What is the cause and what is the reason for so earnestly extolling the paramount tactful method and the very profound mysterious Law, difficult to understand, of the buddhas? I have never before heard such a discourse from the Buddha. At present all in this assembly are altogether in doubt. Will the World-honored One be pleased to explain these things?"

Then Śāriputra, desiring to emphasize what he had said, repeated the same thing in verse. But the Buddha said to Śāriputra: "Enough, enough, there is no need to say more. If I explain this matter, all the worlds of the gods and men would be startled and perplexed and become discouraged in their practice. It would be better not to explain it."

Śāriputra burned with ardor for the truth and was not discouraged from asking the Buddha to explain it. Śāriputra again said to the Buddha: "World-honored One! Be pleased to explain it! Be pleased to explain it! Wherefore? Because in this assembly there are numberless living beings who have already seen the buddhas, whose perceptions are keen and whose wisdom is clear. If they hear the Buddha's teaching, they will be able to believe and practice it respectfully."

The Buddha again said: "Enough, Śāriputra! If I explained this matter, arrogant people would have doubts about it and might sneer that it is impossible for them."

Śāriputra, persistent, once again asked the Buddha the same question. The Buddha gazed intently at Śāriputra for a little while. Then, nodding his head with an air of satisfaction, he addressed Śāriputra: "Śāriputra! Since you have already three times earnestly repeated your request, how can I refuse to speak? I will discriminate and explain it to you. Do you now listen attentively to, ponder, and remember it!"

FIVE THOUSAND LEAVE THE ASSEMBLY. When the World-honored One had spoken thus, some five thousand *bhikshus, bhikshuṇīs, upāsakas,* and *upāsikās* in the assembly immediately rose from their seats and, saluting the Buddha, withdrew. This was because the root of sin in these people was so deep and their haughty spirit so enlarged that they imagined they had attained what they had not attained, and that they had proved what they had not proved. In such error as this, they would not stay.

The World-honored One was silent and did not stop them. This was because he thought that even if he forced them to remain, they could not understand his teaching and it would tend instead to produce an adverse result. He also considered that they would wish to seek a true teaching sometime in the future, and would in time develop the capacity to understand it. His preaching to them at that time would be the quickest way to save them.

At first glance this attitude of the Buddha seems to indicate indifference to others, but his mind in its profundity was filled with the great wisdom and benevolence of the Buddha. This is clear from the incident recounted in chapter 8, "The Five Hundred Disciples Receive the Prediction of Their Destiny": when he gave a great many *arhats* the prediction that they would become buddhas in accordance with their practice, he said to Kāśyapa, "The other band of *śrāvakas* will also be like them. To those who are not in this assembly, do you proclaim my words." The Buddha's words "those who are not in this assembly" refer to the five thousand monks who had risen from their seats and left the assembly earlier. The fact that he purposely did not stop them at that time demonstrates his great power in tactful means.

When the haughty monks had left and only the true and earnest seekers remained in the congregation, the Buddha addressed Śāriputra: "The *udumbara* flower is said to be seen but once in three thousand years. The wonderful Law that I am now preaching to you is as rare to hear as is the blooming of this flower to see. All the buddhas preach only when they consider that the time is right. All of you have happened to meet with a very good opportunity. Śāriputra, believe me, all of you; in the Buddha's teaching no word is false. Now listen carefully to my teaching.

"The Buddha expounds the laws by numberless tactful ways and with various reasonings and parables. The purpose for which these laws have been preached cannot be understood clearly. The fact is that the buddhas, the world-honored ones, appear in the world only in order to preach the one very great cause. What is the one very great cause? It is nothing other than what the buddhas desire to cause men to realize as being the purpose for which they live—that is, the Buddha-knowledge. If each person understands this, he will become a buddha and will be able to attain true happiness.

"For this purpose, all living beings must first realize that they all equally possess the buddha-nature. As they become able to understand that they have the same nature as the Buddha, they will naturally rid themselves of their small selfish ideas and will have pure minds. The buddhas appear in the world because they desire to cause all living beings to open their eyes to the Buddha-knowledge. To those who can realize the Buddha-knowledge, the buddhas desire to show, indicating clearly, what the world is in the Buddha's eyes and in his wisdom. Having been able to understand the real state of the world, if they have the Buddha-knowledge they come to realize that this world is a quiet and peaceful state, with no suffering. The buddhas appear in the world because they desire to cause all living beings to apprehend the Buddha-knowledge. But living beings cannot attain such a state of mind naturally. It is a mental state that they cannot enter until they have devoted themselves to their practice with assiduity. The buddhas appear in the world because they desire to cause all living beings to enter the way of the Buddha-knowledge.

"Through the tactful order of letting all living beings open their eyes to the Buddha-knowledge, showing it to them, letting them apprehend it, and letting them enter into its Way, the buddhas desire to cause all living beings to attain the Buddha-knowledge, and they teach that man must truly understand the purpose for which he lives—the buddhas for this one very great purpose alone appear in the world."

A Buddha Teaches Only Bodhisattvas. After preaching thus, Sakyamuni Buddha said to Śāriputra in a serious and sharp tone: "The buddha-*tathāgata* teaches only bodhisattvas."

We are apt to take these words to mean, "The buddhas teach only bodhisattvas, so *śrāvakas* and *pratyekabuddhas* are not the true disciples of the Buddha." We are also liable to think that somehow such words as these are inconsistent with the Buddha's having said, "The buddhas appear in the world to cause all living beings to apprehend the truth." However, when we carefully consider the meaning of his words, we realize that they are always consistent.

Among the teachings of the Buddha there are many that apparently contradict each other. Many seeming contradictions are also found in the Lotus Sutra. However, the Buddha never made contradictory statements in his teachings. It is only that he speaks frankly, without mincing matters. Taking a shallow view of his words, we cannot guess what great hidden meaning they hold and so we think that they contain contradictions. When our understanding of his words is shallow, we become confused and think, "I cannot possibly understand the Buddha's teachings," or "His teachings are unreliable because of their inconsistency."

We must read the sutras deeply. Those who find this difficult should read them over and over, and then they will be able to understand something of the true meaning of the sutras. If they still cannot understand them, they should ask a competent person for instruction. They should realize that it would be a great mistake to think, "The Buddha's teachings have no interest for me because of their contradictions." We must receive and keep firmly the Lotus Sutra. Even if the sutra seems so difficult that we cannot understand it, with perseverance we will come to understand it eventually, at which time we have only to hold to it earnestly.

The true meaning of the Buddha's words, "The buddhas teach only bodhisattvas," should be interpreted as follows: "As long as you think that the fact that you have been able to obtain enlightenment for yourself alone is enough, you cannot attain real enlightenment. If you feel that you yourself have attained enlightenment though many other people have not, such a feeling is positive proof that you are keeping yourself aloof from others. Such a feeling is not a blending with others; it is, rather, isolation from them. You cannot enter the state of 'Nothing has an ego' because your egoistic feeling still remains. Therefore, your enlightenment is not real. One can obtain enlightenment for one's own self, and by the same token, all others can do the same. One can be saved from one's own suffering, and at the same time, all others can be saved from theirs. Your salvation together with that of others is your real salvation—at the very time that you understand this, you can be said to have attained real enlightenment and to have been set free from the bonds of illusion and suffering in the world."

Indeed, our first step toward enlightenment makes a crucial difference to our lives. In the example of the mathematician Yōichi Yoshida, mentioned in the Preface, as a child he found that one cannot be divided exactly into three through decimal arithematic. Though an effective way to calculate the fraction "one-third" existed all along, he could not possibly know this before studying fractions. But he was able to grasp it as soon as he was taught that fractions were another way of considering numbers.

We can say the same thing of attaining enlightenment. As long as even a man of great wisdom, such as Śāriputra, only desired to obtain enlightenment for himself and to be saved for his own sake, he could not possibly bridge the great gulf between his own and the Buddha's enlightenment, though he had already nearly attained the Buddha's enlightenment. However, he was able to leap the gulf at the moment when he realized that real salvation consists in one's own salvation together with that of all other people.

This is the true meaning of the Buddha's words, "The buddhas teach only bodhisattvas." He said this in order to explain that only bodhisattvas, those who practice to save all living beings, can grasp the true teachings of the Buddha.

ONLY ONE BUDDHA-VEHICLE. If *śrāvakas* and *pratyekabuddhas* should generate the intention to practice the bodhisattva-way, they would at that moment become the true disciples of the Buddha. The Buddha did not ignore them, but said what he did in order to lead them to true Buddha-knowledge. In evidence of this, the Buddha next addressed Śāriputra as follows: "Śāriputra! The Tathāgata, by means of the One Buddha-vehicle, preaches the Law to all living beings; there is no other vehicle, neither a second nor a third."

The One-vehicle means: All people can become buddhas. The enlightenment obtained by *śrāvakas, pratyekabuddhas,* and bodhisattvas alike is one by which they become buddhas, and it is the same in origin. Some can obtain the enlightenment of a *śrāvaka* and others can obtain that of a *pratyekabuddha*. Both aspects of enlightenment are gates to the Buddha-knowledge.

This is allegorically explained as follows: A person who has entered this gate cannot enter the inner room of the Buddha-knowledge until he has first passed through the porch of the bodhisattva practice. At the same time, it cannot be said that the gate and the porch are not both included within the residence of the Buddha. However, if a person stays at the gate, he will be drenched when it rains and chilled when it snows. "All of you, come into the inner room of the Buddha's residence. The eastern gate, the western gate, and the porch, all are entrances that lead to the inner room of the Buddha-knowledge." This is the meaning of the Buddha's words, "Besides the One Buddha-vehicle, there is neither a second vehicle nor a third. I have shown the existence of these two vehicles by my tactful power. There is only one true goal for all."

If we can grasp the true meaning of the Buddha's words, we will come naturally to understand the meaning of the latter part of chapter 2. Here only the principal points, which include some difficult terms that may be confusing, will be explained.

As mentioned before, the buddhas appear in the world only for the one very great purpose of causing all living beings to attain the Buddha-knowledge; in other words, for the sake of causing living beings to obtain enlightenment, realizing that they can become buddhas. The truth is that the Buddha's teaching is only one, but because in the evil ages of the five decays all living beings are greedy and alienated from the Buddha, the buddhas, by tactful powers, through the One Buddha-vehicle discriminate and expound the three vehicles—*śrāvaka, pratyekabuddha,* and bodhisattva.

All living beings have many kinds of desires deeply rooted in their minds. Even if man's illusions seem to have been removed from his conscious mind, they remain in the subconscious mind and will arise again through force of fixed habit, given the right conditions. The Buddhist term for this phenomenon is *jikke,* meaning the innate seeds that we possess within us. For example, we suddenly feel angry when someone insults us, though we had decided never to lose our temper and had thought we had become very even-tempered. This happens because of deeply rooted desires. As long as we do not remove them from our subconscious mind, we cannot be said to be truly free from the bonds of illusion and suffering.

The subconscious mind has a great influence on physical health, as medical science has verified. This fact, which psychologists and doctors now acknowledge, Sakyamuni Buddha had recognized twenty-five hundred years ago.

THE EVIL AGES OF THE FIVE DECAYS. The Buddha said to Śāriputra: "The buddhas appear in the evil ages of the five decays—the decay of the *kalpa,* decay through tribulations, decay of all living beings, decay of views, and decay of lifetime."

The decay of the *kalpa,* the first of the five decays, is the decay that takes place because of a very long lapse of time. When the status quo is maintained over a long period, various evils arise, just as hardening of the arteries exerts an unfavorable influence upon physical health. For this reason, sometimes the world needs to enter a new age in order to restore its health.

Decay through tribulations means that men come to act stupidly because of their illusions. This is the reason that criminal acts increase with time.

Decay of all living beings refers to the conflicts that arise because of the superficial differences in people's natures. Disputes break out among people and lead eventually to trouble in their families and in society in general because they do not realize that all people are permeated by one great life-force, so they focus on surface differences, and each asserts his own self.

Decay of views indicates the public conflicts that arise because of different viewpoints. Everything works against people, as all of them take a narrow view of matters because of their own selfish aims. But if all adopted a right way of looking at things, as expounded in the Buddha's teachings, a peaceful world without disputes would come about naturally.

Decay of lifetime means the uneasy state of the world caused because, due to their short lives, people seek immediate results and profit from their ideas and conduct, and they become anxious over trifles. If they could only awaken to the truth of man's eternal life, they would be saved from their sufferings without fail.

In such evil ages of the five decays, all living beings are too deeply attached to their illusions to understand the supreme teaching if it is preached to them directly. Therefore the buddhas gradually lead all living beings to enlightenment by their tactful power of dividing the teaching into the three vehicles: the *śrāvaka*-vehicle, in which one listens to the Buddha's teachings and removes illusions from one's mind; the *pratyekabuddha*-vehicle, in which one is not satisfied with listening to the Buddha's teachings but realizes the truth for oneself through one's own experience; and the bodhisattva-vehicle, in which one is saved and becomes a bodhisattva as the result of the religious practice of saving others. When all living beings realize that these three divisions stem from the tactful powers of the buddhas, the tactfulness shown by the buddhas itself becomes a great way leading to the truth.

All living beings can enter the Buddha-way from any point: from worshiping the buddhas' relics, from building stupas and memorials, from building temples and shrines to the buddhas in the wilderness, or even from heaping sand in play to form a buddha's stupa. All living beings can enter the Buddha-way by doing anything good. As they increasingly strive after virtue and develop the great mind of benevolence, they finally become buddhas.

The words of the Buddha that we must be particularly careful to understand correctly here are: "I predict that such men as these / In the world to come will accomplish the Buddha-way." We should pay special attention to the phrase "the world to come." This does not mean "after one's death" but "sometime in the future, when one will gradually have advanced, step by step."

The Lotus Sutra teaches us that when one attains enlightenment, one becomes a buddha immediately and this world instantaneously becomes the Land of Eternally Tranquil Light. The sutra also teaches us not that we cannot go to paradise until we die but that the Buddha dwells in our minds and paradise exists in our daily lives.

In the last verse portion of chapter 2, we find the following lines: "The buddhas never by a smaller vehicle / Save all living creatures." These lines are often misinterpreted to mean: "In the end the buddhas did not save all living beings by a smaller vehicle." Some people consider that this is inconsistent with the Buddha's benevolence. However, the true meaning of these words is: "The buddhas could not save all living beings finally by a smaller vehicle alone." That is, the buddhas save all living beings to some degree even by a smaller vehicle, but by that vehicle alone the buddhas cannot lead them to the final salvation, that is, the supreme salvation.

The Buddha concluded his preaching in chapter 2 with strong words: "Know, Śāriputra! The Law of the buddhas is thus: by innumerable tactful ways, they proclaim the Law as opportunity serves. The essential thing is to learn it repeatedly and to practice it in your daily lives. Those who will not do so are not able to realize perfectly the one very great purpose, that the buddhas preach their teachings to all living beings by degrees and finally lead them to attain the same state as the Buddha. But you already know the expedient tactful ways of the buddhas. If so, you have no further doubts and rejoice greatly in your hearts, and you are also able to realize for yourselves that you will become buddhas."

CHAPTER 3

A Parable

IN THE PREVIOUS CHAPTER, after Śāriputra had three times earnestly repeated his request to Sakyamuni Buddha, who said to him, "Enough, enough, there is no need to say more," he was taught clearly the relation between the teaching of the One Buddha-vehicle and the tactful ways of the buddhas. Śāriputra felt ecstatic with joy when he realized that there was an open gate for him to enter into the real enlightenment of the Buddha the instant he regarded the buddhas' tactful ways themselves as valuable.

Then Śāriputra instantly rose up, folded his hands, and, looking up into the Buddha's face, spoke to the Buddha, saying: "Ah, I am grateful to the World-honored One! Now, hearing the sound of the Law from you, I have my eyes opened toward the Law for the first time. How imperfect a man I have been! When I heard of such a Law as this from the Buddha and saw the bodhisattvas whose attainment of buddhahood was predicted, I was not prepared for these things and was greatly distressed, saying, 'Ah, will I end without discovering the Buddha's knowledge?' Constantly when dwelling alone in mountain forests or under trees, whether sitting or walking, I was occupied with this thought: 'I have listened to the Buddha's teachings like these bodhisattvas, and I have been able to realize them to some extent. But why does the Buddha preach to me only the small-vehicle law?'

"I have been wrong in my judgment of this. Wherefore? Because if I had attended to the Buddha's preaching in regard to the accomplishment of Perfect Enlightenment, I should certainly have been delivered by the Great-vehicle. It is my own fault that I have been impatient for it and have felt myself unfairly treated. Not understanding the Buddha's tactful method of opportune preaching, on first hearing the Buddha-law I only casually believed, pondered on, and bore witness to it. Ever since then I have passed whole days and nights in self-reproach because I saw the bodhisattvas who were predicted to become buddhas. But now my eyes are opened for the first time. Today I indeed know that I am really a son of the Buddha, and I am quite another man now. I have a changed way of looking at things because of the supreme teaching of the Buddha. Moreover, I have obtained a place in the Buddha-law. I am truly grateful to you."

Then Śāriputra, desiring to announce this meaning again, spoke in verse and repented his past imperfection, expressing thoroughly his present state of mind.

Greatly satisfied with Śāriputra's words, the World-honored One said to him: "Śāriputra! You have well realized what I have preached. If you maintain your present mental attitude for a long time, serve countless numbers of buddhas, and complete the Way that bodhisattvas walk, you will surely become a buddha."

Speaking thus, the Buddha gave a title to this future buddha, Flower Light Tathāgata, and announced the name of his buddha-domain as Undefiled. He also named the period when that buddha would appear as Ornate with Great Jewels.

PREDICTION OF BUDDHAHOOD. The prediction of buddhahood, called *juki* in Japanese, is a term that will appear frequently later in this book. The most important fact to bear in mind here is that this is not a casual assurance given by the Buddha that one can become a buddha without making any effort.

When a religion decays, it is likely to be rejected by thinking people because it teaches that one can be reborn in paradise by merely uttering a magic formula. If that were all, it would not be so bad; but sometimes it preaches that no matter what evil one does, one can be saved and go to paradise if only one buys a certain talisman. The real salvation of the Buddha is not such an easy matter. We cannot be saved until we not only learn the Buddha's teachings but also practice them and elevate ourselves to the stage of making othres happy by means of them. The Buddha's teachings can be clearly understood by anyone and are consonant with reason and common sense; they are not a matter of magic or superstition.

When all in the great assembly saw that Śāriputra had received his prediction to Perfect Enlightenment, they rejoiced greatly and worshiped the Buddha from the depths of their hearts. Heavenly beings also paid homage to the Buddha with wonderful heavenly robes and celestial flowers. Thereupon all of them declared in verse that they believed themselves definitely able to become buddhas.

The heavenly beings paid homage to the Buddha because all creatures in the universe are disciples of the Buddha. In other words, because all things are given life by the universal truth, they cannot help worshiping and admiring the truth. The "heavenly beings" are beings who live in paradise. They seem to have no trouble or anxiety and so apparently have no need to listen to the teachings of the Buddha, but in fact that is not the case. As already mentioned, because the ideal way of human life is always to advance, not even heavenly beings can feel true joy unless they listen to the still higher teaching of the Buddha. They cannot truly feel joy unless they constantly practice good for the sake of the people who live in the *sahā*-world. This is a distinctive and profound feature of Buddhism. To suppose that one can be free from care forever and lead an idle life once one has gone to paradise is a naive and shallow belief.

Thereupon Śāriputra spoke to the Buddha, saying: "World-honored One! I now have no doubts or regrets. In person, before the Buddha, I have received my prediction to Perfect Enlightenment. Many self-controlled ones, who of yore abode in the state of learning, were always instructed by the Buddha, who said: 'My Law is able to cause men to raise the mind to be free from the various changes of the world, and is able to give them the power to extinguish suffering and distress.' These people consider that they have attained enlightenment because of being free from illusion. But now the World-honored One says: 'This is not the real enlightenment. You cannot attain real enlightenment unless you raise the mind of the bodhisattva to sincerely serve others and keep practicing this.' Finding that what you have said now is greatly different from what they had heard before, they have all fallen into doubt and perplexity. World-honored One! Please state the reasons for this to them more fully so that they may be free from doubts and regrets."

Then the Buddha spoke to Śāriputra: "Have I not said before that the buddhas by various reasonings, parables, and terms preach the Law tactfully, so that their teachings seem to be shallow in some parts and deep in other parts, but that their purpose is always only one, namely, to lead all people to the enlightenment of the Buddha? Though the various buddhas' teachings appear to be different in form and content, these teachings all have the purpose of saving those who desire to obtain enlightenment and who endeavor to do so, and these teachings all reach the same conclusion.

"Śāriputra! Let me now again in a parable make this meaning still clearer, for intelligent people reach understanding through parables."

The Buddha then told the following story.

THE PARABLE OF THE BURNING HOUSE. There was a great elder in a certain kingdom. Old and worn as he was, he possessed boundless wealth, many fields, houses, slaves, and servants. His house was spacious, having only one gate, and with many people dwelling in it. Its halls and chambers were old and decayed, its walls crumbling, the bases of its pillars rotten, the beams and rooftree leaning dangerously.

Fires suddenly started on all sides at the same moment, and the house was enveloped in flames. His many sons, to whom the elder was very much attached, were all in this dwelling. When the elder, who was outside the house, realized that fire had broken out and returned to the house, he was greatly startled to see his children absorbed in play. They had no apprehension, knowledge, surprise, or fear. Though the fire was spreading toward them and pain and suffering were imminent, they had no care nor fear and felt no urge to escape from the house.

The elder pondered: "My body and arms are strong. Shall I get them out of the house by means of a flower vessel, or a bench, or a table?" Again he pondered: "This house has only one gate, and it is narrow; my children are too young to know yet that they must go out the gate. Perhaps they will be burned in the fire because they are attached to their place of play. I must speak to them about this dreadful matter, warning them that the house is burning and that they must come out instantly lest they be burned."

Though the elder tried to lure and admonish the children with kind words, still the children, joyfully attached to their play, were unwilling to believe him and felt neither surprise nor fear, nor any need to escape; moreover, they did not know what was the fire, nor what the house, nor what he meant by being lost, but only ran hither and thither in play. Though sometimes glancing at their father, they only thought, "Our father is saying something," and they did not listen to him in earnest.

Then the elder reflected: "This house is burning in a great conflagration. If I cannot get them to leave at once, they will certainly be burned. I have no choice but to cause them to escape this disaster by some tactful means because they will not leave the house in spite of my warnings. I know! My children like toys. They are always attracted by such things when they are told about them."

The father shouted to the children: "Your favorite playthings—goat carts, deer carts, and bullock carts—are now outside the gate for you to play with. I will give you whatever you want, but all of you must come quickly out of the burning house. These things, which you are fond of playing with, are very rare and precious. If you do not come and get them now, you will be sorry later. Come quickly out of the burning house and play with these attractive toys." Thereupon the children, hearing their favorite playthings mentioned by their father, and because it suited their wishes, eagerly began pushing and racing against each other and came scrambling out of the burning house.

Then the elder, seeing his children had safely escaped and were all in the square, sat down in the open, no longer troubled, but with a mind at ease and filled with joy. Then the children said to their father: "Father! Please give us now those lovely things you promised us to play with, goat carts, deer carts, and bullock carts." The elder then gave each of his children equally a great white-bullock cart, larger and more wonderful than any of the three kinds of carts he had mentioned before.

Needless to say, the elder as father corresponds to the Buddha. The decayed house indicates the dangerous and miserable state of the human mind in the *sahā*-world. It goes without saying that the Buddha is beyond the miserable illusions of man, but he never forgets his children—all living beings—who are in such a state. The dangerous state of the *sahā*-world is shown faithfully in the description of the decayed house. The miserable state of the human mind is vividly depicted in the first part of the last verse section of chapter 3 of the Lotus Sutra. All sorts of evil creatures run about in every direction. There are places stinking with excrement and urine, overflowing with uncleanness, where dung beetles and worms gather. Foxes, wolves, and jackals bite and trample each other to gnaw human carcasses, scattering their bones and flesh. Following these, troops of dogs come to snatch and grab at the remains and, gaunt with hunger, skulk about seeking food everywhere. On the other hand, *kumbhāṇḍa* demons seize dogs by their feet, striking them so that they lose their voice, twisting their legs around their necks, and torturing the dogs for their own amusement. This description is an allegory of the human world in the age of decadence in which we live.

The fire that breaks out in this decaying old house symbolizes all human suffering, including old age, disease, and death. Human beings, absorbed in sensual pleasures and material satisfactions, are not aware that these sufferings will befall them sooner or later, much less that they are imminent.

The Buddha wants to get all living beings out of the burning house. However, the house has only one gate, and it is so narrow that they cannot pass through it easily. This means that there is only one way of salvation for men and that the gate leading to their salvation is so narrow that it is not easy to pass through it. This point teaches us that truth is one alone and that we cannot possibly attain it with a doubting or lukewarm attitude.

The Buddha considers getting his children out of the burning house by means of a flower vessel, a bench, or a table. This may be interpreted to mean that he thinks first of saving all living beings by means of his compassion and supernatural powers. But even if he wants to do so, there is the possibility of their being excluded from the Buddha's salvation because they are too engrossed in pleasures of the senses and material things. The Buddha's compassion is useless unless all living beings can realize it. For this reason, he purposely does not use his divine power.

If we penetrate further beneath the surface of this meaning, we can see that if the Buddha were to lead all living beings straight to enlightenment, they could not understand his teachings and would lapse because they are so absorbed in pleasures of the senses and material things. Therefore, he desires to lead them from the first step, which is to cause them to realize the dreadful state of this world.

In spite of the compassionate consideration of the Buddha, living beings often only glance at their father's face (the Buddha's teachings); they do not consider how these teachings concern their own lives, and they do not listen to them wholeheartedly. We have often experienced this, which shows clearly the mental state of ordinary people.

Then the Buddha as a final measure displays goat carts (the *śrāvaka*-vehicle), deer carts (the *pratyekabuddha*-vehicle), and bullock carts (the bodhisattva-vehicle). Now all living beings are attracted to the Buddha's teachings for the first time. Hearing his words, "Take whichever teaching of these three that you like; I will give you any of them," they run out of the burning house while imagining these attractive playthings to themselves.

To imagine attractive playthings to oneself means that one has already entered into the mental state of *śrāvaka, pratyekabuddha,* or bodhisattva. To run out of the burning house means that one is already seeking after the Buddha's teachings. When living beings remove illusions from their minds, they can immediately escape from the burning house of suffering in this world.

However, they do not yet think of being saved from the burning house. Their minds are filled with the desire to obtain one of the attractive carts—the enlightenment of a *śrāvaka,* a *pratyekabuddha,* or a bodhisattva. Then they ask the Buddha for these carts. This means that each asks for his own enlightenment. Then quite unexpectedly, beyond the enlightenment of the three vehicles, they see the supreme teaching, that is, the enlightenment of the One Buddha-vehicle (the great white-bullock cart), shining brilliantly.

The Buddha really wishes to give this great cart to all living beings. So he gives the same thing unsparingly and equally to anyone who has advanced to the mental state of seeking supreme enlightenment. How wonderful the Buddha's consideration is! All can attain the Buddha's enlightenment equally—this is the great spirit of the Lotus Sutra.

After relating the Parable of the Burning House, the World-honored One expounded fully the meanings included in this parable, and then, desiring to preach the same teaching over again in different words, he spoke in verse. Following is the gist of what he said.

"I tell you, Śāriputra! I am in the same position as the elder in the parable. I am the most honored of all the sages and the father of the world. All living beings are my sons. They are deeply attached to earthly pleasures and they do not have enough wisdom to realize the true aspects of all things. So I am ready to save them.

"The triple world is not a safe place for ordinary men. It is like the burning house, full of all kinds of suffering, and is greatly to be feared. Always there are various human sufferings, including the distress of birth, old age, disease, and death. Such fires as these are burning ceaselessly. Since ancient times, I have been free from the triple world full of illusions and have been abiding in a peaceful state that is not influenced by earthly troubles. But I cannot forget the triple world for even a moment. This is because all this triple world is my domain, and all the living beings in it are my sons. But now this place abounds with distress and suffering. I cannot help entering into the world of suffering and saving my sons. And I alone am able to save and protect them."

"All this universe is my domain, and all the creatures in it are my sons. And I alone am able to save and protect them." What great words of firm confidence these are! How full of his great benevolence they are! However, the word "I" is not confined to Sakyamuni, the historical Buddha who lived in India some 2,500 years ago. It refers rather to the Buddha in the sense of "one who has realized the truth." Therefore, the Buddha's words are a great proclamation that for those who have realized the truth, all the universe is their domain. When even we, who are not equal to Sakyamuni Buddha, close our eyes quietly and think with pure minds, "All the universe is our domain," we sense the vastness of space and feel an inner peace.

There was a recent fashion among some people to purchase land on Mars. Though this fad seemed to be half a joke, it can be considered an effective way to broaden man's mind, in a sense. When we really think of the stars hundreds of millions of light years away, these stars immediately fly into our minds and thus come into our possession. When we think of things tens of thousands of years ago or tens of thousands of years in the future, we realize that the world includes these things; they become part of our own minds. It is our mind that enables us to ignore time and space and to reach out everywhere.

If we could realize the truth of the universe just as the Buddha did and unite with the universal life, how much more would this world become our own! This is not a matter of asserting ownership but of feeling as if we have melted into the whole of the universe. In short, it means that we have reached a mental state of "nonself." It means that we have abandoned the small self and found the self that lives as the whole.

At such a time, self expands to fill the whole universe. Nonself is the only way that we can realize the idea that "all the universe is our domain." If we can attain this mental state, our minds will have perfect freedom. We will be free from everything, and even if we act as we wish, everything we do will result in enhancing others' lives. This is the mental state of the Buddha.

Even though we cannot reach such a state of mind in one leap, we must strive toward it by beginning to follow the Buddha's example. We cannot attain the mind of the Buddha unless we enter into the Buddha-way by following his example. To recite the sutras, to listen to preaching, to think calmly, and to serve others—all this can be said to be our practice for the purpose of abandoning our self and melting into the whole. This is the spirit of harmony. If we maintain such a practice for even an hour each day, we can approach the Buddha to a slight degree, step by step, and through perseverance we can become buddhas sometime in the future. We must abandon the spineless attitude that we cannot possibly attain buddhahood. We will readily understand why this is important when we read the next chapter, "Faith Discernment."

FOURTEEN SINS OF SLANDERING THE LAW. In the final verse portion of chapter 3, the Buddha teaches us what we ought to know in preaching the Lotus Sutra to others and what recompense we are bound to receive if we go against the sutra. Here the Buddha's words, "Do not recklessly proclaim it," are apt to be misunderstood. These words do not mean not to preach the Lotus Sutra unnecessarily, but never to preach it wrongly and always to find suitable ways of preaching it.

The Buddha teaches us, "Do not preach this sutra to those who have the following kinds of evil minds," and expounds the fourteen sins against the spirit of the Lotus Sutra. Here, he means not that we should refuse to deal with such evil-minded people but that we should preach the Lotus Sutra to them carefully after first removing their sins of slandering the Law, because unless we do this first, preaching the sutra not only will have no good effect but will in fact have an unfavorable effect.

The fourteen sins of slandering the Law are the following:

(1) haughtiness, or *kyōman* (to be conceited and to think one has understood what one has not understood);
(2) neglect, or *kedai* (to be lazy and to be absorbed in trivial things);
(3) self-centeredness, or *keiga* (to act only for selfish ends);
(4) shallowness, or *senshiki* (to look only at the surface of things, not trying to grasp their essence);
(5) sensuality, or *jakuyoku* (to be deeply attached to the desires of the senses and to material things);
(6) irrationality, or *fuge* (to interpret everything according to one's own limited viewpoint and to not understand important points);
(7) unbelief, or *fushin* (not to believe in the sutra and to vilify it because of one's shallow understanding);
(8) sullenness, or *hinshuku* (to frown upon the sutra and to show ill feeling toward it);

(9) doubting, or *giwaku* (to harbor doubts of the truth of the sutra and to hesitate to believe in it);
(10) slander, or *hibō* (to speak ill of the sutra);
(11) scorning goodness, or *kyōzen* (to despise those who read and recite, write and keep the sutra);
(12) hating goodness, or *zōzen* (to hate those who practice the abovementioned goodness);
(13) jealousy of goodness, or *shitsuzen* (to envy those who practice this goodness);
(14) grudging goodness, or *konzen* (to grudge those who practice this goodness).

Next the recompense of the various sins of slandering the Law are mentioned. What we must pay special attention to here is that such recompense is not meted out by the Buddha as a punishment. The Buddha does not have this kind of relationship with man. Because he is the truth that gives life to all things in the universe, it is hardly possible that he would perform an action running counter to man's life, such as letting him fall into hell or letting him become an animal or a deformed person. Who brings such punishment on man? Needless to say, man brings it upon himself. His own illusion brings it upon him. Illusion is like a dark cloud that covers our intrinsic buddha-nature. When the light of our buddha-nature is covered with illusions, darkness arises in our minds and various unpleasant things happen to us. This state is the punishment that we have meted to ourselves. If we blow away the dark clouds of our own illusions, our buddha-nature will immediately begin to shine forth. Therefore we have nothing to fear in the Buddha. We must keep firmly in mind and truly believe that the Buddha is that which enlivens all beings at all times.

CHAPTER 4

Faith Discernment

THE MEANING OF FAITH AND DISCERNMENT. Faith (*shin*) is the working of one's emotions, and discernment (*ge*) that of one's reason. Though people often say that a religion or faith ought to be believed in instead of argued about, it is very dangerous to believe blindly in a religion without having any knowledge of it. If this religion is a worthless or wrong teaching, blind belief will result in not only ruining ourselves but also exerting an extremely harmful influence on our families and on society in general.

Even if a religion is a good teaching, as long as we believe in it blindly our faith is liable to be easily shaken by circumstances. Let us suppose that one believes that he will recover from a disease or that his circumstances will improve if only he has faith in a particular religion, without understanding its teachings. He does recover from his illness, believing that his cure is due to his religion, but he suffers a relapse and then begins to doubt. Suppose that then his son fails his university-entrance examination; the father forsakes the faith to which he has so firmly adhered regardless of others' opinions. This kind of thing is a common occurrence.

This kind of faith is not a firm faith in the true sense of the term but merely a narrow faith. A true religion can always be understood through reason; this kind of understanding is called discernment. When we give a clear-cut explanation of a religion, this alone is also an incomplete faith. Though we can advance spiritually to a certain degree by means of such an incomplete faith, we cannot go beyond that degree. A true religion is extremely profound. For example, even if we can understand through reason that the Buddha is the truth of the universe, when we try to penetrate this truth completely we find it to be limitlessly profound and cannot grasp it through reason alone.

A famous scientist said, "The scientific universe in our time is so mystical that we have never found it in any history of thought." His words mean that the universe as scientifically considered is much more mystical than the mystery felt by primitive man in the presence of the sun, the moon, volcanoes, storms, and other natural phenomena, or the mystery felt by man at all periods in the face of religion. The more scientific knowledge increases, the more mystical the universe seems to become. To pursue this mystery through theory and experiment to wherever it may lead is the mission of science, and this is as it should be. On the other hand, through believing in religion we can enter the world of mystery directly, not merely theoretically. The mental state generated by the firsthand encounter with mystery is called faith. A religion whose teachings a person tries to explain entirely by reason has no power to move others because this person has only a theoretical understanding and cannot put his theory into practice. Such a religion does not produce the energy to cause others to follow it. True faith has power and energy. However uneducated a person may be and however humble his circumstances, he can save others and help them promote his religion if he only has faith. But if he has faith in what is fundamentally wrong, his energy exerts a harmful influence on society and those around him. Therefore faith and discernment must go together. A religion cannot be said to be true unless it combines faith and discernment. The Buddha's teachings can be understood by reason. They do not demand blind, unreasoning faith. We must understand the Buddha's teachings by listening to preaching and by reading the sutras. As we advance in our discernment of these teachings, faith is generated spontaneously.

When a person who has a flexible mind is not advanced in discernment, he develops faith as soon as he is told, "This is a true teaching." So far as the teaching of the Lotus Sutra is concerned, that is all right, because he will gradually advance in discernment through hearing and reading its teaching.

In short, we can enter a religion from the aspect either of faith or of discernment, but unless a religion combines both aspects, it does not have true power. With this basic knowledge of the components of a true religion, let us consider the text of chapter 4.

The World-honored One had given a *śrāvaka bhikshu,* Śāriputra, the prediction that he would become a buddha, and he had clearly expounded the reason in the Parable of the Burning House. At that time, such *śrāvaka bhikshus* in the assembly as the Wisdom-destined Subhūti, Mahā-Kātyāyana, Mahā-Kāśyapa, and Mahā-Maudgalyāyana came to realize the value of the Law more and more, and became ecstatic with joy. Thereupon they bowed in reverence, and with one mind and folded hands addressed the Buddha, saying: "We are senior monks among your disciples, and we are advanced in years. We considered ourselves free from earthly troubles and sufferings and that there was nothing more for us to strive for, so we did not press forward to seek after Perfect Enlightenment.

"The World-honored One has been preaching the Law for a long time, and all the while we have been seated in our places; our bodies have become weary and we have become neglectful and have felt there was no necessity to hear your preaching anymore. We thought only of the void, of the formless, and of nonfunction. But in regard to the Law that the bodhisattvas point out to others with great compassion, preaching freely according to others' capacity, causing them to display their true character, saving them equally and purifying the world, our hearts have not taken delight. We have no words to apologize for our imperfect understanding. Hearing the prediction that the Buddha has now given to Śāriputra as to our fellow *śrāvakas,* saying, 'You can obtain Perfect Enlightenment,' we are extremely glad. Unexpectedly we now suddenly hear this rare Law. Profoundly do we congratulate ourselves on having acquired so great and good a gain, such an inestimable jewel, without seeking for it. World-honored One! We have understood thus the teaching that you have now preached to us. Now let us have the pleasure of speaking in a parable to make plain this meaning." Then the four great *śrāvakas* told the following story.

THE PARABLE OF THE POOR SON. A young man left his father and ran away. For a long time he lived in a distant country, until finally he was fifty years old. The older he grew, the poorer he became. Roaming here and there in search of work, he wandered until he approached his native country. The father, who had been very sorrowful over his son's leaving home, had searched for him all over the country but in vain. Meanwhile, the father had settled in a certain city. He had become very rich, his goods and treasures incalculable. He had many slaves, retainers, and attendants.

At that time the poor son, wandering through village after village and passing through many cities and countries, at last reached the city where his father had settled. He found himself standing before the gate of his father's house, not knowing whose dwelling it was.

While the father constantly thought of his son, he never spoke of this to anyone. Pondering his loss and harboring regret in his heart, he reflected: "Old and worn, I own much wealth, but I have no son. Someday my end will come and my wealth will be scattered and lost. If I could only get my son back and commit my wealth to him, how contented and happy I would be!" About that time, the poor son, who had worked for wages here and there, stopped unexpectedly at his father's house in the hope of being hired. Standing by the gate, he saw from afar a dignified elderly man seated on a couch, surrounded and revered by many respectable-looking people. The poor son, seeing this powerful man, was seized with fear and thought, "He must be a king or someone of royal rank. This is no place for me to find work. I had better go to some poor village where I can hire out my labor, and where food and clothing are easier to get. If I stay here long, I may be seized and forcibly put to work." And he hastily ran away.

In the meantime, the rich man had recognized his son at first sight and with great joy had thought, "Ah! Suddenly my son has come back. My longing is satisfied. I have found my son, to whom I can leave all my wealth." Surprised to see his son suddenly run away, the father immediately sent attendants to rush after him and bring him back. The poor son, surprised and afraid, loudly cried, "I have committed no offence against you; why should I be seized?" But the messengers grabbed him and compelled him to return. The son thought that though he was innocent, he would be imprisoned and that this would certainly mean his death. He became so terrified at the thought that he fainted and fell to the ground. The father, seeing this from afar, ordered the messengers: "There is no need for this man. Do not bring him by force. Sprinkle cold water on his face to restore him to consciousness and do not speak to him any further." The father knew that his son's disposition was servile because of his long life of deprivation and that his own lordly position had frightened his son. Though he was sure that this was his son, he said nothing to others but decided to attract his son gradually.

After sprinkling cold water on the son's face to bring him to his senses, a messenger said, "I now set you free; go wherever you will."

The poor son was delighted and departed, repeatedly making respectful bows. He went to a humble village in search of food and clothing, as was his habit. Then the father, desiring to attract his son, devised a plan. Secretly he sent two men poorly dressed and humble in appearance, telling them: "You go and visit that place and gently say to the poor man, 'There is a place for you to work here; you will be given double wages.' If the man agrees, bring him back and give him work. If he asks what work do you wish him to do, then you may say to him, 'We hire you to remove a heap of dirt, and both of us will work along with you.' "

The poor son, thinking this to be work fit for him and having entrusted himself to the two messengers, received his wages beforehand and joined them in removing the dirt heap. His father, watching him, was struck with compassion. One day he saw through a window his son's distant figure, gaunt and filthy, by the piles of dirt and dust. Thereupon the father, who was unable to bear this feeling of pity for his son, put on a coarse, torn, dirty garment, smeared his body with dust, took a dustpan in his hand, and joined the laborers. He said to them, "Get on with your work, don't be lazy." The father then said to his son, "I hear you are a poor fellow. You have nothing to live on, have you? You may depend upon me hereafter. My man, you stay and work here. Don't go elsewhere. I will increase your wages. You may use without hesitation whatever you need—bowls, utensils, rice, flour, salt, vinegar, and so on. Besides, there is an old and worn-out servant whom you shall be given if you need him. Be at ease. I am like your father; do not worry anymore. I am old, but you are young and vigorous. All the time you have been working, you have never been deceitful, lazy, angry, or grumbling. I have never seen in you any of the vices like those of the other laborers. From this time forth you shall be like my own son."

Thereupon the elder gave him a new name and called him his son. The poor son, though he rejoiced at this, still thought of himself as a humble hireling. For this reason, for twenty years he continued to be employed to remove dirt. After this period, there was mutual confidence between father and son, and the latter came and went as he pleased, though his servile spirit had not yet changed.

Then the elder became ill, and knowing that he would shortly die, he entrusted the son with the management of all his wealth. Though the son had gained his father's confidence, he still could not eradicate his sense of inferiority. After a short time, the son had become familiar with his father's household and all the treasure, and his thinking gradually broadened so that he could imagine managing all his father's house by himself. He now despised his previous state of mind.

The father was greatly relieved at this. Seeing that his end was near, he commanded his son to come and at the same time gathered together his relatives and the kings, ministers, *kshatriyas,* and citizens of the country. When they were all assembled, he proclaimed to them, "This is really my son and I am really his father." He explained why this was so and told them, "All the wealth that I possess entirely belongs to my son."

When the poor son heard these words, great was his joy at such unexpected news, and he thought, "Without any intention or effort on my part, these treasures have now come to me of themselves."

This is the Parable of the Poor Son, the second of the seven parables in the Lotus Sutra. As soon as the four *śrāvakas* finished relating the parable, they said to the World-honored One, "The very rich elder is the Buddha and we all are as his sons." Then they praised the Buddha's compassion and his tactful power, which had led them to the teaching of the Great-vehicle even though they had been satisfied with a lesser enlightenment.

Chapter 4 of the Lotus Sutra ends with the verses spoken by Mahā-Kāśyapa, which repeat the story.

From our point of view, the poor son symbolizes all living beings. But here let us regard the son as these four *śrāvakas* and try to apply the parable to their case.

The poor son, who originally knew that the rich elder (the Buddha) was his real father but ran away from him and wandered through human suffering, indicates the usual state of living beings in the world. In this stage, the four *śrāvakas* were ordinary people like us. However, there is no denying the ties of father and son. Even though the son did not know that he possessed the buddha-nature and wandered in the world of human sufferings, he unexpectedly approached the Buddha. Standing at the gate of the Buddha's house, living beings do not know that he is their father. But the Buddha recognized his son immediately. The Buddha is always close to us; the truth is everywhere, and the Buddha waits for us to find him. We have only to attune our minds to him. The Buddha tries to lead living beings to the truth, but they turn their backs on him because of their servile feeling that his teachings are too high for them and that it is impossible for people like them to approach him.

Then the Buddha, desiring to attract living beings, devises a plan. He sends messengers (the servants who work in the Buddha's house and obtain mental peace there, namely, the *śrāvakas* and *pratyekabuddhas*) having the same appearance as ordinary men but having attained a higher spiritual stage than ordinary human beings, and he causes them to raise the level of men's minds so that they can associate with such people as the messengers. To have the son remove the dirt heap means that the Buddha leads living beings to be free from their illusions by means of the practice of the small vehicle. This part of the Parable of the Poor Son applies to the process of the practice of the four great *śrāvakas* rather than to the state of living beings in general.

After gradually making the four *śrāvakas* familiar with his teachings in this way, the Buddha desired to call them his sons and tried to improve them through his true teachings. Meanwhile, the four *śrāvakas* were still under the impression that the Buddha's teachings had no connection with them but belonged to a higher plane, and they drew a line between the Buddha and themselves. So they continued to practice the small-vehicle teaching assiduously for twenty years.

This is the point that ordinary people find difficult to emulate. For twenty long years, Subhūti, Kātyāyana, Kāśyapa, and Maudgalyāyana continued assiduously to remove the dirt heap without weariness, negligence, anger, or quarreling with their fellows. On this point they fully justify their fame as great disciples of Sakyamuni Buddha. In this way they finally obtained freedom of mind and became well acquainted with the Buddha's teachings.

Then the Buddha opened the door of the treasury of his teachings and said to them, "You can have everything in the treasury of my teachings." This was the Buddha's way of saying that because they were his real sons, they might take whatever they wished. But they still thought of themselves as servants and could not abandon their servile spirit. Therefore, though they performed their duties, such as preaching in place of the Buddha, perfectly and faithfully as managers (the Buddha's disciples), they did not realize that all the wealth actually belonged to them. They still could not abandon the mentality of the two vehicles and were very well content with their present status.

The Buddha preached the Lotus Sutra just before his death, proclaiming, "The relation between the Buddha and all living beings is that of father and son. All can become buddhas." The disciples at first were surprised by this great proclamation of the Buddha, and they were overjoyed to realize that unexpectedly the Buddha's wealth (the Buddha's enlightenment) was sure to belong to them.

This parable illustrates the process of long practice of these four *śrāvakas* and also the working of the Buddha's compassion and his tactful power, through which he steadily watched over his disciples and gradually raised them to a higher degree. However, fortunately we can encounter the Lotus Sutra without going through this long process first. For this reason, we can fly straight to the Buddha's arms. But various mental attitudes are necessary if we are to do so. These mental attitudes are also discussed in this chapter.

ARROGANCE AND HUMILITY. The first mental attitude that we learn from this chapter is to abandon a servile spirit. To think of ourselves as useless is to deny our own buddha-nature, and accordingly it is to deny the Buddha. It is thus an affront to the Buddha.

We should free our minds. We should always tell ourselves, "I can become a buddha too; I am united with the universe." We should recite this over and over to ourselves. When we recite this wholeheartedly for a set period, thinking of nothing else, we can enter into the state of perfect spiritual concentration. This state makes us acquire increasing confidence. This kind of confidence is quite different from arrogance. To be arrogant means to think one has realized what one has not yet realized, that is, to judge things according to one's limited discernment.

On the other hand, when we have truly realized something, we are usually not immediately aware of the fact of our own realization. One who has reached a very advanced spiritual state can sense this realization for himself, but most of us are not immediately aware of our realization. We only gradually become aware of it through its results. For example, somehow we feel light at heart; we feel relieved; we have become open-minded; we are no longer angry over or afraid of mere changes in circumstances; we feel that everything turns out as we wish. When we have such vague feelings, though not truly aware of them, we have attained the first stage of enlightenment. Therefore, it is not arrogant to think, "I can become a buddha," or "I am united with the universe," for we have come truly to experience this to some extent.

On the other hand, we must adopt a humble attitude when we listen to the Buddha's teachings and when we transmit them to others. Both our inner and our outer attitudes must always be humble. But it is permissible to be as proud as we like when we think about the truth. We may cherish such seemingly inflated ideas as "I am heir to the universe because I am the Buddha's son. The universe itself is our own, so I can own it, too." To think thus is a shortcut, helping us fly straight to the Buddha's arms, and to make us do so is the sole purpose of the appearance of the Buddha in this world.

The second mental attitude that we learn from chapter 4 is to maintain both faith and discernment toward the Lotus Sutra. Without both, we cannot fly surely to the Buddha's arms. We are liable to deviate from the right course, either to a wrong one or to a blind alley in human life. If this should happen to us, we need to read the Lotus Sutra over again. In that way we can be sure of finding the way to return our lives to the right course, because the Lotus Sutra includes teachings that are applicable to people in all situations; we can come to our senses by beginning with any portion of the sutra. This is how we can escape from blind alleys in human life.

The third important thing to learn from chapter 4 is that those who are fortunate enough to have encountered the Lotus Sutra and have been able to understand it and believe in it can fly straight to the Buddha's arms. However, today's world, in the evil ages of the five decays, is filled with "poor sons." We cannot be said to have actually practiced the spirit of the Lotus Sutra unless we save as many of these poor sons as possible. The only thing we can do to save them and lead them is to understand the spirit of the Buddha's tactful means as illustrated in this chapter. At the same time, we must follow the Buddha's example in using tactful means; we must not forget that to follow another's good example is a shortcut to reaching the goal.

The fourth lesson that we learn from chapter 4 is that an excellent way to progress from faith to discernment is revealed here. The four *śrāvakas* listened to the Parable of the Burning House and understood it. They not only thought that they had understood it but demonstrated their understanding to the Buddha in another parable. Not only to receive the teaching passively but also to announce actively what we have been able to realize is a very good way both to deepen our discernment and to elevate our faith. Moreover, it also helps to deepen others' discernment and elevate their faith. We must not overlook the importance of telling others of our own religious experiences, as demonstrated in this chapter.

CHAPTER 5

The Parable of the Herbs

In the previous chapter, the four great *śrāvakas* showed their admiration for the Buddha's great compassion and tactful power through the Parable of the Poor Son, then they told the Buddha that they understood that though he had preached his teachings in various ways according to the capacity of living beings and the stage of their enlightenment, his preaching had always been based on the One Buddha-vehicle, and that they had aimed at the same vehicle. When they announced their own faith and discernment thus, the World-honored One spoke to them as follows: "Good! Good! Kāśyapa; you have well proclaimed the real merits of the Buddha. Truly they are as you have said. The Buddha, in addition, has infinite, boundless, innumerable merits, which if you spoke forever you could not fully express.

"Know, Kāśyapa! The Buddha is the king of the Law. He knows fully the real state of all things. Whatever he declares leads wholly to the way of the truth. In expounding all the laws, he discerns and discriminates by wise tactfulness and preaches them according to the hearers and the occasion. The Law preached by him all leads to the stage of perfect knowledge.

"The Buddha sees and knows the merit of all the laws and also knows what all living beings in their inmost hearts are thinking and feeling. He penetrates them without hindrance. Moreover, he has the utmost understanding of the real state of all things in the world. He reveals to all living beings the wisdom that he can discern, both the discriminative and the equal aspects of all things."

THE PARABLE OF THE HERBS. With this preamble, the Buddha then preached the Parable of the Herbs. "Kāśyapa! Suppose there are growing on the mountains, along the rivers and streams, in the valleys and on the plains, plants, trees, thickets, forests, and medical herbs of various and numerous kinds, all with different names and colors. A dense cloud, spreading over and covering the whole world, pours down its rain equally at the same time.

"Its moisture universally fertilizes plants, trees, thickets, forests, and medicinal herbs, with their tiny roots, tiny stalks, tiny twigs, and tiny leaves; their medium roots, medium stalks, medium twigs, and medium leaves; their big roots, big stalks, big twigs, and big leaves; every plant big or little, according to its superior, middle, or lower capacity, receives its share. From the rain of the one cloud each develops appropriately according to the nature of its kind, opening its beautiful blossoms and bearing its fruit. You must know that though produced in one soil and moistened by the same rain, yet these plants and trees are all different."

Roots, stalks, twigs, and leaves indicate faith, precepts, meditation, and wisdom. Roots are the most important part of plants. Without roots, they cannot grow stalks, twigs, or leaves. Therefore "roots" means faith. One cannot keep the precepts without faith. Because of keeping the precepts, one can enter into the mental state of meditation and can also obtain wisdom.

Conversely, however strong the roots may be, they will eventually die if the twigs and leaves wither or if the stalks are cut. In the same way, if man does not have wisdom, his faith will become corrupt. In short, in believing in a religion, man begins with faith and attains wisdom through the precepts and meditation. However, these four steps of his religious practice are always interrelated and exist together. When any one of the four steps is lacking, his religious practice cannot be perfect, and it will not progress to the next stage. Just as a tree may be big or little, superior, middle, or low, so different people are large- or small-minded, wise or ignorant.

But we must make clear that a big tree cannot always be said to be superior to a little one, nor a little plant inferior to a bigger one. A cedar has its proper role, and a box tree also has its own role. The small violet is beautiful, and the larger pampas grass has its own kind of beauty. In the same way, though there seem to be various differences in people's external appearance, intelligence, ability, character, and bodily strength, all one's qualities become beautiful and honorable when he displays his own strength to the full according to his particular nature and ability. This is the meaning of the equality preached by the Buddha.

However, it is another matter to receive the Law. In the previous chapter, we were taught that we must not have the servile idea that we have the capacity to understand the Buddha's teachings only to a certain limited extent. We should abandon such trifling discriminations and devote ourselves to hearing and receiving the Law. The Parable of the Herbs states that every effort of ours will be surely rewarded. That is, though various kinds of plants and trees are produced in the same soil and moistened by the same rain, each develops according to its own nature. In the same way, though the Buddha's teachings are only one, they are understood differently according to each hearer's nature, intellect, environment, and so on.

Even if we have only a shallow understanding of the Buddha's teachings or can practice only a part of them, this is never useless. Every effort will be surely rewarded with the merits of the Law. But we should not be satisfied with this reward. We must always desire and endeavor to deepen our understanding and to elevate ourselves further. Thus we can use shallow faith and discernment as the first step in advancing ourselves to a higher level of faith and discernment. Ascending step by step, we can unfailingly reach a superior state of mind. We should understand this well when we read the latter part of this chapter. It is stated here that though the Buddha's teachings are one, there are differences in faith and discernment according to one's capacity to understand the teachings. But we must not interpret this as stating an absolute condition.

One tree receives too much rain, while another does not receive enough. One tree can grow in a year, but another takes many years to reach maturity. One tree can bear fruit in a year, but another cannot bear fruit until seven or eight years have passed. Suppose that when such a tree sees a tree that can bear its fruit in a year, it thinks, "I am useless because I cannot possibly bear my fruit in such a short time." It would be nonsensical for the tree to think this, wouldn't it? And suppose that there is a tree that is content to say, "That tree has borne its fruit in a year, while I have barely managed to grow my twigs and leaves in a year. But I am very well off as I am, because all are moistened by the same rain. I am doing all I can." It would be just as nonsensical for the tree to express such satisfaction on the basis of its limited judgment alone.

A tree that requires seven or eight years to bear its fruit must work hard and practice without impatience, discouragement, or bitter feelings toward others. The time will come when it will surely bear its blossoms and fruit. If fruit borne in a year is sweet, so will fruit borne in eight years be good. What both of them achieve is the same: the Buddha's enlightenment.

Then the World-honored One said: "Know, Kāśyapa, the relation between the Buddha's teachings and the enlightenment of living beings." The point of the Buddha's teaching of the Parable of the Herbs is that the Buddha is like the great cloud that sheds its rain equally on all. He leads all living creatures, including human beings, to his universal teachings, just as that great cloud covers the entire world.

THE TEN EPITHETS OF THE BUDDHA. The Buddha then explained his identity with the following ten titles: "I am the Tathāgata, the Worshipful, the All Wise, the Perfectly Enlightened in Conduct, the Well Departed, the Understander of the World, the Peerless Leader, the Controller, the Teacher of Gods and Men, the Buddha, the World-honored One." These are called the ten epithets of the Buddha, each of which represents an aspect of the Buddha's virtue and power.

Tathāgata (*nyorai*) means "one who has come from the world of truth"; the Worshipful (*ōgu*), "one who deserves offerings in the human and the celestial worlds"; the All Wise (*shōhenchi*), "one who has the right and perfect wisdom"; the Perfectly Enlightened in Conduct (*myōgyō-soku*), "one who completely combines knowledge with practice"; the Well Departed (*zenzei*), "one who is free from everything"; the Understander of the World (*sekenge*), "one who can understand people in all circumstances"; the Peerless Leader (*mujōji*), "one who is unsurpassed"; the Controller (*jōgo-jōbu*), "one who is infallible in controlling men's minds"; the Teacher of Gods and Men (*tennin-shi*), "one who leads all lives of creatures in the human and the celestial worlds"; and the Buddha, the World-honored One (*butsu-seson*), "the enlightened one who is most honored by the people of the world." One who is possessed of these ten virtues and powers is called Buddha.

Because of such perfect virtues and powers, those who have not yet reached the mental state of being uninfluenced by changes in their circumstances, the Buddha causes to reach that state of mind; those who have not yet understood why their illusions occur and how they can be removed, he causes to understand; those who have not yet been comforted after their illusions are extinguished, he causes to be comforted;

those who have not yet obtained true enlightenment, he causes to obtain it.

The Buddha also knows the present, the past, and the world to come as they really are. He is the one who knows everything perfectly (*issai-chisha,* the All Knowing), the one who discerns the real state of all things (*issai-kensha,* the All Seeing), the one who knows the true Way (*chidō-sha,* the Knower of the Way), the one who makes all living beings understand the Way and leads them to it (*kaidō-sha,* the Opener of the Way), and the one who preaches the Way to them (*setsudō-sha,* the Preacher of the Way).

THE THREE ACTIONS OF BODY, MOUTH, AND MIND. To know the Way, to open it, and to preach it are indispensable practices for followers of the Lotus Sutra. One knows the Way with one's mind, one opens it with one's body, and one preaches it with one's mouth. These are called the three actions of body, mouth, and mind, and they are the standards of the daily conduct of those who practice the Lotus Sutra by following the Buddha's example.

The Buddha, who had such perfect virtues and powers, addressed all creatures, urging them to come to him to hear the Law. At that time numberless classes of living beings gathered and did so. Thereupon the Buddha, observing the natural powers of all these beings, keen or dull, zealous or indifferent, according to their various capacities, preached to them the Law in varying ways, causing them all to rejoice and joyfully obtain much merit. He proclaimed that all living beings that have well understood this Law, have believed in it, and have practiced it are comforted in the present life and afterward will be born in happy states where they will be made joyful by the truth and will also hear the Law.

COMFORT IN THE PRESENT LIFE. To be comforted in the present life means to lead a peaceful life in this world. People of old interpreted this as meaning simply that they would easily recover from disease and would be free of worries about their livelihood. The common opinion more recently has been that "to be comforted" refers only to spiritual problems and that it means that one's mind will never be influenced by whatever suffering one undergoes. This interpretation may have developed because people have come to think that to seek material happiness in the present life is a goal unworthy of people of religion or because they fear that they would be looked down on unless they considered mind and body as separate entities, a tendency encouraged by a superficial understanding of modern science.

However, such ideas are mistaken. Research in psychosomatic medicine has made it clear that many physical disorders disappear if one's mental and emotional state improves. When one's mind is free, one's way of life naturally changes for the better. Therefore, it is no wonder that such people actually can and do lead relatively comfortable lives. Belief in a religion for the sake of receiving divine favors in the present life is attended with various evils. With such an attitude toward religion, one cannot obtain freedom of mind. So it seems plausible to regard "being comforted" as a purely mental and emotional matter. However, to consider that the fact that mental freedom leads also to material freedom has nothing to do with the Buddha's teachings is also a lopsided view and is a denial of the Buddha's power.

The words "All living beings afterward will be born in happy states where they will be made joyful by the truth and will also hear the Law" are highly significant. Our lives have continued since the time when the earth was a ball of fire—no, since much longer ago than that—and they will continue into the infinite future. Therefore, even though our bodies will die, if we attain a state of mind such that we are not influenced by our circumstances, our minds will be reborn in "happy states" and will have peaceful lives in the world to come, where they will be made joyful by the truth, because by practicing the truth we can set our lives in the right direction.

This teaching was misinterpreted in former times as referring only to one's rebirth in the Pure Land after death; in reaction to this, people now show a strong tendency to limit the interpretation to spiritual problems in the present life. But the Buddha's teachings are not so narrow and limited. We must not forget that they teach us the ideal way to live our lives, which extend from the infinite past to the infinite future.

Having thoroughly understood this Law, all living beings can gradually become free from mental hindrances and disturbances, and from the various teachings of the Buddha they can choose for themselves a teaching that they can understand according to their own capacity and by means of which they can enter the Buddha-way, just as the great cloud rains on all plants equally and nourishes them so that each grows and develops perfectly in accordance with its own nature.

The Buddha then declared: "The Law preached by the Tathāgata is of one form and flavor, that is to say, deliverance, abandonment, extinction, and finally the attainment of perfect knowledge." This means that though his teachings are all the same essentially, they can be analyzed into three parts: deliverance (*gedatsu-sō*), abandonment (*ri-sō*), and extinction (*metsu-sō*).

"Deliverance" is the mental state of being no longer influenced by changes in circumstances or things. If one reaches this state, one can consider all things equally, unmoved by whatever happens. On the other hand, those who are convinced that they cannot look at things equally wish to rise above the world of phenomena, and so they lose the feeling of kinship with people who are suffering and distressed. We should abandon such self-righteousness and strive instead to save people from their sufferings. This attitude is called "abandonment."

UNITING ONESELF AND OTHERS. "Extinction" means to extinguish false discrimination between oneself and others, that is, to feel the unity of oneself and all creatures in the universe. We cannot reach this state of mind as long as we think only that we must save people who are suffering and distressed. We must wish to stretch out our hands to others spontaneously and embrace them. This feeling is the mental state of the unification of oneself and others.

We do not consider saliva at all dirty when it is in our mouth. This is because saliva is part of our body. On the other hand, once we spit it out, we feel it to be unclean because we have lost the feeling of its being part of us. A person with true affection has a strong feeling of unity with others. There are historical instances of the ideal affection that demonstrates the unity of oneself and others. For example, a man touched his mouth to the mouth of his wife, who was so ill with tuberculosis that she was too weak to spit, and sucked out a hard mass that was blocking her throat. Empress Kōmyō of Japan sucked the pus oozing from sores on the back of a leper. We cannot reach such a mental state at one bound. But if we could come to feel spontaneously that another's suffering is our own suffering and that we must try to help the sufferer, or to feel that another's joy is our own joy, how comfortable to live in, how bright and peaceful this world would be.

The Buddha's teachings lead us progressively to a higher state of mind in this order: deliverance, abandonment, extinction, and finally the attainment of perfect knowledge. The wisdom that unites the ability both to see the equality of things (void) and to discern the differences among things (existence) is the attainment of perfect knowledge.

Then the Buddha's preaching continued as follows: "If there be living beings who hear the Law of the Tathāgata and keep, read, recite, and practice it as preached by him, their achievements will not enable them to understand their own natures. Only the Tathāgata in reality sees, clearly and without hindrance, the stages in which all living beings are, just as those plants, trees, thickets, forests, medicinal herbs, and others do not know whether their own natures are superior, middle, or inferior." With these words the Buddha affirms the inevitability of man's receiving divine favors in the present life. He also declares that people themselves do not understand such divine favors; only the Buddha knows them. When man believes in the Law and practices it, various changes take place in him. As one who lives in the *sahā*-world, such changes may be unpleasant to him. But from a broader viewpoint, they indicate that his life has been set in the right direction. If he yields at once to these internal changes, although they may seem to be disagreeable at the time, the changes themselves are sure to lead him to happiness.

One of Aesop's fables tells us that a crow drowned because he disliked his black color and tried to wash it off. If a hedgehog is not pleased with the spines growing all over his body and pulls them out, he will soon be eaten by a wild cat or some other animal. As the proverb says, "Everything is as you see it"; true deliverance lies in our mental attitude to accept willingly what we are and to receive obediently what we are given.

The Buddha says that the Law preached by him is of one form and flavor, that is, it is the same essentially though it is preached in various ways. John is different from Mary, but both are originally the same as human beings. To use the terminology of science, a red flower is composed of subatomic particles, such as electrons, protons, and neutrons; the green leaf of a willow is also formed from the same particles: the two are the same in essence. The Buddha also says that his unitary essential Law ends in a return to the void. In this case, the void means equality; thus he indicates that everything is essentially equal.

Though all things are equal, as phenomena they are manifested as red flowers, or as green leaves, or as John who is skilled with his hands, or as Mary who is clear-headed. The subtle working of the universal life-force is seen in the generation of distinction from equality. If we can thoroughly develop the natural potential of our own lives according to the Buddha's teachings, this results in vitalizing others' lives, and we can reach a state of mind in which we realize the unification of ourselves and others and the essential unity of the diverse living beings.

In the last part of this chapter, the World-honored One stated that all his teachings culminate in causing all living beings equally to attain the same state of mind as the Buddha but that he does not immediately declare this to them because he observes the differences in their dispositions. He concluded his preaching by saying that Kāśyapa's ability to realize this truth is the rarest and greatest faculty.

Then the World-honored One, desiring to proclaim this teaching over again, repeated it in verse. In the final stanzas he gave strong encouragement to the *śrāvaka* disciples, saying:

"What I have now said to you all
Is the veriest truth.
All *śrāvakas*
Have not yet attained nirvana.
The Way in which you walk
Is the bodhisattva-way;
By gradually practicing and learning,
All of you will become buddhas."

CHAPTER 6

Prediction

As already explained, "prediction" means that the Buddha gives us the assurance, "You will surely become buddhas." The term "prediction" (*juki*) includes three meanings of great importance and subtlety, which it is essential that we understand. The first important point is that Sakyamuni Buddha says not "You are buddhas" but "You will become buddhas." In the sight of the Buddha, all living beings have the buddha-nature, and any one of them can definitely become a buddha. But if the Buddha says merely, "You are buddhas," this statement will be greatly misunderstood by ordinary people. They will be liable to take these words to mean that they are already perfected as buddhas while in a state of illusion, and will have the idea that they can become buddhas without any effort, like riding an escalator.

The prediction given by the Buddha is often compared to an admission permit to a school, and this comparison is quite just. It is not a diploma but only an admission permit. This assurance signifies, "You have passed the entrance examination of the highest university, which leads to the degree of buddhahood. If you study here for some years, you will surely graduate and will become buddhas." Having this assurance, ordinary people must hereafter practice all the more, and must make ever greater efforts to realize this goal.

What a joyful thing it is for ordinary people to have obtained admission to the Buddha's university—to have received the Buddha's prediction, "You will become buddhas." In chapter 3 of the Lotus Sutra, Śāriputra was the first *śrāvaka* to receive this prediction from the Buddha, and it is natural that all the great assembly, witnessing Śāriputra receiving this prediction, rejoiced in unbounded ecstasy.

The rejoicing of the great assembly is the same as our rejoicing. We have already gained admission to the Buddha's university; we will understand this fact still better when we discuss chapter 8, "The Five Hundred Disciples Receive the Prediction of Their Destiny," and chapter 9, "Prediction of the Destiny of Arhats, Training and Trained." Those who believe sincerely in the Lotus Sutra and practice its spirit faithfully have already received admission to the highest, universal university, that of buddhahood. Knowing this, how proud we feel and how worthwhile our life becomes!

Our natural joy and pride in this fact must never lead to self-satisfaction, however. If we make this feeling our own personal joy alone, it is meaningless. This is the second important point of the Buddha's prediction. At the end of the second verse portion of chapter 6, Maudgalyāyana, Subhūti, Kātyāyana, and others spoke in unison as follows: "Great Hero, World-honored One! / Thou dost ever desire to pacify the world; / Be pleased to bestow our prediction, . . ." What they are saying is: "The Buddha always desires to make all the people of the world feel at ease. We also desire to become buddhas and to make them live in peace. Please give us your assurance of becoming buddhas." They do not mean that they alone be saved and become buddhas, or that they alone become buddhas and attain peace of mind. Their final purpose is to make all the people of the world happy. This is a most important point. We must understand that the real intention of these disciples in earnestly requesting that the Buddha give them his assurance of becoming buddhas lies in the fact that they wanted to obtain such freedom and power as to be capable of making others happy. If we do not realize this, we are likely to receive the mistaken impression that they asked the Buddha for only their own personal enlightenment and mental peace.

The third major point of the Buddha's prediction is that the Buddha's disciples must already have well understood that they would become buddhas, through the teachings that the Buddha had already preached. Therefore, some people wonder why the disciples so persistently asked the Buddha for his prediction. This is where religion differs from knowledge. Buddhism is a teaching that we can understand through reason. For knowledge, it is enough to understand something by reason, but in religion it is not enough to understand by reason alone. When understood, the knowledge must inspire man. It must generate faith, which will spontaneously cause one to wish to act for the benefit of other people and of society in general.

When understanding develops into service to society and to other people, we can call it faith or religion. A true religion has this kind of power. Where does inspiration, the foundation of this power, come from? Inspiration comes not from theories but from the contact of one's spirit with other spirits. When we meet a person of great character and listen to his words, our hearts are touched with joy. We ardently determine to emulate him even at the risk of our lives. The ability to give us such determination is the greatness of Sakyamuni as the appearing Buddha. When we take as the universal truth the words of Sakyamuni Buddha, whom we revere as the ideal human being, we receive a great power, which is beyond mere understanding and which gives us strength and uplifts us.

This is why the Buddha's disciples were eager to hear the Buddha's words, "You will become buddhas," directly from his lips. Such words were a stronger encouragement to them than the support of ten million people. "Be pleased to say a word to us! If you should say something to us, we would sacrifice ourselves for your teachings and would follow them to the end. We would never turn away or be neglectful in our practice. So be pleased to say a word to us!" Thus were the disciples asking Sakyamuni.

This innocent and trusting attitude shows true faith. The disciples' manner of asking is a good example for our religious lives, so we should bear it well in mind. The understanding of the Buddha's teachings gained by reading books and listening to preaching is still shallow. If we do not have a sense of being inspired or the feeling of flying straight to Sakyamuni's arms of great compassion, our understanding will not produce the power to save others as well as ourselves. Worshiping the Buddha's image and repeating the title of the Lotus Sutra are not mere idol worship and magical incantations. The purpose of these actions is nothing other than the merging of ourselves with the mind of Sakyamuni, whom we revere as our teacher and our parent, and through him with the great salvation of the Eternal Original Buddha.

If we keep in mind these three essential points of the Buddha's prediction in reading chapter 6, we can clearly understand the Buddha's teachings in this chapter. Let us proceed to the text of the chapter.

After pronouncing the last verse of chapter 5, the World-honored One addressed the great assembly in the following way: "This my disciple

Mahā-Kāśyapa, who has well understood the Buddha's teachings and has firmly determined to follow the practices of the bodhisattvas for the sake of the people of the world, in the world to come shall pay homage to innumerable buddhas and widely proclaim the infinite, great Law of the buddhas. In his final bodily state he will become a buddha, whose name will be Radiance Tathāgata, Worshipful, All Wise, Perfectly Enlightened in Conduct, Well Departed, Understander of the World, Peerless Leader, Controller, Teacher of Gods and Men, Buddha, World-honored One, whose domain is named Radiant Virtue, and whose period is named Great Magnificence. The lifetime of that buddha will be a hundred and twenty thousand years, his Righteous Law will abide in the world for two hundred thousand years, and the Counterfeit Law will also abide for two hundred thousand years."

When Kāśyapa earlier expressed his deep emotion and his great gratitude for the Buddha's teachings through the Parable of the Poor Son, the World-honored One understood that Kāśyapa had already realized almost all his teachings, had deepened his faith, and had achieved a determined will. This can also be seen in the Buddha's words to Kāśyapa at the beginning of chapter 5: "Good! Good! Kāśyapa; you have well proclaimed the real merits of the Tathāgata. Truly they are as you have said."

When the Buddha predicted the attainment of buddhahood to all the great assembly, he designated the future buddhas' names, their domains, and their periods. He gave Kāśyapa the ten epithets of a buddha, beginning with "Radiance Tathāgata." The ten epithets of the Buddha demonstrate that he perfectly combines virtues with powers. Therefore, the Buddha was stating here that Kāśyapa through his practice could become the same buddha as Sakyamuni. In short, he made it clear that if anyone can truly realize the Buddha's truth, he will become the same buddha as himself. It may be gathered from this how high a value Sakyamuni Buddha placed on truth.

The Buddha continued his discourse: "His domain called Radiant Virtue will be beautiful, devoid of dirt, potsherds, thorns, and unclean ordure; its land will be level and straight, with no uneven places, neither pitfalls nor mounds, its ground of lapis lazuli, lined with jewel trees and golden cords to bound the ways, strewn with precious flowers, and with purity reigning everywhere. In that domain the bodhisattvas who practice the Buddha's teachings will be infinite, with numberless people who seek after the teachings. No Māra deeds will be there, and though there are Māra and Māra's people, they all will protect the Buddha-law."

This description depicts the ideal state of the world. The former half resembles the description of a beautiful city in a highly developed country of today's world, but the latter half gives the impression of a realm exactly the opposite of today's world. Indeed, the world has advanced remarkably in material aspects, while it has made only slow progress in spiritual aspects. The Buddha's description shows us clearly that this is the greatest defect of modern society. Realizing this, how can we avoid cooperating with each other to spread the spirit of the Lotus Sutra among as many people as possible, with the firm resolution of realizing as soon as possible, in this world, the ideal realm shown by the Buddha?

DEVILS AND DEVILISH DEEDS. We must not ignore the following words of the Buddha: "No Māra deeds will be there, and though there are Māra and Māra's people, they all will protect the Buddha-law." Māra, or "devil," includes all creatures that obstruct the righteous way. "Māra's people" means the followers of the devil. They have such great powers that they may appear in succession before those who endeavor to realize the righteous way, lead them into temptation, and confuse them. These devilish people conspire to obstruct and intimidate those who try to practice the righteous way. They may be likened to a gang of hooligans or racketeers. The power of evil-minded speech and writing is a still greater devil.

A devil and its followers appeared before Sakyamuni Buddha when he was deep in meditation shortly before his enlightenment, and tried to throw various obstacles in his way. If he had been an ordinary man, he would have yielded immediately. However, he was able to withstand the temptations, obstructions, and threats by which the devils tested him, and then his enlightenment became unshakable. Judging from the results Sakyamuni Buddha achieved, these devils' hindrances can even be said to have spurred his enlightenment.

"Devil" has two meanings. The first is the "devil in the body," meaning instinctive impulses or wicked ideas that disturb our righteous minds. The second is the "devil outside the body," meaning temptation or pressure from the outside.

In an ideal domain like Radiant Virtue, there are people who practice the Buddha's teachings or seek them sincerely. Even if such people are sometimes tempted by the "devil in the body," that is, a wicked idea or instinctive impulse, such a temptation acts to strengthen their will to seek the Way. As a result, the "devil in the body" protects the Buddha-law. For this reason, though there are the devil and devilish people, no devilish deeds will exist in the ideal domain.

The "devil outside the body" means the speech and conduct of those who offer temptation, criticism, disturbance, and threats to those who endeavor to practice the Buddha's teachings and spread them. As the saying goes, "Extremes in wickedness make for extremes in goodness." In an ideal domain like Radiant Virtue, even extremely wicked people completely change and use their powers to protect the Buddha's teachings. As all sentient beings have innate buddha-nature, once a devilish person awakens to his own buddha-nature, he can distinguish himself more brilliantly than a good but weak person.

The Buddha teaches us that the "devil," whether in the body or outside the body, displays its ability for harm when it lives in illusion. But if it should realize the righteous way, it will immediately exercise its faculties for good. Therefore, we should not think of Radiant Virtue as an ideal domain far removed from the world in which we live but should interpret it in terms of spiritual matters in our own religious lives and as practical problems in our own society. Understanding this, we must devote ourselves to enlightening "devils" and to removing "devilish deeds," and moreover, to changing these "devils" so that they will show their good abilities.

How can we do so? There is one course open to us: to seek the righteous teachings of the Buddha, and to believe and practice them. If we do so, no devilish deeds will exist in society. The devilish deeds that cling to our minds and bodies will disappear like mist before the morning sun, and our infinite life will shine in its purity.

Then the World-honored One, desiring to proclaim his teaching again, repeated it in verse and ended by giving his prediction to Kāśyapa. Thereupon Mahā-Maudgalyāyana, Subhūti, Mahā-Kātyāyana, and others tremblingly folded their hands and with one mind, gazing up into the World-honored One's face, not for an instant lowering their eyes, and with united voice, spoke thus: "Great Hero, World-honored One who can drive out all evils! The Buddha who is endowed with the power to lead all men! Be pleased to grant us the Buddha-announcement out of your compassion for us. Be pleased to encourage us to be more and more assiduous in our practice in the future. If you know the depths of our minds and predict our destinies, saying, 'You will become buddhas,' we will feel as if you were pouring sweet dew over us to allay the heat.

"We are like people from a land of famine, suddenly finding a royal repast, yet harboring doubt and fear, not daring to eat it at once. But when instructed by the king, then we dare to eat his repast. In the same way, we have become sufficiently aware of our errors that we are able to free ourselves from our own illusions and sufferings, and at the same time we have understood the supreme wisdom of the Buddha. But we do not know how to obtain it. Though we hear the voice of the Buddha, who says we shall become buddhas, our hearts are still anxious and afraid of attaining buddhahood, just as those starving people dare not eat the royal repast before their eyes. But if we receive the Buddha's prediction of becoming buddhas, then we shall be happy and at ease. Great Hero, World-honored One! You do ever desire to pacify the people of the world. Be pleased to bestow our prediction. If you do so, just like the starving people instructed by the king to eat the repast, we can devote ourselves to the bodhisattva-way and render service to people and society."

Thereupon the World-honored One, knowing the thoughts in the minds of those senior disciples, instantly complied with Subhūti's request and gave his prediction to him. He declared his name as a buddha to be Name Form Tathāgata, his period Possessing Jewels, and his domain Jewel Producing. Next the World-honored One bestowed his prediction on Mahā-Kātyāyana and declared his name as a buddha to be Jambūnada Golden Light Tathāgata. He also gave his prediction to Mahā-Maudgalyāyana, naming him Tamālapattra Sandal Fragrance Tathāgata, his period Joyful, and his domain Glad Mind.

Most of you who have read to this point may feel as if the story above is far removed from your own lives because it relates an incident concerning Sakyamuni Buddha and his senior disciples in ancient India. But in fact this story is not at all removed from our lives today, as we will understand when we read the last portion of the final verse section in this chapter. The World-honored One spoke in verse to the following effect: "Among my many disciples, there are five hundred in number who possess high virtues and exert great influence upon those around them. All of them will receive their prediction to become buddhas after their accumulation of practice in a life to come. I will now declare my and your development in previous worlds. Do you all listen well!"

"My and your development in previous worlds" includes not only Sakyamuni Buddha and his five hundred disciples but all the buddhas and their disciples who have appeared or will appear, from the infinite past to the eternal future. This is because one who has truly understood the Buddha's teachings never fails to tell them to others and to have the urge to save others. By continuing this, he himself can become a buddha. Moreover, those who have been saved by him can themselves become buddhas by transmitting the Buddha's teachings to many other people and by continuing the practice of saving others. In this way, numberless buddhas have appeared from the infinite past to the present, and these numberless buddhas have produced innumerable more buddhas. Thus a continuous proliferation of people's enlightenment by the buddhas has been occurring incessantly. This is the true meaning of the words "my and your development in previous worlds."

Today, we are fortunate to be able to encounter the Lotus Sutra. That we have means that we have been given the Buddha's prediction of becoming buddhas if we practice. Though Sakyamuni the historical Buddha passed away some two thousand five hundred years ago, Lord Sakyamuni the Eternal Original Buddha is with us forever. He gives us his prediction of attaining buddhahood through the Lotus Sutra.

THE IMPORTANCE OF REPETITION. When the Buddha gave his prediction to Kāśyapa, his domain was described as a beautiful and ideal land, and the description of this realm was repeated in the verses that the Buddha spoke afterward. Though slightly different in wording, basically the same description was repeated in the predictions given to Subhūti, Maudgalyāyana, and Kātyāyana.

In chanting the Lotus Sutra, we should not think, "These are the same words as before," nor should we recite them carelessly. Repetition has a very important function in religious life.

To do something repeatedly makes a deep impression on our minds. But this repetition must be done wholeheartedly. Anyone who tries reciting chapter 6 with his whole heart will find himself repeating the description of man's ideal state as symbolized by the ten epithets of the Buddha, and the ideal human society as symbolized by the description of the beautiful lands of the buddhas. Through frequent repetition these ideals will penetrate the depths of his mind.

Such expression as "as mentioned above" or "the aforesaid" are excusable in business documents and official reports. Such shortcut expressions pass muster in today's busy world. However, when it comes to Buddhist practice, we must not shirk repeating everything exactly. Unless one repeats the same thing wholeheartedly as often as possible in studying music or in practicing baseball, he will never improve. It is the same with religion.

When we recite the title of the Lotus Sutra, it seems well enough in theory to recite it only once if we do so with complete sincerity. But in reality, if we do not repeat the title from three to ten times, the idea of taking refuge in the Buddha does not penetrate completely. Nevertheless, although repetition is very important, if we recite it a thousand or ten thousand times, unless we are superhuman we will become bored or our minds will wander, and we will find ourselves merely mouthing the title without understanding it. This results in the defect of formalism, the lazy belief that merely by reciting the title we can be saved.

We must realize that real Buddhist practice has three requisites: (1) a good practice, (2) wholehearted conduct, and (3) constant repetition.

CHAPTER 7

The Parable of the Magic City

THE BUDDHA USED three methods of preaching. The first was the theoretical method, or "preaching by theory" (*hossetsu*). If his audience found it difficult to understand his teachings when presented in this way, he then used the figurative method, called "preaching by parable" (*hi-setsu*). If his hearers were still unable to grasp the Buddha's true meaning, he used the method called "preaching by causality" (*innen-setsu*), preaching by means of the story of the life of a past buddha. The Lotus Sutra uses all three methods, so that people of all dispositions can understand the teaching.

Chapter 7, "The Parable of the Magic City," falls into the category of preaching by causality. It begins with the Buddha's explaining the relationship between the Buddha and his disciples from the remotest past to the present.

In the last part of chapter 6, the World-honored One said, "I will now declare my and your development in previous worlds. Do you all listen well!" With this introductory remark, the World-honored One again addressed the *bhikshus:* "In the remotest past, there was a buddha named Universal Surpassing Wisdom Tathāgata, whose domain was named Well Completed and whose period was named Great Form. Since that buddha became extinct, an inexpressibly long time has passed. For instance, suppose the earth of this whole world was ground into ink by someone, and he was to pass through a thousand countries in an eastern direction and then let fall one drop as small as a grain of dust; again, passing through another thousand countries, to let fall another drop. Suppose he thus proceeds until he has finished the ink made of the earth —can you count the number of countries he has passed through? All these countries—is it possible for mathematicians or their disciples to know their end and confines so as to know their number?"

"A thousand countries" in today's terms means all the heavenly bodies of the universe. Imagine that one drop of ink as small as a grain of dust was let fall on a star, and after passing a thousand stars, another drop was let fall.

Asked what they thought, the *bhikshus* answered unanimously, "Oh no, World-honored One! It is quite impossible for us to know their number."

Nodding to himself, the World-honored One continued: "*Bhikshus!* Suppose all those countries [stars] which that man has passed, where he has let fall a drop and where he has not, are ground to dust, and let one grain of the dust be a *kalpa*.[1] Can you imagine how long it will take to finish grinding the whole universe to dust? The time since Universal Surpassing Wisdom Tathāgata became extinct till now still exceeds that number by innumerable and unlimited years. By the power of my Tathāgata-wisdom, I observe that length of time as if it were only today."

The Buddha used this simile of earth ground into ink in order to make his disciples realize clearly the idea of the unlimited duration of eternity. The idea of eternity or infinity does not come home to us unless we can establish a standard of limitedness. Even if we look up at the cloudless azure sky and think of the sky as unlimited, we have no clear idea of this unlimitedness. But when we see a tiny wisp of cloud high in the sky, we sense something of the unlimitedness of the sky. We feel infinity when we look up the starry sky at night and realize that the stars we see are millions of light years distant from the earth.

THE MEANING OF "TODAY." The Buddha's words "I observe that length of time as if it were only today" suggest to us that human life is unlimited. The Buddha gives us hints to realize that our lives continue from the unlimited past to the endless future; "today" does not exist in isolation but is like a deep pool or a shoal of the endless river of life. If we defile our body and mind of today, we exert a bad influence upon the lower reaches of the stream of unlimited life. If we purify our body and mind

1. An eon; a period of time of extremely long duration.

of today, we cause a favorable change farther down the same stream.

Before we proceed with the discussion of this chapter, we should understand that it was from his thoughtful consideration that the World-honored One said, "I observe that length of time as if it were only today," and then told the story of the life of a past buddha. Repeating this teaching in verse, the World-honored One continued: "The lifetime of the Buddha Universal Surpassing Wisdom Tathāgata is five hundred and forty myriad *koṭis*[2] of *nayutas*[3] of *kalpas*. At the beginning when that buddha, seated on the wisdom throne, had destroyed the army of the devil, though he was on the point of attaining Perfect Enlightenment, the Buddha-laws were not yet revealed to him. So for about a hundred thousand years he sat cross-legged with body and mind motionless; but the Buddha-laws were not yet revealed to him.

"Then the gods of Indra's heavens[4] spread for the Buddha Universal Surpassing Wisdom a lion throne, which was a *yojana*[5] high, under a Bodhi tree. As the gods requested that buddha to sit on this throne in order to attain Perfect Enlightenment, he sat on it, complying willingly with their request. No sooner had he sat on that throne than the Brahma heavenly kings rained down celestial flowers on the throne. A fragrant wind arose from time to time, sweeping away the withered flowers and raining down fresh ones. Thus incessantly, for a full hundred thousand years, they paid honor to the buddha, while the gods belonging to the four heavenly kings,[6] in order to honor the buddha constantly, beat celestial drums while other gods played celestial music for a full hundred thousand years and continued to do so until that buddha's extinction."

This description shows that the gods of the heavens wished fervently for the attainment of Perfect Enlightenment by the Buddha Universal Surpassing Wisdom and that they worshiped and revered this buddha. The image of a fragrant wind sweeping away the withered flowers and

2. A *koṭi* is a very large number, variously interpreted as ten million, one hundred million, and so on.

3. A *nayuta* is one hundred *ayutas;* an *ayuta* is one hundred *koṭis.*

4. The heaven of the thirty-three gods. This is the heaven of Indra, the second highest of the six heavens of the Realm of Desire, situated between the four peaks of Mount Sumeru.

5. A unit of distance equivalent to 64, 120, or 160 kilometers.

6. These kings protect the worlds from demons, each guarding one quarter of the compass around Mount Sumeru. They are the representatives of Śakra (Indra). They include Dhṛtarāshtra Mahārājā, governor of the east; Virūḍhaka Mahārājā, governor of the south; Virūpāksha Mahārājā, governor of the west; and Vaiśravaṇa Mahārājā, governor of the north.

raining down fresh ones indicates that the gods' hope, worship, and admiration of that buddha continued constantly.

"*Bhikshus!* After the lapse of many very long years, the Buddha Universal Surpassing Wisdom attained the Buddha-laws, and Perfect Enlightenment was revealed to him. Before that buddha left home, he had sixteen sons, the eldest of whom was named Wisdom Store. Each of his sons had various kinds of amusements and lived happy lives, but on hearing that their father had accomplished Perfect Enlightenment, they all gave up the things they valued and went to pay their regards to the buddha, their weeping mothers escorting them without expecting that they would return home again.

"Their grandfather, Sacred Wheel-Rolling King, with his grandsons, his many ministers, and many of his citizens, followed them to the Buddha Universal Surpassing Wisdom. After serving that buddha in various ways, they paid homage by prostrating themselves and touching his feet with their heads, and after making procession around him, with folded hands and with one mind, they gazed up at the buddha and praised him in verse. They spoke to the following effect: 'Though now the Buddha, you were formerly the same kind of ordinary man as we, and after the practice of measureless years, you have now become a buddha to save all living beings. You have a very holy appearance. Now seeing it, there seems to be hope even for us ordinary men to become buddhas according to our practice. We have attained good fortune and congratulate ourselves with great joy. All the living beings are suffering and without a leader; they are unaware of the way to end pain, knowing not how to seek deliverance. Their evil ways have increased more and more.

" 'But now the Buddha is free from all illusions and has attained the supreme and peaceful state of mind. You have set a good example for us so that we, together with the gods and men, will receive the Buddha's teachings and will attain enlightenment. This is the greatest good fortune that we have gained. Therefore we all offer our lives to you, the peerless honored one. Be pleased to lead us!' Thereupon all these sixteen royal sons, when they had extolled the buddha in verse, entreated him to roll on the Law-wheel, saying, 'Please preach the Law for all living beings.' " Here occurs the phrase "roll on the Law-wheel." In this case, the Law means the teaching of the truth. Once the teaching is preached, it is transmitted to one after another just as ceaselessly as a wheel rolls.

Therefore, to preach the teaching of the truth is called "to roll on the Law-wheel" in Buddhism.

Then in a more solemn tone, the Buddha said to the *bhikshus:* "When the Buddha Universal Surpassing Wisdom attained Perfect Enlightenment, each of the five hundred myriad *koṭis* of buddha-worlds in all directions was shaken in different ways; even the dark places between those realms, where the august light of the sun and moon could not shine, all became brilliant. All the living beings in their midst could see each other and unitedly exclaimed, 'From where have all these living beings suddenly come?' "

EMANCIPATION FROM THE HELL OF ISOLATION. The above words call for some explanation. In those places to which the Buddha's teachings have not spread, people assert themselves against each other and cannot open their minds. Though father and sons or brothers and sisters live together, each is isolated in the depths of his or her mind. They lead lonely lives, as they have no one but themselves to depend upon. But once the Buddha's teachings spread among them, they can all become friends. A person who has been lonely immediately becomes happy, surrounded by many good friends.

"Moreover, the palaces of the gods in all those regions shook in different ways and a great light universally shone, filling all the worlds, surpassing the light of heaven. Then, eastward, all the palaces of the Brahma heavens in many domains were brilliantly illuminated with double their normal brightness. And each of the Brahma heavenly kings reflected thus: 'For what reason does this sign appear, that our palaces are now illuminated as they never were of yore?' Then those Brahma heavenly kings all visited each other to discuss this happening. Meanwhile, among those assembled there was a great Brahma heavenly king, named Savior of All, who addressed the host of Brahmas in verse to the following effect: 'Why does this sign appear in such shining brightness as has never before been in all our palaces? Let us together investigate it. Is it that a great virtuous god is born? Is it that a buddha appears in the world? Why does this great light everywhere illuminate the universe?'

"Thereupon the Brahma heavenly kings from many domains, each with all his palace train, each taking a sack filled with celestial flowers, went together to visit the western quarter to investigate this sign. There they saw the Buddha Universal Surpassing Wisdom on the wisdom terrace under the Bodhi tree, seated on the lion throne, surrounded and revered by gods and human and nonhuman beings. And they saw his sixteen royal sons entreating the buddha to roll along the Law-wheel. Then all the Brahma heavenly kings bowed to the ground before the buddha, made procession around him hundreds and thousands of times, and then strewed celestial flowers upon him. The flowers they strewed rose liked Mount Sumeru and were offered also to the buddha's Bodhi tree. When they had offered the flowers, each presented his palace to the buddha and spoke thus: 'Out of compassion for us and for our good, condescend to accept the palaces we offer!' "

To honor the Buddha with an offering symbolizes one's worshiping the buddha and thanking him. The expression "the flowers were offered also to the buddha's Bodhi tree" has a very deep meaning. This tree protected the Buddha from the hot sun while he was meditating. The ground under the Bodhi tree is a natural place for attaining the highest enlightenment. For this reason, those who have deep devotion to the Buddha also pay honor to the Bodhi tree that protected him and to the place under this tree where he was seated when he attained enlightenment.

"Thereupon all the Brahma heavenly kings before the buddha, with one mind and one voice, praised him in verse to the following effect: 'A world-honored one rarely appears in this world and it is hard for us to meet him. He is perfect in infinite merit and is able to save all. As a great teacher of gods and men, he has compassion and leads all the creatures in the world. All the living beings in the universe hear his teaching and receive his aid. We have come from many heavens and have left deep meditative joys for the sake of serving the buddha. Our palaces are magnificently adorned as rewards for our former lives. Now we offer them to the world-honored one and beg him in mercy to accept them.' "

CREATION IS JOY IN HUMAN LIFE. The point here is that the heavenly kings have left their deep meditative joys and have descended from heaven to the human world for the sake of hearing the buddhas' teachings. This important point is at the core of the teaching of the Lotus Sutra.

A worthwhile life does not consist in merely spending one's life in peace and quiet but in creating something good. When one tries to become a better person through his practice, this endeavor is the creation of good. When he does something for the benefit of other people, this is the creation of a still higher standard of good. The various arts are the creation of beauty, and all honest professions are the creation of various kinds of energy that are beneficial to society.

Creation is bound to bring with it pain and hardship. However, one finds life worth living when one makes a strenuous effort for the sake of something good. He endeavors to become a little better a person and to do just a little more for the good of other people—through such positive endeavor we are enabled to feel deep joy in our human lives.

If we lived for a week in a world where we did not have hardships and the joy of creating something, we would tire of it. If we did not become bored with such a world, it would show that we were basically lazy in nature. Such people are sunk in illusion, and even if they rise to a heavenly world, at any moment they may fall immediately to the world of demons (*shura*) or to hell (*jigoku*).

Though heavenly beings have attained a peaceful state of mind and body, as long as there is a human being who is suffering, if they are concerned to save him from his suffering and if they practice positively to help the buddhas for the sake of the salvation of all living beings, they rise to the world of the buddhas (*bukkai*), the highest realm of living beings. This is because even heavenly beings make strenuous efforts for the sake of serving others, making them happy, and saving them from their sufferings. In such merciful actions and creative lives they feel a deep joy, and this is the way that leads them to the enlightenment of the buddhas.

As illustrated by the diagram of the ten realms of living beings (*jikkai*) on page 103, the way to enter the world of the buddhas starts in the world of human beings (*ningen-kai*). It is concerning this point that Nichiren said, "A hundred years' practice in the Pure Land is not equal to the merit of a day's practice in the impure land." Unless heavenly beings continually come down to the world of human beings and practice to save all living beings from their sufferings, they cannot become buddhas. For this reason, all the Brahma heavenly kings descended from the peaceful heavens, desiring to receive the Buddha's teachings so much that they gave up their palaces, that is, their peaceful lives.

Then the Brahma heavenly kings from all directions gathered, and all made the same request of the buddha. As here, similar descriptions are often repeated in the sutras. But as has been mentioned before, in reciting the sutras, wholehearted repetition is most important.

THE CLOSING VERSE OF VOWS. At the end of the fourteenth verse portion of this chapter occur the following lines: "May this deed of merit / Extend to all creatures / That we with all the living / May together accomplish the Buddha-way!" This is called "the closing verse of vows" because not only the practicers of the Lotus Sutra but all believers in Buddhism recite it as a closing verse in their sutra-chanting service. It is said that the spirit of the great vow and practice of Buddhists can be summed up in these few short lines. The words "this deed of merit" mean "this deed of merit of serving the buddhas." This does not mean that the Brahma heavenly kings desire to receive some merit in compensation for their having presented their palaces to the buddhas. It goes without saying that the buddhas are not anxious to have material things. To serve the Buddha by presenting flowers and offerings is an expression of our worship of and gratitude to him. But the most important thing is to serve the Buddha through our practice, namely, to practice the Buddha-way after abandoning our ego, or "small self." The sutra-reciting service that we perform before Buddhist altars is one of our practices in which we forget the small self, abandoning it and devoting ourselves solely to the pursuit of the Buddha-way. Therefore, our sutra-reciting service is also a great way of serving the Buddha.

Serving the Buddha should not be done merely for the sake of mental peace and a comfortable life. It should be our heartfelt desire that the merit of our practice of serving the Buddha extend to all living beings. It should be also our prayer to accomplish the Buddha-way together with all the living. Because the closing verse of vows has this deep significance, we should not merely learn it by heart but recite it earnestly as our great vow as Buddhists.

When the Tathāgata Universal Surpassing Wisdom received the entreaty of the Brahma heavenly kings of the ten regions and of his sixteen royal sons, he taught them the doctrine of the Four Noble Truths through the three ways of preaching.

The three ways of preaching are "show-rolling," or *ji-ten* (to show the Four Noble Truths); "exhortation-rolling," or *kan-ten* (to exhort to the practice of the Four Noble Truths), and "proof-rolling," or *shō-ten* (to witness or prove that the Buddha has accomplished the Four Noble Truths). Because the *tathāgata* preached the Four Noble Truths in these three ways, the sutra says, "the Tathāgata Universal Surpassing Wisdom at once thrice rolled the Law-wheel of the twelve divisions." Then he expounded in detail the Law of the Twelve Causes (*jūni-innen*), one of the fundamental teachings of the Buddha.

THE LAW OF THE TWELVE CAUSES: OUTER CAUSATION. This law, also called the doctrine of the twelve-link chain of dependent origination, teaches that all phenomena in this world constantly change, appearing and disappearing, and that all changes are based on an established rule. Though all things change, this rule is immutable. It is known as the Law of the Twelve Causes because the rule is divided into twelve stages. However, it is easier for us to understand this law by limiting it to man than by trying to apply it at once to all phenomena.

The Buddha preached the Law of the Twelve Causes in detail to Ānanda in the *Dīrghagāma-sūtra* (*Jō-agon-gyō*). This law rules the growth of the human body as well as the changes in man's mind. The former is called the "outer causation" (*gai-engi*) and the latter the "inner causation" (*nai-engi*). It explains the process through which a human being is born, grows, ages, and dies in light of the three temporal states of existence, the past, present, and future. And in connection with this, it shows how man's mind changes and the fundamental method of purifying it and of removing illusions from it.

The twelve links or stages are (1) ignorance (*mumyō*), (2) actions (*gyō*), (3) consciousness (*shiki*), (4) name and form (mental functions and matter; *myō-shiki*), (5) the six entrances (the five sense organs and the mind; *rokunyū*), (6) contact (*soku*), (7) sensation (*ju*), (8) desire (*ai*), (9) clinging (*shu*), (10) existence (*u*), (11) birth (*shō*), and (12) old age and death (*rō-shi*). First we will explain the growth and changes of the human body, the outer causation.

The first link of the Twelve Causes is *ignorance*. Prior to our conception by our parents, nothing is known or sensed. When the ignorant spirit is conceived in the mother's womb through the *action* of sexual intercourse, *consciousness* is produced. Consciousness means "something living." Here something like a human being—a fetus—is produced, although it is still incomplete. As the incomplete consciousness is gradually taking shape, it grows into *name and form* (mental functions and matter). "Name" means an immaterial being, spirit or soul, and "form" indicates a material being, that is, the human body. "Name and form" mean the human body with a soul.

As name and form (mind and body) grow, they develop the five sense organs (eyes, ears, nose, tongue, body) and the mind, by which we perceive the existence of things. At this time, we are still in the mother's womb and incomplete. This stage is called the *six entrances* because the functions of our minds and bodies are on the point of dividing into six different senses.

We are born into this world at the stage of the six entrances. When we grow to the age of two or three, the six entrances are completed and sensibility is developed. That is, we become able to discern shapes, colors, sounds, smells, tastes, physical sensations, and so on. This stage is called *contact*.

When this sensibility is further developed, feelings of like and dislike naturally develop. This state is called *sensation*. These feelings become distinct at six or seven years of age. As this state develops, *desire* is produced. "Desire" implies many things, but here we limit its meaning to the human body and take it only as meaning affection for the opposite sex. As affection for the other sex becomes stronger, we come to have the desire of possessing the other. This is *clinging*. Later we enter into married life; this stage is *existence*. In the course of time children are born as a natural consequence of our marriage. This is *birth*. When we reach this stage, we are attacked in various ways by sufferings in their true sense. This stage continues through life, and finally we come to *old age and death*.

Clinical studies by modern doctors prove that during the nine months from the moment of conception to the birth of a human baby, the body, which was at first like an amoeba, passes through all the major evolutionary stages that occurred before reaching the form of man as he is today. In other words, even today's evolved man is in a state like the amoeba of two billion years ago when he is conceived in his mother's womb. When this fact is compared with the Law of the Twelve Causes taught by the Buddha, we cannot help admiring the fact that the Buddha preached exactly what the studies of twentieth-century scientists tell us.

TRANSMIGRATION. What happens to us after death? Buddhism teaches that we remain for some time in the state of intermediate existence (*chū-u*) in this world after death, and when this time is over, in accordance with the karma that we have accumulated in our previous life, we are reborn in another appropriate world. Buddhism also divides this other world into the following ten realms: hell (*jigoku*), hungry spirits (*gaki*), animals (*chikushō*), demons (*shura*), human beings (*ningen*), heaven

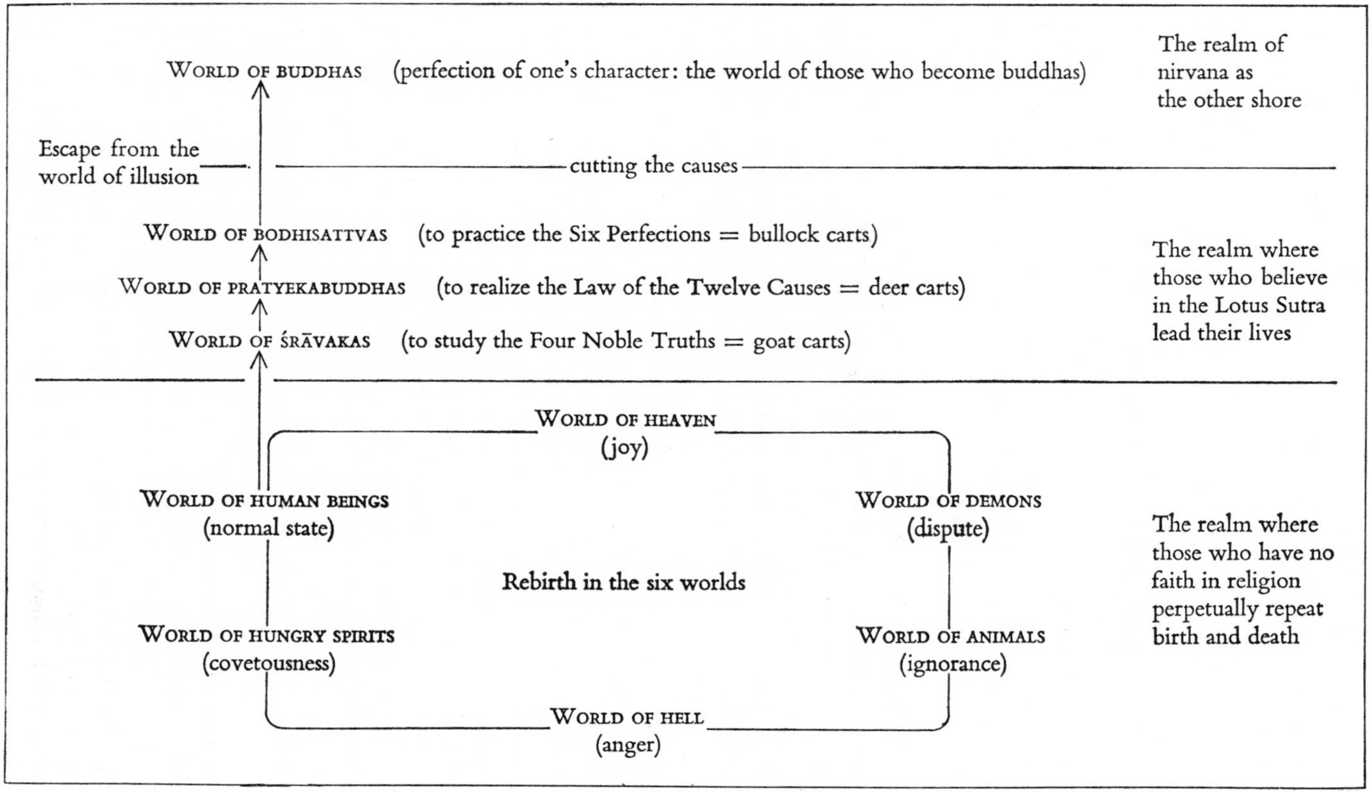

The Ten Worlds

(*tenjō*), *śrāvakas* (*shōmon*), *pratyekabuddhas* (*engaku*), bodhisattvas (*bosatsu*), and buddhas (*butsu*).

If we die in an unenlightened state, our souls will return to the former state of ignorance, will be reborn in the six worlds (*rokudō*) of illusion and suffering, and will finally reach old age and death through the twelve stages discussed above. And we will repeat this round to the end of time. This perpetual repetition of birth and death is called transmigration (*rinne*). But if we purify our souls by hearing the Buddha's teachings and practicing the bodhisattva-way, the state of ignorance is annihilated and our souls can be reborn in a better world. The expression "to cut the causes" applies to this state.

KARMA. Here we will discuss karma (*gō*) to help us attain a better understanding of the Law of the Twelve Causes. Briefly, "karma" means "deed." It is produced by all the deeds we do. Any deed is invariably accompanied by a result. All that we are at the present moment is the result of the karma that we have produced in the past. For example, the fact that you are now reading this book is the result of the causes and conditions that have occurred due to the accumulation of various past deeds. The phenomenon that the results of deeds leaves behind as a residue, as it were, is called "recompense" (*hō*).

Karma is complex and serious. Our deeds, however trifling, leave traces physically, mentally, and environmentally. The traces left in our minds include memory, knowledge, habit, intelligence, and character. They are produced by the accumulation of our experiences and deeds over a long period of time. The traces that our deeds leave on our body are seen, for example, when heavy eating or drinking leads to sickness. They are also seen where a proper amount of exercise trains our body and builds up our constitution. These physical traces are so clearly visible that anyone can perceive them.

Our mental attitudes also leave traces on our body. Most obvious are those on our faces. There is something mean or shady in the face of a person who is low-minded, however handsome he may be. A man who is usually angry has a grim look. A person who is tender-hearted, knowledgeable, and endowed with virtue and influence seems somehow happy-looking, clear-headed, and dignified, even if his features themselves are not particularly striking. It is also generally known that a person's work causes changes in his looks. This is what Abraham Lincoln was referring to when he said, "A man over forty should feel responsible for his looks."

Part of the traces of our deeds that are left on our minds remains on the surface of our minds; this includes memory, knowledge, habit, intelligence, and character. Another portion of the traces remains in the subconscious, in the hidden depths of our minds. Moreover, all the influences of the outer world by which we have been unconsciously affected, which include the experiences that we have had before our birth (indeed, since the beginning of mankind), are sunk in the subconscious mind. Karma includes all this. Though it was simply defined as deeds, in reality karma implies the accumulation of all our experiences and deeds since the birth of mankind, and since even before that time. This is called the "karma of a previous existence" (*shuku-gō*). The action of this karma is called the "power of karma" (*gō-riki*).

This power can be correctly explained by understanding the working of the subconscious mind. Even things that the human race experienced hundreds of thousands of years ago remain in the depths of our minds, as do the much stronger influences of the deeds and mental attitudes of our ancestors.

The "karma of a previous existence" that Buddhism teaches is still more profound, as it includes the karma that our own life has produced through the repetition of birth and death from the infinite past to the present.

What does the idea of karma teach us? There are people who think, "I never asked my parents to bring me into this world," or "I am not responsible for what I am because everything, including my brain, nature, and physical constitution, partake of the nature of my parents."

Such ideas seem to be half reasonable, but they are imperfect. Indeed, one's parents or ancestors must be responsible for half of the nature of their descendants, but the other half is the responsibility of the descendants themselves. This is because, though half of the present self must be the effect of karma produced by one's ancestors and parents, the other half is the effect of the karma that one has produced oneself in one's previous lives. Moreover, the self that exists after one's childhood is the effect of the karma that one has produced oneself in this world. So the responsibility of one's parents is very limited.

The idea of karma teaches us clearly that one will reap the fruits of what he has sown. Suppose that we are unhappy at present; we are apt to lose our temper and express discontent if we attribute our unhappiness to others. But if we consider our present unhappiness to be the effect of our own deeds in the past, we can accept it and take responsibility for it.

Besides such acceptance, hope for the future wells up strongly in our hearts: "The more good karma I accumulate, the happier I will become and the better recompense I will receive. All right, I will accumulate much more good karma in the future." We should not limit this idea only to the problems of human life in this world. We can also feel hope concerning the traces of our lives after death. For those who do not know the teachings of the Buddha, nothing is so terrible as death. Everyone fears it. But if we truly realize the meaning of karma-result, we can keep our composure in the face of death because we can have hope for our next life.

When we do not think only of ourselves but realize that the karma produced by our own deeds exerts an influence upon our descendants, we will naturally come to feel responsible for our deeds. We will also realize that we, as parents, must maintain a good attitude in our daily lives in order to have a favorable influence (recompense) upon our children. We will feel strongly that we must always speak to our children correctly and bring them up properly and with affection.

The word "karma-result" has often been interpreted as something negative, but this is due to a mistaken way of teaching this idea. We should consider the idea of karma-result in a positive and forward-looking way.

THE LAW OF THE TWELVE CAUSES: INNER CAUSATION. Next we shall consider the Law of the Twelve Causes in terms of the growth and changes of man's mind.

Ignorance, the first link of the inner causation of this law, is not to have a right view of life or the world, or to disregard the right view even when one knows it. Because of being ignorant, one repeatedly does things that depart from the truth (the universal law): these are *actions.* In this case, "actions" must be interpreted not only as one's own actions but as the accumulation of all the actions that one has experienced since the distant past, as explained in the discussion of karma.

Consciousness is the fundamental power or function by which man discerns things. All the states of this power or function are decided by the accumulation of one's experiences and deeds of the past, that is, by the karma that one has produced.

As mentioned before, *name and form* mean mental functions and matter, respectively. The former refers to an immaterial being, the soul or spirit, and the latter to a material being, the human body. Taking the

1. IGNORANCE OR PASSION (*mumyō*; illusion) 2. ACTIONS (*gyō*)	sexual intercourse of parents	the past
3. CONSCIOUSNESS (*shiki*)	moment of conception	the present
4. NAME AND FORM (*myō-shiki*; mental functions and matter)	growth after conception	
5. SIX ENTRANCES (*rokunyū*; the five sense organs and the mind)	growth of these in the womb	
6. CONTACT (*soku*)	stage of two- or three-year-old children	
7. SENSATION (*ju*)	stage of six- or seven-year-old children	
8. DESIRE (*ai*; affection for the opposite sex)	stage of seventeen- or eighteen-year-old youths	
9. CLINGING (*shu*; desire for the opposite sex)	mental state of adults	
10. EXISTENCE (*u*; possession of the opposite sex)	marriage	
11. BIRTH (*shō*)	birth of a child	the future
12. OLD AGE AND DEATH (*rō-shi*; occurrence of suffering)	grief, lamentation, suffering, and distress	

The Law of the Twelve Causes

two together, "name and form" refer to our existence. It is through consciousness that we are enabled to have a faint idea of our existence. If there is no consciousness, we do not understand our existence. The expression "Consciousness causes name and form" in the Lotus Sutra expresses this.

The *six entrances* mean the function of the six sense organs: eyes (sight), ears (hearing), nose (smell), tongue (taste), body (touch), and the mind, by which we perceive the existence of the things sensed through these five organs.

Though we are aware of our own existence (name and form) through consciousness, it is still too vague an awareness to constitute true knowledge. But then the five functions of sight, hearing, smell, taste, and touch develop, and at the same time the mind, by which we perceive the existence of things sensed through these functions, matures. At this point we first gain the power to discern things clearly. This stage is called *contact.*

There are two major interpretations of this stage. Some are of the opinion that this is the stage before we have feelings of like or dislike and is called contact because our minds merely come in contact with things. Others say that contact means the stage when consciousness, name and form, and the six entrances have reached a relationship conducive to the clear-cut development of the function of our mind. Setting aside such scholastic opinions, it is enough for us to understand that contact indicates the stage at which our mind can clearly discern things. With such mental development, feelings of pain, pleasure, like, and dislike are produced. This is *sensation.*

When such feelings appear, *desire* for things arises spontaneously. The desire referred to here means attachment, whose meaning is little different from that of love as this word is commonly used. In other words, this is a state of mind that has preferences and that clings to what it likes. When we have desire for something, we try to hold onto it. Conversely, we try to avoid what we considers unpleasant or undesirable. This state of mind is called *clinging.*

Clinging leads to various feelings, ideas, and assertions. This is *existence*, which means the discriminating mind. Due to this discriminating mind, opposition and struggle occur among people, and human life as suffering unfolds before one. Such human life is called *birth.* Leading such a life of suffering, *old age* comes before one knows it, and finally one encounters *death.*

Man's life develops in this way, so that the basic cause of a life of suffering is fundamental ignorance. Suffering occurs because man does not know the law applicable to all things and does not have a right view of the world and of life; even when he is aware of it, he disregards it. Only if man can rid himself of this ignorance and set his mind in the direction of the law will his deeds (practice) be correctly directed. When his mind is set on the right track, his sufferings in this world disappear, and eventually he will attain peace of mind. This is the conclusion reached through the Law of the Twelve Causes.

In short, the Law of the Twelve Causes teaches that man is born as an ordinary human being because of his ignorance in his previous life.

The Law also teaches that if he eradicates his ignorance in the present world, the essential form of his life as it was meant to be will be revealed in his future life. Here we should not limit the meaning of "future life" to life when we are reborn after death but should regard it rather as the life before us in the future. If we abandon fundamental ignorance and set our minds in the direction of the Law, a bright and serene future life will open up before us. To the extent that we do not do this, our life will be accompanied by suffering, however rich we may be and however much honor we may gain, and our minds will continue to revolve in the track of the six worlds of illusion. The six worlds in this case refer to states of mind, as explained in chapter 2 of the Sutra of Innumerable Meanings.

Through the Law of the Twelve Causes, we have considered the vertical development of life (our ancestors, ourselves, and our descendants; or ourselves in a previous life, in the present world, and in the world to come). However, the fact is, the mind and human life do not comprise merely such vertical relationships. Both are also greatly influenced by horizontal relationships, that is, by complex connections with the whole of society.

The idea of the ten worlds, the six worlds of ordinary men and the four worlds of saints (the worlds of *śrāvakas, pratyekabuddhas,* bodhisattvas, and buddhas), thus develops into the teaching of the Three Thousand Realms in One Mind (*ichinen-sanzen*).

THE THREE THOUSAND REALMS IN ONE MIND. This doctrine forms the essence of the *Makashikan* (*Mo-ho-chih-kuan*), a twenty-section work in which T'ien-t'ai Chih-i of China systematized various teachings included in the Lotus Sutra. This was his new interpretation of the Lotus Sutra. Nichiren regarded Chih-i's doctrine of the Three Thousand Realms in One Mind as the essence of the Buddha's teachings.

In the second section his work *Kaimoku-shō* (Essay on the Eye-opener), Nichiren extolled this doctrine in the following words: "Unless man attains buddhahood through the teaching of the Three Thousand Realms in One Mind, his attaining nirvana and becoming a buddha will be little more than a mere name." In the first section of the same work, he also praised the doctrine as follows: "The very doctrine of the Three Thousand Realms in One Mind of the Tendai sect appears to be the way to lead man to buddhahood." Nichiren specifically extolled this doctrine a total of eighteen times in his works.

What is the teaching of the Three Thousand Realms in One Mind? As has been mentioned, our minds revolve ceaselessly in the six worlds of hell (anger), hungry spirits (covetousness), animals (ignorance), demons (dispute), human beings (normality), and heaven (joy). Thus our sufferings continue endlessly.

However, even an ordinary person sometimes rises to the level of the four realms of the saints. He conceives the desire to study the right way to live (*śrāvaka*), realizing it intuitively from his experiences (*pratyekabuddha*), and wishing to live for the benefit of people and society (bodhisattva). But he will seldom if ever reach such a mental state of absolute compassion that he completely forgets himself. It would be a great thing if he could maintain such a mental state constantly. But soon his mind returns to that of an ordinary person without his having made any lasting improvement.

THE TEN REALMS OF BEING FOUND IN ONE ANOTHER. Everyone's mind possesses the ten realms, the six of the ordinary person and the four of the saint. These ten realms exist in the minds of heavenly beings, as well. The ten realms exist in the mind of each person in each of the ten realms. This is *jikkai-gogu,* or "the ten realms of being found in one another."

The seed of the buddha-nature is also possessed by those who are in the worlds of hell and demons, although it is very undeveloped. The doctrine of the Three Thousand Realms in One Mind teaches that even those who are in such a state of mind have the possibility of attaining buddhahood and that the chance of salvation can be found anywhere. In other words, this doctrine teaches plainly that the Buddha's compassion extends to all living beings. On the other hand, even when one thinks he has realized and become free of the bonds of illusion and suffering, by studying the doctrine he will become able to reflect on his remaining seeds of illusion and will come to wish to devote himself still more to his practice.

Each of the ten realms exists in the mind of everyone in each of the ten worlds. Ten multiplied by ten equals one hundred. One hundred minds appear in the ten ways according to the doctrine of the Ten Suchnesses (*jū-nyoze*).

THE TEN SUCHNESSES. This doctrine consists of ten words prefaced by "such a" or "such an": "such a form" (*nyoze sō*), "such a nature" (*nyoze shō*), "such an embodiment" (*nyoze tai*), "such a potency" (*nyoze riki*), "such a function" (*nyoze sa*), "such a primary cause" (*nyoze in*), "such a secondary cause" (*nyoze en*), "such an effect" (*nyoze ka*), "such a recompense" (*nyoze hō*), and "such a complete fundamental whole" (*nyoze hommatsu kukyō-tō*). This doctrine reveals the deepest reality of the existence of all things in the universe, which is called the principle of the Reality of All Existence (*shohō jissō*). Modern science has analyzed physical substances to the extent of subatomic particles. But the principle of the Reality of All Existence is much more profound than such an analysis, extending even to the mental world. The Chinese character read *nyo* means *shinnyo*, meaning "that which is constant and unchanging." *Nyoze* means "such" or "thus," and also "invariably," "without fail," or "without error."

The existence of all things invariably has form. This is called "such a form." That which has a form invariably has a nature. This is called "such a nature." That which has a nature invariably has an embodiment. This is called "such an embodiment." That which has an embodiment invariably has potency (energy). This is called "such a potency." When it has potency, it invariably produces various outwardly directed functions. This is called "such a function."

Innumerable embodied substances exist in the universe. For this reason, their outward-directed functions are interrelated with all things. Nothing in the universe is an isolated existence having no relation to other things. All things have complicated connections with one another. They are interdependent and through their interaction cause various phenomena. A cause that produces such phenomena is called "such a primary cause."

Even when there exists a cause, it does not produce its effect until it comes into contact with some occasion or condition. For instance, there is always vapor in the air as the primary cause of frost or dew. But if it has no secondary cause that brings it into contact with the ground or the leaves of a plant, it does not become frost or dew. Such an occasion or condition is called "such a secondary cause." When a primary cause meets with a secondary cause, a phenomenon (effect) is produced. This is called "such an effect."

An effect not only produces a phenomenon but also invariably leaves some trace or residue. For example, the effect of frost forming will give a pleasant feeling to one person who enjoys the patterns it makes on the windowpanes, while the same effect will give an unpleasant feeling to

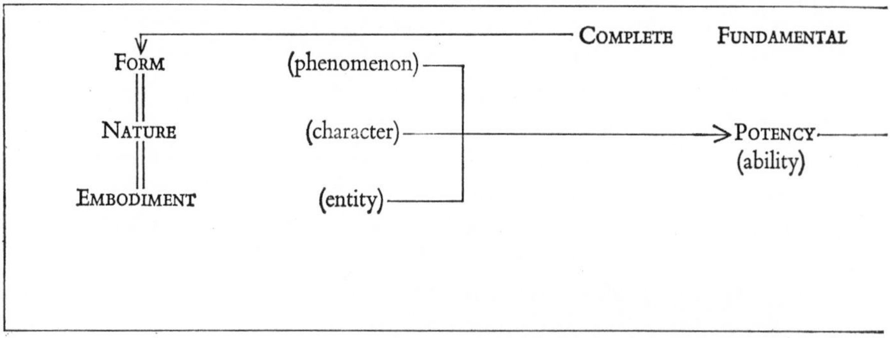

someone else whose crops have been damaged by it. The function of an effect leaving a trace or residue is called "such a recompense."

It will be helpful to explain primary cause, secondary cause, effect, and recompense in more detail. Suppose a man has offered his seat in the train to an old woman. In his mind he possesses, as a primary cause, the potential of wishing to be kind to others. When such a primary cause comes into contact with a secondary cause, in this case his seeing an old woman staggering while trying to stand in the train, it produces the effect of his offering his seat to her. Afterward he feels refreshed, thinking, "I have done something good." This is recompense. This recompense comes from one's mind as well as from outside. The former comes first to him, and it is the most important recompense.

The nine suchnesses mentioned above occur incessantly in society and in the universe as a whole. They are interconnected in a complex manner, so that in most cases, man cannot discern what is a cause and what is an effect. But these suchnesses never fail to operate according to the law of the universal truth, and no one, no thing, and no function can depart from this law. Everything functions according to the Law of the Ten Suchnesses, from form to recompense, namely, from beginning to end. This is the meaning of "such a complete fundamental whole." The fact that all things, including man, and their relations with one another are formed by this law is called the Reality of All Existence.

The hundred worlds mentioned earlier operate in the ten ways shown in the law of the Ten Suchnesses. Ten multiplied by one hundred is one thousand; therefore one hundred minds have one thousand functions.

THREE CONSTITUENTS OF THE WORLD. We have been discussing the

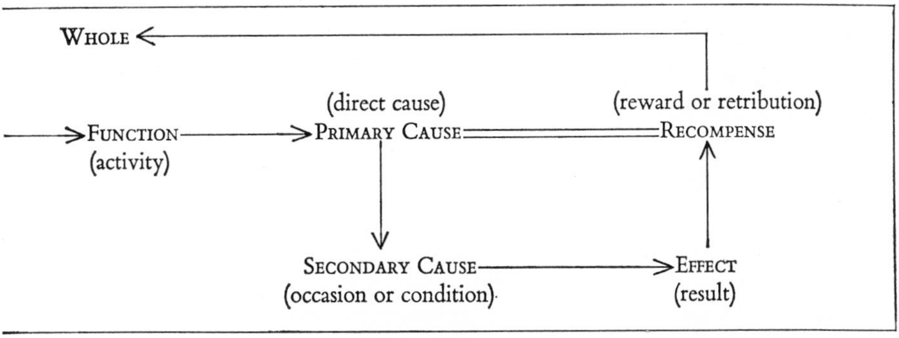

The Ten Suchnesses

mind of an individual, but we must always think of an individual in connection with society because there is no one who exists isolated from it. Buddhism teaches that there are three ways of thinking about society. The first is *go'on seken,* or the world where an individual mind exerts an influence upon others, in other words, environment in the narrow sense. The second is *shujō seken,* or the world of which its living beings are regarded as a constituent. Generally speaking, this is a society or nation. The third is *kokudo seken,* or the world consisting of many societies and countries. This is commonly considered to be the whole world.

We all form part of these three kinds of worlds, which coexist, whether we like it or not. The one thousand functions of our minds are spread over these three kinds of worlds. One thousand multiplied by three is three thousand; thus, all relations in the three constituents of the world (*sanzen*) are included in a single momentary thought (*ichinen*) of a human being in his daily life. Hence the term "Three Thousand Realms in One Mind" (*ichinen sanzen*).

Suppose that the following thought has occurred in one's mind: "A man is coming toward me. What an unpleasant face he has!" Also suppose the following idea has flashed into one's mind: "How beautiful the flowers on the hedge are!" When we analyze this thought, we find that its occurrence includes the vertical influences on our mind from the remote past until the present and the horizontal influences of people, society, and all other things in this world.

This thought also includes one's personal nature, which leads one to fall into hell or become a buddha. One's dislike of the man's face is also part of one's nature inclining one to buddhahood, just as one's appreciation of the beauty of the flower is also part of one's nature inclining one to fall into hell. This may seem strange, but actually it is quite natural. If one's dislike of the man's face develops into a wish to hit him in the face, one will soon fall into the mental state of hell. But if one thinks, "My feeling this way is due to my insufficient practice. I feel dislike because I have the seed of dislike in my mind. I must practice more in order to remove this seed [illusion]," one has attained the mental state of the self-enlightened (*pratyekabuddha*).

Moreover, if one has the firm resolution, "A person with such a face must surely have some great personal problem that affects his daily life; it is my duty to spread the Buddha's teachings so widely that no one will wear such an expression," this person is in the mental state of a bodhisattva and has the possibility of becoming a buddha.

When one thinks, "How beautiful the flowers on the hedge are," one's untainted admiration for their beauty reflects the mental state of a saint who has merged with heaven and earth. But if one thinks, "I will pick a spray to take home and put on my desk," one is beginning to fall into the world of hungry spirits (covetousness). If one becomes angry, thinking, "I wonder how rich that person is, that he can have a beautiful hedge around his house. He must lead a carefree life, while I have to keep my nose to the grindstone. Bad luck to him!" one has fallen completely into the realm of hell.

THEORETICAL DOCTRINE OF THE THREE THOUSAND REALMS IN ONE MIND. The question arises as to how we should consider the doctrine of the Three Thousand Realms in One Mind. When we understand this doctrine only theoretically, it cannot generate the power capable of saving others as well as ourselves. This is called the theoretical doctrine of the Three Thousand Realms in One Mind (*ri no ichinen-sanzen*). Far from saving others, we are unconsciously enslaved by the philosophical theory of the doctrine and eventually may become so obsessed with the thought of the myriad implications of our every act that we become mentally paralyzed, as it were. We must accept this doctrine with an open-hearted, optimistic, and positive attitude.

The doctrine of the Three Thousand Realms in One Mind teaches us that we have the infinite possibility of moving both upward and downward. If we resolve firmly to practice the Buddha's teachings, we can go upward without fail. Secondly, this doctrine lets us realize clearly that in all the universe, there is no individual existing apart from the whole and that all things are interconnected like the meshes of a net. Individual salvation alone is not true salvation.

PRACTICAL DOCTRINE OF THE THREE THOUSAND REALMS IN ONE MIND. When we understand these two teachings not only theoretically but also in the depths of our hearts, we cannot help elevating ourselves and practicing in order to help others. This is called the practical doctrine of the Three Thousand Realms in One Mind (*ji no ichinen-sanzen*). Unless we thoroughly understand the doctrine of the Three Thousand Realms in One Mind in this way, it does not become a living doctrine.

Nichiren spoke in the highest terms of the doctrine of the Three Thousand Realms in One Mind. He derived his teachings from this doctrine, but ultimately he passed beyond a theoretical understanding and realized that for Buddhists the doctrine should result in faith and practice. Indeed, if we can thoroughly understand the theoretical doctrine, we should awaken to the fact that we must be concerned as long as there is a single person in the world who is suffering. Unlike the worries of an ordinary man, this is a great worry, the Buddha's worry. This is the meaning of the expression, "When living beings are taken ill, the Buddha suffers pain." It is also the significance of Nichiren's words, "Although Nichiren does not weep in reality, tears of worry for others always flow from his eyes."

If we must be worried about something, we should have the same worry as the Buddha and Nichiren. Such a worry gives us courage and makes us find life worth living. After all is said and done, there is no work that is more valuable in this world than to save people who are suffering. To elevate human beings is the loftiest work. Our own consciousness of having taken part in this work, small as we are—this consciousness alone should brighten our lives.

Let us now return to the text of chapter 7. The Buddha continued his preaching as follows: "The Buddha Universal Surpassing Wisdom preached the Law of the Four Noble Truths and the Law of the Twelve Causes amid the gods, men, and all the great host. The numberless people were not subject to the changing phenomena in their surroundings [temporary laws]; their minds were freed from faults and they did not become agitated by anything around them any time or any place. Likewise at a second, a third, and a fourth preaching of the Law, the

Buddha Universal Surpassing Wisdom repeated the Law of the Four Noble Truths and the Law of the Twelve Causes, and innumerable living beings equally reached the same state of mind [Hīnayāna enlightenment].

"Meanwhile, the sixteen royal sons, seeing that the numberless people had become free from illusions, left home and became *śrāmaṇeras*[7] of keen natural powers, wise and intelligent. As they gradually received the teachings, they came to understand them thoroughly. They reached the understanding that each teaching of the Four Noble Truths and the Twelve Causes was a path leading to the Mahāyāna teaching, and that they must study this and practice the bodhisattva-way in order to attain the true enlightenment of the Buddha. They asked the Buddha Universal Surpassing Wisdom to preach to them the teaching of Perfect Enlightenment [the supreme enlightenment of the Buddha]. Then the subjects of the holy wheel-rolling king also sought to leave home, whereupon the king consented.

"Then the Buddha Universal Surpassing Wisdom, on the entreaty of the *śrāmaṇeras,* when two myriad *kalpas* had passed, in the presence of many of his disciples, including monks, nuns, and lay devotees, preached this Great-vehicle Sutra named the Lotus Flower of the Wonderful Law, the Law by which bodhisattvas are instructed and which the buddhas watch over and keep in mind."

The words "the Law by which bodhisattvas are instructed" mean "the Law teaching the bodhisattva-way," and the words "the Law which the buddhas watch over and keep in mind" imply that one cannot rashly preach the Law, because the buddhas watch over it and keep it in mind. Both expressions apply to the Lotus Flower of the Wonderful Law.

The Buddha continued: "When he had preached this sutra, the sixteen *śrāmaṇeras,* for the sake of Perfect Enlightenment, all received, kept, practiced, and penetrated it, and preached it to others. While this sutra was being preached, besides the sixteen bodhisattva-*śrāmaṇeras,* there were also those among the host of *śrāvakas* who believed and discerned it, but most of the other living beings harbored doubts and perplexities, being convinced that they could not possibly become buddhas.

"The buddha preached this sutra incessantly for eight thousand *kalpas.* When he had finished preaching it, he entered a quiet room and re-

7. A male novice who has received the ten precepts, after which he may become a *śramaṇa,* a monk or ascetic.

mained in meditation for eighty-four thousand *kalpas*. Thereupon the sixteen bodhisattva-*śrāmaṇeras*, knowing that the buddha was absorbed in meditation, were concerned about what would happen if they did not preach the Law on behalf of the buddha. Each of them ascended a Law throne and according to the capacity of his listeners extensively preached and expounded to them the Sutra of the Lotus Flower of the Wonderful Law. Each of them showed, taught, benefited, and gladdened them, leading them to develop the mind leading to Perfect Enlightenment."

A brief explanation should be given here of the words "Each of them showed, taught, benefited, and gladdened them." These words indicate the order of preaching the Law. First, one must show the general meaning of the teaching to people. Then, when one knows that they have generated the desire to enter the teaching, one must teach its profound meaning. Next, seeing that they appear to understand it, one must lead them to practice it and to obtain the benefit of the teaching. Lastly, one must so act toward them as to gladden them in keeping the teaching.

The Buddha continued: "The Buddha Universal Surpassing Wisdom, who arose from his meditation after eighty-four thousand *kalpas* had passed, went up to the Law throne and quietly sat down on it.

"Universally addressing the great assembly, he said: 'Rare are such bodhisattva-*śrāmaṇeras* as these sixteen, keen in their natural powers and clear in their wisdom. They have paid homage to an infinite number of buddhas, constantly practiced religious conduct under those buddhas, received and kept the Buddha-wisdom, and revealed it to the living beings, leading them to enter into it. Do you all, again and again, draw nigh and worship them. Wherefore? Because if you do so, all the people who are in the mental state of *śrāvakas, pratyekabuddhas,* and bodhisattvas will attain Perfect Enlightenment.' "

The Buddha then addressed all the *bhikshus,* saying: "These sixteen bodhisattvas take delight in preaching this Sutra of the Lotus Flower of the Wonderful Law. Numberless living beings whom each of these bodhisattvas converted, reborn generation after generation, all following these bodhisattvas, heard the Law from them, and all believed and discerned it. For this cause they succeeded in meeting four myriad *koṭis* of buddhas, world-honored ones, and at the present time have not ceased so to do."

Some people consider that because this chapter is only the seventh sermon of the Buddha in the Lotus Sutra, and Sakyamuni Buddha has not yet finished preaching the sutra, it is odd that he should have said that the Buddha Universal Surpassing Wisdom and the sixteen bodhisattvas had preached the Lotus Sutra in the past. This mistaken idea comes from their thinking that the Sutra of the Lotus Flower of the Wonderful Law is just the title of this specific sutra, like the title of a book.

"The Sutra of the Lotus Flower of the Wonderful Law" actually indicates the following idea: the supremely sacred truth that dwells in the minds of ordinary men living in this corrupt world but untainted by their evils, just as the lotus is untainted by the mud in which it grows, and which leads them to buddhahood. Such a truth is always one; it cannot be divided into two or three. Therefore it is quite natural that Sakyamuni Buddha should have said that the Buddha Universal Surpassing Wisdom and the sixteen bodhisattvas had once preached the Lotus Sutra. The truth has obviously existed from the infinite past, before Sakyamuni Buddha appeared in this world, and the enlightenment realized by a truly enlightened person cannot exist except as the one truth. For this reason, it is no wonder that the Buddha said that some hundred thousand people preached the truth in their previous lives. From such words of the Buddha, we can clearly gather his intention to cause people to understand thoroughly the fact that the truth is one.

Then the Buddha said: "*Bhikshus!* Listen carefully to my words. I tell you now a very important matter: the sixteen *śrāmaṇeras* have all attained Perfect Enlightenment, and in all countries in every direction they are at the present time preaching the Law." Then he mentioned the name of each buddha and his realm. With the ninth, the name of a familiar buddha appears with the words, "Of the two buddhas in the western quarter one is named Amita. . . ." But the Tathāgata Amita is the buddha in the Pure Land of the western region, and he is not in charge of instructing us in this world.

The Buddha declared, "The sixteenth is I myself, Sakyamuni Buddha, who has accomplished Perfect Enlightenment in the *sahā*-domain." He first reveals here his own history and the cause of his eventual enlightenment.

We should take note of the declaration that Sakyamuni is the Buddha who has accomplished Perfect Enlightenment in the *sahā*-domain. The Buddha alone is the great teacher for the people of this *sahā*-world. We cannot but call again to mind here how irreplaceable and important the man Sakyamuni is for us as the historical Buddha.

The Tathāgata Sakyamuni, the Eternal Original Buddha, as the first cause of this appearing Buddha, is the Buddha of non-beginning and non-end who appears everywhere in the universe at all times. These two Buddhas are originally the same, but their significance is different. Unless we understand this, we will not be able to grasp Sakyamuni's words hereafter.

The Buddha continued his preaching: "*Bhikshus!* When we were *śrāmaṇeras,* each of us taught and converted infinite living beings, and those who heard the Law from me attained Perfect Enlightenment. Among these living beings there are some who still remain in the stage of *śrāvakas.* I constantly instruct them in Perfect Enlightenment, so that all these people will, through this Law, gradually enter the way of buddhahood. This is because the Buddha-wisdom with its profound meaning is hard to believe and hard to understand when it is preached suddenly. Therefore, people gradually advance from the teaching with the shallow meaning to that with the profound meaning. All those living beings, innumerable as the sands of the Ganges, whom I converted at that time, are yourselves, *bhikshus,* and will be my *śrāvaka*-disciples in future worlds after my extinction."

Our concept of the Buddha will be confused unless we understand the difference between the Tathāgata Sakyamuni as the historical Buddha and the Tathāgata Sakyamuni as the Original Buddha. A detailed explanation of this difference will be given in chapter 16, "Revelation of the [Eternal] Life of the Tathāgata."

The Buddha continued: "After my extinction there will also be disciples of mine who, not hearing this sutra, nor knowing nor apprehending the course that bodhisattvas pursue, will, through their own merits, conceive the idea of extinction and enter what they think is nirvana. But in other domains to which they may go, I will still be Buddha though under different names. These people, though they conceive the idea of extinction and enter what they call nirvana, yet in those lands will seek after the Buddha-wisdom and will succeed in hearing this sutra. Only by the Buddha-vehicle will they attain real nirvana. There is no vehicle other than the tactful teachings of the Tathāgata."

This is a very important teaching. Buddhahood, that is, attainment of the ideal state of mind as a human being, cannot be realized only by our practice throughout our entire life or in our next life. Some will be able to become buddhas in this world, but such people have practiced the Buddha-way for many previous lives. As has been repeatedly said, because man's life is eternal, even granted that he cannot reach the mental state of a buddha in this world, if he should continuously hear the Buddha's teachings in future worlds and devote himself to the bodhisattva-way of saving others, he will eventually become a buddha. For a person who has come into contact with the Buddha-way in this world, a secondary cause of the attainment of buddhahood is produced. A person who can perfectly accomplish the practice of the bodhisattva-way in this world has already passed through the mental state of *śrāvaka* or a *pratyekabuddha* previously. For one who has thus been able to encounter the Lotus Sutra, a secondary cause of attaining buddhahood in the future has been generated. For this reason, he should receive and keep this sutra continuously until his death and even beyond.

"*Bhikshus!* The Tathāgata does not exist in this world indefinitely. After preaching all his teachings, he will leave to enter nirvana at some time. When he himself knows that the time of nirvana has arrived and the assembly is pure, firm in faith and discernment, penetrated with the Law of the Void, and profound in meditation, then he will gather together all bodhisattvas and *śrāvakas* to preach this sutra to them.

"In the world there is no second vehicle through which to attain extinction; there is only the One Buddha-vehicle for attaining extinction. The tact of the Tathāgata reaches deeply into the nature of all living beings, and knows that they are bent on trifling pleasures and deeply attached to the five desires. For their sake he preaches nirvana tactfully so that they can remove their illusions and obtain mental peace. It is the most suitable teaching for the people at such a stage, and if they hear it, they will receive it in faith. For your better understanding, I will tell you the following parable, *bhikshus*."

THE PARABLE OF THE CITY IN A VISION. Then the Buddha related the Parable of the City in a Vision, the fourth of the seven parables in the Lotus Sutra. The substance of the parable is as follows. Suppose there is a fearful region, five hundred *yojanas* in extent, through which runs a perilous and difficult road, far from the abodes of men. Suppose there is a large company wishing to pass along that road to the Place of Jewels, and they have a guide, wise and astute, who knows the perilous road well, where it is passable and where closed.

The guide leads the company that wishes to cross this wilderness. Suppose the company, including both slow walkers and impatient people, become tired on the way and say to the leader, "We are utterly exhausted and are afraid. We can't go any farther; the road before us stretches far; let us turn back."

The leader, who is well known for his tactfulness in leading people according to the circumstances, thinks: "These people are to be pitied. How can they give up such great treasure when it is within reach and want to turn back? They should have a little more patience." Reflecting thus, in the midst of the perilous road he mystically creates a city over three hundred *yojanas* in extent and says to the company, "Do not fear, and do not turn back. Here is this great city in which you may rest and do as you please. If you enter this city, you will soon be rested; and if you then are able to go forward to the Place of Jewels, you may proceed."

Thereupon the exhausted company greatly rejoice, and they proceed into the magic city. When the leader perceives that the company are completely rested, he makes the magic city disappear and says to the company, "Come along, all of you, the Place of Jewels is at hand. I only created this city for you to rest in."

Thus the leader encourages the company, and finally he succeeds in leading them to the Place of Jewels.

After he finished telling this parable to the *bhikshus,* with the prefatory statement, "So is it with the Tathāgata," the Buddha explained the meaning of the parable. As a great leader, the Tathāgata is acquainted with all the distresses, the evils, the perils, and the long-continued processes of mortality from which living beings must be freed. If they only hear of the One Buddha-vehicle, they will not desire to see the Buddha nor wish to approach him. They will be discouraged and will think, "The Buddha-way is long and far; only after long suffering and arduous labor can the goal be reached." The Buddha, knowing that they are timid and ignorant, through his tact, while they are on the way, in order to give them a rest preaches the two stages of nirvana, namely, the enlightenment of the *śrāvaka* and of the *pratyekabuddha.* When the people thus have obtained mental peace, the Buddha then makes them proceed to the supreme enlightenment, the One Buddha-vehicle. Although there is no vehicle other than the One Buddha-vehicle, he speaks of the two vehicles, *śrāvaka* and *pratyekabuddha,* in order to give rest to them on the way, just like the leader who, in order to rest his company, magically creates a great city and after they are rested says, "The Place of Jewels is at hand; this city is not real, but only my magic production." Though the two vehicles are sacred as the steps (tactful means) leading living beings to the One Buddha-vehicle, we realize from this parable that we must not remain in the stage of these two vehicles.

Chapter 7 ends with a verse section in which the Buddha repeats this teaching.

CHAPTER 8

The Five Hundred Disciples Receive the Prediction of Their Destiny

THIS CHAPTER STATES that Sakyamuni Buddha gave the prediction of attaining enlightenment to many of his disciples, including Pūrṇa, one of his ten great disciples. The Buddha had perceived clearly that they had attained a high spiritual level through his preaching as recorded in the first seven chapters of the Lotus Sutra. (The figure "five hundred" should not be taken literally but just as indicating a very large number of disciples.)

Pūrṇa was so eloquent that he has been described as "the personification of eloquence"; "to speak as eloquently as Pūrṇa" became a common figure of speech in later times. However, he never showed off his superiority but led the same kind of life as ordinary men. He was such a great man that though he seemed mild, he had true mental courage. The following story about Pūrṇa has been handed down from old times.

When Sakyamuni Buddha permitted certain of his disciples to preach his teachings, Pūrṇa, desiring to preach in Śroṇāparanta, a region he knew well, asked the Buddha's permission to do so. The Buddha said, "It will be very difficult for you to do missionary work in Śroṇāparanta, where the people are very stubborn. What would you do if they didn't listen to your preaching however hard you tried?" Pūrṇa answered, "Even if they didn't listen to my preaching, I would not be disappointed. I would consider myself fortunate not to be made fun of." Then the Buddha asked, "What if you were derided?" Pūrna replied, "If I were, I would consider myself fortunate not to be slandered." When asked, "What if you should be slandered?" he answered, "Even if I were, I would consider myself fortunate not to be beaten with sticks or stoned." Asked, "What if you were beaten or stoned?" he replied, "I would consider myself fortunate not to be wounded by a sword." Then asked, "What if you were wounded by a sword?" he answered, "Even if I were, I would consider myself fortunate not to be killed." Next asked, "What if you were mortally wounded?" he replied, "I would consider myself fortunate to give up my life in spreading your teachings." Thereupon the Buddha permitted Pūrṇa to go to Śroṇāparanta, saying, "You may go there if you have such a firm determination in doing your missionary work." From this story, we can well understand that Pūrṇa was no common preacher.

Having heard the Buddha's many preachings and having seen the prediction of the great disciples to Perfect Enlightenment, having heard the stories of their former lives, and having realized the sovereign, transcendent powers of the buddhas, Pūrṇa received such an unexampled teaching that his heart was purified and ecstatic.

Immediately he rose from his seat, went before the Buddha, prostrated himself at the Buddha's feet, then withdrew to one side, gazing upon Sakyamuni's face without turning away his eyes for a moment, and reflected thus: "Wonderful is the World-honored One. Rare are his doings according to the many kinds of earthly dispositions. By tactful wisdom, he preaches the Law to and lifts all beings out of every condition to let them get rid of selfish attachment. No words of ours can declare the Buddha's merits. Only the Buddha, the World-honored One, is able to know the inclinations of our inmost hearts."

Thereupon the Buddha addressed the *bhikshus,* saying: "Do you see this Pūrṇa, Son of Maitrāyaṇī? I have always styled him the very first among all the preachers of the Law and constantly praised his varied merits. He has been zealous in guarding and helping to proclaim my Law. Among the many people, he has been able to display the Law through the correct process of preaching it. Perfectly interpreting the Righteous Law of the Buddha, he has greatly benefited his fellow followers of brahma-conduct. Excepting the Tathāgata, no one is able to equal the lucidity of his discourse.

"Do not think that it is only my Law that Pūrṇa is able to guard and help to proclaim. He also guarded and helped to proclaim the Righteous Law of the buddhas under ninety *koṭis* of buddhas in the past. Among those preachers of the Law he was also the foremost. And in regard to the Law of the Void[1] preached by the buddhas, he was clear-minded and penetrating; knowing the capacity of the people to understand the Buddha's teachings, he has ever been able to preach the Law freely and thoroughly according to his hearers' capacity. In preaching the Law, he has had such an unselfish mind as not to request any reward nor make a display of his greatness, and he has earnestly kept a pure attitude of mind without doubt and perplexity. Perfect in transcendent bodhisattva-powers, he has all his lives ever maintained his brahma-conduct.

"All the people around Pūrṇa spoke of him as 'the true *śrāvaka* disciple' because, though he realized the Law to such a degree, he did not show the slightest sign of it. They were on familiar terms with him and listened to him with good will. Thus Pūrṇa, by such tactfulness, has benefited innumerable living beings and converted innumerable people so that they would achieve Perfect Enlightenment. For the sake of purifying his buddha-land, he has constantly done a buddha's work and instructed the living."

THE PRINCIPLE OF HALF A STEP. In doing missionary work or leading others, we can learn something very important from Pūrṇa's attitude, which he maintained both inwardly and outwardly. If one were a person of great virtue and influence, such as Sakyamuni Buddha, even though he never assumed an air of self-importance everybody would throw himself on his knees and concentrate his mind upon hearing that person's teaching. However, in the case of one who is not endowed with so much virtue and influence, people do not always listen earnestly to his preaching of the Law. If he gives himself the airs of a great man, some will come to have ill feeling toward him, while others will feel that he is unapproachable. Pūrṇa's attitude is a good example for us.

It goes without saying that we must not look down on people or think, "They are unenlightened," but it is dangerous for us even to fancy ourselves to have gone a step farther than others. We must preserve the attitude of keeping pace with other people. But we cannot lead others if we completely keep pace with them, that is, if we behave exactly the same as those who know nothing of the Buddha-way. We should go not a step but only half a step farther than others. If we do this, those around us will still feel that we are one of them and will keep pace

1. This bears a resemblance to the Western concept of the realm of pure spirit.

with us. While accompanying us, they will be influenced by us and led in the right way without realizing it.

On the other hand, if we preach the teaching to others with a high-handed attitude when we ourselves have not realized it, or if we threaten them with violence and force them to follow the teaching, we cannot truly instruct them.

This principle of half a step is very important in our preaching the Law. We can say the same thing about the content of the Law preached. Even Sakyamuni Buddha led living beings gradually, from a simple teaching to a more advanced one, because he knew that a sudden preaching of the supreme teaching would only perplex them all the more; how much less effective would it be if we, who do not have the great persuasive power of the Buddha, should try to preach the most profound teaching from the start.

In some cases it can be a tactful means of leading someone to enter into the Buddha-way and of giving him peace of mind from the start if we preach that the teaching brings immediate benefits, such as most diseases being cured or one's daily life improving. In the case of intellectuals, it is often effective to begin preaching the Buddha's Law by giving examples of its being the teaching of humanism. And in the case of a Marxist, it may be best to lead him to Buddhism from the theory of the Three Thousand Realms in One Mind.

In any case, we must never look down on other people as being unenlightened while we are enlightened. Based on the fundamental truth that everyone equally possesses the buddha-nature, we must lead many people to the teachings of the Buddha with the compassionate attitude of wishing to disclose the buddha-nature of others as far as possible. In this respect, Pūrṇa is indeed a model for lay believers of the Lotus Sutra.

Finally, the World-honored One gave Pūrṇa the prediction of attaining buddhahood: "*Bhikshus!* Pūrṇa was the foremost among the preachers of the Law under the past Buddhas[2] and now is again the foremost among the preachers of the Law under me. Among the preachers of the Law under future buddhas,[3] he will also be the foremost and will guard and help to proclaim the Buddha-law. In the future he will do

2. The so-called Seven Buddhas: Vipaśyin, Śikhin, Viśvabhū, Krakucchanda, Kanakamuni, Kāśyapa, and Sakyamuni. The first three are the last three of a thousand buddhas who appeared during the previous *kalpa,* named Glorious; the last four are the first four of a thousand Buddhas who appear during the present *kalpa* of the sages.

3. The 996 future buddhas of the present *kalpa.*

the same thing that he did in his past lives. Gradually fulfilling the bodhisattva-course, after infinite *asaṃkhyeya kalpas* he will attain Perfect Enlightenment and his title will be Radiance of the Law Tathāgata. That buddha will have a buddha-land of worlds as numerous as the sands of the Ganges, and it will be an ideal country that is beautiful and peaceful. The palaces of the gods will be situated nearby in the sky, where men and gods will meet and behold one another."

That men and gods meet and behold one another indicates a state in which there is a high degree of communication between the realm of heaven and that of human beings shown in the diagram on page 103. It also indicates that the world of human beings has approached that of the Pure Land.

The Buddha continued: "There will be no evil ways and no womankind, for all living beings will be born transformed and have no carnal passion. They will have mental freedom; their will and memory will be firm; they will be zealous and wise, all golden-hued and self-adorned with the thirty-two signs. All the beings in his domain will always have two articles of food—one the food of joy in the Law, the other the food of gladness in meditation."

This implies that though a person has a human body, it is as if he did not have a body; the Pure Land is surely such a place. But as the expression "one the food of joy in the Law, the other the food of gladness in meditation" indicates, no being can lead a worthwhile life if he does not hear and practice the Law, even in the Pure Land.

The Buddha continued his description: "In that domain, there will be an infinite host of bodhisattvas who have excellent ability in instructing all kinds of beings. The domain of that buddha will be adorned and perfected with boundless excellences. That buddha's title will be Radiance of the Law Tathāgata; his period will be named Jewel Radiance, and his domain Excellent Purity. The lifetime of that buddha will be infinitely long, and the Law will remain long. After the extinction of that buddha, stupas of the precious seven will be erected throughout all that domain for the veneration of his virtue." Then the World-honored One proclaimed this teaching again in verse. With this his prediction to Pūrṇa ended.

The twelve hundred *arhats*, having freed themselves from all defilements and being of self-reliant mind, on having seen the prediction by the Buddha of Pūrṇa's Perfect Enlightenment and being greatly delighted with it, reflected "If the World-honored One would predict for each of us our future destiny, as for the other great disciples, how glad we would be!" The Buddha, knowing the thoughts in their minds, addressed Mahā-Kāśyapa, saying: "These twelve hundred *arhats,* let me now in their presence and in order predict for them Perfect Enlightenment." Then the Buddha gave the prediction of the destiny of the great disciples, saying that after paying homage to many buddhas, all would become buddhas with the same title, Universal Light Tathāgata. Following this the World-honored One, desiring to proclaim this teaching over again, repeated it in verse.

The last portion of the verse section has a very important meaning:

"Kāśyapa! You now know
Of these five hundred self-reliant ones.
The other band of *śrāvakas*
Will also be like them.
To these, who are not in this assembly,
Do you proclaim my words."

In other words: "These five hundred self-reliant *arhats* will become buddhas in the future, as will the many other *śrāvakas*. Kāśyapa! Do you proclaim what I have now said to those who are not in this assembly, and do you lead them to the way of attaining buddhahood." "Those who are not in this assembly" indicates the five thousand arrogant monks who left the assembly saying that since they had already attained enlightenment it was not necessary for them to listen to the Lotus Sutra. As already mentioned, because of his great wisdom and compassion, the World-honored One was silent and purposely did not stop them. Here he gives his prediction that even they will surely become buddhas according to their practice.

We must not feel that this is merely a story set in the remote past. The great compassion of the Buddha suggests that, although the other band of *śrāvakas* left the assembly, they would also become buddhas named Universal Light Tathāgata, like those who heard the Buddha's proclamation through Kāśyapa and further endeavored to practice the way to buddhahood. This is the Buddha's assurance that if we enter the path of his teachings through the Lotus Sutra and accumulate the practices of the bodhisattva-way, we too will surely become Universal Light Tathāgata. This is the meaning of so many people being predicted to become buddhas with the same title, Universal Light Tathāgata. The designation "Universal Light Tathāgata" means a person who emits light from his body and by it brightens all of society. We often see people around us like Universal Light Tathāgata or his followers. Somehow just seeing or talking with them makes us feel more cheerful. Such *tathāgatas* are necessary in our lives in the *sahā*-world. We ought at least become the followers of Universal Light Tathāgata, who can brighten our surroundings.

Thereupon the five hundred *arhats* present before the Buddha, having received this prediction, ecstatic with joy, instantly rose from their seats, went before the Buddha, made obeisance at his feet, repented of their errors, and rebuked themselves, saying: "World-honored One! We have constantly been thinking that we had attained final nirvana only by removing illusions from our minds. Now we realize for the first time that this was a great mistake; now we know that we were just like foolish unenlightened people. Why is this? Because we ought to have realized our own buddha-nature and to have obtained the Tathāgata-wisdom according to our practice, and yet we were content with the inferior status of just removing our illusions."

Then desiring to reinforce this statement, they told the following parable. This is the Parable of the Gem in the Robe, the fifth of the seven parables in the Lotus Sutra.

THE PARABLE OF THE GEM IN THE ROBE. A man went to a close friend's house, got drunk, and fell asleep. Meanwhile his friend had to leave suddenly on business. Not wanting to rouse the man from sleep, the friend tied a priceless jewel within his garment as a present and departed. The other man, being in a drunken sleep, knew nothing of it. On arising he traveled onward till he reached another country, where he worked hard for food and clothing, underwent great hardship, and was content with even a little.

Later, his friend happened to meet him again and said: "How is it you are scraping so for food and clothing? Wishing you to be in comfort and able to satisfy all your five senses, in such and such a year and month and on such and such a day, I tied a priceless jewel within your garment. It is still there, and you in ignorance are slaving and worrying to keep yourself alive. How very stupid! Go now and exchange that jewel for what you need and do whatever you will, free frem all poverty and need."

After telling this parable, Ājñāta-Kauṇḍinya and the others heartily expressed their thanks to the Buddha: "The Buddha is like this friend.

When he was a bodhisattva, he taught us to think that because everyone is endowed with the buddha-nature [the jewel], he can attain enlightenment through his practice. But we soon forgot, neither knowing nor perceiving it. Having merely removed our illusions, we said we had reached nirvana. But our aspiration after the true enlightenment of the Buddha still remained hidden in the depth of our minds. Somehow we have felt something lacking. Now the World-honored One arouses us. Now we know we are really bodhisattvas who will serve people in society and have the possibility of finally becoming buddhas. For this reason we greatly rejoice in our unprecedented gain." They then repeated this in verse.

CHAPTER 9

Prediction of the Destiny of Arhats, Training and Trained

THIS CHAPTER RECORDS the Buddha's prediction of the attainment of Perfect Enlightenment by his two great disciples Ānanda and Rāhula, as well as by other disciples. Ānanda, a cousin of the Buddha, was a younger brother of Devadatta, who at first was a follower of the Buddha but later left him and even attempted to kill him. Unlike Devadatta, Ānanda was a warmhearted man who had become a disciple of the Buddha in childhood. He was called "Ānanda, attendant always following the Buddha," because he accompanied the Buddha, looking after him and attending him as a favorite disciple until Sakyamuni's death.

Rāhula was the son of the Buddha, born before his renunciation of the world. The Buddha, who expected Rāhula to have the quality of goodness, summoned him from the palace when he was fifteen years old and added him to his group of disciples. To prevent Rāhula from considering that he had a special status because he was the Buddha's son, the Buddha placed Rāhula under the care of Śāriputra, one of his ten great disciples.

The word "training" (*gaku*) in the title of this chapter refers to the stage in which one must undergo religious exercises, while "trained" (*mugaku*) refers to the stage in which one no longer need undergo any religious exercise and is beyond learning.

Having seen the prediction of many *arhats* to Perfect Enlightenment, Ānanda and Rāhula, who were the only two of the direct disciples of the Buddha not yet to have received a prediction, felt left out and sad. They reflected: "If our future were only foretold, how happy we would be!" Therefore they rose from their seats, went before the Buddha, made obeisance at his feet, and together spoke to him, saying: "World-honored One! Let us have your prediction of us to Perfect Enlightenment. We have only the Tathāgata in whom to trust. We are known to and acknowledged by all the worlds, including gods, men, and devils. Ānanda is always your attendant, protecting and keeping the treasury of the Law, and Rāhula is the Buddha's son. If the Buddha sees fit to predict Perfect Enlightenment for us, our desire will be fulfilled and the hopes of many will be satisfied."

Thereupon the two thousand disciples who were under training and no longer under training all rose from their seats, bared their right shoulders, went before the Buddha, with one mind folded their hands, and gazed upon the World-honored One, wishing as Ānanda and Rāhula had wished, and stood there in line.

Seeing this, the World-honored One, who had already decided to predict for each of these two great disciples his destiny, told Ānanda that he would pay homage to sixty-two *koṭis* of buddhas, protect and keep the treasury of the Law, and finally attain Perfect Enlightenment. The Buddha gave him the title of Sovereign Universal King of Wisdom Mountains and Oceans Tathāgata and named his domain Never-lowered Victorious Banner.

Before the advent of Buddhism, Brahmanism flourished in India. It had more than sixty schools, all of which disputed and criticized each other. It was customary to raise a victory banner at the gate of the temple of a Brahman monk who had defeated his opponent in a religious dispute. Never-lowered Victorious Banner, the name of the domain of Sovereign Universal King of Wisdom Mountains and Oceans Tathāgata, means the proof that the teaching preached by this Tathāgata is the most excellent of all teachings.

Then the Buddha foretold the following: "That buddha's lifetime will be immeasurable thousand myriad *koṭis* of *asaṃkhyeya kalpas.* His teaching will abide in his world twice his lifetime. This buddha will be extolled and his merits praised by universal unlimited buddhas." Thereupon, because the Buddha gave Ānanda, a *śrāvaka,* more gracious words than those given to the senior bodhisattvas who had received the prediction of buddhahood, the eight thousand bodhisattvas in the assembly who had newly started on the road all entertained doubts about it. The

World-honored One, knowing what the bodhisattvas were thinking, addressed them, saying: "Good sons! I and Ānanda together, under the Buddha Firmament King, at the same time conceived the thought of Perfect Enlightenment. But there was a difference in our way of practicing the teaching. Ānanda took constant pleasure in learning, while I was devoted to active progress. For this reason I have already attained Perfect Enlightenment, while Ānanda, who is my disciple in this world because of former lives, has been taking care of my Law, as he will take care of the Law-treasuries of future buddhas and will instruct and bring to perfection the host of bodhisattvas. Such was his original vow, although all of you may have thought that he must be a *śrāvaka* because he seems to take constant pleasure in learning. So he has received this prediction."

The difference that the Buddha pointed out in his way of practice and that of Ānanda is a very important point. The Buddha taught that to realize Perfect Enlightenment, one should practice by taking the Buddha as an example. The practice of benefiting others is the highest reach of religion, as the Buddha here clearly shows.

As the term "original vow" (*hongan*) appears here, an explanation must be given of the word "vow" (*gan*) as used in Buddhism.

ORIGINAL VOW. The word "vow" is casually used in our time, but the word in its true sense is not one to be used lightly. "Vow" means setting up one's own ideal and devoting oneself to its realization. Needless to say, from the standpoint of Buddhism, our ideal is to benefit others. The desire to attain buddhahood does not become a vow unless we entertain it for the purpose of saving others from their sufferings. A vow for the particular aim of benefiting others is called the "original vow" of Buddhists.

GENERAL VOW. In Buddhism, there are two kinds of vow: "general vow" (*sōgan*) and "special vow" (*betsugan*). "General vow" means the vow common to all people. The common desire of all Buddhists is to study the teachings of the Buddha and to extinguish illusions. Their desire is also to benefit many others through attaining enlightenment. This desire is called the general vow. It is divided again into four parts, which are known as the four great vows of the bodhisattva (*shi gu-sei-gan*). These four great vows are explained on page 180.

SPECIAL VOW. A special vow, as opposed to the general vow, is a vow made according to one's individual character, ability, and vocation. For example: because I am a talented painter, I will make this world as beautiful as I can by painting beautiful pictures; because I am musically talented, I will use music to give people peace of mind; because I am a farmer, I will render service to society by raising the best crops possible; because I am a merchant, I will be of use to my customers by supplying them with goods as inexpensive and fine as possible. These are good instances of special vows.

Besides the general vow to save all living beings, each of the buddhas has his own special vow, such as the forty-eight vows of the Tathāgata Amitābha (Amita) and the five hundred great vows of the Tathāgata Sakyamuni. In addition to the general vow that is common to all of us as people in this world, we should formulate our own special vow or vows throughout our lives. When we work to fulfill such a vow, we discover the value of human life and enrich our daily lives. Buddhism teaches not only one's eternal and great ideal but also one's ideal in daily life. Thus, it is both a very profound teaching and a very intimate one.

Of course, merely making vows is of no use; we must work to fulfill them. Our vows must never be made with a lukewarm attitude. Once we have pronounced our vows in our minds, we must be zealous and persistent enough to fulfill them at all costs. If we maintain such a mental attitude, we can surely achieve our vows.

Some people think that things never actually turn out as we wish. But this is mistaken. If our minds are concentrated on our vows over a long period of time, our vows will invariably be achieved eventually. If they are not realized in this world, they will be in the world to come. An earnest desire generates great energy. When we continuously endeavor to concentrate our minds even on something that is thought to be almost impossible, such endeavor produces a result that makes the seemingly impossible possible. One's vow will definitely be achieved if one has an unshakable belief and makes constant efforts to realize it.

The World-honored One, after predicting Ānanda's Perfect Enlightenment, gave the same prediction to Rāhula. The Buddha gave him the title of Treader on Seven-Jeweled Lotuses Tathāgata. He told Rāhula that he would pay homage to buddhas equal in number to the atoms of ten worlds, always becoming the eldest son of each of those buddhas, just as he was at present. He also foretold that the splendor of the domain of Treader on Seven-Jeweled Lotuses Tathāgata, the duration of his lifetime, and so on would be the same as those of the Tathāgata Sovereign Universal King of Wisdom Mountains and Oceans.

Thereupon the World-honored One, desiring to proclaim this teaching over again, spoke thus in verse:

"When I was a prince royal,
Rāhula was my eldest son.
Now that I have accomplished the Buddha-way,
He is the Law-heir receiving the Law.
In worlds to come,
Seeing infinite *koṭis* of buddhas,
To all he will be eldest son
And with all his mind seek the Buddha-way.
Of the hidden course of Rāhula
Only I am able to know.
At present as my eldest son
He is revealed to all.
Infinite thousand myriad *koṭis*
Are his merits, beyond calculation.
Peacefully abiding in the Buddha-law,
He seeks the supreme Way."

THE HIDDEN COURSE. This moving verse reveals the Buddha's affection as a teacher of the Law and as a father. Hearing the Buddha say, "Of the hidden course of Rāhula / Only I am able to know," how glad Rāhula must have been! The hidden course means that when one has achieved something, one does not reveal it to others by one's look or manner but joins them as an ordinary person and leads them naturally in a better direction. This is the same as the principle of half a step exemplified by Pūrṇa. Though Rāhula had attained a very high spiritual level, he did not show the slightest sign of it but silently guided people from behind the scenes. Only Sakyamuni Buddha, who was his teacher and his father, knew the truth about Rāhula. For him, the Buddha's recognition must have been a double joy.

Why did Sakyamuni Buddha give the prediction of Perfect Enlightenment to such great disciples as Ānanda and Rāhula later than to the other disciples? We may imagine that the Buddha reasoned in the following way: Ānanda was always the attendant to the Buddha, while Rāhula was the Buddha's son. Both of them were thus the disciples closest to the Buddha, who had manifested himself for the benefit of unenlightened living beings. Having due regard for these two disciples' special circumstances, which could hinder rather than aid their practice, and in order to show this to all living beings, the Buddha intentionally deferred the prediction of these two great disciples to Perfect Enlightenment.

We must not think that because these two disciples were closest to him, the Buddha hesitated to give them the prediction out of consideration for the feelings of the many other disciples in his order. Sakyamuni Buddha was not such a small-minded man. When, like Ānanda, one always accompanies the Buddha and waits on him personally, it often happens that he becomes unable to discriminate between his master's greatness as the Buddha and the sacredness of his teachings on the one hand and the Buddha as a man on the other, and that for this reason he will have difficulty in revering the Buddha with the same pure mind as other disciples. The same thing can be said of the relation between father and son. However great a father may be, his own son will find it hard to treat his father with the same respect as outsiders. The Buddha taught that for a person who personally attends and follows a great man, this will become a hindrance to his practice unless he draws a strict line in his mind between public and private matters. Though Ānanda and Rāhula were placed in a very delicate situation, they constantly behaved respectfully, and their behavior bore witness to their high virtue.

It is most difficult for us to lead those closest to us—our wives, husbands, sons, daughters, and parents—to the Law of the Buddha. If we try to guide them merely by what we say, we can never be completely successful. We have no alternative but to influence them through our practice in our daily lives. If our conduct is ignoble and selfish most of the time, being good only on rare occasions, it will not influence others. Unless we constantly set a good example to the members of our families, they cannot possibly follow us. Sakyamuni Buddha was alluding to this in his teaching.

At that time the World-honored One looked upon the two thousand men under training and no longer under training, gentle in mind, tranquil and calm, who were observing the Buddha single-mindedly. The Buddha addressed Ānanda: "Do you see these two thousand men under training and no longer under training?" Ānanda replied, "Yes, I see them." Ānanda's answer here means "Yes, they look excellent," to the

Buddha's implied question, "How do they look to you?" This is the so-called tacit understanding in question and answer between the Buddha and Ānanda.

Then the Buddha gave the following prediction to these two thousand men: if they pay homage to innumerable buddhas, revere and honor them, and care for their treasuries of the Law, finally in the same hour, in domains in every direction, each of them will become a buddha with the same title, Jewel Sign Tathāgata. Thereupon the two thousand men under training and no longer under training, hearing the Buddha's prediction, became ecstatic with joy and offered deep thanks to the Buddha, speaking thus in verse:

> "World-honored One!
> Bright Lamp of Wisdom!
> We, hearing his voice of prediction,
> Are filled with joyfulness,
> As if sprinkled with sweet dew."

Though short, this is a famous verse. It is filled with so deep a sense of gratitude and reverence for the Buddha that we should read and recite it daily.

CHAPTER 10

A Teacher of the Law

THIS CHAPTER DECLARES what the teacher of the Law ought to know and practice. "Teacher" is not limited to monks but means any person who devotes himself to spreading the Lotus Sutra, whether monk, nun, or lay devotee, man or woman.

At that time the World-honored One addressed the eighty thousand great leaders through the Bodhisattva Medicine King, saying: "Medicine King! Do you see in this assembly innumerable gods, dragon kings, demons, human and nonhuman beings, as well as *bhikshus, bhikshuṇīs,* male and female lay devotees, seekers after enlightenment in various stages of mind? All such beings as these, in the presence of the Buddha, if they hear a single verse or a single word of the Wonderful Law-Flower Sutra and even by a single thought delight in it, I predict that they will all attain Perfect Enlightenment."

If we delight in a single verse or a single word of the Lotus Sutra by a single thought but become no better than we were before, it is of no use. The assurance of our becoming buddhas is conditional on the result of practice over a long period of time. Why then did the Buddha say that he would predict Perfect Enlightenment for anyone who by a single thought delights in a single verse or a single word of the Lotus Sutra? This is because the mind that one raises through delighting in the Lotus Sutra by a single thought will become the seed of his attaining buddhahood. One must incessantly nurture this seed, making it bud by watering it diligently, making it grow, flower, and bear fruit. However, when we understand that we are assured of becoming buddhas if we hear a single verse or a single word of the Lotus Sutra and by a single thought delight in it, we should be inspired with redoubled courage. Such an understanding is a great encouragement to us in this corrupt age. The Buddha referred to this as follows: "Moreover, after the extinction of the Tathāgata, if there be any people who hear even a single verse or a single word of the Wonderful Law-Flower Sutra, and by a single thought delight in it, I also predict them to Perfect Enlightenment."

The following words of the Buddha concern mainly the corrupt age in which we now live: "Again let there be any who receive and keep, read and recite, expound and copy even a single verse in the Wonderful Law-Flower Sutra, and look upon this sutra with reverence as if it were the Buddha, and make offering to it in various ways, as well as revere it with folded hands; know, Medicine King, these people have already paid homage to ten myriad *koṭis* of buddhas and under the buddhas have performed their great vows; therefore out of compassion for all living beings, they are born here among men."

THE FIVE PRACTICES OF TEACHERS OF THE LAW. Receiving and keeping the sutra (*juji*), reading and reciting it (*doku-ju*), expounding it (*gesetsu*), and copying it (*shosha*) are called the five practices of teachers of the Law (*goshu hosshi*). These are most important practices for those who spread the Lotus Sutra. The description of these five practices of the teacher of the Law is the first of the seven essentials mentioned in the chapter "A Teacher of the Law."

Of these five practices of the teacher, "receiving and keeping" (*juji*) is called "the intensive practice" (*shōgyō*), while the other four practices are called "the assisting practices" (*jogyō*). The reason we must set apart "receiving and keeping" as the intensive practice is that this is the most important and fundamental practice of the five; without it, the other four practices mean little. "Receiving" (*ju*) indicates believing deeply in the teachings of the Buddha, and "keeping" (*ji*) means to adhere firmly to that belief.

"Reading" (*doku*), the first of the assisting practices, means actually reading the sutra; this practice includes reading it aloud, reading it silently, and listening intently to others' reading of it.

"Reciting" (*ju*) means to recite the sutra from memory. This practice includes the repetition of the words of the sutra that we have learned by heart and the mental repetition of their meaning. The teaching becomes deeply rooted in our minds through repeated recitation from memory.

"Expounding" (*gesetsu*) means to explain the meaning of the sutra to others. This is both an indispensable practice for spreading the teaching and also a practice for our own benefit. It is difficult for us to preach the teaching to others, and for this reason we must study the sutra over and over again. While preaching it to others, we will often be led to reflect upon the insufficiency of our own faith and discernment.

"Copying" (*shosha*) means to copy the sutra by hand. This practice is significant in two ways. One is its practice for propagating the teaching and the other is its practice for deepening our own faith and discernment. Before the art of printing was invented, copying the Lotus Sutra by hand was indispensable in order to spread it. In modern times, we must spread the teaching making the best use of printing, movies, records, tape recorders, and other audio-visual aids. The first meaning of "copying" has been enlarged in this way. However, the practice of copying must not be limited to the first meaning only. When we copy carefully each word of the sutra with a calm and concentrated mind, the spirit of the sutra becomes firmly rooted in both our body and our mind. Copying the sutra in this sense is still an important practice.

The Buddha continued: "Medicine King! If there be any people who ask you what sort of living beings will become buddhas in future worlds, you should show them that those are the people who will certainly become buddhas in future worlds. Wherefore? If my good sons and good daughters receive and keep, read and recite, expound and copy even a single word in the Law-Flower Sutra, and make offerings to it in various ways, as well as revere it with folded hands, these people will be looked up to by all the worlds; and as you pay homage to the tathāgatas, so should you pay homage to them."

The Buddha preached this repeatedly. By this frequent repetition we are deeply impressed by how seriously the Buddha regarded it. We should especially learn the following passage so that we can recite it from memory: "If these good sons and good daughters, after my extinction, should be able even by stealth to preach to one person even one word of the Law-Flower Sutra, know these people are Tathāgata-apostles sent by the Tathāgata to perform Tathāgata-deeds. How much more so those who in great assemblies widely preach to others."

This passage includes the second essential point mentioned in chapter 10. Those who practice the Lotus Sutra must keep its words in mind morning and night.

Next the Buddha spoke as follows: "Medicine King! Even if there be some wicked person who from an evil mind throughout a whole *kalpa* appears before the Buddha and unceasingly blasphemes the Buddha, his sin is still light, but if anyone, even with a single ill word, defames the lay devotees or monks who read and recite the Law-Flower Sutra, his sin is extremely heavy."

This and the following comprise the third essential point in this chapter: "Medicine King! In every place where this sutra is preached or read or recited or copied or its volumes kept, one should erect a *caitya*[1] of the precious seven, making it very high, spacious, and splendid. But there is no need to deposit relics. Wherefore? Because in it there is the whole body of the Tathāgata."

THE TRUE MEANING OF WORSHIP. Through these words the Buddha teaches us that it is much more important to revere the Law itself than to worship idols. What he is saying is: However much a person may blaspheme the Buddha, his sin is still light. There is no need to deposit the Buddha's relics in pagodas. The greatest veneration of the Buddha is to practice the Lotus Sutra, and the heaviest sin is to defame the lay devotees or monks who practice the sutra.

However, we must be careful in our understanding of this teaching. It would be a great mistake to think that it does not matter if we blaspheme the Buddha, or that we should ignore the Buddha's relics. Sakyamuni Buddha was a great man who left us his precious teachings, and for this reason we cannot revere him too much. We worship the image of the Buddha in order to show our boundless gratitude to the Buddha, who left us his precious teachings. As mentioned repeatedly in this book, it is also done for the sake of deepening our reverence for the Buddha as our ideal, which we wish to approach little by little.

Moreover, through the image of Sakyamuni as the historical Buddha, we worship the Tathāgata Sakyamuni and the Eternal Original Buddha, namely, the Law preached by him. Worshiping the image of the Buddha is not idol worship. Idol worship indicates the idea of regarding the thing itself as the object of worship, believing, for example, that if one worships some object one's disease will be cured, one will be spared from suffering, or one's desires will be fulfilled. There is all the difference in the world between true worship and idol worship.

The Buddha continued: "He who reads and recites the Law-Flower

1. A *caitya* is a pagoda in which sutras are deposited. From this chapter on, the Lotus Sutra stresses erecting *caityas* instead of stupas, or pagodas for relics.

Sutra—know! That man has adorned himself with the adornment of the Buddha, and so is carried by the Tathāgata on his shoulder." Indeed, the appearance of a person who absorbedly reads and recites the Lotus Sutra is dignified and beautiful, like that of a buddha. Observing his appearance with divine eyes, he will appear to be tinted with a golden color.

The fact that such a person will be always protected by buddhas is stated as follows: "After the Tathāgata is extinct, those who are able to copy, keep, read, recite, worship, and preach it [the Lotus Sutra] to others will be invested by the Tathāgata with his robe. Those people shall dwell with the Tathāgata, and the Tathāgata shall place his hand upon their heads."

The Buddha's frequent repetition of such words shows that we must be keenly aware of how sacred the teaching of the Lotus Sutra is and how perfectly our practice of it conforms to the intention of the Tathāgata. Whatever difficulties and whatever persecution we may meet with, the Tathāgata promises surely to protect us.

The Buddha makes the following gratifying and reassuring promise to us in this evil world: "Because a person who practices the Lotus Sutra is as honorable as a buddha, the Buddha is sure to protect him." The Buddha also proclaims: "Why is a person who practices the Lotus Sutra honorable? It is because this sutra is the foremost among all the sutras I have preached." These two important statements are the fourth essential point of this chapter.

So far, the merits gained by one who practices the Lotus Sutra have been expounded. Next the mental attitude with which he must practice it is stressed. This mental attitude is divided into three major parts, in accordance with the following words of the Buddha.

The Buddha addressed Medicine King, saying: "Infinite thousand myriads of *koṭis* are the sutras I preach, whether already preached, now being preached, or to be preached in the future; and among them all, this Law-Flower Sutra is the most difficult to believe and the most difficult to understand. Medicine King! This sutra is the mystic, essential treasury of all buddhas, which must not be distributed among or recklessly delivered to men. It is watched over by buddhas, world-honored ones, and it has never been revealed and preached. And this sutra while the Tathāgata is still here has aroused much enmity and envy; how much more after his extinction!"

First, the Buddha says that infinite thousand myriads of *koṭis* are the sutras he preaches, whether already preached, now being preached, or to be preached in the future, and that among them all, this Lotus Sutra is the most difficult to believe and the most difficult to understand. The reason that this sutra is the most difficult to believe and to understand is that the fundamental teaching of the Lotus Sutra, that everybody becomes a buddha according to the accumulation of his practice, is so difficult to believe and to understand.

We can understand the Lotus Sutra in theory, but this kind of understanding is liable to be shaken by any adverse change in our circumstances. The person who can truly understand and believe the sutra from the bottom of his heart is one who is spiritually sensitive to the teaching and who is ripe to bear the fruit of the accumulated karma of his former lives. For that reason, we must continually strive to grasp the teaching of the Lotus Sutra more deeply and must patiently receive and keep it regardless of whatever doubts we may have in our minds or whatever persecution and slander we may suffer from outsiders.

Secondly, the Buddha teaches that this sutra is deeply treasured in the minds of all buddhas and must not be recklessly distributed among or delivered to people. As mentioned in chapter 3, it is most important here too that we not misinterpret this teaching of the Buddha as meaning that we should not preach the sutra to others.

Thirdly, the Buddha proclaims: "This sutra is watched over by buddhas, and I have never revealed and preached it before the people in the world. And this sutra, while I am still here, has aroused much enmity and envy; how much more after my extinction!"

Some people may think it strange that this sacred teaching should incur enmity and envy, but it is not really strange, because whenever a better teaching is preached or believed in, those who believe in a lower teaching tend to envy it and are irritated and upset by it. Others scorn the teaching when they know nothing of its content. Still others denounce a good teaching as heresy and persecute it. When Sakyamuni Buddha, Jesus Christ, and Nichiren began to preach their teachings, all were attacked by enemies and underwent religious persecution.

As mentioned before, the Buddha promises us: "Even if the Lotus Sutra arouses much enmity and envy, endure this and receive, keep, and practice the sutra. Such a person will be protected and invested by the Tathāgata with his robe." This is the fifth essential point of this chapter.

THE PARABLE OF DIGGING IN A TABLELAND. Next, the Buddha teaches us through the Parable of Digging in a Tableland that one who practices the Lotus Sutra must earnestly seek after the Law with hope and unremitting zeal. A man who is extremely thirsty searches for water by digging in a tableland. So long as he sees dry earth, he knows that water is still far off. Continuing his labor unceasingly, in time he sees moist earth and then gradually reaches mud. Then he knows that water is near at hand. So he digs still more earnestly, without being discouraged or doubting. Bodhisattvas are like this. If they have not heard, nor understood, nor been able to observe this Law-Flower Sutra, they are still far from Perfect Enlightenment. But if they hear, understand, ponder, and observe it, they are near Perfect Enlightenment.

Once we have known the Lotus Sutra, we never have to be at a loss as to what to do. If we give up the sutra after only a little practice of it, as though starting to dig somewhere else because water does not appear immediately, we cannot realize the sutra, just as we cannot quench our thirst by digging only a little. The Buddha teaches here that if we endeavor patiently to attain Perfect Enlightenment, just as when we continue to dig unceasingly, we can assuredly reach enlightenment, just as we can reach the mud. This is the sixth essential point of this chapter.

THE ROBE, THE THRONE, AND THE ABODE OF THE TATHĀGATA. The seventh and final essential point of this chapter is shown in the following words of the Buddha describing the three rules of the robe, the throne, and the abode of the Tathāgata: "Medicine King! If there be any good son or good daughter who, after the extinction of the Tathāgata, desires to preach this Law-Flower Sutra to the four groups, how should he preach it? That good son or good daughter, entering into the abode of the Tathāgata, wearing the robe of the Tathāgata, and sitting on the throne of the Tathāgata, should then widely proclaim this sutra to the four groups of hearers.

"The abode of the Tathāgata is the great compassionate heart within all living beings; the robe of the Tathāgata is the gentle and forbearing heart; the throne of the Tathāgata is the voidness of all laws [the spirituality of all existences].[2] Established in these, then with unflagging

2. Literally, the voidness of all phenomena (laws); this is interpreted in terms of the truth of the Middle Path—that things are neither existent nor nonexistent, that there is a realm between these two that can only be a spiritual realm.

mind to bodhisattvas and the four groups of hearers he will preach this Law-Flower Sutra."

The abode of the Tathāgata means the possession of a heart so great and compassionate that one desires to save all people, both good and evil, even those who try to harm one. This compassionate heart is compared to the great abode of the Tathāgata, which any person can enter.

The robe of the Tathāgata means such a gentle and forbearing heart that one never becomes angry at whatever bitter experiences one may undergo, and also is never swayed by whatever compliments one may be paid. This kind of heart is compared to the robe of the Tathāgata, which is never affected by any evil influence from the outside. This means that one who practices the Lotus Sutra must maintain a firm determination to spread it.

The throne of the Tathāgata means to view all things equally. As already explained in chapter 5, this indicates that though the differences among all things are recognized as they are, one must view things equally by rising above this discrimination. For example, though John has a slow mind, he is quick with his hands. Though Mary is not clever with her fingers, she is clear-headed. Although the difference between the two is rightly recognized, they are seen as equal as human beings in the sight of the Buddha. To view things thus is the meaning of the "voidness of all laws" (the spirituality of all existences).

The Buddha teaches us that we must faithfully keep these three rules concerning the virtue of the Tathāgata and untiringly preach the Lotus Sutra based on them.

This chapter does not take the form of a story or drama as do the other chapters of the sutra but is in the form of a sermon from beginning to end.

CHAPTER 11

Beholding the Precious Stupa

LIKE CHAPTER 2, this chapter relates stories that sound strange at first. As already explained in the Introduction, the Lotus Sutra often represents abstract ideas in the form of concrete images in order to help people grasp them. This entire chapter is a case in point.

First we must explain the description of the Stupa of the Precious Seven springing from the earth. This stupa symbolizes the buddha-nature that all people possess. Buddha-nature (the stupa) springing from the earth implies unexpectedly discovering one's buddha-nature in oneself (the earth), which one had been predisposed to regard as impure. Hence the title of this chapter, "Beholding the Precious Stupa."

In this stupa is the Tathāgata Abundant Treasures, who symbolizes the absolute truth that was realized by the Tathāgata Sakyamuni. This truth never changes, and it has existed throughout the universe forever. The truth is revealed in the form of the various teachings of the Buddha, and it guides people everywhere. This is symbolized by the buddhas who have emanated from the Buddha and who are preaching the Law in worlds in all directions.

When the Tathāgata Abundant Treasures within the Precious Stupa shares half his throne with Sakyamuni Buddha, saying, "Sakyamuni Buddha! Take this seat!" Abundant Treasures testifies that all the teachings of the Tathāgata Sakyamuni are true. This testimony is delivered by truth itself. It may be difficult to understand the idea of the truth itself testifying to the truth, but in brief, this means that all that Sakyamuni Buddha has said is sure to come true eventually. To come true eventually is to testify that what the Buddha said is the truth. There can be no testimony more definite than this.

There is a deep meaning in the image of the Tathāgata Abundant Treasures as the truth and the Tathāgata Sakyamuni as its preacher sitting side by side cross-legged on the lion throne in the Stupa of the Precious Seven. This symbolizes the fact that were it not for a person who preaches the truth, ordinary people could not realize it, and that a preacher of the truth is as much to be honored as the truth itself.

Lastly, the great assembly reflected thus: "The Buddhas are sitting aloft and far away. Would that the Tathāgata by his transcendent powers might cause us together to take up our abode in the sky." Then immediately Sakyamuni Buddha, by his transcendent powers, transferred the great assembly to the sky. This signifies that if people discover their buddha-nature in themselves, they will be able immediately to make their abode in the world of the buddhas.

In this chapter, grasping the meaning of the text as a whole is more important than understanding the meaning of specific verses or words. Therefore our discussion will be limited to an outline of the chapter, together with explanation of its essential points.

After hearing the Buddha's preaching in chapter 10, those in the great assembly made the firm resolution: "As the Buddha says, whatever may happen, we will endeavor to spread the sacred teachings of the Buddha and to render service to people and to society." Just then, in front of them a huge stupa made of the precious seven suddenly sprang from the earth and abode in the sky. Decorated with all kinds of precious substances, it was of incomparable beauty. All the beings in the world, both human and nonhuman, gathered around the stupa, paid homage to it, and revered, honored, and extolled it.

The description of the stupa springing from the earth has a very deep meaning. The earth symbolizes our bodies and minds as ordinary people. It also means this *sahā*-world, which consists of ordinary people. The enlightenment and salvation of the buddhas do not drop out of the clouds but spring from within ourselves. Enlightenment and salvation that spring from within ourselves are truly valuable and powerful, as the Buddha teaches us clearly here. His teaching is realistic and positive.

Then from within the Precious Stupa there came a loud voice, saying: "Excellent! Excellent! World-honored Sakyamuni! Thou art able to preach to the great assembly the Wonderful Law-Flower Sutra of universal and great wisdom, by which bodhisattvas are instructed and which the buddhas guard and keep in mind. So is it, so is it, World-honored Sakyamuni! All that thou sayest is true."

This great voice came from the Tathāgata Abundant Treasures, although he was invisible. All in the great assembly wondered who was in the stupa. Meanwhile, the Bodhisattva Great Eloquence, perceiving the uncertainty in the minds of the people, asked the Buddha on their behalf the reason for this stupa's springing from the earth and for such a voice being emitted from within it.

Then the Buddha told the Bodhisattva Great Eloquence: "In this stupa there is the whole body of the Tathāgata." "The whole body of the Tathāgata" means the whole of the virtue and the power that the Tathāgata possesses. The Buddha proclaimed here that once one awakens to his own buddha-nature, he becomes an eternal being like the Tathāgata; he comes to possess supreme wisdom and to exercise infinite compassion.

The Buddha continued as follows: "Of yore in the past, there was a buddha entitled Abundant Treasures. When that buddha was treading the bodhisattva-way, he made a great vow, saying: 'After I become a buddha and am extinct, if in any country in the universe there be a place where the Law-Flower Sutra is preached, my stupa shall arise and appear there, in order that I may hearken to that sutra, bear testimony to it, and extol it, saying, "Excellent!" ' When that buddha had finished his course, he, his extinction approaching, in the midst of gods, men, and a great host, instructed his *bhikshus*. In the stupa which has now sprung up from the earth is none other than the Tathāgata Abundant Treasures."

Thereupon the Bodhisattva Great Eloquence said to the Buddha: "World-honored One! We earnestly desire to see this buddha's body." Confirming this desire, the Buddha addressed the Bodhisattva Great Eloquence thus: "This Buddha Abundant Treasures has a profound and grave vow: 'When my stupa appears in the presence of any of the buddhas for the sake of hearing the Law-Flower Sutra, if he desires to show my body to the four groups, let the buddhas who have emanated from that buddha and who are preaching the Law in the worlds in all directions return all together and assemble in one place, and then shall my body appear.' "

On behalf of all in the great assembly, Great Eloquence replied to the Buddha: "World-honored One! We would also see the buddhas emanated from the World-honored One and worship and pay homage to them."

Then the Buddha sent forth a ray from the circle of white hair between his eyebrows, whereupon all the buddhas of the domains in all directions became visible. Wherever the ray from the circle of white hair shone, it revealed the beautifully adorned domains of the buddhas. Then each of the buddhas addressed the host of his bodhisattvas, saying: "Good sons! We must now go to Sakyamuni Buddha in the *sahā*-world and pay homage to the Precious Stupa of the Tathāgata Abundant Treasures." Thereupon the *sahā*-world instantly became a beautiful world of purity and adornment.

This story indicates clearly that the Pure Land is not located in some faraway place but is here in the *sahā*-world where we live. For an enlightened person, the *sahā*-world is identical in essence with the Pure Land of Tranquil Light.

The buddhas from the ten directions all arrived and assembled in the *sahā*-world. Each sent his attendants to pay homage to Sakyamuni Buddha, and the buddhas unitedly expressed their desire that the Precious Stupa be opened. Thereupon Sakyamuni Buddha with his right hand opened the door of the Stupa of the Precious Seven, when there was a great sound like that of withdrawing the bolt on opening a great city gate. Thereupon all the congregation saw the Tathāgata Abundant Treasures sitting on the lion throne in the Precious Stupa. And they heard him say, "Excellent! Excellent! Sakyamuni Buddha! Speedily preach this Law-Flower Sutra. I have come hither in order to hear this sutra."

All the congregation praised this unprecedented marvel and strewed on the Buddha Abundant Treasures and on Sakyamuni Buddha heaps of celestial jewel flowers. Thereupon the Buddha Abundant Treasures shared half his throne with Sakyamuni Buddha, saying, "Sakyamuni Buddha! Take this seat!" Whereon Sakyamuni Buddha entered the stupa and, sitting down on the throne, folded his legs.

At first the great assembly was deeply moved by this marvelous scene, but when they saw the two Buddhas sitting cross-legged in the stupa in the sky, they felt forlorn, as if the two Tathāgatas were suddenly aloof and far away. Each reflected that he wished the Tathāgatas by their transcendent powers might cause them also to take up their abode in the sky. Immediately Sakyamuni Buddha, perceiving their feelings, by his transcendent power received all the great assembly up into the sky.

THE TWO PLACES AND THREE ASSEMBLIES OF THE LOTUS SUTRA. From this part of this chapter, the setting of the Lotus Sutra shifts from Vulture Peak to the assembly in the sky. Sakyamuni Buddha is said to have expounded this sutra at two places and three assemblies. First it was preached at the assembly on Vulture Peak, next at the assembly held in the sky, and last again at the assembly on Vulture Peak. The spiritual significance of the two places and the three assemblies is as follows.

On receiving the teachings of the Buddha, at first we cannot understand them unless they are closely linked with our present actuality. The first preaching of the Lotus Sutra on the earth means that the Buddha first revealed his teachings based on actuality. This is the teaching of wisdom. Next, the preaching of the sutra in the sky, away from the earth, indicates the Buddha as the ideal that takes a step beyond actuality. This is possible through the absolute compassion shown by the Buddha. But his compassionate teaching is meaningless unless we demonstrate it in our actual lives. Therefore, the final preaching of the Lotus Sutra returns to actuality (the earth). As often mentioned in this book, the strange stories in the Lotus Sutra are not descriptions of some dreamlike world but contain well-reasoned spiritual significance.

THE DOCTRINE OF SIX DIFFICULTIES AND NINE EASY PRACTICES. Thereupon, with a great voice, the Tathāgata Sakyamuni universally addressed the four groups from within the Precious Stupa, saying: "Who are able to publish abroad the Wonderful Law-Flower Sutra in this *sahā*-world? Now indeed is the time. The Tathāgata not long hence must enter nirvana. The Buddha desires to bequeath this Wonderful Law-Flower Sutra so that it may ever exist." The Buddha, using various similes, then expounded the difficulty of preaching the Lotus Sutra in the age of degeneration. This is generally called the doctrine of six difficulties and nine easy practices.

If one picked up Mount Sumeru and hurled it to another region of numberless buddha-lands, that would not be hard. If one were to move a great-thousandfold world with his toes and hurl it afar to another land, that also would not be hard. If one, standing on the Summit of All Beings,[1] were to expound to all beings the countless sutras other than the Lotus Sutra, that also would not be hard. But if one, after the Buddha's extinction, is able to preach this sutra in the midst of an evil world, this indeed is hard. Though there were a man who grasped the sky in his hand and wandered about with it, that would not be hard. If one

1. The highest heaven, also called the Summit of All Existence.

took the great earth, put it on his toenail, and ascended to the Brahma heaven, that would still not be hard. Though one, in the final conflagration at the end of the world, carried a load of dry hay on his back and entered the fire unseared, that would still not be hard. But after the Buddha's extinction, in the midst of an evil world, if anyone keeps the Lotus Sutra, reads it aloud, and proclaims it to but one other person, that indeed will be hard.

Simply because the Buddha preached thus, however, we must not lose heart through the fear that we cannot possibly carry out such a difficult task. Here the Buddha points out the difficulties that we will have in perfectly receiving and keeping the Lotus Sutra, reading and reciting it, and expounding it. Though we must incessantly strive toward perfect practice, we have already understood some of the difficulties mentioned above. So we need not feel discouraged. The very fact that we actually study this sutra, remember it, and are ready to practice it within the limits of our ability bears witness to the possibility of our accomplishing such a difficult task. We should, rather, encourage each other in our practice in these difficult times so that all the buddhas will rejoice in us.

CHAPTER 12

Devadatta

SO FAR WE HAVE READ that the Buddha directly predicted the attainment of buddhahood of many disciples. All these people, however, were males and were the Buddha's immediate disciples, who had iron wills and devoted themselves absolutely to their religious disciplines. If only such people can attain Perfect Enlightenment, however, the principle that all living beings equally possess the buddha-nature is not fully attested.

In this chapter, however, the vastness and perfection of the Buddha's teachings are clearly revealed through the teaching of the attainment of buddhahood by evil men and by women.

Devadatta was a cousin of the Buddha, but as is well chronicled in stories of the life of the Buddha, he was a most wicked and cruel man. He was jealous of the fact that Sakyamuni was looked up to as the Buddha and adored by many people. Being ambitious to take the place of the Buddha, he often set traps for the Buddha by slandering and defaming him. He even attempted several times to kill the Buddha. Once he rolled a boulder down onto a road when the Buddha was passing; once he tried to make an elephant drunk so that it would run amok and attack the Buddha; once he administered poison to Sakyamuni; once he shot at the Buddha with his bow.

The Buddha predicted buddhahood even of Devadatta, whose name stood first on the list of his enemies. The Buddha's tolerance and generosity toward Devadatta must be acknowledged as extraordinary.

Another peculiarity of this chapter is that a dragon's daughter, only eight years old, was predicted to become a buddha. People in this modern age, especially in the postwar era, may think it unjust for women to be discussed together with evil men in this chapter. But the general public of India in the time of the Buddha considered women to be sin incarnate. Women were regarded as an obstacle to men's practicing religious disciplines, and it was thought that they could never be saved from suffering.

Society in ancient India was highly stratified, being divided into the four major hereditary castes: the highest, the Brāhmaṇa, or priestly caste, was charged with learning, religion, and morality; the second was the Kshatriya, or military caste, including kings and warriors; the third, the Vaiśya, was the caste of peasants, artisans, and merchants; the fourth, the Śūdra, was that of manual workers. As rigid distinctions based on birth were maintained through the caste system, however brilliant a man might be, he could never rise in caste. If he was born a Śūdra, he was fated to remain a Śūdra all his life.

On the other hand, a man who came of a Brāhman family was able to acquire a higher position, ruling many others, even if he was a fool. A person who was descended from the Kshatriyas could gain great power even if he was a coward. Because of their wealth, men who belonged to the Vaiśya conspired with the Brāhmans and ingratiated themselves with the Kshatriyas. The Vaiśyas also wielded a degree of power over the Śūdras and worked them as if they were beasts of burden.

Members of the Śūdra caste comprised an overwhelming majority of the population, but they were scarcely treated as human beings. The upper three castes managed and ruled the society of ancient India. Needless to say, the lower castes were severely oppressed by the more powerful castes. In such a society, the Buddha's proclamation that all men are equal was more revolutionary than we today can imagine.

Sakyamuni Buddha, however, who patiently bore all persecutions, preached the Lotus Sutra as the teaching of human equality with great courage and indomitable spirit. He repeatedly preached the difficulties of receiving, keeping, and proclaiming the Lotus Sutra because of the social conditions of his time in India.

Concerning the Buddha's prediction of women to buddhahood, we must think of this in terms of the state of society and the general attitudes of the Buddha's time. The Buddha declared, "Women can become buddhas, too; there is no distinction of sex in essence; all human beings are equal," at the time when women were considered as intrinsically sinful. This was indeed an epochal declaration.

Since the French Revolution, the idea of human equality has taken root in men's minds, and as a result, the ideal of democracy has been resurrected in the West. However, more than two thousand years before that time, Sakyamuni Buddha had preached human equality, although the meaning of equality as preached by him was far more profound than that of equality in modern times. However, people in the centuries following the Buddha's death were unable to accept this teaching of the Buddha and spread it. We certainly owe those of past ages many apologies for the long delay in the realization of the Buddha's ideal of human equality.

Let us now proceed to the text of this chapter.

First the Buddha addressed the bodhisattvas, the celestial beings, and the four groups, and spoke about the relationship between himself in a previous life and a certain hermit: "For many *kalpas* in a previous existence, I was king of a country and vowed to seek the supreme wisdom. Desiring to fulfill the Six Perfections, I earnestly bestowed alms with an unsparing mind—the precious seven, countries, cities, wives, children, not grudging even my body and life. For the sake of the Law, I gave up the throne of my domain, deputed my government to the crown prince, and sought everywhere for the truth, proclaiming, 'Whoever is able to tell me of a Great-vehicle, I will provide for him all my life and be his servant.'

"At that time a hermit called Asita came to me and said, 'I have a Great-vehicle named the Wonderful Law-Flower Sutra. If you will not disobey me, I will explain it to you.' I, hearing what the hermit said, became ecstatic with joy and instantly followed him and provided for his needs, gathering fruit, drawing water, collecting fuel, preparing his food, even turning my body into his seat and bed, yet never feeling fatigue of body or mind. While I thus served, a millennium passed, and for the sake of the Law I zealously waited on him so that he should lack nothing."

After telling this story to all the *bhikshus,* the Buddha revealed that while the king was he himself, the hermit Asita was the present Devadatta. The Buddha declared to all the four groups that Devadatta, after innumerable *kalpas* had passed, would become a buddha.

EVIL MEN WILL BECOME BUDDHAS. It would be a great mistake to take lightly the Buddha's declaration that even Devadatta, who had attempted to kill him, would become a buddha. We must not forget that Devadatta's attainment of buddhahood was conditional on the fact that he be free from illusion and practice religious disciplines. Any evil man certainly possesses the buddha-nature. If such a man comes in contact with the Law of the Buddha and sweeps away the dark cloud of illusion covering his mind, his true nature, his buddha-nature, will begin to shine forth. The Buddha's teaching, which clearly indicated this, is a great salvation for men in the age of degeneration.

In this section of the Buddha's preaching, besides his teaching that even evil men can become buddhas, two more teachings are included. One is that if a man endures all persecution and adversity and continues to practice religious disciplines, his hardships will become an indirect cause of his becoming a buddha. The Buddha said, "My attainment of Perfect Enlightenment, and my widespread saving of the living—all this is due to the good friendship of Devadatta."

This is a most important declaration. When we receive scorn, abuse, and obstruction from others, we are apt to become angry with them, feel sad, and begin to doubt the Law. We must instead endure such hardships and divert them to a positive force because the teaching of the Lotus Sutra is the supreme Law in this world. Many ancient teachers and leaders, including both Sakyamuni Buddha and Nichiren, have proved by their example that man can thus transform drawbacks into advantages.

Do Not Return Hatred for Hatred. Another teaching is that we must not return hatred for hatred. Sakyamuni Buddha not only did not feel resentment toward Devadatta, who inflicted so many injuries on him, but even thanked him for his "good friendship." Some people may think that such attitude will not work in today's world, where we must struggle so hard for existence. But the Buddha's idea is corroborated by the following recent happening.

At the plenary session of the Japanese Peace Treaty Conference held in San Francisco in 1951, J. R. Jayewardene, the Ceylonese finance minister and chief Ceylonese delegate to the conference, made a speech declaring that Ceylon renounced its demand for reparations from Japan, quoting the following words of the Buddha from the *Dhammapada:* "Hatred is never appeased through hatred in this world; by love alone is it appeased. This is an ancient law." His speech is reported to have evoked a storm of applause.

Diplomatic skill includes threatening an opposing country, deceiving it, bargaining with it, secretly winning some of its citizens over to one's own side, and betraying one's friends at the last moment. From the viewpoint of personal relationships, such diplomatic skill is quite as shameful as that of a criminal. How impressive is the fact that at the peace conference, attended by veteran diplomats, the Buddha's teaching was set forth by the delegate of Ceylon as his country's foreign policy! Moreover, the fact that the other delegates accorded the speech of the Ceylonese delegate thunderous applause clearly shows that there is only one way for mankind to be saved. From this incident, we can feel great hope for the future of mankind.

Indeed, if we return our opponents hatred for hatred, they will also feel more bitter toward us. Thus hatred will beget more hatred and will continue forever in a vicious circle. In the *Dhammapada,* the Buddha teaches that man's hatred will cease forever when it is abandoned by him, and in the Lotus Sutra he teaches man's positive attitude, in which he takes a further step forward to transform hatred into gratitude.

Some may think that it is very difficult for an ordinary person to do this. Therefore Sakyamuni Buddha spoke as follows: "If there be in a future world any good son or good daughter to hear this Devadatta chapter of the Wonderful Law-Flower Sutra with pure heart and believing reverence, and is free from doubt, such a one shall not fall into the hells or become a hungry spirit or animal, but shall be born into the presence of the buddhas of the universe. Wherever he be born he will always hear this sutra; and if he be born amongst men or gods, he will enjoy marvelous delight. As to the buddha into whose presence he is born, his birth shall be by emanation from a lotus flower."

Then a bodhisattva-attendant of the Tathāgata Abundant Treasures named Wisdom Accumulation said to the Buddha Abundant Treasures: "Let us return to our own land!" But Sakyamuni Buddha said to Wisdom Accumulation: "Good son! Wait a while! Here is the Bodhisattva Mañjuśrī. First meet and discuss with him the Wonderful Law and then return to your own land." Thereupon Mañjuśrī sprang up from the ocean, together with the bodhisattvas who accompanied him. To a question from the Bodhisattva Wisdom Accumulation, Mañjuśrī said that he had instructed many people in the palace of the undersea dragon king. Then the Bodhisattva Wisdom Accumulation extolled Mañjuśrī for the results of his instruction in the ocean.

Mañjuśrī replied: "This is not all due to my greatness. That which I, in the midst of the ocean, always proclaimed was none other than the Wonderful Law-Flower Sutra. My instruction of the bodhisattvas does not amount to much. Actually, I have a very delightful thing to tell you." Then Mañjuśrī told Wisdom Accumulation that he had preached the Lotus Sutra to the eight-year-old daughter of the dragon king and caused her to obtain enlightenment. He extolled the greatness of the dragon king's daughter.

The Bodhisattva Wisdom Accumulation said: "I have seen how Sakyamuni Tathāgata, during innumerable *kalpas,* doing arduous and painful deeds, accumulating merit, and heaping up virtue, sought the Way of Bodhi ceaselessly and without rest. I have observed that in the three-thousand-great-thousandfold world there is not a spot as small as a mustard seed where he has not laid down his body and life as a bodhisattva for the sake of the living; and only after that did he attain Bodhi. It is incredible that this girl in but a moment should become perfectly enlightened."

Before he had ceased talking, the daughter of the dragon king suddenly appeared before them and after making reverent obeisance to the Buddha, withdrew to one side, extolled the Buddha in verse, and said: "I believe that I can surely attain Bodhi. Only the Buddha may bear witness to that. I will reveal the teaching of the Great-vehicle, which delivers creatures from suffering."

The congregation could not understand her declaration. Śāriputra said to the daughter of the dragon king: "You state that in no length of time you attained the supreme Way. This thing is hard to believe." He listed several reasons that a woman cannot become a buddha.

The dragon's daughter possessed a precious pearl, which she then held up and presented to the Buddha, and which the Buddha immediately accepted. The Buddha's immediate acceptance of her pearl is evidence that he had recognized her attainment of buddhahood. She then said to the Bodhisattva Wisdom Accumulation and Śāriputra: "I have offered my pearl, and the World-honored One has accepted it—was this action speedy?" They answered: "Most speedy."

She said: "By your supernatural powers behold me become a buddha even more rapidly than that!" At that moment the entire congregation saw the dragon's daughter suddenly transformed into a male, perfect in bodhisattva-deeds, who instantly went to the world Spotless in the southern quarter, where she universally proclaimed the Wonderful Law to all living creatures in the universe.

WOMEN WILL BECOME BUDDHAS. Then the *sahā*-world of bodhisattvas, *śrāvakas,* gods, dragons, and human and nonhuman beings, all from afar beholding the dragon's daughter become a buddha and universally preach the Law to the gods, men, and other beings, rejoiced greatly and made reverent salutation. The countless multitude on witnessing her preach the Law and become a buddha as a woman were aroused to realization and attained the stage of never sliding back into mortality. They also received their prediction of attainment of the perfect Way. Three thousand living beings set their minds on Bodhi and obtained their prediction of it. The Bodhisattva Wisdom Accumulation and Śāriputra and all the congregation silently and deeply believed in the greatness of the power of the Buddha's teachings. The chapter on Devadatta ends with this.

Women of today may feel dissatisfied that the dragon's daughter was suddenly transformed into a male and then became a buddha. Such an expression was used merely because of the idea of women in ancient India. The sudden transformation of a woman into a male means nothing but the transcendence of the difference between male and female. Sakyamuni Buddha asserted that animals, birds, worms, plants, and trees, as well as human beings, possess the buddha-nature. How could he then discriminate between men and women? It is impossible. Observed with the Buddha's eyes, all living beings are equal. We must never misunderstand this.

CHAPTER 13

Exhortation to Hold Firm

THIS CHAPTER IS CALLED *Kanji-hon* in Japanese. *Kan* means to exhort or urge others to the teaching, while *ji* means to hold or to receive and keep. This chapter relates how the virtuous bodhisattvas, who had well understood through the Buddha's preaching hitherto how precious the teaching of the Wonderful Law-Flower Sutra is, made a firm resolution to spread abroad this sutra after the extinction of the Buddha, no matter what difficulties they might encounter, and how they vowed to practice it in the presence of the Buddha. One must be firmly resolved to preach the teaching oneself before one exhorts others to it. It is noteworthy that the title, "Exhortation to Hold Firm," does not refer to the exhortation of others to the teaching but to the resolution and vow of the bodhisattvas themselves. This is an essential point that we must not overlook.

In this chapter the Perfect Enlightenment of two women, the Gautamī and the Bhikshuṇī Yaśodharā, was predicted. The Gautamī was the sister of the Buddha's mother, Mahāmāyā, who died soon after giving birth to the Buddha, and the Gautamī raised Sakyamuni. She nurtured him with no less affection than a true mother and so was named the Bhikshuṇī Mahāprajāpatī (the way of great affection). The Bhikshuṇī Yaśodharā was the wife of Sakyamuni before he renounced the world, and the mother of Rāhula. These two women earnestly wished to become the immediate disciples of the Buddha when his father, King Śuddhodana, died. They accumulated religious disciplines as irreproachable *bhikshuṇīs.*

It may seem strange that the Buddha in his predictions had left them until last and that before mentioning them he had given his prediction to the dragon king's daughter, who was, so to speak, an indirect disciple instructed by Mañjuśrī, and only an eight-year-old girl. This priority has the following meanings. First, as already mentioned in the explanation of the Buddha's prediction to Ānanda and Rāhula, for those closest to the Buddha, like the Bhikshuṇī Mahāprajāpatī, who had brought up Sakyamuni from babyhood, and the Bhikshuṇī Yaśodharā, who had been his wife and had given birth to his son, such intimacy could have become a hindrance rather than a help to their practice. The Buddha teaches us that someone like the dragon king's daughter, who is a perfect stranger to the Buddha, can receive the Law with ease, while we may find great difficulty in instructing those closest to us, such as our parents and spouses. The delay of the Buddha's prediction to the Bhikshuṇī Mahāprajāpatī and the Bhikshuṇī Yaśodharā does not mean that they were considered inferior to the dragon king's daughter.

All Creatures Will Become Buddhas. Another meaning is that as long as the teaching is transmitted rightly and as long as it is received with an obedient mind, anyone can obtain the enlightenment of a buddha. Whoever one may be, whether a direct disciple of the Buddha, someone born after the Buddha's lifetime, or someone in a foreign country, none of these conditions has any bearing on the possibility of one's attainment of buddhahood. If a person receives the right teaching as it is, he can be saved. The eight-year-old daughter of the dragon king symbolizes an obedient mind like that of a child. She symbolizes the vastness and boundlessness of the Buddha's teaching, showing that all are equally saved regardless of nationality and of whether they are human beings or not. We must realize that the Buddha's preaching in this chapter has a much deeper meaning than just the indication of women's attainment of buddhahood.

In the present age, women seem to be much more religiously inclined than men. There are various reasons for this, but the deepest and greatest reason is considered to be that women have the duty to give birth to the life of the next generation. Most men are harried by business affairs. To put it briefly, one must work as hard as he can just to support his family, while another devotes himself to making his shop or company prosperous. On the other hand, women think instinctively of their next life and their eternal life in the depths of their minds, although they are not conscious of it. Thus their religious feeling becomes strong, which is quite natural.

Women practice religious disciplines eagerly. We can view their practice thus. Women have the strong point of being very patient in repeating the same thing over and over. They never tire of repeatedly making the same stitch thousands of times in knitting. As mentioned before, a discipline is nothing but seeking one's elevation by patiently repeating something beneficial to one's mind or body. In their religious disciplines, women exhibit their special characteristics.

Meanwhile, it should not be thought that men are entirely lacking in the characteristics found in women. When I enlisted in the Japanese navy and lived on board ship, I used to knit, together with my fellow sailors. I could knit gloves and stomach warmers as skillfully as a woman. When men enter such a life-environment, they may turn out to have characteristics that enable them to repeat something as patiently as women. Men do not have to feel discouraged at their lack of patience in doing things that women can do. As preached in chapter 5, all have the possibility of being equally saved, whatever their individual differences may be.

Now let us proceed to the main subject of chapter 13.

All in the great assembly were deeply moved by the vivid scene of the dragon's daughter becoming a buddha. At that time the Bodhisattva Medicine King and the Bodhisattva Great Eloquence, with their retinues of many bodhisattvas, all in the presence of the Buddha made this vow: "Be pleased, World-honored One, to be without anxiety! After the extinction of the Buddha we will devote ourselves to spreading abroad this honorable teaching. In the evil age to come, living beings will decrease in their good qualities, while they will increase in utter arrogance and in covetousness of gain and honors, develop their evil qualities, and be far removed from emancipation. Though it may be difficult to teach and convert them, we, arousing our utmost patience, will observe this teaching and spare not our body and life to preach it." The motto of believers of the Lotus Sutra, "Not to spare body or life for the cause of the Law," comes from this verse.

Thereupon the five hundred *arhats* in the assembly and the eight thousand *arhats,* training and trained, made this vow: "World-honored One! We also will publish abroad this teaching in other lands because the virtuous bodhisattvas have undertaken to teach and convert the people in the *sahā*-world, where there will be many difficulties."

Then the aunt of the Buddha, the Bhikshuṇī Mahāprajāpatī, with many *bhikshuṇīs,* training and trained, rose up from their seats, with one mind folded their hands, and gazed up at the honored face without removing their eyes for a moment. Then the World-honored One addressed the Gautamī: "Why, with sad countenance, do you gaze at the Tathāgata? Are you not thinking that I have not mentioned your name and predicted you to Perfect Enlightenment? Gautamī! I have already inclusively announced that the future of all *śrāvakas* is predicted. Everyone who desires to obtain the enlightenment of a buddha and devotes himself to doing so will surely become a buddha regardless of being man or woman."

Speaking thus, the Buddha gave his prediction of Perfect Enlightenment to the Bhikshuṇī Mahāprajāpatī and the six thousand *bhikshuṇīs,* training and trained.

Thereupon the mother of Rāhula, the Bhikshuṇī Yaśodharā, reflected thus: "The World-honored One in his predictions has left my name alone unmentioned. But I have the determination to endeavor to practice the bodhisattva-way as hard as I can. I wish the Buddha would predict my Perfect Enlightenment." Then the World-honored One, perceiving her thoughts, immediately gave her his prediction of buddhahood. Thereupon the Bhikshuṇī Mahāprajāpatī and the Bhikshuṇī Yaśodharā together with their retinues rejoiced greatly and offered him their heartfelt thanks. The *bhikshuṇīs* declared to the Buddha that they would endeavor to spread the Lotus Sutra in other lands.

Thereupon the World-honored One looked upon the infinite bodhisattvas. All these bodhisattvas were of the stage *avaivartika,*[1] who rolled the never-retreating Law-wheel, never neglecting to preach the teaching, and had attained the *dhāraṇīs,* that is, the power of checking all evils by all virtues. Having seen that the Buddha was gazing at them, they immediately rose from their seats, went before him, with one mind folded their hands, and reflected thus: "If the World-honored One commands us to keep and expound this sutra, we will proclaim abroad this Law as the Buddha has taught it. The Buddha now is silent. We are not commanded; what shall we do?"

Then these bodhisattvas, respectfully obeying the Buddha's will and themselves desiring to fulfill their original vow, raised a lion's roar before the Buddha and uttered this vow: "World-honored One! After the extinction of the Tathāgata we will compass and travel through the

1. The stage of nonretrogression from the degree of perfection already attained.

worlds in all directions in order to lead all the living to believe in this Law and to exhort others to practice it as their law and rightly keep it in mind, all by the Buddha's might. Be pleased, World-honored One, after your extinction, to behold and guard us!"

Then the bodhisattvas all together raised their voices, speaking in verse to the following effect: "Be pleased to be without anxiety! After the Buddha's extinction, we will proclaim abroad this Law in the last dreadful evil age. Though in their ignorance many will curse and abuse us and persecute us, we will endure it all. *Bhikshus* in that evil age will be heretical, suspicious, and warped, claiming to have attained what they have not, and will have minds full of arrogance. Others in *āraṇyas*[2] will wear patched garments[3] and live in seclusion, pretending that they walk the true path and scorning other people."

THREE KINDS OF POWERFUL ENEMIES. Three kinds of arrogance are mentioned in these words of the bodhisattvas. First, some people irresponsibly curse and persecute believers of the Lotus Sutra even though they know nothing about the teaching. These are the "people of worldly arrogance" (*zokushū-zōjōman*).

Secondly, some men of religion take it for granted that even a worthless teaching is good, abuse the Lotus Sutra, and obstruct those who preach it. They are the "people of religious arrogance" (*dōmon-zōjōman*).

Thirdly, some men of religion inwardly have the desire for fame and wealth, although they assume as grave an air as saints. Since they pretend to have transcended the world, many influential people follow them. They lead negative religious lives and preach negative teachings. For this reason, they feel somewhat embarrassed by the Lotus Sutra as a positive teaching that can save ordinary people and they try to oppress believers of the sutra and obstruct them in their preaching. These are the "people of excessive arrogance" (*senshō-zōjōman*) toward the believers of the Lotus Sutra. This third group, the "people of excessive arrogance," are said to be the most injurious to others.

The bodhisattvas declared: "The people of excessive arrogance, though they try to appear enlightened, are greedily attached to worldly desire, and lust for power and fame. They preach the Law to rich laymen and are revered by the world just like *arhats* of transcendent powers.

2. *Āraṇya* is a general term for Buddhist monasteries.
3. That is, monk's garments made of patches of cloth sewn together.

These men, harboring evil minds, ever thinking of earthly things, love to calumniate those who preach the Lotus Sutra to the people.

"These men of arrogance say such things of us as, 'All these *bhikshus* preach a heretical doctrine from love of gain; they have themselves composed this sutra to delude the people of the world.' In order to ruin us, they are always in the assemblies and slander us to kings, ministers, Brahmans, and citizens and to the other groups of *bhikshus*. They say, 'These are men of false views, who proclaim heretical doctrines.' "

However severely the three kinds of powerful enemies may persecute the believers of the Lotus Sutra, the latter should preach the sutra widely without retrogressing from the stage of perfection they have attained. Such determination is shown in the following strong words of the bodhisattvas: "But we, from reverence for the Buddha, will endure all these evils. We will revere this sutra of the highest teaching as much as the Buddha. In order to keep it and spread it widely, we will put up with whatever persecution comes to us. Others contemptuously address us as 'All you buddhas!' We will patiently endure even this scorn and arrogance.

"Various fears and dreads abound in the evil age of the corrupt. Devils will take possession of them to curse, abuse, and insult us. But we, revering and believing in the Buddha, will wear the armor of perseverance and will protect the Law with a nonviolent but dauntless attitude. We will endure all these hard things for the sake of preaching this sutra. We will not love body and life, but care only for the supreme Way.

"Throughout all ages to come, we will guard what the Buddha bequeaths. Vicious *bhikshus* in the corrupt ages, knowing not the laws so tactfully preached by the Buddha as opportunity served, will abuse and frown upon us; repeatedly we will be driven out and exiled afar from the monasteries. Such evils will be our ills for remembering the Buddha's command, but we will endure all these things.

"Thus we do not fear whatever difficulties and whatever persecutions may befall us. If there are those who seek after the Law whether in villages and cities or wherever a strong enemy watches, we will all go there and preach the Law bequeathed by the Buddha. We are the apostles of the World-honored One and we have nothing to fear amid the multitude. We will rightly preach the Law. Be pleased, O Buddha, to abide in peace. In the presence of the World-honored One and the buddhas from all directions we thus make our vow, and the Buddha knows our hearts. Permit us to preach this Law in the corrupt age."

Indeed, these words were a lion's roar of self-confidence and courage. "We, revering and believing in the Buddha, / Will wear the armor of perseverance; / For the sake of preaching this sutra / We will endure all these hard things."—whenever believers read and recite this portion of the closing verse of chapter 13, they will be heartened and feel courage well up anew from the depths of their hearts. For believers of the Lotus Sutra, this can be said to be one of the most important verses in the sutra.

CHAPTER 14

A Happy Life

IN CHAPTER 13, all the bodhisattvas made great vows to spread the teaching of the Lotus Sutra no matter what persecution they might suffer. Agreeing with their pledge and deeply moved by it, the Bodhisattva Mañjuśrī asked the Buddha on behalf of the bodhisattvas: "World-honored One! How are we bodhisattvas to be able to protect, keep, and preach this Law in the evil age to come?" The chapter "A Happy Life" shows how, in answering the question put by the Bodhisattva Mañjuśrī, the Buddha instructed the believers of the Lotus Sutra with painstaking care.

"A Happy Life" means always to maintain a peaceful and happy mind and willingly to practice religious disciplines. So long as a person faces religious persecution with resentment, his mental attitude does not embody the ideal way of a true believer of the Lotus Sutra; whatever misfortune may befall him, he must maintain a peaceful and calm mind for the sake of the Law and must voluntarily practice religious discipline and preach the Law.

Man's mental strength is little short of miraculous. For instance, in a movie we see a man carrying a pack weighing thirty or forty kilograms on his back and climbing a mountain, bathed in perspiration. Viewers of such a film must feel how arduous it is to climb the mountain. Sometimes it takes three or four hours to advance only twenty or thirty meters. Moreover, the climber risks his life with every step. If it grows dark while he is scaling a rocky cliff, he must hang from the rock and sleep in place in subzero temperatures. If a man were obliged to undergo such an ordeal on the orders of his employer, then indeed he could bring a complaint against the employer for infringing his human rights. However, a mountain climber does this voluntarily. Though he certainly feels pain, his mind is peaceful, and his pain even contributes to his pleasure and enjoyment.

In practicing the teaching of the Lotus Sutra, so long as a person forces himself to endure persecution and the scorn of outsiders though filled with anger and resentment, he is a beginner in Buddhist disciplines. A person who has attained the Way can maintain a peaceful and calm mind even while suffering, and can feel joy in the practice itself. Until a person attains such a state of mind, he must take scrupulous care not to be tempted or agitated by the various setbacks in his daily life. The chapter "A Happy Life" teaches us this. The bodhisattvas declare with great ardor their resolution to withstand persecution from outside in the chapter "Exhortation to Hold Firm," while the Buddha, like a father, gently admonishes the bodhisattvas not to yield to inward temptation in the chapter "A Happy Life." In a sense, these two chapters state the contrast between a kindly father who knows the world and a son who is young and high-spirited.

Before proceeding to the central theme of this chapter, we must warn readers not to misunderstand the words "do not consort with" so-and-so, which often appear in this chapter. These words do not mean not to approach or associate with someone. The Buddha, who had made a great vow to save all living beings equally, could not have said such a thing. The true meaning of "do not consort with" so-and-so is that we must not fawn upon others or compromise ourselves in dealing with them through excessive familiarity or from some ulterior motive. Should we be dealing with a king or minister, we must not defer to their station in life in order to curry favor, because there is only one truth, and it applies to kings just the same as to ordinary citizens. On the other hand, if we are too familiar with others, we are liable to forget to draw the line between public and private life. The Buddha warns us of this danger.

The Buddha also warns us not to consort with people whose profession is to kill living beings, such as hunters and fishermen, or with prostitutes. However, this warning is generated by his parental affection and means that, although it is such people whom we must instruct, we must not be influenced by their environment. If we do not read this chapter with such preliminary knowledge, we will be in danger of harboring doubts because it includes many expressions that are open to misunderstanding.

THE FOUR PLEASANT PRACTICES. The Buddha answered Mañjuśrī's question by saying that if any bodhisattva desires to preach this sutra in the evil age to come, he should be steadfast in the "four pleasant practices" (*shi anraku-gyō*): first, the pleasant practice of the body (*shin anraku-gyō*); second, the pleasant practice of the mouth (*ku anraku-gyō*); third, the pleasant practice of the mind (*i anraku-gyō*); and fourth, the pleasant practice of the vow (*seigan anraku-gyō*). Thus the Buddha teaches us how to behave, how to speak, what kind of mental attitude to maintain, and how to endeavor to realize our ideal.

The Buddha taught the pleasant practice of the body by dividing it into two parts, a bodhisattva's spheres of action and of intimacy. A bodhisattva's sphere of action means his fundamental attitude as the basis of his personal behavior. A bodhisattva is patient, gentle, and agreeable, and is neither hasty nor overbearing; his mind is unperturbed, and unlike ordinary people, he is not conceited or boastful about his own good works ("he has no laws by which to act") but sees all things in their reality. Nor does he take a partial view of things but acts toward all people with the same compassion, never making a show of it ("nor proceeds along the undivided way"). The Buddha preaches here that this is the fundamental attitude of the bodhisattva.

Next, the Buddha teaches a bodhisattva's sphere of intimacy by dividing it into the following ten parts: First, a bodhisattva is not intimate with men of high position and influence in order to gain some benefit, nor does he compromise his preaching of the Law to them through excessive familiarity with them.

Second, he is not intimate with heretics, composers of worldly literature or poetry, nor with Lokāyatas[1] and Anti-Lokāyatas.[2] Thus he is not adversely affected by their impure environment, nor does he compromise the Law. Third, he does not resort to brutal sports, such as boxing and wrestling, nor to the various juggling performances of *nartakas*[3] and others. Fourth, he does not consort personally with those who kill creatures to make a living, such as butchers, fishermen,

1. A non-Buddhist sect whose members believe in following the ways of the world.
2. The opposite of the Lokāyatas, being those utterly opposed to the world.
3. Dancers, singers, and actors.

and hunters, and he does not develop a callous attitude toward engaging in cruel conduct.

Fifth, he does not consort with *bhikshus* and *bhikshuṇīs* who seek the teaching of the small vehicle and are satisfied with their own personal isolation from earthly existence. Moreover, he does not become infected by their selfish ideas, nor develop a tendency to compromise with them in listening to the laws preached by them. If they come to him to hear the Law, he takes the opportunity to preach it, expecting nothing in return. Sixth, when he preaches the Law to women, he does not display an appearance capable of arousing passionate thoughts, and he maintains a correct mental attitude with great strictness. He does not take pleasure in seeing women.

Seventh, he does not become friendly with any hermaphrodite. This means that he needs to take a very prudent attitude when he teaches such a deformed person. Eighth, he does not enter the homes of others alone. If for some reason he must do so, then he thinks single-mindedly of the Buddha. This is the Buddha's admonition to the bodhisattva to go everywhere together with the Buddha. Ninth, if he preaches the Law to women, he does not display his teeth in smiles nor let his breast be seen. Tenth, he takes no pleasure in keeping young pupils and children by his side.

Besides these ten major points, the Buddha admonishes the bodhisattva ever to prefer meditation and seclusion and to cultivate and control his mind.

The matters mentioned above are the sphere of intimacy of a bodhisattva. If he can maintain the bodhisattva's spheres of action and intimacy, his behavior as a bodhisattva is perfect and he can preach the Law with a peaceful mind. The above comprises the pleasant practice of the body.

THE PLEASANT PRACTICE OF THE MOUTH. Following are the Buddha's admonitions concerning one's speech. First, the bodhisattva takes no pleasure in telling of the errors of other people or of the sutras; second, he does not despise other preachers; third, he does not speak of the good and evil, the merits and demerits of other people, nor does he single out *śrāvakas* by name and broadcast their errors and sins; fourth, in the same way, he does not praise their virtues and he does not beget a jealous mind.

If he maintains a cheerful and open mind in this way, those who hear the teaching will offer him no opposition. To those who ask difficult questions, he does not answer with the law of the small vehicle but only with the Great-vehicle, and he explains the Law to them so that they may obtain perfect knowledge. This is the pleasant practice of the mouth.

THE PLEASANT PRACTICE OF THE MIND. Following are the eight admonitions of the Buddha with regard to the mental attitude of the bodhisattva.

First, he does not harbor an envious or deceitful mind. Second, he does not slight or abuse other learners of the Buddha-way even if they are beginners, nor does he seek out their excesses and shortcomings. Third, if there are people who seek the bodhisattva-way, he does not distress them, causing them to feel doubt and regret, nor does he say discouraging things to them. Fourth, he should not indulge in discussions about the laws or engage in dispute but should devote himself to discussion of the practice to save all living beings. Fifth, he should think of saving all living beings from their sufferings through his great compassion. Sixth, he should think of the buddhas as benevolent fathers. Seventh, he should think of the bodhisattvas as his great teachers. Eighth, he should preach the Law equally to all living beings. This is the pleasant practice of the mind.

THE PLEASANT PRACTICE OF THE VOW. In the last ages to come, when the Law is about to perish, the bodhisattva who keeps this Law-Flower Sutra should beget a spirit of great charity toward both laymen and monks, and should have a spirit of great compassion for those who are not yet bodhisattvas but are satisfied with their selfish idea of saving only themselves. He also should decide that, though those people have not inquired for, nor believed in, nor understood this sutra, when he has attained Perfect Enlightenment through his transcendental powers and powers of wisdom he will lead them to abide in this Law. The pleasant practice of the vow means to have a spirit of great compassion and to raise the mind of vowing to lead all people to the Lotus Sutra and to practice its spirit.

The bodhisattva who can perfectly accomplish this pleasant practice of the vow will be free from error when he preaches the Law. He will always be worshiped by all the people. The gods will constantly guard and protect him day and night for the sake of this Law, so that he will be able to cause all his hearers to rejoice.

THE PARABLE OF THE GEM IN THE TOPKNOT. Having preached these four pleasant practices, the World-honored One emphasized the excellence of the teaching of the Lotus Sutra through the following Parable of the Gem in the Topknot, the sixth of the seven parables in the Lotus Sutra.

"It is like a powerful holy wheel-rolling king who desires by force to conquer other domains. When minor kings do not obey his command, the wheel-rolling king calls up his various armies and goes to punish them. The king, seeing his soldiers distinguish themselves in battle, is greatly pleased and, according to their merit, bestows rewards, giving fields, houses, villages, or cities, or giving garments or personal ornaments, or giving all kinds of treasures. Only the crown jewel in his topknot he gives to none because only on the head of a king may this jewel be worn, and if he gave it away, all the king's retinue would be astounded. Mañjuśrī! That the Tathāgata has not prematurely preached the Lotus Sutra is also like this.

"By his powers of meditation and wisdom he has taken possession of the domain of the Law and rules as king over the triple world. But the Māra kings are unwilling to submit. The Tathāgata's wise and holy generals fight against them. With those who distinguish themselves he, too, is pleased, and in the midst of his four hosts preaches the sutras to them, causing them to rejoice, and bestows on them the meditations, the emancipations, the faultless roots and powers, and all the wealth of the Law. In addition, he gives them the city of nirvana, saying that they have attained extinction, and attracts their minds so that they all rejoice; yet he does not preach to them the Law-Flower Sutra.

"Mañjuśrī! Just as the wheel-rolling king, seeing his soldiers distinguish themselves, is so extremely pleased that now at last he gives them the marvelous jewel so long worn in his topknot, which may not carelessly be given to anyone, so also is it with the Tathāgata. As the great Law-king of the triple world, teaching and converting all the living by the Law, when he sees his wise and holy army fighting various kinds of Māras, and doing so with such great exploits and merits, exterminating the three poisons,[4] escaping from the triple world, and breaking through the nets of Māras, then the Tathāgata also is greatly pleased and now at last

4. Greed, anger, and delusion.

preaches this Law-Flower Sutra, which has never before been preached and which is able to cause all the living to reach perfect knowledge, though all the world greatly resents and has difficulty in believing it. Mañjuśrī! This Law-Flower Sutra is the foremost teaching of the *tathāgatas* and the most profound of all discourses. I give it to you last of all, just as that powerful king at last gives the brilliant jewel he has guarded for so long."

Then the World-honored One proclaimed this teaching again in verse. Many merits obtained by those who read this sutra are stated in the middle part of the verse section:

"He who reads this sutra
Will be ever free from worry
And free from pain and disease;
His countenance will be fresh and white;
He will not be born poor,
Humble, or ugly.
All creatures will delight to see him
As a longed-for saint;
Heavenly cherubim
Will be his servants.
Swords and staves will not be laid on him;
Poison cannot harm him.
If anyone curses him,
That man's mouth will be closed.
Fearlessly he will roam
Like a lion king.
The radiance of his wisdom
Will shine like the sun."

The Buddha comes directly to the point by comparing man's wisdom to sunshine. There is no substance in darkness; there is only a lack of sunshine. If the sun shines in the darkness, the darkness will disappear. If a person realizes the wisdom of the Buddha, then his mental darkness will instantly disappear. We must realize fully that the wisdom of the Buddha is absolute and that it is a law which, in opposing darkness, disperses it.

Lastly, this chapter states that a person who perfectly performs the four pleasant practices and preaches the Lotus Sutra will dream various dreams. We should not belittle this statement because it concerns dreams. Modern psychology clearly recognizes the great importance of dreams. Briefly, a dream is said to be a "memory of the daytime." It is said that our experiences in our waking hours accumulate in our subconscious mind and reappear as dreams when we sleep. When one dreams that he sees a sacred image of the Buddha, it is proof that he has become pure to the depths of his mind, has become compassionate, and always calls on the name of the Buddha.

Even a highly respected person may become delirious because of fever or a nightmare. This is evidence that his subconsciousness is not yet purified. It is to be hoped that we will attain such a mental state that even in our dreams we will see buddhas with golden bodies and, finding ourselves in their midst, will extol the Buddha with folded hands.

CHAPTER 15

Springing Up out of the Earth

THIS CHAPTER INCLUDES two especially important points. First, the World-honored One flatly refused the many bodhisattvas who had come from other lands to the *sahā*-world, offering to cooperate with him in instructing all the living beings there. Secondly, he told the many bodhisattvas who sprang up out of the earth that it was their duty to do this.

The bodhisattvas who sprang up out of the earth signify people who have had much suffering and worry during their lives, have accumulated virtues in such an unfavorable environment, and have attained enlightenment while leading ordinary lives. Such people, who have themselves experienced and weathered much suffering and worry, possess real power. They indeed have the power to instruct other people.

That the Buddha entrusted the *sahā*-world to the bodhisattvas who emerged from the earth teaches us that the world in which we live should be purified and made peaceful through our own efforts as dwellers in the world, and that we should realize happiness in our lives through our own efforts. We are responsible for creating the Pure Land where we live. We should bring about our happiness through our own efforts—what a reassuring and positive teaching this is!

Sakyamuni Buddha himself went through such a process of suffering and finally attained supreme enlightenment. Buddhism differs distinctively from other religions in this point. Though all have fine teachings, there is no clear evidence of another case in which the founder of a religion attained his own supreme enlightenment and established his own religion. Some religions proclaim that their founders were sent by God. Others declare that God gave a revelation to the founder or that God descended from heaven to this world.

Unlike these religions, the teaching of Buddhism is the truth that Lord Sakyamuni, who was born as a human being like all of us and experienced human suffering and worry, aspired to enlightenment, practiced ascetic disciplines, and attained enlightenment after six years of spiritual effort. The process through which he attained his enlightenment can be clearly seen. Therefore, we can feel confident that we are sure to reach supreme enlightenment eventually if only we follow the Buddha's teachings and traverse the same path. It is also sure that because this teaching is one that sprang up out of the earth (actual life), we who actually live in this world can follow it. Chapter 15 makes this point emphatically.

Another important point is the introduction of the Law of Origin—the teaching of the Original Buddha—in the latter half of the chapter. The difference between the Buddha appearing in history (*shakubutsu*) and the Original Buddha (*hombutsu*) has already been explained on page xxiv. The former half of chapter 15 is defined as the introductory part of the Law of Origin, and the latter half of chapter 15, all of chapter 16, and the first half of chapter 17 are the main part. Thus chapter 15 occupies a pivotal position in the division of the Lotus Sutra, and we should read it carefully and wholeheartedly.

When the World-honored One finished preaching the chapter "A Happy Life," numerous bodhisattvas who had come from other lands arose in the great assembly, and with folded hands saluted and said to the Buddha: "World-honored One! If the Buddha will allow us, after his extinction, diligently and zealously to protect and keep, read and recite, copy and worship this sutra in this *sahā*-world, we would preach it abroad in this land."

Thereupon the Buddha firmly answered the host of bodhisattvas: "Enough! My good sons! There is no need for you to protect and keep this sutra. Wherefore? Because in my *sahā*-world there are in fact a great many bodhisattvas, and each one of these bodhisattvas has a great retinue. These are able, after my extinction, to protect and keep, read and recite, and preach abroad this sutra."

When the Buddha had thus spoken, the *sahā*-world trembled and quaked, and from its midst there issued innumerable bodhisattvas. All these bodhisattvas, their golden-hued bodies bearing the same sacred signs as the Buddha, had been dwelling in the infinite space below the *sahā*-world. Hearing the voice of Sakyamuni Buddha preaching, they sprang forth from below.

That these bodhisattvas did not originally dwell in the earth but that they, who were in the infinite space below the *sahā*-world, came out of the earth and rose into the sky has a deep meaning. These bodhisattvas were people who had been freed from illusion in their previous lives by means of the Buddha's teachings. For this reason, they had been dwelling in infinite space. But hearing the Buddha declare that he would entrust the instruction of the *sahā*-world to them, they entered into the earth, namely, this *sahā*-world, experiencing suffering there, and practiced religious disciplines so zealously as to attain the mental state of bodhisattvas. Therefore they rose into the sky again after coming out of the earth. Though the bodhisattvas had been free from illusion in their previous lives, they voluntarily passed through various sufferings and worries in this *sahā*-world for the purpose of saving the people here, endeavored earnestly to become enlightened, and preached the teaching to others. As mentioned before, this is a very important process; without completing such an endeavor, they could not truly acquire the divine power to save the people in the *sahā*-world.

Some of these bodhisattvas were the commanders of great hosts, each leading a retinue that he instructed; some led innumerable followers and others led fewer; and there were also those who were alone, practicing in isolation.

When these innumerable bodhisattvas had emerged from the earth, each went up to the Stupa of the Precious Seven in the sky, where the Tathāgata Abundant Treasures and Sakyamuni Buddha were seated. On their arrival they made obeisance to both the World-honored Ones and extolled them with all manner of bodhisattva hymns. Then they stood to one side, gazing with delight upon both the World-honored Ones. They continued to extol the buddhas thus for fifty minor *kalpas*. During all this time Sakyamuni Buddha sat in silence, and silent also were the four groups, but the fifty *kalpas*, through the divine power of the Buddha, seemed to the great multitude as half a day.

THE FOUR GREAT VOWS OF THE BODHISATTVA. At that time the four groups, also through the divine power of the Buddha, saw the bodhisattvas, who filled the space of innumerable domains. Among this host of bodhisattvas there were four leading teachers: Eminent Conduct (Jōgyō),

Boundless Conduct (Muhengyō), Pure Conduct (Jōgyō), and Steadfast Conduct (Anryūgyō).

As explained in the discussion of the vow (*gan*) in chapter 9, the general vow (*sōgan*) that should be made by all who practice the Buddha-way consists of the following four great vows of the bodhisattva (*shi gu-seigan*), each of which is identified with one of the four great bodhisattvas mentioned above:

1. *Shūjō muhen seigan-do*. However innumerable living beings are, I vow to save them. (Steadfast Conduct)
2. *Bonnō mushū seigan-dan*. However inexhaustible the passions are, I vow to extinguish them. (Pure Conduct)
3. *Hōmon mujin seigan-gaku*. However limitless the Buddha's teachings are, I vow to study them. (Boundless Conduct)
4. *Butsudō mujō seigan-jō*. However infinite the Buddha-truth is, I vow to attain it. (Eminent Conduct)

These four great fundamental vows are thus represented by the above four bodhisattvas. Conversely, the four bodhisattvas can be said to be the symbols of the fundamental vows of all Buddhists.

Each at the head of his great host, these four bodhisattvas with folded hands looked toward Sakyamuni Buddha and inquired of him: "World-honored One! Hast thou few ailments and few troubles, and art thou at ease? Are those whom thou must save readily receiving thy teaching? Do they cause the World-honored One not to become weary?"

Then the World-honored One, in the great assembly of the bodhisattvas, spoke thus: "My good sons! The Tathāgata is at ease, with few ailments and few troubles. These beings are easy to transform and I am free from weariness. Wherefore? Because all these beings for generations have constantly received my instruction and worshiped and honored the former buddhas, cultivating roots of goodness. All these beings on first seeing me and hearing my preaching received it in faith and entered the Tathāgata-wisdom, except those who had previously practiced and learned the small vehicle; but even such people as these I have now caused to hear this sutra and enter the Buddha-wisdom."

Though the Buddha was already advanced in years and had had many difficulties in spreading the Law for the instruction of all living beings, he did not feel this to be a burden or find it difficult. From his attitude we can vividly sense his boundless benevolence.

Thereupon these great bodhisattvas spoke thus in verse:

"Good, good!
Great Hero, World-honored One!
All these living creatures
Are easily transformed by thee,
Are able to inquire into
The profound wisdom of buddhas,
And, hearing, to believe and discern.
We congratulate thee."

Then the World-honored One extolled these supreme chiefs, the great bodhisattvas, saying: "Good, good! My good sons! You may rightly be minded to congratulate the Tathāgata."

Then the Bodhisattva Maitreya and the host of other bodhisattvas all reflected: "From of old we have never seen nor heard of such a host of great bodhisattvas issuing from the earth, standing in the presence of the World-honored Ones with folded hands worshiping and inquiring of the Tathāgata." The Bodhisattva Maitreya desired to resolve his own doubt, so he folded his hands and asked the Buddha in verse:

"These innumerable thousand myriad *koṭis,*
This great host of bodhisattvas,
Are such as we have never seen before.
Be pleased to explain, Honored of Men,
From what places they have come,
For what reason they have assembled.
Huge of body, of transcendent power,
Of wisdom inconceivable,
Firm of will and memory,
With great powers of long-suffering,
Whom all the living rejoice to see:
Whence have they come?"

Meanwhile the buddhas who had emanated from Sakyamuni Buddha and had come from innumerable domains in other quarters eagerly awaited the Buddha's answer to the question put by the Bodhisattva Maitreya. Thereupon Sakyamuni Buddha addressed Maitreya: "Good, Good! Ajita![1] You have well asked the Buddha concerning so great a matter. Do you all, with one mind, don the armor of zeal and exhibit

1. Ajita, "Unconquered," is a title of the Bodhisattva Maitreya.

a firm will, for the Tathāgata now intends to reveal and proclaim the wisdom of buddhas, the sovereign and supernatural power of buddhas, the lion-eagerness of buddhas, and the awe-inspiring forceful power of buddhas."

Then the World-honored One, desiring to proclaim this teaching over again, said in verse that he was about to expound what he had never revealed before and called upon the bodhisattvas to listen to it single-mindedly. Having spoken these verses, he again addressed the Bodhisattva Maitreya: "Ajita! All these great bodhisattvas, innumerable and numberless, who have issued from the earth, and whom you have never seen before—I in this *sahā*-world, after attaining Perfect Enlightenment, instructed and led all these bodhisattvas, controlled their minds, and caused them to set their thoughts on the Way." Thus the Buddha extolled the fact that these bodhisattvas had practiced many religious disciplines and that they possessed high virtues.

Then the Bodhisattva Maitreya, the numberless bodhisattvas, and other beings were seized with doubt and perplexity, wondering at this rare thing and reflecting: "How has the World-honored One, in so short a time, instructed such innumerable, countless great bodhisattvas and caused them to abide in Perfect Enlightenment?" Then, addressing the Buddha, they said: "World-honored One! The Tathāgata, when he was a prince, left the Śākya palace and not far from the city of Gayā took his seat on the wisdom terrace, and attained Perfect Enlightenment. From that time but forty years have passed. World-honored One! In so short a time how hast thou done such great Buddha-deeds, and by Buddha-power and Buddha-merit taught such an innumerable host of great bodhisattvas to attain Perfect Enlightenment?

"World-honored One! This host of great bodhisattvas, even if a man counted them for numberless years, he could not come to an end or reach their limit. All these from the far past under innumerable and countless buddhas have planted their roots of goodness and accomplished the bodhisattva-way, constantly living the noble life. World-honored One! Such a matter as this the world will find it hard to believe. It is just as if there were a man of fine complexion and black hair, twenty-five years old, who pointed to centenarians and said: 'These are my sons,' and as if those centenarians also pointed to the youth and said: 'This is our father who begot and reared us.' This matter is hard of belief. So also is it with the Buddha, whose attainment of the Way is really not long since. Yet this great host of bodhisattvas, for numberless thousands of myriads of *koṭis* of *kalpas*, for the sake of the Buddha-way, have devoted themselves with zeal, and they have well perceived all of it; they are treasures amongst men and of extreme rareness in all worlds.

"Today the World-honored One has just said that when he attained the Buddha-way he from the beginning caused them to aspire to enlightenment, instructed and led, and caused them to proceed toward Perfect Enlightenment. It is not long since the World-honored One became a buddha, yet he has been able to do this great, meritorious deed. Though we still believe that what the Buddha opportunely preached and the words the Buddha uttered have never been false, and also the Buddha's knowledge is all perceived by us, yet if newly converted bodhisattvas hear this statement after the Buddha's extinction, they may not receive it in faith and this will give rise to causes of wrong action to the destruction of the Law. So, World-honored One, be pleased to explain it, removing our doubts, and so that all thy good sons in future generations, on hearing this matter, shall also not beget doubt."

Then Maitreya repeated his request in verse. In the next chapter, "Revelation of the [Eternal] Life of the Tathāgata," the World-honored One replies to the bodhisattvas in detail and reveals to them the entity of the Buddha.

In the verses spoken by the Bodhisattva Maitreya occur the following words: "They have ably learned the bodhisattva-way, / And are as untainted with worldly things / As the lotus flower in the water." These words represent the ideal way of life that the Buddha teaches us in the Lotus Sutra. We should not withdraw from society but should lead beautiful and pure lives within society. The ideal of the Lotus Sutra consists in making all society pure and beautiful. The title *Sutra of the Lotus Flower of the Wonderful Law* expresses this ideal.

CHAPTER 16

Revelation of the [Eternal] Life of the Tathāgata

Is Buddhism Philosophy or Religion? The book *Buddhism* by Christmas Humphreys has been widely read in the West. The author, a distinguished English lawyer and also a devout Buddhist, wrote in his preface: "Indeed, by the usual tests, Buddhism is not a religion so much as a spiritual philosophy whose attitude to life is as cool and objective as that of the modern scientist. But it lives, it lives tremendously. . . ." We cannot help admiring the fact that Mr. Humphreys, a Westerner, has grasped the essence of Buddhism with such accuracy. Indeed, he may have been enabled to understand Buddhism in its true and pure state because he was born and bred in England, which has no tradition of Buddhism.

When we reconsider the teaching of the Law of Appearance in the Lotus Sutra, we realize that though Buddhism is indeed a religion in one respect, which will be made clear later in this chapter, at the same time, with Christmas Humphreys, we can say that Buddhism is a great system of philosophy and ethics. Philosophy is the science of the study of this world, human life, and the fundamental principles of things. Ethics is the path of duty. The teaching of the Lotus Sutra that we have studied so far may be tentatively summed up as philosophy and ethics.

However, when we thoroughly investigate the teaching of the Lotus Sutra, the most profound teaching of the Buddha, we realize that it is also the teaching of a religion that enables us to be saved from our mental suffering, something which cannot be accomplished by learning alone, making human life brighter and leading the world toward peace. The profundity of the Lotus Sutra as a religious teaching is first revealed in chapter 16, "Revelation of the [Eternal] Life of the Tathāgata." While chapter 2, "Tactfulness," is regarded as the core of the Law of Appearance, chapter 16 is considered as the essence of the Law of Origin and also as the key chapter of the entire Lotus Sutra.

THREE IMPORTANT TEACHINGS. From ancient times, the chapter "Revelation of the [Eternal] Life of the Tathāgata" has been held to include three important teachings: "opening up the short and revealing the long" (*kaigon kennon*), "accepting the historical Buddha as a temporary manifestation of the eternal Sakyamuni Buddha and revealing the eternity of Sakyamuni Buddha" (*kaishaku kempon*), and "opening up the expedient teaching and revealing the true teaching" (*kaigon kenjitsu*).

The first teaching, "opening up the short and revealing the long," means that we start from an easily discerned fact, gradually tracing its origin, and discover its ultimate implications. "An easily discerned fact" is that Sakyamuni Buddha appeared in this world, attained enlightenment, and preached to many people to cause them to realize enlightenment. Where did this fact originate? Was Sakyamuni Buddha suddenly awakened to a holy Law having no relationship to past human history? This cannot be. The Law must have existed before the birth of the Buddha and since the origin of human beings—indeed, since the creation of this universe. Because the Law existed, the Buddha perceived it.

Though human beings had been gradually evolving since the origin of human life, they did not know the true Law but lived according to their instincts or by means of a mistaken law. As long as they continued to do so, their true development was impossible. It was only logical that someone should awaken to the correct and true Law, and appear in this world for the purpose of preaching it to other people. The time was ripening for the appearance of such a person, and the culmination was the appearance of the Buddha in this world.

The appearance of the Buddha and his attainment of buddhahood first revealed to people the Law, which no other person had realized, although it had been in existence from time immemorial. This becomes clear in the chapter "Revelation of the [Eternal] Life of the Tathāgata." The teaching of "opening up the short and revealing the long" has a very important meaning because through the easily grasped fact of the appearance of the Buddha in this world and his attainment of buddhahood, we can understand the Law that has existed since the eternal past.

The second teaching is "accepting the historical Buddha as a temporary manifestation of the eternal Sakyamuni Buddha and revealing the eternity of Sakyamuni Buddha." In a broad sense, the term "appearing buddha" (*shakubutsu*) refers to such buddhas as Abundant Treasures and Amitābha, not to mention Sakyamuni Buddha, who appeared as a man in this world. When tracing the principle behind the manifestation of such appearing buddhas, we realize that obviously there must be a buddha as their foundation. Because the truth is only one, it must have a single foundation even if it appears in various different forms. When we thus consider the principle of Sakyamuni Buddha, who was the appearing Buddha in this world, we realize that behind this manifestation is the one Eternal Original Buddha. This is the teaching of "accepting the historical Buddha as a temporary manifestation of the eternal Sakyamuni Buddha and revealing the eternity of Sakyamuni Buddha," which is made clear in this chapter.

The third teaching is "opening up the expedient teaching and revealing the true teaching." The word *gon,* "expedient," means "provisional" or "temporary," as in the term "provisional appearance" (*gongen*), which indicates a buddha's appearing provisionally in the form of a god. This word also means "vice" or "assistant" as opposed to "principal" or "original," as in the term "vice-high priest" (*gon-no-sōjō*), a Buddhist high priest of the second highest rank. The expedient teaching here means the temporary or provisional teaching as the means or way of leading all living beings to the truth. The provisional teaching is very sacred, but it is still a "temporary" teaching as a means of preaching the truth and is also a "secondary" teaching.

The faith of all living beings has been raised to a very high level by means of such a temporary teaching, but they have not yet attained the highest state of mind. The chapter "Revelation of the [Eternal] Life of the Tathāgata" reveals the true and supreme teaching, thus opening up the expedient teaching and revealing the true teaching.

As chapter 16 includes these three important teachings, we should review the teaching of the Law of Appearance in order to realize clearly the inevitability with which the teaching of the Law of Appearance leads to the teaching of the Law of Origin. It is also most important that we understand the essence of religion before proceeding to the main subject of this chapter.

The main reason that the teaching of Buddhism often seems not to be a religion in the usual sense of the word is that Sakyamuni Buddha did not admit the existence of a transcendent god controlling man's destiny. The Buddha never preached belief in a god who created this world and presides over the workings of nature—an absolute being by whom people are saved if they pray to or worship him.

The Sanskrit word *buddha* is derived from the word *bodhi*, indicating the idea of "exercise of reason." The mental state of enlightenment that the Buddha preached can be understood by anyone who has a high enough degree of reason. This enlightenment is not something visionary that only an inspired person can perceive, nor is it something bestowed by an absolute being in whom one simply has faith.

Sakyamuni Buddha did not regard this universe as God's creation or his conquest, but as resulting from the relation of cause and effect by which all phenomena are produced. Causation means a primary cause (*in*) and a secondary cause (*en*) combining to produce an effect (*ka*) and a recompense (*hō*). In this world, there is nothing unchangeable or fixed in form. All things have a direct cause (primary cause, *in*). When this comes into contact with an opportunity or condition (secondary cause, *en*), the result of this conjunction appears as a phenomenon (effect, *ka*). This effect leaves behind traces (recompense, *hō*): thus Sakyamuni Buddha interpreted all things in the world.

THE SEAL OF THE THREE LAWS. The combination of a primary cause and a secondary cause leads every action to have an effect and a recompense. When a primary cause is annihilated or when, even if it exists, it does not come into contact with a secondary cause, it does not produce an effect and a recompense. Therefore, in this world, there is nothing existing in an eternal, fixed, and unchangeable form. This is the law "All things are impermanent." Is there nothing at all unchangeable in this world? Yes, there is one immutable thing—the truth that presides over the existence, the working, and the changes of all things. Only this truth alone is unchangeable.

Sakyamuni Buddha also taught the truth that nothing in this world has an isolated existence, without any relation to other things, but that all things exist in relationship with one another and are interdependent. This is the law "Nothing has an ego." At first glance, there does not seem to be any relation between the earth on which we stand, the sea stretching to the horizon, and the clouds far above in the sky. But when we consider how clouds are produced, why seawater is salt, and how the earth receives moisture, we soon understand the close relationship of earth, sea, and sky. We know that clouds are produced by water vapor that evaporates from the earth, sea, and rivers; clouds precipitate rain or snow that falls on the earth and moistens it; and seawater is salt because river water dissolves salts contained in the earth and carries them to the sea, where the concentration of salt becomes stronger through the evaporation of water. This is an example of how nothing in the universe has a completely isolated existence.

Of course, Sakyamuni Buddha did not preach the formation of the universe as a science or a philosophy. He preached it to cause all people to understand thoroughly how people should live and what human life should be. His teaching always concerned man and humanism.

How should we put the universal truths that all things are impermanent and that nothing has an ego to practical use in our daily lives? It was to answer this question that the Buddha preached the law "Nirvana is quiescence."

We undergo various sufferings in life because we are swayed by changing phenomena and are influenced by immediate gain or loss. If we come to have the spirit of perfect freedom, being detached from these temporary and superficial considerations, we will be in a spiritual condition of peace and calm even when we are in a situation that others consider to be very painful. This is the state of "Nirvana is quiescence" in relation to the law "All things are impermanent."

The reason for our inability to succeed in something, for having a conflict or dispute, or for feeling displeasure, often comes from the fact that we lack harmony in our relations with other people and things. The earth revolves around the sun. The moon revolves around the earth. The innumerable stars twinkling in the night sky have the same kinds of relationships. The sun, the earth, the moon, and the stars all move according to the law of gravitation. They move without colliding because the force of gravitation is balanced, creating a harmony among them. If this harmony were destroyed, the sun, the earth, and the moon would collide. If this kind of thing took place with all planets and stars, the universe would be destroyed.

Human life is the same. Each person is a constituent member of the universe; if he maintained harmony in his various relationships with other people and things so that a balance were maintained among them, dispute and trouble in this world would disappear. But such a state cannot be realized in this world. Why? Because each person has his own small "ego." People differ in their interests and feelings, and are out of harmony with each other because too many people are self-centered and are concerned only with their personal profit, welfare, and comfort. If all human beings abandoned their own small "egos" and devoted themselves to respecting and helping one another, a great harmony would be generated among them and true peace in their daily lives would come about. This is the state of "Nirvana is quiescence" in relation to the law "Nothing has an ego."

These three laws—"All things are impermanent," "Nothing has an ego," and "Nirvana is quiescence"—are the fundamental principles of Buddhism and as such are called the Seal of the Three Laws (*sambō-in*). It is no exaggeration to say that all the teachings of Buddhism are derived from these three laws.

How should we practice the Seal of the Three Laws in our daily lives? The answer to this question is found in the doctrines of the Four Noble Truths, the Eightfold Path, the Law of the Twelve Causes, and the Six Perfections.

In the doctrine of the Four Noble Truths, the Buddha taught first that man must realize that his existence is suffering and must recognize this actual condition of suffering (the Truth of Suffering), not evade or deny it. However, man cannot alleviate his suffering just by recognizing it. So the Buddha taught that he must go further and investigate the cause of suffering, reflecting on it and clearly discerning it (the Truth of Cause). The original cause of suffering is ignorance, as shown in the doctrine of the Law of the Twelve Causes.

Once one has been able to discern the cause of his sufferings, the Buddha taught, if he can remove his ignorance as the original cause of suffering his suffering will be extinguished (the Truth of Extinction). Lastly, the Buddha showed that the way enabling man to be led to the Truth of Extinction is the practice of the Eightfold Path and the Six Perfections (the Truth of the Path).

Here let us review the doctrine of the Eightfold Path, the eight ways of daily life, consisting of right view, right thinking, right speech, right action, right living, right endeavor, right memory, and right meditation.

First we must thoroughly analyze the word "right" because this word may be misunderstood if it is considered according to the index of today's morality. Briefly, the word "right" means "in accord with the truth." For example, if man looks at things from a narrow egoistic viewpoint, he cannot possibly discern the real state of things and his judgment of them will not be well balanced. When he gets rid of his egoistic viewpoint and prejudice and looks at things with a clear mind, he can see the real state of things. This way of looking rightly at things is based on the wisdom of the Buddha.

When thinking about things with a self-centered mind or with a selfish aim, we are liable to fall into mistaken ideas that are not in accord with truth or are even directly opposed to truth. For instance, suppose that someone has the following idea: "To increase the prosperity of our own country, it is all right to sacrifice the people of other countries," or "You must make allowances for our deceiving or injuring others for the sake of our personal welfare." It is obvious that these ideas are wrong when applied to other people. But when a person thinks about things on the basis of his own country, or himself and his family, he adopts such selfish ideas without compunction. There have been many instances of this way of thinking throughout history; in fact, there are innumerable examples today.

When man looks at things not from a selfish standpoint but from a much greater standpoint—from the same standpoint as the Buddha—he can view and evaluate all things on their own merits. The word "right" applies to this way of looking at things. When man views things according to a partial viewpoint, he cannot see the truth. If he puts on red-lensed glasses, the whole world appears red. If he puts on green-tinted spectacles, everything looks green. He cannot have a right view till he looks at things without colored spectacles.

When man perceives the things of this world through his five sense organs or thinks about them with his mind, they seem to be differentiated. To look only at the differentiated state of things (temporality, *ke*) appearing externally and not the equal state (void, *kū*) existing originally is the superficial way of looking at things of ordinary people. That all things in this world are originally equal (void, *kū*) is the important core of the Buddha's teachings, but to view only the original equal state of things and to disregard the differentiated state appearing in external forms is also a one-sided way of looking at things. A philosopher who studies the fundamental principle of things may well be unhappy in his personal life and a failure socially. This may be the result of his lopsided view of things.

To take a right view of things in the true sense, it is necessary to refrain from viewing things exclusively as either temporality (*ke*) or void (*kū*) but to combine these two viewpoints. This third way of looking at things is called *chūtai,* or the "truth of the middle"[1]—a truth that is almost the same as that of the Middle Path (*chūdō*). The Middle Path means not to be one-sided, but it does not imply to take the middle position on every issue, leaning neither right nor left. The Middle Path preached by Sakyamuni Buddha does not mean a rigid path existing exactly in the middle between two extremes. Because it is one of the most important teachings of the Buddha, the truth of the Middle Path will be discussed here.

At the time that Sakyamuni Buddha lived, there were numerous religious teachings in India. One religion insisted that because man's various desires are natural to him, to seek to satisfy them is the way of emancipation from the bonds of illusion and suffering. Another religion preached that an ascetic life strictly suppressing all desires is the only way to lead man to freedom from the bonds of illusion and suffering.

Asceticism was very rigorous at that time in India. An ascetic tried to suppress completely his carnal appetites and his desire for comfort. There was even a school of naked ascetics who regarded wearing clothes as forbidden. Other ascetics mortified their bodies by all kinds of painful practices, including living in a tree for days at a time, burning the skin with fire, slashing themselves with knives, or sitting on sharp stakes driven into the earth. The most extreme group insisted that a person who is free from the bonds of illusion and suffering must eat nothing, and considered death by starvation as the supreme joy.

Sakyamuni Buddha, who was not attracted to the hedonistic extreme, first tried to pursue enlightenment by means of asceticism. He visited two famous ascetics in succession, and after practicing their teachings under their guidance, he completely mastered them. Though he was earnestly asked to remain by each of these two ascetics, he found their teachings insufficient to enable him to attain true enlightenment, and turned away. Next Sakyamuni tried ascetic practices by himself. He underwent such extreme austerities as eating only one grain of rice and sesame seed a day.

Such ascetic experience may not have been useless, but when Sakyamuni eventually realized that asceticism was not the right way to lead him to enlightenment, he abruptly gave up such practices. He then went to the Nairañjnanā River and cleansed his body. Then he drank a bowl of milk gruel that a village girl gave him, and gradually regained his

1. *Kūtai, ketai,* and *chūtai*—the truth of the void, truth of temporality, and truth of the middle—are the three kinds of truth (*santai*) in the Tendai teaching.

strength. He proceeded to a place near the village of Bodhgayā by way of Mount Pragdodhi, and sat down under the Bodhi tree. There, sitting quietly alone, he entered into deep meditation and finally attained enlightenment.

After that, he went to the Deer Park near Vārāṇasī (Benares), where were gathered the five ascetics who had accompanied him in his austerities. The teaching that he preached to these five ascetics in his first sermon included the doctrines of the Four Noble Truths, the Middle Path, and the Eightfold Path.

Sakyamuni Buddha said to the five men: "Monks! In this world there are two extremes that you must avoid." The two extremes are those of hedonism and of asceticism. The Buddha, who rejected these two extremes as unreasonable, proclaimed the following: "By avoiding these two extremes, the Tathāgata has attained full enlightenment—the Middle Path." It is significant indeed that the Buddha preached the Middle Path in the very first of as many as eighty-four thousand sermons.

Then Sakyamuni preached the following: "What is the foundation of the Middle Path? It is the Eightfold Path: right view, right thinking, right speech, right action, right living, right endeavor, right memory, and right meditation. This is the Middle Path, which the Tathāgata has realized. It opens man's eyes, gives rise to right wisdom, and leads him to mental peace and quiet and, further, to nirvana."

As shown plainly here, the Middle Path realized by the Buddha has the following meaning: To lead a life of extreme hedonism or to practice extreme asceticism is just like looking at the world through red- or green-colored glasses; it is not the way of looking rightly at all things in the world. It is, so to speak, the way of a viewpoint covered with the clouds of illusion. This is not the way to reach nirvana. Man must not take such a biased and fixed position but must view things, and act, according to the truth.

The word "right" that is prefixed to every word in the doctrine of the Eightfold Path has the same meaning as "middle" in the doctrine of the Middle Path. "Right" means to be in accord with the truth, as mentioned above, and also indicates the idea of being in harmony with the truth. Following is a parable related by the Buddha to explain this idea.

THE TEACHING OF THE HARP. This is a story from the time that Sakyamuni Buddha was staying on Vulture Peak near Rājagṛha (Rajgir). In the nearby forest was an ascetic called Srona, who devoted himself to rigorous spiritual disciplines. His austerities were so severe that he was said to be supreme in asceticism among the many disciples of the Buddha. But he was not able to free himself from the bonds of illusion and suffering, because his austerities were too exaggerated.

Finally Srona succumbed to the following illusion: I am so wonderful that I am known as the foremost disciple in assiduous disciplines. Nevertheless I cannot attain enlightenment. I cannot go any further than this in assiduous discipline. Had I not better give it up and go home? I have enough property to live comfortably for the rest of my life. Should I take this way rather than lead a life of religious disciplines? Srona was tormented by this mental dilemma. Perceiving that his disciple was going through a great spiritual crisis, Sakyamuni Buddha called on Srona in the forest and asked him about his mental state in an ordinary, everyday tone of voice full of benevolence. Srona told the Buddha what he was thinking, concealing nothing.

Then the Buddha said, "Srona! I hear that you were very good at playing the harp before becoming a monk. Is that true?" Srona replied that it was as the Buddha had said. Then the Buddha continued: "You know the harp well. Does it produce good music if the strings are stretched too tight?" Srona answered, "No." Then the Buddha asked, "Well, does the harp make music if the strings are too loose?" Srona again answered, "No." The Buddha asked once more, "How about when the strings are stretched just right? Can it produce good music?" Srona answered, "Yes, it can."

The Buddha then instructed Srona: "Srona! Training for enlightenment is just like adjusting the strings of a harp. If you are inclined toward extreme assiduity, the strings of your mind will be stretched too tight, and the mind will not be in a state of peace. If you are not assiduous enough, the strings of your mind will be loose, and this will lead to idleness. Srona! Remain in a moderate assiduity and maintain equality among your senses. Try to maintain moderation in yourself, without inclining toward the extreme of assiduity."

Thus the Buddha taught Srona, carefully and affectionately. From this short story, we can feel keenly how unfathomably great a personality Sakyamuni Buddha had.

In the Sutra of the Forty-two Chapters, the Buddha taught:

"A harp emits no sound

If the strings are stretched too much.
It also sounds nothing
If they are stretched too little.
Only when the strings are stretched just right,
All music is in tune."

With a superficial understanding of these words of the Buddha, we can take them to mean: "Just maintain a middle position, being neither too strict nor too lax." When we apply this interpretation to the practice of religious discipline, we find that it means the middle way between extreme hedonism and extreme asceticism, and the result is our acknowledgement of these two extremes. This implies that the extreme of hedonism should be admitted to some extent, and also the extreme of asceticism. The most moderate way exists between these two extremes. To speak in much plainer language, if extreme hedonism is zero and extreme asceticism is ten, the moderate state would exist at about five.

However, this is a mistaken interpretation. When we play a harp, the strings cannot sound sweetly if they are either too loose or too tight; both indicate, so to speak, a state of zero. The harp will produce its best sound when its strings are stretched moderately. But the optimum tautness of the strings is a matter of great delicacy. The harp will produce a discordant sound with the strings at any state of tension except this exact degree, also indicating a state of zero. But if the tautness of the strings is just right, the harp will be in tune, producing a sweet sound. This implies a change from zero to ten. Such a state is that of being in harmony. The exact tension of the strings resulting in good harmony means that this particular degree of tautness suits perfectly the tune that the harp is intended to produce. In short, such a condition perfectly fits its purpose. Therefore, the idea of being in accord with the truth expresses that of being fit for the purpose.

The same thing can be said of human life. The person who has really attained enlightenment is one who attains a way of life that is in accord with the truth. His thought and conduct are naturally fit for the purpose. He can also choose a way of life that is always in harmony with everything in the world. Thus it is impossible for us to find the "right" or "middle" path simply by choosing the midpoint between two extremes. Each extreme represents a fundamental difference. If we conduct ourselves based on the truth of causation, discussed on page 188, without adhering to fixed ideas, we can always lead a life that is perfectly fit for its purpose, and one that is in harmony with the truth. This is the teaching of the Middle Path.

How can we attain such a mental state? The teaching in which the Buddha shows us concretely how to attain this in our daily life is none other than the doctrine of the Eightfold Path. Following is a brief explanation of this doctrine: Look at things rightly (right view), think about things rightly (right thinking), speak the right words (right speech), perform right conduct (right action), lead a right human life (right living), endeavor to live rightly (right endeavor), constantly aim the mind in the right direction (right memory), and consistently keep the right mind and never be agitated by anything (right meditation). As mentioned above, the word "right" has the same meaning as "middle" in the doctrine of the Middle Path.

Next we shall briefly discuss the doctrine of the Six Perfections. This teaching shows us the six kinds of bodhisattva practices for the benefit of society and other people, while the doctrine of the Eightfold Path is chiefly the way of individual practice by which we are able to free ourselves from illusion. The Six Perfections include donation, keeping the precepts, perseverance, assiduity, meditation, and wisdom.

To render service to others in all spheres—spiritual, material, and physical—is donation. To remove illusion from one's own mind in accordance with the precepts taught by the Buddha, leading a right life and gaining the power to save others by endeavoring to perfect oneself, is keeping the precepts. Always to assume a generous attitude toward others, enduring any difficulty and maintaining a tranquil mind without arrogance even at the height of prosperity, is perseverance. To proceed straight toward an important goal without being sidetracked by trivial things is assiduity. To maintain a cool and unagitated mind under all circumstances is meditation. And to have the power of discerning the real aspect of all things is wisdom. The doctrine of the Six Perfections teaches us the right way to practice in order to save other people and society through these six practices.

TRUE MEDITATION. A full explanation has not yet been given of meditation as one of the Six Perfections. Indeed, this word has such a profound meaning that we cannot generalize concerning it.

From the standpoint of its result, "meditation" means to maintain a cool and unagitated mind under all circumstances. But it also means the practice necessary in order to attain this result. In other words, it indicates the idea of contemplation, or concentration of the mind on a single object while sitting quietly alone.

On what should we concentrate? That is the important question. And this indeed is the point at which religion differs from philosophy and morality.

However hard we may concentrate on something, we cannot become absolutely free from our sufferings as long as we are absorbed only in immediate phenomena with a self-centered attitude. For example, if we devote ourselves to thinking of such a selfish matter as wishing to be rid of uneasiness and irritation concerning the management of our business, or wishing to recover from illness, it is obvious that we cannot be freed from such trouble for a moment, because our mind is swayed by our business or our illness. This kind of mental absorption is not meditation but a mere struggling with illusion.

To reflect on our past conduct, criticizing ourselves for what we think to be wrong and determining to correct it, is a kind of meditation. It can be said to be meditation from a moral point of view. This is a very fine practice that is useful for improving our character.

To think still more deeply than this about a subject is meditation without a self-centered idea. To probe deeply into such matters as the formation of the world, the way of human life, and the ideal society—this is meditation from the philosophical point of view. This kind of meditation is also a fine practice that enhances our character, adding depth to our ideas and in turn benefiting society.

However, regrettably, we cannot obtain a true state of mental peace (nirvana) through the forms of meditation mentioned above. This is because we can go only as far as the range of human knowledge permits, however sternly we may reflect on ourselves and however deeply we may probe philosophically into the ideal way of the world and human life. If we say that man cannot lead himself to nirvana even though he reflects on his conduct, repents of wrong conduct, and determines to practice good conduct, the following question will naturally arise: "That must be so when reflecting on morality and society and making resolutions on the basis of that reflection. But is it not the way to nirvana to reflect on oneself in the light of the Buddha's teachings and to determine one's actions according to them?" Indeed, this is one process by which we progress toward nirvana, but the way to attain nirvana is not as easy as that. If it were only a matter of understanding and controlling one's superficial, conscious mind, the problem would be relatively simple. Most people can control their conscious mind by means of the Buddha's teachings through practice of religious disciplines. But man also has a mind of which he is not aware. He cannot grasp it because he is unconscious of it. He cannot control it because of being unable to grasp it. This kind of mind is called *ālaya* or *manas* in Sanskrit and corresponds to the subconscious mind in scientific terminology.

All that one has experienced, thought, and felt in the past remains in the depths of one's subconscious mind. Psychologists recognize that the subconscious mind not only exerts a great influence on man's character and his mental functions but even causes various disorders. Because it is normally beyond our reach, we cannot control the subconscious mind by mere reflection and meditation.

Here let us recall the problem of karma (*gō*), mentioned in chapter 7. The karma that we have now is very deep-rooted and complex, and includes the "former karma" (*shuku-gō*) that human beings have accumulated since their beginning. We also possess the "former karma" that we have produced ourselves in previous existences and to some extent the "former karma" that our ancestors have produced. And of course we possess the "present karma" (*gen-gō*) that we have produced ourselves in this life. Is it possible for an ordinary person to become free from these karmas and enter the mental state of perfect freedom (escape from the world of illusions) by means of his own wisdom? This is clearly out of the question. What then, if anything, can we do about it?

Here let us recall the doctrine of the Three Thousand Realms in One Mind, also discussed in chapter 7. This doctrine teaches us that the three thousand realms with all their relationships are included in a single random thought, and that the mental states leading us to the realms both of hell and of the buddha are included in that one thought. Practically speaking, how can we control such random thoughts? This is not a question that can be answered by human knowledge. One random thought arising out of innumerable thoughts—no scholar, however learned, can teach us to cope with each thought that we hit upon. How should we cope with each one of these thoughts that occur?

This kind of problem is beyond the sphere of philosophy and cannot be answered in terms of morality, either. What can solve this kind of problem? Only religion can do so. There is nothing else that can do this. Confronting a problem of this scope and profundity, we can grasp clearly the true value of religion. We realize that our true salvation must be brought about ultimately by religion.

A religion, especially an advanced religion like Buddhism, includes philosophy, morality, and ethics. Indeed, Buddhism can be said to consist almost entirely of the teaching of philosophy and morality. However, when we make a profound study of the teaching, we find there is something beyond this that touches our hearts directly. It is like a light that envelops us warmly and shines brightly, illuminating our way. It is something that enlivens us and allows us to develop fully according to our true potential. This "something" is nothing other than faith. Christmas Humphreys points this out plainly in the preface of his book *Buddhism:* "But it lives, it lives tremendously. . . ."

WHAT RELIGION SHOULD BE. What in fact is religion? We must consider religion from its very origin. In all periods men have felt fear of things more powerful than they. In the course of time, their fears changed to feelings of worship and awe.

Primitive man feared the moon and stars, not to mention the sun. They had the same feeling toward the snow-capped mountains soaring above them, the great rivers that sometimes flow quietly and at other times overflow their banks and cause heavy floods that ravage the land, and the boundless ocean stretching to the horizon. They revered birds because of their wonderful ability to fly, and stood in awe of powerful beasts like elephants and lions. Man's fear of natural things changed gradually to the feeling of awe and finally to that of worship of such forces and beings as gods. This kind of faith is called nature worship or animism.

Next, people came to believe that in the heavens and in the air there were spirits that had such supernatural power that human beings could not control them. These spirits were not characterized by love and compassion but only by the possession of power. Therefore people were afraid of being cursed by these forces unless they worshiped and propitiated them. They believed these spirits could both cause and prevent such calamities as diseases, bad harvests, storms, and rough seas. They trembled in fear of these spirits and worshiped them, praying to be spared misfortune and granted blessings. This kind of faith is called spirit worship.

Primitive man believed that such spirits dwelt within physical things either temporarily or permanently. This abode might be a nonliving thing, such as a stone, a feather, or an implement, or it might be a great tree, an animal or bird, or even a human being. They regarded these things as protecting them, their families, and their villages from harm, and they worshiped them earnestly. This kind of faith is called fetishism. Some primitive men considered a specific animal, plant, or nonliving thing as their ancestor. They worshiped it to be spared harm and to obtain happiness. Such a faith is called totemism.

A more advanced form of religion than the above is primitive pantheism, whose believers regard everything in the universe as god. There is also a primitive monotheism, which proclaims that one and only one god exists in this world and presides over all things, including good and evil, in this world.

These religions remain at so low a stage of spiritual development that modern people consider them mere superstitious beliefs. This is because they establish something as an absolute, to be worshiped and prayed to, although religion should be originally related to man. It is odd to worship such an animal, plant, or nonliving thing and to pray to it. Such things should not be worshiped and prayed to but should be freely put to practical use by people for the promotion of their happiness.

For example, the sun is an absolute necessity for man's existence, but it is only a thing, not a god. When in the future human knowledge has advanced much further than at present, there is a fair chance of his being able to produce a substitute for the sun. The moon is a mere thing, too, although it was worshiped as a god in ancient times. But now manned spacecraft have landed several times on the moon. This lunar exploration will culminate in practical application of its findings to human life. Rivers, seas, and mountains are nothing but things whose power should be put to practical use by human knowledge to enrich human life. The same can be said of the various animals and plants. If the words "put to practical use" seem to be too anthropocentric, they can be replaced by the expression "be coexistent and coprosperous" by making the best use of the life of natural things.

These matters belong to the sphere of science (human knowledge) in a broad sense and should never become the object of religion, although such primitive religion is popular even today. From the preceding brief survey of the origin and development of religion, we can understand why this kind of religion is mistaken and superstitious.

Problems that can be solved by human knowledge should be so solved to the last. This is not a new idea but is an unchangeable truth. From this viewpoint, it is no wonder that a religious organization should have a general hospital that uses the most highly advanced modern medical techniques and equipment to treat its patients.

Sakyamuni Buddha has taught this truth in various sutras. For instance, in the *Śīgalovāda-sūtras* (*Shikara-otsu-roppōrai-kyō*), the Buddha instructed a young man in Rājagṛha as to how he should be filial to his parents, saying, "If your parents suffer from disease, you must soon place them under a doctor's care and must nurse them."

In chapter 17 of the Lotus Sutra, "Discrimination of Merits," the Buddha preaches as follows: "Ajita! If anyone, after my extinction, hears this sutra, and is able either to receive and keep, or himself copy or cause others to copy it, he has already erected monasteries and built red sandalwood temples of thirty-two shrines, tall as eight *tāla* trees, lofty, spacious, splendid, in which abide hundreds, thousands of *bhikshus;* adorned also with gardens, groves, and bathing pools, promenades and meditation cells; with clothing, victuals, bedding, medicaments, and all aids to pleasure provided to the full therein." From the use of the word "medicaments" in the sutra we can judge that it was natural even for monks to take medicine, not to rely on prayers, when they fell ill.

This attitude is not confined to illness and medicine. In the case of economics, for example, the Buddha never teaches us to worship something in order to escape from poverty. In the *Saṃyuktāgama-sūtra* (*Zō-agon-gyō*) he spoke to the following effect: "First study hard at a technical skill and then earn an income by using it as a right means. Having gained an income, without wasting it, you divide it into four parts, of which one-fourth is allowed for living expenses, two-fourths for business expenses, and the remaining one-fourth for savings as a safeguard against loss of income. . . . If you work rightly and seek money with right wisdom, money will accumulate about you day by day. However, from such money, you must give some to public welfare and must accommodate your friends and relatives in need."

What a pragmatic and moral teaching this is! Thus Sakyamuni teaches us to try to solve our problems by human knowledge whenever this is possible.

Plants, animals, and stones are not objects of worship to which one prays to be healed of illness. They are natural things to be used appropriately for their medical properties through human knowledge and endeavor. Nearly all physical suffering can be eliminated not by the force of the spirit of such an animal as a fox or a snake but by human knowledge, technology, and endeavor.

THE SUFFERING OF DEATH AND LIFE. There is one problem of human life that cannot be solved through human knowledge and endeavor. This is the problem of death. Man's life expectancy has increased considerably with the development of medical science and undoubtedly will be further prolonged in the future. Nevertheless, death invariably comes to us all. We instinctively feel death to be undesirable and frightening. Young people do not feel so horrified by death because they are so full of vitality and strong feelings that they do not think of death as it really is. They are not afraid of death because they do not think about it. If they gave it serious consideration, they would probably tremble with fear.

A friend of mine said to his twelve-year-old daughter, "There is a chance that hydrogen bombs will be dropped upon us in Japan." His daughter innocently asked him, "If that happened, what would become of us?" He answered her half-jokingly, "Well, we would all die. We would all die in an instant. Probably we would die an easy, gentle death." The girl suddenly turned pale and cried, "I hate death! I hate it!" He told me that he had never seen her face filled with such horror.

Even a twelve-year-old girl reacts this way when she thinks seriously of death. How seriously must people past middle age think of it! However healthy a person may be, he sometimes thinks of death when he reaches middle age. The dark shade of death occasionally flits through his mind. At such moments, he feels an indescribable thrill of horror, as though an icy wind were blowing on his neck.

How much more fear must a person who is seriously ill feel! His heart must almost burst with horror and loneliness when he thinks of death, which may come upon him at any moment. Moreover, the pain of his illness will torment him. The thought of death will double his pain during his remaining days.

Someone may say that he is not especially afraid of death. But he says this when he is not confronted by death. He will surely not be able to keep his composure when the moment of death actually approaches. Sometimes, though, the suffering of pain actually makes us forget the true pangs of death. When we feel extreme pain our minds are so filled with the desire for freedom from pain that often we are able to forget our terror of death.

When we think of a condemned criminal who is in good health, we can easily imagine how keenly he must feel the pangs of death. A condemned criminal who is healthy does not have either sufficient suffering or sufficient pleasure to make him forget death. He constantly sits within the walls of his solitary cell and waits quietly for the coming of death. He is truly confronted by death; his suffering must be great beyond comparison.

In a sense, however, all people are just like criminals sentenced to death. The time will come when they will all surely die. When medical science makes further progress, their physical suffering at the time of death may be alleviated. But even so, they will not be free from the terror, anxiety, and suffering of death itself.

There is only one way to be free from the threat of death. This is a religion through which we can believe in eternal life—that we do not die, our lives only change in form. When we can perfect our consciousness through religion, we will be truly free from the terror and suffering of death.

We are shadowed not only by the pangs of death but also by the suffering of life. We are assaulted day and night by material, physical, spiritual, and other sufferings. Among these many sufferings, two, material and physical sufferings, should be alleviated through human knowledge and endeavor. Although these two forms of suffering cannot be entirely abolished in our present state of knowledge, they are being lessened bit by bit with the development and elevation of human knowledge. In fact, these kinds of suffering may almost disappear in time.

Spiritual suffering whose cause we can perceive with our conscious mind may be abolished through the eradication of its cause or through moral cultivation. However, there remains the spiritual suffering that we cannot control by our own power however hard we may strive for moral improvement. As mentioned earlier, when the subconscious mind erupts in violence, one cannot control it with the conscious mind however hard one may try.

Thinking earnestly that we do not hate some person, our hatred for him is growing in our minds. Warning ourselves sternly that we must not get angry, we suddenly burn with rage. Realizing that we do not have to be afraid of something, we cannot free ourselves from a feeling of terror or anxiety. We ordinary people often experience such conflicts. We cannot control even such sufferings of life, much less the terror and anxiety of death.

When people encounter a serious suffering that they cannot resolve however hard they may try, they feel as if they must depend upon something more powerful than themselves, something absolute, and they ask for help. They entrust themselves body and mind to this absolute power, as if to say, "Do as you please. I leave everything up to you."

What should we depend upon? To what should we entrust our body and mind? As mentioned before, primitive people prostrated themselves before the sun, mountains, animals, plants, or other human beings and the spirits dwelling within them. But such behavior is out of the question now. Believers in a more advanced form of religion depend on its "absolute power," on a god that is considered to be the almighty being who creates and governs everything in heaven and on earth. They manage to obtain a certain degree of mental peace by praying to this god and asking his help.

But even this peace of mind is limited. We cannot obtain absolute assurance and peace from such a god because this god exists externally, in some transcendental sphere like heaven. A god who majestically looks down on the world from heaven, a god who mercilessly punishes evil and rewards good—the more absolute the power this god possesses, the more dependent we become and at the same time, the more fear we feel because we do not know when we may be forsaken by the god or when we may be punished by him. For this reason, we live in great fear of the god, although we depend upon him with our whole heart. With such mental dependence on an external force, we cannot attain true mental peace (nirvana).

Can we depend upon anything inside ourselves? No, this is also unreliable because our mind is always subject to illusion. Our body is also unreliable, being destined to disintegrate eventually. If we could depend wholly upon something within us, we would have no need of religion and should be able to save ourselves by our own efforts.

What then should we depend upon for our salvation? We must here remember the Buddha's teaching "Make the self your light, make the Law your light" (*Ji-tōmyō, hō-tōmyō*), the words Sakyamuni spoke to Ānanda, one of his ten great disciples, before dying. Ānanda felt anxious, reflecting, "When the World-honored One, who is an unparalleled leader and teacher, dies, who on earth should we depend upon in our practice and life?" In response to Ānanda's anxiety, the Buddha taught him as follows: "Ānanda! In the future, you should make yourself your light and depend upon your own self. You must not depend upon other people. You should also make the Law your light and depend upon the Law. You must not depend upon others."

There is no better teaching than this to sum up the essence of a right religion in a few words. The Buddha first taught, "You can depend upon your own self." When we depend upon other people, we do not know what to do if we are forsaken by them or if they disappear. Therefore, the Buddha admonished us to depend upon ourselves and walk the Way through our own efforts. But what should we depend upon in living our lives? The Buddha taught that this is nothing other than the Law, namely, the truth, and that we must not depend absolutely upon others. Here the word "others" means "gods," beings who are considered to exist outside ourselves and to be our masters. The Buddha taught emphatically that we must not depend upon such gods but only upon the Law, the truth.

Indeed, his words carry great weight. A single word of the teaching "Make the self your light, make the Law your light" is more valuable than all the innumerable teachings concerning human life and religion that have been promulgated by the many great men of past ages.

Through this teaching, we understand that what we depend on, the Law, exists both within and outside us. It is the truth that permeates the entire universe, not establishing a distinction between inside and outside. Our body is produced by this truth and is caused to live by it. Our mind is also produced by it and caused to work by it. All things, including society, heaven, earth, plants, birds, and beasts, are produced by this truth and are caused to live by it.

A person who feels the word "truth" to be somewhat cold and abstract can replace it with the term "the great life," which makes everything in this world exist and live. When we are firmly aware in the depths of our mind that we are given life by this great life that permeates the universe, we can obtain the true mental peace that is not disturbed by anything.

In what way can we gain such consciousness? Needless to say, the way is to study the teachings of the Buddha repeatedly and to root them deeply in our minds by meditating on them. We must keep firmly in mind the realization that our lives should be unified with the universal life (the Buddha). This indeed is meditation from the religious point of view. Through this kind of meditation, we can purify even the mind of which we cannot be conscious ourselves, that is, our subconscious mind, and we can make our thought and conduct harmonize spontaneously with our surroundings. If our thought and conduct are in harmony with our surroundings, sufferings and worries cannot trouble us. This mental state is true peace of mind; it is the stage of "Nirvana is quiescence," the absolutely quiet stage in which we cling to nothing. This state of mind is not limited to a passive mental peace. Our consciousness of being enlivened by this great universal life gives us great hope and courage. Energy springs form this consciousness so that we advance to carry out our daily lives, our work, and our bodhisattva-way for the benefit of others in this world.

Our awareness of being caused to live is our true salvation. Our absolute devotion to the truth that imparts life to us, so that we utter "Namu" in our hearts, must be said to be the highest reach of faith. *Namu* comes from the Chinese transliteration of the Sanskrit word *namas,* and means to take refuge in the Law wholeheartedly, with utter faith and trust. The state of religious exaltation in which we feel inexpressible gratitude to and joy in the Law is also included in the word *namu.* We do not worship a thing, a person, a spirit, or a god existing outside ourselves, but devote ourselves to the Law, which causes us to live and unites us with it—this is the purest and the supreme faith. Uttering the sacred title *Namu Myōhō Renge-kyō* is the expression of our practice of taking refuge in the Law with our entire heart and mind. No form of religion is purer than this; this is the highest form of religion.

It is natural that understanding of the Law is different in each period and according to the capacity of each person. As most people today receive a scientific education, they have a tendency to believe only that which is clearly visible or which has been scientifically proved. They are apt to doubt such concepts as the Law and "that which causes everything to live" as mere ideas produced by religious leaders. But they should think of the composition of all physical substances as elucidated by nuclear physics: all substances in this universe are composed of electrons, protons, neutrons, and other subatomic particles, and the differences between various substances are caused by different combinations of these basic particles.

Granted that subatomic particles are regarded as the minimum units of matter, so long as such particles exist as matter, as things, they should be still further divisible. However, modern science cannot do this, so scientists say that these elemental particles are produced by "energy."

Energy is generally considered as "the force through which matter functions." But before matter can function, there must already exist the energy that produces matter. This is the theory advanced by the engineer Dr. Yōichi Yamamoto.

We cannot see energy with our naked eyes or otherwise discern it as a physical entity. Energy seems at first to be "nothingness," but it does exist and it is a kind of matter. The accumulation of this "kind of matter" produces such particles as electrons, protons, and neutrons. The accumulation of these particles produces various kinds of atoms. The accumulation of these atoms produces such elements as hydrogen, oxygen, and carbon. The accumulation of these elements produces air, water, minerals, plants, and the human body. Thus, matter is originally produced from a kind of energy or force.

Scientists in the Soviet Union have propounded the theory that time is also energy. They assert that the sun and other stars will never stop burning because they use time as energy. This is the very limit that modern science has been able to ascertain. It is considered impossible to trace the origin of matter beyond that.

Sakyamuni Buddha, however, taught about matter correctly more than two thousand years ago. He proclaimed it as *shiki soku zekū* and *kū soku zeshiki.*[2] *Kū,* or *śūnyatā,* literally "emptiness" or "void," does not mean "nothingness" but "equality " *Shiki* implies "phenomena." *Shiki soku zekū* indicates the idea that all things, including matter, the human mind, and events, originate from the same foundation. Though these things seem to be different from one another in the eyes of man, their real state is equal. When analyzed to the utmost possible limit, all things are equal because they are energy (force) of some kind. Similarly, *kū soku zeshiki* means that all things, including matter, mind, and events, are produced by *kū,* and therefore *kū* is identical with *shiki.* In short, all phenomena are produced from an equal kind of energy or force.

Kū (energy) accumulates through conditions (secondary causes, *en*) and produces a substance. Differences in the conditions lead to the production of water, air, stone, or the human body. When the conditions change, the substances produced change and take another form. When water comes into contact with a high temperature as a condition, it

2. Two famous sentences in the *Prajña-pāramitā-hṛdaya-sūtra* (*Hannya-haramitta Shingyō*), or Heart Sutra. They indicate that form or matter is identical with voidness (*shiki soku zekū*) and that the void, or *śūnyatā,* is identical with matter (*kū soku zeshiki*).

evaporates. When vapor comes into contact with cold air as a condition, it condenses and forms a cloud. Events and the function of the mind are similar; there is nothing that does not follow this basic rule.

Sakyamuni Buddha expounded this rule through the doctrine of *pratītya-samutpāda* (*engi*), or dependent origination, meaning that all phenomena are produced and annihilated by causation. This term indicates the following: a thing arises from or is produced through the agency of a condition (a secondary cause, *en*). A thing does not take form unless there is an appropriate condition. This truth applies to all existence and phenomena in the universe. The Buddha intuitively perceived this so profoundly that even modern science cannot probe further.

Thinking thus, our lives may seem to be capricious. That *kū* is produced by a secondary cause (*en*) seems to indicate that all things are the products of mere chance. But this is not so. When we look carefully at things around us, we find that water, stone, and human beings are produced each according to a certain pattern with its own individual character. Through what power or direction are the conditions generated that produce various things in perfect order from such an amorphous energy as *kū?* When we consider this regularity and order, we cannot help admitting that some rule exists. It is the rule that causes all things to exist. This indeed is the Law taught by the Buddha.

We do not exist accidentally, but exist and live by means of this Law. As soon as we realize this fact, we become aware of our firm foundation and can set our minds at ease. Far from being capricious, this foundation rests on the Law, with which nothing can compare in firmness. This assurance is the source of the great peace of mind that is not agitated by anything. It is the Law that imparts life to all of us. The Law is not something cold but is full of vigor and vivid with life.

Just consider that billions of years ago, the earth had no life; volcanoes poured forth torrents of lava, and vapor and gas filled the sky. However, when the earth cooled about two billion years ago, microscopic one-celled living creatures were produced. It goes without saying that they were produced through the working of the Law. They were born when the energy (*kū*) forming the foundation of lava, gas, and vapor came into contact with appropriate conditions (a secondary cause, *en*). It is the Law that provided the conditions for the generation of life. Therefore, we realize that the Law is not cold, a mere abstract rule, but is full of vivid power causing everything to exist and live.

Conversely, everything has the power of desiring to exist and to live.

Two billion years ago, even lava, gas, and vapor possessed the urge to live. That is why one-celled living creatures were generated from them when the conditions were right. These infinitesimal creatures endured all kinds of trials, including extreme heat and cold, tremendous floods, and torrential rains, for about two billion years, and continued to live. Moreover, they gradually evolved into more sophisticated forms, culminating in man. This evolution was caused by the urge to live of these first microscopic creatures. Life had mind, through which it desired to live, from the time even before it existed on earth. Such a will exists in everything in the universe. This will exists in man today. From the scientific point of view, man is formed by a combination of elementary particles; and if we analyze this still more deeply, we see that man is an accumulation of energy. Therefore, the mind desiring to live must surely exist in man.

However, this is a mind so deep that we cannot grasp, isolate, or control it. It is the mind existing in the origin of life, even deeper than the subconscious mind. What is this mind that desires to live, and what is the origin enabling us to live? We cannot isolate it by means of science or explain it by some theory. Even the most eminent scientists regard it as a problem beyond human knowledge. Philosophers have attempted to explain it as "the blind will toward life." We can call it "the universal will" or "universal life." We can also describe it as "the power that makes everything live" or "the rule that makes everything exist." Sakyamuni Buddha taught this point in the following way: all things in the universe are *kū*, and they are produced and annihilated by *en*. Nothing exists in a fixed eternal form; only the Law permeating them is an existence that never changes.

It is difficult, however, for an ordinary person to perceive clearly the Law, which is invisible and intangible. For those who lived during the Buddha's lifetime, it must have been extremely difficult for anyone but a person of very superior intellect to grasp it theoretically. Therefore Sakyamuni Buddha manifested the Law or truth in the form of the Buddha, whom man can view directly. He preached that the Buddha has absolute power and is an immortal existence that is present in all things and causes them to live. This Buddha is, of course, the Eternal Original Buddha.

The Original Buddha is the power that makes everything live and is omnipresent in the universe. There is no place where the Buddha does not exist. It is natural that the Original Buddha appear in a form appropriate to the object that he causes to live, because he is the power that makes everything live. When he appears in the world of man, he takes a shape suited to it.

If we superficially interpret the words "the Original Buddha appears," we may wonder why, then, everybody cannot see him when he makes his appearance. But this doubt is unfounded. It means replacing the realization of his existence with the words "he appears," nothing more. As long as the Original Buddha is the truth and the power that makes all men live, he always exists in each of us. We can all realize his existence in some way. To do this is to see the Buddha.

Lord Sakyamuni was the first human being who clearly realized the truth that makes all things live. An ordinary person cannot understand it even when it is explained to him as "the Law" or "truth." But when we think of the truth in the form of the Buddha, who perceives our minds and gives all of us life, we can realize the loving power of the Buddha that enables our minds to unite with his mind, and which causes us to live. The Buddha's power causing us to live is his benevolence.

The Lotus Sutra often mentions that the Buddha exists everywhere and appears in various forms in order to save people—that is, to cause them to live. The sutra also teaches indirectly that the Buddha has existed since the eternal past. However, in the Lotus Sutra so far, the Buddha has not explicitly preached this truth in its full depth. In order to guide his disciples to understand the truth in its utmost profundity, he tried to alter their minds little by little and to make them change their direction. If he had not done so but had suddenly preached the profound and real state of all things, his disciples could not have understood or believed what he said but would have been thrown into confusion.

When he judged the time to be ripe, the Buddha finally began to preach this most important teaching. This is the substance of chapter 16, "Revelation of the [Eternal] Life of the Tathāgata," in which the Buddha's entity and life are manifested. He proclaimed that the entity of the Buddha is not the Sakyamuni seen by his disciples but the Eternal Original Buddha. He also revealed that the Original Buddha always exists, from the infinite past to the infinite future, and is omnipresent in the universe. In other words, he taught that the power that causes all things to live exists constantly in all places and at all times.

That the Buddha's life is infinite means that our lives, too, are infinite. By realizing the infinity of the Buddha's life we can obtain limitless hope and courage. Therefore chapter 16 is not only the core of the Law of

Origin but is also regarded as the living spirit of the entire Lotus Sutra.

This chapter contains such a profound teaching that we cannot possibly grasp its essence if we interpret it literally. Therefore I have tried to introduce the chapter by reviewing the teaching of the Law of Appearance and then defining the essence of religion. I have also tried to explain the meaning of the Original Buddha in terms that modern people can understand. Now let us proceed to the content of chapter 16 itself.

In chapter 15, "Springing Up out of the Earth," the host of bodhisattvas entertained doubts when they heard that the innumerable great bodhisattvas who issued from the earth had all been instructed by Sakyamuni Buddha since his enlightenment. Then on behalf of these bodhisattvas the Bodhisattva Maitreya asked the Buddha to resolve their doubts. Chapter 16 of the Lotus Sutra begins at this point.

At that time the Buddha said to the bodhisattvas and all the great assembly, "Believe and discern, all you good sons, the veracious word of the Tathāgata." Again he said to the great assembly, "Believe and discern the veracious word of the Tathāgata." And a third time he said to all the great assembly, "Believe and discern the veracious word of the Tathāgata."

The Buddha repeated the words "Believe and discern the veracious word of the Tathāgata" three times to emphasize how important was the teaching that he was about to expound.

"The veracious word of the Tathāgata" means the truth in the most profound depths of his mind; this is the opposite of the "tactful teaching." As shown repeatedly in the teaching of the Law of Appearance in the first half of the Lotus Sutra, the tactful teaching expounds the truth in plain language in various ways, according to the capacity of those listening to the Buddha's teachings. An ordinary person cannot realize the truth without going through this process of tactful teaching. In contrast to this, the veracious word of the Tathāgata is the truth as it really is, the unadorned truth.

Why does the Buddha here reveal for the first time "the truth as it really is"? It is partly because he was now confident of his disciples' understanding of the Law and partly because his teachings would not be perfected unless he preached the most profound truth before his extinction.

The Buddha's saying "Believe and discern it" instead of commanding "Believe it" has an important meaning. Sakyamuni Buddha never forced his ideas upon his disciples or other people. He preached the truth as it was and exhorted his listeners, saying, "You, too, behold it." He led them on the way of the truth and coaxed them, saying, "You, too, come to me." His exhortation to "behold the truth" instead of saying only "Believe it" is a very important point. This short phrase of the Buddha speaks for the character of his teachings. His words "Behold it" are equivalent to the "scientific spirit" in today's parlance. The Buddha shows in these few words that if anyone thoroughly views the truth, studies it, and discerns it, he will surely be able to accept it to his satisfaction.

His words "You, too, come to me" include the same important idea. They mean: "Come to me and practice the Law as much as I do. Then you are sure to understand the value of the Law." The Buddha could never have uttered these words unless he had absolute confidence in the Law and the Way.

Because Sakyamuni Buddha was a reasonable person, he did not say even to his leading disciples, "Believe the truth," but said, "Believe and discern it," that is, "Believe it after understanding it." In this emphasis on belief based on understanding, Buddhism differs fundamentally from many other religions.

THE THREE CATEGORIES OF WISDOM, COMPASSION, AND PRACTICE. Then the great host of bodhisattvas, Maitreya at their head, folded their hands and said to the Buddha, "World-honored One! Be pleased to expound the matter, and we will believingly receive the Buddha's words." Thus they spoke three times, repeating the words, "Be pleased to expound the matter, and we will believingly receive the Buddha's words."

The repetition of these words by the great host of bodhisattvas illustrates their ardent desire to hear the Law and their firm determination to practice it after hearing it. Their determination is shown in their declaring, "We will believingly receive the Buddha's words." They thus express their intention not only to believe the Buddha's words but also to remember them.

Another thing that we must not forget is that, on behalf of the great host of bodhisattvas, the Bodhisattva Maitreya asked the Buddha to expound the teaching. In chapter 1 of the Lotus Sutra, the Buddha sent forth from the circle of white hair between his eyebrows a ray of light that illuminated all the lands in the universe. At that time the Bodhisattva Maitreya wondered at this marvel and asked the Bodhisattva Mañjuśrī to explain it. Then, on the basis of his past experience, the Bodhisattva Mañjuśrī predicted, "The World-honored One now intends to preach a very important law, the truth in the utmost depth of his mind."

From this episode we can judge that Mañjuśrī was the most senior bodhisattva. In chapters 12 and 14 the Bodhisattva Mañjuśrī again requested the Buddha to instruct the host of bodhisattvas. However, from the latter half of chapter 15 onward, the Bodhisattva Maitreya represents the host of bodhisattvas, and the Bodhisattva Mañjuśrī does not appear in the later chapters of the Lotus Sutra. This change is not incidental but has deep significance.

As indicated by the saying "the wisdom of Mañjuśrī," the Bodhisattva Mañjuśrī is regarded as the idealization or personification of the wisdom of the Buddha. Therefore, in the Law of Appearance as the teaching of wisdom, this bodhisattva usually represents the host of bodhisattvas. The Bodhisattva Maitreya, on the other hand, is believed to represent the Buddha's compassion. Therefore, in the Law of Origin as the teaching of compassion, which begins with the latter half of chapter 15, the Bodhisattva Maitreya is the representative of all the bodhisattvas. However, in chapter 28, "Encouragement of the Bodhisattva Universal Virtue," the last chapter of the Lotus Sutra, the Bodhisattva Universal Virtue acts as the representative of the bodhisattvas. This is because Universal Virtue typifies the practice of the Buddha. This bodhisattva is actually regarded as representing the teaching, practice, and attainment of the Buddha, but in the Lotus Sutra he most strongly represents the practice of the Buddha.

The appearance of these three bodhisattvas—Mañjuśrī, who represents the wisdom of the Buddha; Maitreya, who typifies the compassion of the Buddha; and Universal Virtue, who personifies the practice of the Buddha—reflects the organization of the Lotus Sutra itself.

Man needs wisdom before all else in order to become a good person. As is commonly said, "Ignorance is a sin"; evil occurs because man lacks true wisdom. Wisdom here does not mean human knowledge. People may consider a man wise who is familiar with the inner workings of government or industry and who makes a large profit or escapes punishment for wrongdoing through his cleverness. But this is not true wisdom. True wisdom enables man to see the essential qualities of all things in this world and to know the law of causation and of change affecting all phenomena. If man is possessed of such wisdom, he cannot help practicing rightly in everything he does. He cannot do wrong even if he is asked to. He also does not do wrong as the result of being deceived or led into temptation by others. The more people who can acquire such wisdom, the brighter, more peaceful, and richer society will become. For this reason, Sakyamuni Buddha taught us that we must acquire true wisdom first of all.

When we have true wisdom, we understand that all things in the world are related and interdependent (the law that nothing has an ego), and that if we alone are possessed of wisdom or we alone are right, the world as a whole will not become better. Therefore, when we see the many people who lack wisdom and therefore depart from the path of righteousness, we feel the urge to save them from such a situation. The spirit of compassion wells up in our hearts.

If we have the spirit of compassion, we cannot help showing it in our actions. We preach the Law to those who do not know it; we return those who have departed from the path of righteousness to its course; we have the wish to protect and instruct those who are assiduous in practicing the Law. When we can perfectly perform the three practices of wisdom, compassion, and practice, the teaching of the Buddha will be perfected in us and this world will become the Pure Land. The teaching of the Lotus Sutra has such a perfected organization. Here is the reason that we cannot grasp the true meaning of the sutra by reading only bits and pieces, skipping here and there.

THE THREEFOLD BODY OF THE BUDDHA. Then the World-honored One, perceiving that the bodhisattvas thrice repeated their request, addressed them, saying: "Listen then all of you attentively to the secret, mysterious, and supernaturally pervading power of the Tathāgata."

The word "secret" means not something hidden but something so profound that it is difficult to fathom. The boundless power of the Tathāgata's entity, which causes everything to live, influences all living beings. There is nothing that can completely obstruct its influence. This power to influence everything freely is what is called the supernaturally pervading power of the Tathāgata. "Secret" refers to the entity of the Tathāgata, and "supernaturally pervading power" signifies the compassionate working of the Tathāgata.

Here the Tathāgata is divided into two parts: his entity and his working. The entity of the Tathāgata is his original power and the working of the Tathāgata the expression of his power. Nothing is achieved satisfactorily unless both original power and expression are complete. Some people are fond of displaying their "expression," that is, their way of working. Some companies and groups even encourage this in their members. However, such ostentatious display of expression never bears valuable fruit in the true sense because their "working" does not come from their real abilities but from their "false," superficial activities. Therefore, their activities soon peter out, just as a shallow well runs dry. At the same time, however substantial one's original power may be, it will not produce any result unless it is attended by expression. An infinite quantity of water underground is of no use in our daily lives unless it gushes out as a spring or we pump it up out of the earth.

The entity of the Tathāgata, his power that causes everything to live, is infinite, and the working of the Tathāgata, the expression of his power, has perfect freedom. It is clear that the salvation of the Tathāgata is absolutely perfect and faultless. Here "Tathāgata" (*nyorai*) does not indicate the historical Buddha but the Eternal Original Buddha. *Nyo* means *shinnyo* (*tathatā*), that is, absolute truth, the true form of things, reality. However, an ordinary man cannot understand by his own power of thought what *shinnyo* actually is. To explain it to him as that which makes all men live does not make a vivid impression but seems vast and abstract.

However, *shinnyo* can take any form because it is the only thing really existing in this world. In what form can we imagine it when we think of it with our human minds? We cannot help imagining a person with absolute power. When we think that such a person has existed in this world for all time, from the infinite past to the infinite future, and that he causes all of us to live, we feel in a concrete way the warm, compassionate mind of the Buddha. We cannot know what form *shinnyo* takes in appearing to beings other than men, but for us, it realizes its true power of salvation when it appears in human form.

Shinnyo necessarily takes a human form in appearing in the human world. This personification of *shinnyo* is called the Tathāgata (*nyorai*), one who has come from *tathatā* (*shinnyo*). This is why one epithet of the Buddha is "Tathāgata." The entity of the Buddha is *tathatā,* and when we consider this as the personification of one who has realized *tathatā,* we see the vivid image of the Buddha as the entity of his compassion, which causes us to live and which leads us in the right direction.

Since ancient times, the Buddha has been said to have a threefold body (*trayaḥ kāyāḥ, sanjin*): the Law-body (*dharmakāya, hosshin*), the reward-body (*saṃbhogakāya, hōjin*), and the mutation-body (*nirmāṇakāya, ōjin*).

The Buddha as *tathatā* itself is called the Law-body, which is the entity of the Buddha. When his entity appears in a form that is comprehensible, this is known as his reward-body. "Reward-body" means a buddha who has become endowed with perfect wisdom in reward for his religious practices over a long period of time. The Buddha who appeared as a man in this world for the purpose of instructing and leading all living beings is called the mutation-body. The Buddha in this body manifests himself for the purpose of saving all living beings. Sakyamuni Buddha, who preaches the Law to the host of bodhisattvas, is the mutation-body. The Tathāgata mentioned by Sakyamuni indicates his Law-body, and his reward-body is its representation.

Then the World-honored One preached as follows: "All the worlds of gods, men, and *asuras* consider: 'Now has Sakyamuni Buddha come forth from the palace of the Śākya clan, and seated at the training place of enlightenment, not far from the city of Gayā, has attained Perfect Enlightenment.' But, my good sons, since I veritably became Buddha there have passed infinite, boundless hundreds of thousands of myriads of *koṭis* of *nayutas* of *kalpas*."

Here the entity of the Buddha is revealed at last. An ordinary person believes the existence of what is visible to his eyes. He considers the Sakyamuni before his eyes as the Buddha and depends upon him in his mind and his religious discipline. He makes a great mistake in thinking so, however, because the Buddha is the existence of non-beginning and non-end, as is clearly declared here.

The Buddha addressed himself not only to his disciples and other human beings but also to heavenly beings and nonhuman beings, such as *asuras*. This is because even heavenly beings have not yet been able to obtain true nirvana but remain in a temporary world of joy and a provisional world of peace. Therefore, they also must hear the Buddha's teachings for the sake of obtaining true salvation. Even the most evil person can be sure of being saved if only he has the chance to learn the teachings of the Buddha. Nonhuman living beings are also equal in the sight of the Buddha.

It is profoundly significant that the Buddha included the heavenly beings and *asuras* in his message. "The training place of enlightenment" does not refer to a special building for religious discipline. The Buddha sat under the Bodhi tree in the forest and entered meditation. This expression refers to the place where the Buddha was seated at the time of attaining the highest enlightenment. There are holy places of learning and practicing the Way everywhere. All places, including homes, offices, trains, and playgrounds become holy places for attaining enlightenment according to one's mental attitude there. That does not mean that we should not have special training places for seeking the Way. We need an environment suitable for religious discipline to help us in our practice. Even Sakyamuni Buddha first sat in a quiet forest and entered meditation. In other words, he chose a suitable environment as the training place of his enlightenment. Our minds are apt to become distracted in our daily environment. For this reason, it is necessary for us to have as many chances as possible to visit a special training place where people of the same faith gather for the sake of purifying their minds. As we gradually accumulate virtue by means of religious disciplines, we can attain a mental state that will allow us to realize that our daily environment is identical with the holy place of learning and practicing the Way.

Sakyamuni Buddha said that infinite time had passed since he had actually become the Buddha. In order to help men realize such a long period of time, he said: "For instance, suppose there were five hundred thousand myriad *koṭis* of *nayutas* of *asaṃkhyeya* three-thousand-great-thousandfold worlds; let someone grind them to atoms, pass eastward through five hundred thousand myriad *koṭis* of *nayutas* of *asaṃkhyeya* countries, and then drop one of those atoms; suppose he thus proceeded eastward till he had dropped all those atoms—what do you think, my good sons, is it possible to imagine and calculate all those worlds so as to know their number?"

The three-thousand-great-thousandfold worlds mentioned here include the world in which we now live. Five hundred thousand myriad *koṭis* of *nayutas* of *asaṃkhyeya* countries indicates the innumerable stars in the universe. A person grinds the three-thousand-great-thousandfold worlds to atoms and drops one atom when he has passed eastward through five hundred thousand myriad *koṭis* of *nayutas* of *asaṃkhyeya* stars. In this way, he proceeds eastward till he has finished dropping those atoms. *Nayuta* is an Indian numerical unit said to be equivalent to one hundred *ayutas*. An *ayuta* is one hundred *koṭis,* and a *koṭi* is an astronomical number variously interpreted as ten million, one hundred million, and so on. *Asaṃkhyeya* means numberless, innumerable, countless. It is impossible for us to imagine five hundred thousand myriad *koṭis* of *nayutas* of *asaṃkhyeyas.*

Maitreya Bodhisattva and the others all said to the Buddha: "World-honored One! Those worlds are infinite, boundless, beyond the knowledge of reckoning, and beyond the reach of thought. Not all the *śrāvakas* and *pratyekabuddhas,* with their faultless wisdom, would be able to imagine and know the bounds of those numbers. And to us also, who are dwelling in the stage of *avaivartika,* these matters are beyond apprehension. World-honored One! All such worlds as these are measureless and boundless." For anyone other than the Buddha, the existence of such measureless and boundless worlds is utterly beyond understanding. We know this from the expression, "All such worlds as these are measureless and boundless."

A *śrāvaka* is one who listens to the Buddha's teachings and attains enlightenment, while a *pratyekabuddha* is one who obtains emancipation for himself. However, even those who have attained the mental state of these two vehicles live in this finite world. They are satisfied with personal purification and emancipation from illusion. There is a limit to their wisdom so long as they remain in such a limited mental world. Therefore the Bodhisattva Maitreya said, "Not all the *śrāvakas* and *pratyekabuddhas,* with their faultless wisdom, would be able to imagine and know the bounds of those numbers."

A bodhisattva is one whose mind reaches a higher stage than that of a *śrāvaka* or a *pratyekabuddha,* and who seeks enlightenment with the desire to save all people. This kind of person is open-minded and deep in feeling, and he reaches the stage of *avaivartika.* In terms of Buddhist religious practice, *avaivartika* means not to retrogress from the stage of attainment one has already reached. The expression "are dwelling in the stage of *avaivartika*" signifies having attained a mental stage from which one will never retrogress and in which one is not agitated by anything in any circumstances. But even one who has already attained such a state of mind is still engaged in religious practice for enlightenment. He cannot yet free himself from "self." In his mind somewhere there still remains the selfish idea that he himself can save others and make society good. If he remains in this state, he cannot reach the mental stage of perfect freedom. There is a limit to where his mind can reach. The Bodhisattva Maitreya himself averred this.

However, the Buddha is completely selfless. When one has attained the same state of mind as the Buddha, he is truly free from the idea of "self" because he realizes that everything in the universe is united with him. In attaining this mental state, he feels that everything in the universe exists in his mind, and he perceives everything clearly. It is impossible for us to reach such a mental state in our entire life or even our next life. But the more often we remove "self" or "ego" from our minds and the stronger is our desire to benefit others and society, the more will our wisdom increase and the further will it extend. We learn this from the Bodhisattva Maitreya's answer to the Buddha.

After the Bodhisattva Maitreya answered the Buddha thus, the Buddha gave a slight nod and addressed all the bodhisattva-*mahāsattvas:* "Good sons! Now I must clearly announce and declare to you. Suppose you take as atomized all those worlds where an atom has been deposited or where it has not been deposited, and count an atom as a *kalpa,* the time since I became the Buddha still surpasses these by hundreds of thousands of myriads of *koṭis* of *nayutas* of *asaṃkhyeya kalpas.*"

THE BUDDHA AS ABSOLUTE EXISTENCE. The measureless and boundless worlds that the Buddha mentioned indicate the idea of infinite space. This was the premise for the subsequent mention of infinite time. We are not able to imagine such infinite and boundless worlds. Much less can we reckon the duration of time in which each atom dropped represents a *kalpa.* Here we must transcend the concept of number and say simply "absolute."

Sakyamuni Buddha did not use such a way of preaching for the purpose of making people imagine an extraordinarily large number. He used this imagery simply to put across the idea of something absolute and infinite. These concepts have no meaning to an ordinary person if he thinks of them abstractly. Therefore the Buddha established the standard of something relative or finite, such as this world and the stars, which are concepts comprehensible to an ordinary person, and through this tried to make people realize the idea of something absolute and infinite.

The Buddha then replaced the concept of infinite number with that of infinite time. To say that when a person takes as atomized all those worlds where an atom has been deposited or where it has not been deposited, and counts an atom as a *kalpa,* the time since Sakyamuni became the Buddha still surpasses these by hundreds of thousands of myriads of *koṭis* of *nayutas* of *asaṃkhyeya kalpas* is nothing but an indication of the idea of the infinite past.

It is undeniable that the Buddha is an absolute existence, because he preaches that he has existed in this world since the infinite past. This absolute existence is more important than anything else. As mentioned earlier in this chapter, that on which we depend must be an absolute existence. Even the greatest man is relatively connected with us so long as he is a man. He is also a limited existence because he will die sometime. Therefore, we cannot truly depend upon him. However delicately and exquisitely made a machine may be, it will eventually deteriorate and rust. Machines are also relative and limited.

However huge a sum of money we may have, we will spend our last penny sometime. However high a position we may occupy, eventually we will have to retire. Therefore, these things are also relative and limited. Even the heavenly god who is considered to exist outside ourselves is relatively connected with man. He is a limited existence, too, because we do not know when we may be deserted by him.

We cannot truly depend upon any of these things. But the Buddha is an absolute existence. He exists everywhere inside and outside us and is constant, from the infinite past to the infinite future. He is an existence inseparable from us even if we want to part form him. Therefore, he is an absolute existence.

The Buddha can be compared to the air. Air always exists around us and even within our bodies. We cannot live for a moment without air, though we usually do not think about its existence. When we are confined in a small room and feel claustrophobic because of stale air, we open the windows and let in fresh air. At such times we are aware of the importance of air.

In the same way, the Buddha is the existence from which we cannot separate ourselves even if we want to, and which always causes us to live. He is an absolute and infinite existence. For this reason, we can devote ourselves to believing in the Buddha, depending upon him, and leaving everything to him.

The Buddha continued as follows: "From that time forward I have constantly been preaching and teaching in this *sahā*-world, and also leading and benefiting all living beings in other places in hundreds of thousands of myriads of *koṭis* of *nayutas* of *asaṃkhyeya* domains."

These words have a very important meaning. Here the Buddha reveals that the Original Buddha as his entity has been constantly preaching and teaching in this *sahā*-world since the infinite past, although it is only forty-odd years since he attained enlightenment as the appearing Buddha. He also shows clearly that the Tathāgata Sakyamuni, the Eternal Original Buddha, has been leading all living beings everywhere in all worlds.

Each buddha, as the reward-body of the Eternal Buddha, has a world that is under his charge for instruction. This world is called *kedo* in Japanese, a "temporary land" where the Buddha is present for instruction. The Tathāgata Healing has his *kedo* in the World of Pure Emerald in the east; the Tathāgata Amitābha in the Pure Land in the west; and the Tathāgata Sakyamuni in the *sahā*-world. However, the Tathāgata Sakyamuni, the Eternal Original Buddha, is not limited to such a temporary land for instruction but is omnipresent and causes everything to live.

All the buddhas are the reward-body of the Original Buddha, who appears in different shapes in various situations. Though each buddha is honorable in himself, he originates in the Tathāgata Sakyamuni, the Eternal Original Buddha, and is united with him. From this we can establish the object of worship of our faith. Risshō Kōsei-kai follows this teaching in enshrining the Image of the Great Beneficent Teacher and Lord Sakyamuni, the Eternal Buddha, as its object of worship. The correctness of this way is clearly testified by the sutras themselves.

Another important point mentioned in this passage is that the Buddha did not proclaim from the beginning that he had been preaching everywhere in this universe but first said that he had been teaching in the *sahā*-world, then added that he had been leading and benefiting all living beings in other places. This may seem a minor point, but it contains the great lesson of "extending the Buddha's teachings from the short to the long."

Since the Buddha shows his compassion for everyone equally, he cannot be making the point that he first instructs the living beings in the *sahā*-world and then extends his salvation to other places. However, when we think of instructing others from our own standpoint, there is a correct order of teaching in our carrying out the bodhisattva practice. We cannot save the whole world at once. For this reason, we begin with saving those around us, then extend this salvation to others who have some relationship to those close to us and to each other. This is the order indicated to us by the Buddha's example. We first set about improving our own villages and towns, then extend this improvement to countries and provinces or states. When we accumulate enough power, we must reach out our hands of instruction and salvation to the whole country in which we live and then still farther, to foreign countries.

Some people boast, "I will save the world myself," when they have been deeply moved by the wonder of the Buddha's teachings. Ambition is certainly a good thing, and to save the entire world is a worthy goal. But however great our ambition or desire, we cannot realize it just by wishing but only if we can actually implement it through concrete measures. A person who cannot save even one of his friends cannot save the world. Even if he has this great desire at first, he will soon give it up when things do not go smoothly. This is because he lacks power proportionate to his ambition.

Power should be accumulated little by little for this aim. Nobody has enough power to instruct all the people of the world immediately. We can gain the power to enlighten others while saving, leading, and instructing only one, two, or three people around us, just as a tiny snowball gradually becomes larger as we roll it through the snow until finally it is big enough to make a fine snowman. The words "extending the Buddha's teachings from the short to the long" should be understood not only in terms of space or numbers of people but also from a spiritual point of view so that they will constitute the backbone of our instruction. We must fully realize this point. Therefore, the Buddha's instruction is divided into two parts: first, "I have constantly been preaching and teaching in this *sahā*-world," and second, "and also leading and benefiting all living beings in other places." This is how we should understand these words of the Buddha.

The Buddha continued to preach as follows: "Good sons! During this time I have ever spoken of myself as the Buddha Burning Light and other buddhas, and also have told of their entering into nirvana. Thus have I tactfully described them all. Good sons! Whenever living beings come to me, I behold with a Buddha's eyes all the faculties, keen or dull, of their faith and so on. And I explain to them, in stage after stage, according to their capacity and degree of salvation, my different names and the length of my lives, and moreover plainly state that I must enter nirvana. I also, in various tactful ways, preach the Wonderful Law which is able to cause all the living to beget a joyful heart."

THE FIVE ORGANS OF GOOD CONDUCT. Here we realize anew the importance and value of the Buddha's tactful teaching. We also realize that not only the Buddha's various tactful teachings, all worthy of honor and reverence in themselves, but also his appearance in this world itself were tactful means adopted by the Eternal Original Buddha for the sake of saving all living beings. The appearance of other buddhas is also a tactful means of the Eternal Original Buddha.

As explained earlier, the Original Buddha can be compared to the electric waves of television. Though they fill our surroundings, we cannot directly see or hear them. But through the medium of a television set, corresponding to a tactful method of the Buddha, we can see images and hear sounds. In the same way, we can come into contact with the true teachings of the Buddha through his tactful means.

These "television sets" owned by living beings are graded from highly sensitive sets to insensitive ones. The Buddha can discern the sensitivity of the various television sets and act to increase or lessen the voltage accordingly. He preaches his teachings according to the mental capacity of his listeners. This is the tactful way of the Buddha's compassion, coinciding with his words: "Whenever living beings come to me, I behold with a Buddha's eyes all the faculties, keen or dull, of their faith."

The words "faculties of their faith" refer to the five organs (*pañcendriyāni, go-kon*) that lead man to good conduct—the sense of belief (*śraddhendriya, shin-kon*), sense of endeavor (*vīryendriya, shōjin-kon*), sense of memory (*smrtīndriya, nen-kon*), sense of meditation (*samādhīndriya, jō-kon*), and sense of wisdom (*prajñendriya, e-kon*). All five are fundamental to our religious lives.

"Sense of belief" means the mind of faith. As pointed out in the explanation of belief in chapter 4, a religion, unlike intellectual learning, does not enable a believer to have the power to save others as well as himself if he understands it only in theory. When he believes from the depths of his heart, his belief produces power. His faith cannot be said to be true until he attains such a mental state.

"Sense of endeavor" means the spirit of endeavoring purely and incessantly. Faith alone is not enough. Our religious lives cannot be true unless we maintain our faith purely and constantly endeavor so that our religious spirit does not weaken or lose its power.

"Sense of memory" indicates the mind that always focuses upon the Buddha. Practically speaking, of course, it is impossible for us to completely forget the Buddha for even a moment. When a student devotes himself to his studies or when an adult is entirely absorbed in his work, he must concentrate on one object. Doing so accords with the way to buddhahood. While devoting ourselves to a particular object, we reflect, "I am caused to live by the Buddha." When we complete a difficult task and feel relieved, we thank the Buddha, saying, "How lucky I am! I am protected by the Buddha." When an evil thought flashes across our mind or we suddenly feel angry, we instantly examine ourselves, thinking, "Is this the way to buddhahood?" The mind that thus keeps the Buddha in mind at all times is "sense of memory."

"Sense of meditation" implies a determined mind. Once we have faith in a religion, we are never agitated by anything, whatever may happen. We bear patiently all persecution and temptation, and we continue to believe only in one religion. We must constantly maintain such firm determination, never becoming discouraged. We cannot be said to be real people of religion unless we have such a mental attitude.

"Sense of wisdom" means the wisdom that people of religion must maintain. As frequently mentioned in this book, this is not a self-centered wisdom but the true wisdom that we obtain when we perfectly free ourselves from ego and illusion. So long as we have this wisdom, we will not take the wrong way. We can say the same thing of our belief in religion itself, not to mention our daily lives. If we are attached to a selfish, small desire, we are apt to stray toward a mistaken religion. However earnestly we may believe in it, endeavoring to practice its teaching, keeping it in mind, and devoting ourselves to it, we cannot be saved because of its basically wrong teaching, and we sink farther and farther into the world of illusion. There are many instances around us of people following such a course. Although "sense of wisdom" is mentioned as the last of the five organs leading man to good conduct, it should be first in the order in which we enter a religious life.

THE FIVE KINDS OF EYES. With his eyes the Buddha can discern to what extent each living being possesses the five senses of belief, endeavor, memory, meditation, and wisdom, and according to his discernment the Buddha uses various ways of guiding each living being.

The Buddha's eyes are the eyes of compassion. When the Buddha views a person with his compassionate eyes, desiring to save him, the Buddha perceives all things, including the person's character, intellect, and mental attitude. The five kinds of eyes (*pañca cakṣūṃṣi, go-gen*) or ways of viewing things are the following: the eye of a material body (*māṃsa-cakṣus, niku-gen*), the divine eye of celestial beings (*dirya-cakṣus, ten-gen*), the eye of wisdom (*prajñā-cakṣus, e-gen*), the eye of the law (*dharma-cakṣus, hō-gen*) and the eye of the Buddha (*Buddha-cakṣus, butsu-gen*).

The eye of a material body means the way of viewing things of an ordinary person, who can perceive only material shapes and forms. Such a person often has a wrong or partial view of things. He mistakes oil for water and a whale for a fish.

The eye of celestial beings means the viewpoint from which we investigate matters theoretically and discern their essential qualities. This is the scientific way of looking at things. When we take this view, we realize that water is formed by the combination of oxygen and hydrogen. From such a point of view, we can foretell when there will be a conjunction between two stars down to the year, month, day, hour, minute, and second. At the same time, we can estimate exactly how many millions of tons of petroleum are buried underground. Such a person, who has the ability of seeing things that an ordinary man cannot see, was called a clairvoyant in ancient times.

The eye of wisdom means to discern the entity of things and their real state. This is, in a sense, a philosophical way of looking at things. A person with the eye of wisdom can observe things that are invisible to the average person and can perceive matters that are beyond imagination. He realizes that all things in this world are always changing and there is nothing existing in a fixed form (all things are impermanent); nothing in the universe is an isolated existence, having no relation to other things; everything exists in relationship with everything else like the meshes of a net (nothing has an ego).

The eye of the law is the artistic way of looking at things. To the average man, a mountain is just a mountain and a cloud is merely a cloud. But a poet feels that the mountain speaks to him and the cloud teaches him. He feels that a beautiful flower, a dignified tree, and a little stream talk to him, each in its own special language. Unlike the average person, an outstanding artist can directly touch the lives of such natural phenomena. In the case of man himself and his human life, such an artist can also perceive truths that the ordinary person cannot. This is why in Japan the title of Hōgen, literally meaning "eye of the law," was given to certain outstanding artists as a special rank, as in the case of the famous artists Kanō Masanobu (1434–1530) and his son Motonobu (1476–1559).

The eye of the Buddha is the highest of all viewpoints. A person with this kind of insight not only can perceive the real state of all things (wisdom) but can observe it with compassion. He penetrates the real state of all things with the desire to make all of them develop to the full extent of their potential, each according to its own original nature. In other words, he is endowed with the divine eye of celestial beings, the eye of wisdom, and the eye of the law while also possessing the mind of great compassion; it is he who takes a religious view of things in the true sense.

If we view all living beings with the eye of the Buddha, we can naturally discern the means most suitable to guide each one. The Buddha can do this perfectly. Granted that we as ordinary people cannot possibly attain such a mental state, we can approach it step by step through our accumulation of practice in the way to buddhahood. As people of religion, we must always try to view everything with a mental attitude based on the compassionate mind of the Buddha.

Then the Buddha continued to preach as follows: "Good sons! Beholding the propensities of all the living toward lower things, so that they have little virtue and much vileness, to these men the Tathāgata declares: 'In my youth I left home and attained Perfect Enlightenment.' But since I verily became Buddha, thus have I ever been, and thus have I made declaration, only by my tactful methods to teach and transform all living beings, so that they may enter the Way of the Buddha."

The expression "the propensities of all the living toward lower things" refers to those who are satisfied with the enlightenment of *śrāvaka* and *pratyekabuddha*. Toward such people the Buddha spoke of his life as the appearing Buddha and encouraged them to be more assiduous in their practice by taking his own experience as an example.

From our point of view, no encouragement is better than that of the Buddha. A teaching that we must follow according to the orders of an invisible god who exists in heaven is too vague for us to grasp. In Buddhism, however, Sakyamuni himself sets a living example for all living beings. All Buddhists should appreciate how much they owe to the Buddha. They have only to pursue the great guidelines the Buddha has left for them and earnestly follow his example. There is no other teaching that is so thoroughly believable or that gives such a feeling of security.

Because of the propensities of all living beings toward lower things, Sakyamuni Buddha declared, "Follow me!" This declaration of his in itself is a great salvation and encouragement to us in the age of degeneration. Needless to say, we must advance toward higher things, but while doing so, we must not forget to follow constantly in the track of the Buddha, step by step.

The Buddha then revealed his tactful methods in detail: "Good sons! All the sutras which the Tathāgata preaches are for the deliverance of the living. Whether speaking of himself or speaking of others, whether indicating himself or indicating others, and whether indicating his own affairs or the affairs of others, whatever he says is all real and not empty air." This passage is difficult for us to understand correctly but is very important indeed. In the phrase "speaking of himself," "himself" (*ko-shin*) means the Buddha's entity, that is, the Original Buddha. In the phrase "speaking of others," "others" (*ta-shin*) indicates other buddhas who appear as the reward-body of the Original Buddha, such as the Buddha Burning Light and the Tathāgata Amitābha. In the words "indicating himself," "himself" means Sakyamuni himself, who appeared in the world as the historical Buddha. In the words "indicating others," "others" indicates the Buddha as he appears as other saints and sages in this world.

In the expression "indicating his own affairs or the affairs of others," the correct meaning of "his own affairs" (*ko-ji*) and "the affairs of others" (*ta-ji*) is especially difficult to grasp correctly. In fact, these words seem to have been misinterpreted for the most part. Their true interpretation is as follows. In brief, the Buddha's salvation lies in enabling us to set our minds in the direction of the truth and to give harmony to our life-power. However, his salvation appears in two different ways: the "direct appearance" and the "reverse appearance."

Suppose that a man suffers from unhappiness in love, failure in business, and family trouble, and that he has reached a state in which he is always anxious and on edge, diverted from the truth and lacking harmony in his life-power. If he could attain a correct mental attitude through the Buddha's teachings, his mind would come to harmonize with his life-power and would begin to work correctly and clearly. This is the "direct appearance" of the Buddha's salvation, in which his salvation appears in a direct and straightforward manner. This is what is meant by "his own affairs" (*ko-ji*). But the Buddha's salvation does not always appear in this way. It sometimes appears as a "reverse phenomenon." Suppose that you begin to have a stomachache. This pain warns you of some disharmony in your life-power. It may come from eating or drinking too much, or it may be the symptom of a disease. When you have a stomachache you take medicine or consult a doctor in order to get rid of it, and you are temperate in eating and drinking until you feel better. Suppose you did not feel any pain. If something was wrong with your stomach or intestines because of neglecting your health, you would continue to remain unaware of it and the condition would gradually worsen until your health was seriously impaired. Thus, though pain and suffering seem to be disagreeable and unwelcome, the fact is that without them we cannot know that a serious disharmony of our life-power is occurring within us.

This is not limited to the body. As shown in the Parable of the Burning House, people do not awaken to the hellish fire burning their bodies and minds when they remain in the world of the five desires. They only examine themselves when they feel mental affliction, suffering, anxiety, and emptiness. Then they reflect on their lives, asking themselves, "Is this a good state for me?" or "What will become of me if I remain in such a mental state forever?" Their awareness of affliction and suffering paves the way for their future salvation.

The feeling of suffering in our human life is nature's warning, showing us the disharmony of our mind and life-power. If we awaken to this situation and realize, "This is not good for me," and if we then follow a correct teaching, we spontaneously set our mind in the direction of the truth. Therefore, even if we cannot immediately recover from illness or extricate ourselves from poverty, we come not to feel this as suffering. This is the great salvation of the Buddha. Thus his salvation sometimes appears in a form that does not at first seem to be salvation. This is the meaning of the expression "indicating the affairs of others."

In Risshō Kōsei-kai, when a member is admonished by a leader, he calls it "merit" (*kudoku*). It is indeed an unpleasant and unwelcome thing for anybody to be scolded or admonished by others. But since the Buddha's salvation is often extended to us through such scoldings and admonitions, our salvation is realized when we receive these warnings with gratitude. The words "indicating the affairs of others" are most important, and we should always bear them in mind in our daily lives.

THE NATURE OF BUDDHISM. Sakyamuni Buddha revealed that he instructed living beings occasionally by speaking of himself or speaking of others, occasionally by indicating himself or indicating others, and occasionally by indicating his own affairs or the affairs of others. Whatever he says is all real and not empty air—that is, there is nothing useless in what he says; all is for the purpose of elevating people and leading them to real enlightenment.

Here lies the vastness and profundity of the Buddha's teaching. Buddhism is not opposed to Christianity, Islam, and other teachings of great sages, such as Confucius, Mencius, and Lao-tzu. We understand that such saints and sages are the appearance of the Buddha in other forms and that their teachings are the manifestation of the Buddha's teachings in other forms. I do not say this because I am a Buddhist but because so long as the Buddha is the great truth and great life of the universe, there can be no truth that is not included in the Buddha, and no law other than that of the Buddha. Accordingly, a narrow-minded Buddhist who indiscriminately criticizes other religions and thinks, for example, that Buddhism is a true religion, while Christianity is not, cannot claim to be a true Buddhist.

A right teaching is right regardless of who preaches it. Truth is truth regardless of who proclaims it. Buddhists revere a person who leads all living beings by such a right and true teaching as "the Buddha." It follows naturally that they should not set themselves in opposition to other religions.

To cite a down-to-earth example, nutrition does not exist separately from such foods as rice, bread, beans, vegetables, milk, fish, and salt. All are nourishing and necessary for good health. All together constitute "nutrition." Someone who says, "I don't need 'nutrition' because I have bread, milk, and vegetables," has completely missed the point of what nutrition is. The teachings of the Buddha are like "nutrition" in this example. The teachings of all saints and sages correspond to the various foods—rice, vegetables, milk, and so on. The origin of all these various teachings is the Buddha's teachings. Accordingly, they are, so to speak, a well-balanced meal full of nutritious elements to nourish the human spirit. We have only to eat such a meal without worrying ourselves unnecessarily. We do not have to argue over the relative merits of rice, milk, and the other ingredients. We will come automatically to understand this if we can discern plainly the difference between the Original Buddha and the appearing Buddha.

As the teachings of the Buddha are vast and boundless, Sakyamuni as the appearing Buddha did not exclude the teachings of other religions. Brahmanism, the most influential religion at that time in India, included many deities and other beings believed to possess supernatural powers. But the Buddha added these heavenly beings to the living beings who were saved by listening to his teachings, and he regarded them as benevolent deities protecting the Buddha-law with their supernatural powers.

A powerful general in Vaiśālī, who had been a believer in Jainism, another Indian religion, was deeply impressed with the Buddha's teachings and soon became a disciple. Though the general wanted to declare his conversion from Jainism to Buddhism throughout the land, Sakyamuni dissuaded him, saying that it was not necessary. He even went so far as to tell the general, "You should continue to revere the Jain order, as you have practiced it all this while." There are many such episodes in the life of the Buddha.

Such ideas of the Buddha were transmitted to people during the period when the Righteous Law was still living. For example, Aśoka, a great king who brought most of India under his sway, and who was also a devout believer in Buddhism, did not persecute other religions but permitted freedom of religion.

One may well wonder whether Nichiren did not go contrary to the Buddha's intention when he criticized the other sects of Buddhism in the Kamakura period (1185–1333), saying, "The Jōdo sect will go to hell; the Zen sect is made by devils; the Shingon sect will ruin the state; the Ritsu sect is traitorous." But there was a good reason for such criticism of the other sects at that time. Japan was then already in the period of the *mappō* (last Law),[3] and the various sects of Buddhism were mutually antagonistic. They were apt to lose sight of the true intention of the Buddha. Therefore Nichiren urged that all Buddhists give up the consciousness of their particular sects and practice according to the true intention of the Buddha. He used harsh language in criticizing the other sects because the people of that time could not be brought to their senses in any other way. This was a tactful means in the true sense. It was nothing other than an indication of the "affairs of others" in the Buddha's salvation.

Since Buddhist priests and the general public today are more sophisticated in their thinking, we need not use the same kind of tactful means as Nichiren. As has already been explained, "tactful means" signifies a suitable enlightening method, in accord with the capacity of the people to understand the teachings of the Buddha. It is stupid to repeat the same tactful means when the people's capacity has changed for the better. To do so is to practice wrongly the teachings of the Buddha. This is an important point to keep in mind.

THE MEANING OF THE TRIPLE WORLD. Next the Buddha preached as follows: "Wherefore? Because the Tathāgata knows and sees the character of the triple world as it really is; to him there is neither birth nor death, or going away or coming forth; neither living nor dead; neither reality nor unreality; neither thus nor otherwise. Unlike the way the triple world beholds the triple world, the Tathāgata clearly sees such things as these without mistake."

This is a very difficult paragraph to understand. First we must explain

3. It is said that Buddhism will go through three periods following the Buddha's decease. The *mappō* is the last of these three periods. The period of the last Law is the period when Buddhist doctrine remains but there is neither true practice nor enlightenment.

the meanings of the words. The word "wherefore" here means: "I have preached that although the Tathāgata's teaching varies in its appearance, whatever he says is all real and not empty air; the reason is that . . ."

The words "triple world" have been variously interpreted since ancient times, but according to the usual interpretation, the triple world means the world of unenlightened people (including both visible and invisible realms) divided into three parts: the world of desire (*yoku-kai*), the world of form (*shiki-kai*), and the formless world (*mushiki-kai*). The world of desire means the world whose inhabitants have the five desires for property, sex, eating and drinking, fame, and sleep. The world of form indicates the idea of a world whose existence is imagined in one's mind in terms of specific shapes and forms, namely, all the things we ordinarily think about. The formless world is one whose inhabitants have no physical form. This is the world of pure mind, which we can attain when we concentrate upon a particular object in meditation or through other religious practices. Only the Tathāgata can see the state of the triple world as it really is.

In the expression "There is neither birth nor death, or going away or coming forth," "neither birth nor death" means not changing; "going away" expresses the idea of things disappearing, while "coming forth" indicates that of things appearing. Taken all together, this expression means: "All things seem to be changing, but they appear to be doing so from a phenomenal and relative point of view. When the Tathāgata sees the real state of all things, they neither disappear nor appear, and they are immortal and eternal."

When this idea is applied to the human body, "coming forth" means birth and "going away" means death. Although man seems to be born, grow old, suffer from disease, and finally die, these phenomena are only produced by superficial changes in the substances that form the human body; true human life continues eternally. The Buddha points this out in his next words, "neither living nor dead." His words appear to indicate something miraculous, but actually this is not so. The same idea can be expressed from a scientific point of view. As a simple example, we can take the law of the indestructibility of matter, through which science confirms that matter neither decreases nor disappears. The snow on the ground seems to melt away as the days go by, but in reality, it merely changes into water and sinks into the ground or evaporates into the air. The snow only changes its form; the quantity of fundamental elements that constitute it do not decrease, much less disappear. When water vapor in the air comes into contact with cold air as a condition (secondary cause, *en*), it becomes a tiny drop of water. These drops accumulate to form a cloud. When these tiny drops of water join to form large drops of water, they become rain and fall on the earth. They will fall not as rain but as snow when the temperature falls below a certain point. Thus, though matter seems to disappear, in actual fact it does not disappear but only changes in form.

The same thing can be said of man. In the sight of the Tathāgata the birth and death of man are merely changes in form; man's life itself remains eternally. Seen with the eyes of the Buddha, man's existence is "neither living nor dead."

In the next expression, "neither reality nor unreality, neither thus nor otherwise," "reality" means that we perceive things as if they were really there. "Unreality" means that we perceive them as not being there. To regard a tangible thing as surely existing is a one-sided way of considering matter. On the other hand, to regard an intangible thing as not existing is also a partial viewpoint.

For example, while we confidently affirm the existence of water because it is visible and tangible, it evaporates without our being aware of it. Conversely, while we do not recognize the existence of vapor because it is invisible, it becomes rain and falls on the earth. To be swayed by either "reality" or "unreality" is a superficial way of looking at things. The right way to look at them is with the Tathāgata's eyes: "neither reality nor unreality."

In the next expression, "neither thus nor otherwise," "thus" indicates the idea of always existing without change and "otherwise" means the opposite, the idea of change. Taken as a whole, this expression means that to view matter either as unchanging or as changing is a partial way of considering matter. An ordinary person is apt to take such a one-sided view, but the Tathāgata can discern equally both the unchangeable and the changeable states of things. In other words, he can see things as they truly are.

However, we can leave the philosophical subtleties concerning the changes in matter in the hands of scholars. Here let us try to apply the Buddha's words to our daily lives. All things seem changeable when viewed from a certain standpoint, and they seem unchangeable when viewed from another angle. For example, the view of human relationships today is quite different from that of feudal times. The relationship between parents and children has greatly changed, but there has been almost no change in parents' feeling of affection for their children or in children's feeling of love for their parents.

All people are different in looks, physique, and mental attitudes, but they have certain features in common, such as two eyes, a mouth, two hands, and two feet.

Thus we should think of things neither as changeable nor as unchangeable. To see only the distinctions between things is not a perfect way of looking at them, and to view them as equal is also an imperfect viewpoint. We must see all states of matter from a larger standpoint, and at the same time, we must view them with compassion—"We make all things live."

For example, if we adhere to the idea, "Our own body is changeable and true life exists in its depth," we are led into the mistaken idea of being indifferent to our own body. On the contrary, we should think that because our present body is the manifestation of our eternal life, to pay careful attention to our health is to value our eternal life, and it is natural for us to do so. This is the mental attitude through which we are hindered by nothing; this is the way of looking at matter with the intention, "We make all lives live."

The Buddha taught that the Tathāgata sees the real state of all things from a universal standpoint and has a free and unhindered view of them. He never takes a partial and narrow view of things in the way that ordinary people living in the triple world see that world.

A PRACTICAL THEORY OF DAILY LIFE. In the paragraph discussed above, the Buddha preached the wisdom of the Tathāgata, which contains a most profound teaching. In the first place, this teaching shows us that we must not misunderstand things by taking the changeable as the unchangeable. Suppose that we devote ourselves to golf, parties, and other amusements, thinking that we can relax because we have succeeded in laying the foundation of our business solidly enough to be ready for whatever may come. Nevertheless, circumstances that we would never dream of may arise. As the economics of the whole world are intricately interrelated, no one can know what influence a sudden change in another country may exert upon his own. Therefore, however solidly one succeeds in laying the foundation of his business, it will never attain an unchangeable state. He must take into consideration the possibility of change at any time and not neglect his work.

Though every businessman should know such things, the fact is that countless people have failed in business because of complacency or negligence. Even the richest man, the greatest businessman, and the ablest statesman should follow the Buddha's teachings selflessly.

It would be a great mistake to think that the teachings of the Buddha have nothing to do with our actual lives, because they are the fundamental principle of the universe and of human life. They apply to every case in our actual lives because of this fundamental principle. Something that is not applicable to our actual lives is something that is not true to this fundamental principle.

We can say the same thing of our bodies. We are not aware of physical changes when we are in good health. This is because the body changes very slowly and quietly. We are liable to overestimate our health and to be overconfident of our own strength. Suppose that a man continues to drink as heavily as when he was younger without regard for his aging body; of course it will be adversely affected. His fault is in regarding the changeable as the unchangeable. We are normally aware of our bodily changes over a period of time, but a person who drinks heavily disregards the changes in his body. He ignores or defies his body's warnings. A person who correctly understands the Buddha's teachings accepts these natural warnings with a flexible mind and therefore can live out his natural span of life.

If we have a flexible mind, we can perceive natural warnings clearly. For instance, we never minded running risks in our youth, but as we get older, we gradually come to feel fearful of taking leaps in the dark. This is normal; it is a natural warning to us to slow down.

A young man can run downhill when descending a steep mountain path, while an old man prudently descends step by careful step. This is because the human body itself knows that wounds heal soon when one is young but that healing is slow when one is old, and for this reason the body warns us, "Take care of yourself." A person who has a flexible mind accepts this warning and descends the mountain path slowly. But one who tries to keep up with young people by running downhill may have a bad fall and break his leg.

The Buddha's teachings instruct us not to regard the changeable as the unchangeable. If we view things thoroughly and clearly, we can see all changes. To act according to changes with a flexible mind is the right way of living. At the same time, we should not be too bound by change, either. To feel that we cannot do anything as well as young people because we have grown older, are too old to work efficiently any longer, and want only to live in comfort for the rest of our days is a way of thinking that is too influenced by change. There should be something unchanging within us even as we grow older. To make the best use of our experience, brains, technical skills, leadership, dignity, and other qualities, and to work for the benefit of people and society for our entire life is the right way to live.

Sir Winston Churchill wrote his great six-volume work *The Second World War* after he had retired from active politics, and he won the Nobel Prize for literature in 1953 at the age of 79. Nakamura Utaemon IV, a famous Kabuki actor, appeared on the stage with the help of others even when he was so old that he had difficulty in walking, and he gave moving performances while remaining seated. These are examples of people who have not been adversely influenced by the changes of old age.

So far we have been considering elderly people; let us now give some examples involving young people. Women have come to have equal rights with men under the law since the postwar constitution of Japan was promulgated. This was a dramatic change from the prewar days. In the new constitution women have been granted equal human rights, but they have not changed in their physical structure, which enables them to give birth to and nurture babies. They are unchangeable in this respect. If women try to behave like men in everything simply because equality of the sexes has been guaranteed in the constitution, it represents a way of thinking that is restricted by change and is inconsistent with reason. Though there may have been some Japanese women who intentionally behaved like men, most have assumed a modest manner. Among them, some women who have listened to the teachings of the Buddha have lived in a reasonable and womanly manner and have indeed been women worthy of Buddhism.

The words "neither reality nor unreality" include a very important teaching concerning our way of life. We must not be overconfident when we perceive the existence of things, nor pessimistic when we perceive their nonexistence. While perceiving the existence of a thing, we must provide against the time when we will perceive its nonexistence. Conversely, even though we may think a thing is nonexistent, it is really existent, and we should seek it. This is true of everything regardless of its substance and of man's ability. We must always do our part well without being rigidly bound by the idea of either the existence or the nonexistence of things. Thus we can maintain calm minds and lead vigorous lives.

Take the case of a river. Water is incessantly flowing in the river. Although we see a wide expanse of water stretching before us, the water that was seen a second ago now exists no longer. The water seen in the present moment no longer exists in the next moment. For all that, the river does not disappear but really exists.

The same thing applies to human life. Strictly speaking, our self of yesterday is not the same as our self of today. The cells of our body are reborn moment by moment. The state of our mental powers and techniques are different today from yesterday. At the same time, we cannot say that our self of yesterday is one thing and our self of today is quite another, for our lives continue unceasingly from yesterday to today.

We can no more say, "This is the river," when we see one section of it before us than we can consider our life aside from its parts. For this reason, we cannot adopt the attitude that if we can only pass the present moment pleasantly, never mind the consequences. Yesterday was yesterday, and today is today. Tomorrow will take care of itself. The karma that we produced yesterday continues to exist today, iust as the river goes on and on. The karma that we produce today is certain to affect tomorrow. If someone pours poison in the river, the fish downstream will die. If he stirs up the water, the river will become muddy downstream.

At the same time, we must not continually worry about what happened yesterday. We cannot go forward when we are bound by the past. Though the past really exists, we should not be swayed by it. What then should we do? We have only to live today well, fully, and without regret. To live in this way will lead us to extinguish the evil karma that we produced yesterday and to accumulate good karma for tomorrow.

The "present" disappears momentarily, but it really exists, so we should attach great importance to this time that seems to be so transient. This attitude embodies the idea of the Buddha's words "neither reality nor unreality."

In this way, if we follow the example of the Buddha-knowledge and try to view the real state of all things without being bound by their surface appearances—that is, their changes, existence, nonexistence, and differences—we can lead correct and positive lives and can accomplish the mission for which we were born into this world.

Then the Buddha preached as follows: "Because all the living have various natures, various desires, various activities, various ideas and reasonings, so desiring to cause them to produce the roots of goodness, the Tathāgata by so many reasonings, parables, and discourses has preached his various truths. The Buddha-deeds which he does have never failed for a moment."

In this passage, "natures" means one's character; "desires," one's cravings; "activities," one's actions; and "ideas," one's thoughts. "Reasonings" implies reading one's own interpretation into everything. Because all living beings differ in various ways, the Buddha has preached the truth in many ways so as to cause all of them to produce the roots of goodness. The roots of goodness are a person's fundamental mind, which produces a good nature, good desires, good activity, good ideas, and good reasoning. These qualities are like the roots of a plant, from which grow its good stem, branches, and leaves.

In what various ways does the Buddha preach the truth? Sometimes he preaches it by reasonings, that is, he speaks of the past in association with himself. On other occasions he preaches the truth through parables. At other times he preaches it by discourses, that is, he expounds it with words appropriate to the occasion and the listener.

Next the Buddha says, "The Buddha-deeds which he does have never failed for a moment." "Buddha-deeds" means the Buddha's work, which instructs all people, saves them from their sufferings, and leads them to nirvana. His deeds include the following: he instructs all the living beings everywhere in various ways—whether speaking of himself or speaking of others, whether indicating himself or indicating others, and whether indicating his own affairs or the affairs of others. It would be a great mistake for us to consider only the Buddha's own work as Buddha-deeds. To convey the Buddha's teachings to others or to listen to them or read them are also Buddha-deeds. Our Buddha-deeds must continue incessantly, just as the Buddha never neglected them for a moment. This is our great responsibility.

Next the Buddha preached as follows: "Thus it is, since I became Buddha in the very far distant past, that my lifetime is of infinite *asaṃkhyeya kalpas,* forever existing and immortal. Good sons! The lifetime which I attained by pursuing the bodhisattva-way is not even yet accomplished but will still be twice the previous number of *kalpas*. But now, in this unreal nirvana, I announce that I must enter the real nirvana. In this tactful way the Tathāgata teaches all living beings."

In the first part of this passage the Buddha refers to the Eternal Original Buddha: "Thus it is, since I became Buddha in the very far distant past, that my lifetime is of infinite *asaṃkhyeya kalpas,* forever existing and immortal." Following this he refers to himself as the appearing Buddha: "The lifetime which I attained by pursuing the bodhisattva-way is not even yet accomplished but will still be twice the previous number of *kalpas.*"

Sakyamuni Buddha had pursued the bodhisattva-way in his previous existences, not only in this present life. He declared that the lifetime that he had attained as compensation for his practice of the bodhisattva-way was infinitely long. The Eternal Original Buddha is the existence of non-beginning and non-end. Even the lifetime that Sakyamuni Buddha had attained in his present existence was not yet accomplished, but now, in this unreal nirvana, he announced that he must enter the real nirvana.

Why must the Buddha enter nirvana, leaving living beings behind, in spite of his remaining lifetime being infinitely long? This is solely a tactful means used for the instruction of living beings; it is nothing but the expression of his compassion. He made this clear in the next statement: "Wherefore? If the Buddha abides long in the world, men of little virtue who do not cultivate the roots of goodness and are spiritually poor and mean, greedily attached to the five desires, and are caught in the net of wrong reflection and false views—if they see the Tathāgata constantly present and not extinct, they will then become puffed up and lazy, and unable to conceive the idea that it is hard to meet the Buddha or a mind of reverence for him."

This is a most important statement. The reference to men who are poor and mean indicates not material but spiritual poverty. In the eyes of the Buddha, all men and all things are equal, and there cannot be any discrimination among them because of their station in life, whether rich or poor. The words "greedily attached to the five desires" refer to the condition in which man is swayed by the joy that he feels through the five sense organs: eyes, ears, nose, tongue, and body. These are such human desires as wishing to see beautiful things, to hear pleasant sounds, to smell pleasant odors, to taste good food, and to touch or feel pleasant things (for example, the desire to be cool in summer, to be warm in winter, to keep from being exposed to rain and wind, and to wear clothes agreeable to the touch).

The desires of the five sense organs are innate and are not wrong in themselves, but they are harmful because illusions arise from being influenced by the pleasures of the senses. They are also dangerous because the urge to seek the Way is disturbed and sullied by them.

This is such an important point that Sakyamuni Buddha taught it on many occasions. It was for this reason that he gave up the practice of asceticism and drank the milk-gruel given to him by a village girl and that he preached the teaching of the Middle Path. The Buddha states clearly that man's instincts are morally neutral (*muki,* literally meaning something existing before the decision of right or wrong, that is, something that we cannot call either good or bad). If our natural appetites and instincts were wrong, we should refrain entirely from eating and starve to death. We should become deaf in order to abandon the desires that come through our ears, and we should put our eyes out in order to deny the desires that come through the sense of vision. The Buddha nowhere preaches such extremes but teaches us that though instincts are not wrong in themselves, the fire of illusion that is produced by a burning attachment to them is not good. Our instincts are morally neutral, but it is not good for us to be greedily attached to them. If we misunderstand this point, we fall into the extreme of either asceticism or hedonism and thus violate the teaching of the Middle Path.

In the words "the net of wrong reflection and false views," "reflection" means to remember what we have already experienced and to imagine what we have not yet experienced. The Buddha suggests here that there is a danger of hindering the spiritual development of living beings if he stays eternally in this world. "False views" means to be unable to view things as they truly are. Man cannot see things as they are because of his self-centered mind.

Suppose that a junior executive, unaware that he has a spot of egg on his chin, walks by the president and the president smiles at the young man. If the man is hoping for a promotion or a raise, he will jump to the conclusion that because the president smiled at him, he will soon get what he desires. On the other hand, if he is lazy or falsifies the books, he will be flustered by the president's smile and will jump to the conclusion that this is a sarcastic smile indicating that some error or dishonesty has finally come to light. In both cases, owing to his egoism, the young man cannot possibly grasp the true reason that the president smiled at him. This is because the man has a self-centered view of things, evaluating everything according to his own standpoint alone. On the other hand, if he has no such egoism, he will ask himself, "I wonder why the president smiled at me. Is something peculiar?" And then he will examine himself in a mirror.

This kind of situation is familiar to all of us. In our daily lives there are many instances in which because of their selfish point of view, people do not recognize the real state of things, worry needlessly, and become unhappy. All such anxieties stem from false views.

The expression "caught in the net of wrong reflection and false views" means that pointless anxiety over the past or future entraps us in the net of taking a wrong view of things, so that we are hampered from acting effectively and freely. When we are greedily attached to the five desires, we are naturally self-centered and produce such results.

The words "become puffed up" refer to man's willful mind. He would feel that he could easily hear the teachings of the Buddha any time he liked, if the Buddha remained forever in this world. He would thus tend to become lazy—"I'll enjoy myself today and listen to the teaching tomorrow." This is the mental state indicated by the words "become puffed up."

People from the country who visit the capital often see more of the city than those who were born and bred there. This is probably because natives of the city put off making a special effort to see the sights, feeling that they can see them whenever they wish. In the same way, if we feel confident of being able to see the Buddha any time we like, we are liable to postpone doing so. Some of us will become lazy to the point of boredom. Others will feel, "Because the Buddha's teachings are always the same whenever I hear them, I do not have to listen to them any longer." If people saw the Buddha constantly present and not extinct, they would be unable to conceive the idea that it is hard to meet the Buddha, nor would they revere him. Therefore the Buddha taught, as a tactful method, that he must enter nirvana before long.

As the Buddha perceived, all people have the tendency to want to have everything their own way. In Japan, people sometimes go to special theaters to hear professional storytellers relate historical or humorous anecdotes. They should pay attention to the entertainment because they have paid admission especially to see and hear the show. However, some people whisper to their neighbors, munch snacks, and appear restless and not quite at ease. Such general restlessness is especially noticeable as one performer leaves the stage and the next one comes on to begin his act. At such a time, as is the custom with Japanese professional storytellers of historical narratives, as soon as he appears on the stage the performer seats himself on a cushion and bows to the audience. He taps with his fan to attract the audience's attention and begins his story in such a low voice that the audience can hardly hear him. Then silence reigns, because everyone wants to hear the story and naturally strains his ears. This demonstrates a tactful method of the storyteller, who has grasped the mental state of the audience and made them want to hear what he is saying. The idea that it is hard to meet the Buddha and that one should have a spirit of reverence toward him is incomparably more important.

Then the Buddha preached as follows: "Therefore the Tathāgata tactfully teaches: 'Know, *bhikshus,* the appearance of buddhas in the world is a rare occurrence.' Wherefore? In the course of countless hundreds of thousands of myriads of *koṭis* of *kalpas,* some men of little virtue may happen to see a buddha or none may see him. For this reason I say: '*Bhikshus!* A *tathāgata* may rarely be seen!' All these living beings, hearing such a statement, must certainly realize the thought of the difficulty of meeting a buddha and cherish a longing and a thirst for him; then will they cultivate the roots of goodness."

The teaching in the chapter "Revelation of the [Eternal] Life of the Tathāgata" can be divided into two main points. The first is the Buddha's revelation of his entity and his immortality. The second is his exposition of the reason that the Tathāgata Sakyamuni, as one of the appearing buddhas of the Original Buddha, must enter nirvana. The core of the second point is expressed clearly in the passage quoted above.

A Buddha Can Rarely Be Seen. When they read the above passage, many people may suspect that it is inconsistent with the idea that the Original Buddha is omnipresent, saving all living beings from suffering and leading them to nirvana. They may also feel that since the Buddha can save all living beings from suffering through his infinite compassion, he should also enable people of little virtue to see a buddha.

Because the Original Buddha is omnipresent, a virtuous person will naturally be able to perceive his teachings that are incomprehensible to ordinary men, just as a television set with good reception transmits a sharp picture. However, ordinary people cannot come in contact with the Buddha's teachings until such great religious leaders as the Lord Sakyamuni, Chih-i, Prince Shōtoku, Saichō, Dōgen, and Nichiren appear in this world and directly preach the Law.

Even if people of little virtue happen to live in the same age as such religious leaders, they cannot come in contact with the teachings preached by them. This is because, as already explained, the appearance of buddhas means that we are aware of them. The same thing can be said of the words "to see a buddha." However often we hear the Buddha's teachings, we cannot see a buddha unless we direct our mind toward him. This is how we should interpret the words "to see a buddha." Although the Original Buddha exists in all times and in all places, his salvation does not appear unless we see a buddha in the true sense. Simply because the Original Buddha always exists close to us, we cannot expect his help if we are idle and lead greedy and self-centered lives.

As mentioned repeatedly, the Original Buddha does not exist apart from us. Therefore he does not treat us with such indulgence as to give happiness to us even when we forget him and violate his teachings. Certainly, he exists at all times and in all places together with us. He is omnipresent both within us and without. But he does not show his salvation to us until we can see him for ourselves. The instant we think of the Buddha, he also intuitively knows us, as expressed in the words of a sutra: "I realize the thought of the Buddha, while he realizes the thought of me."

We must voluntarily seek the Buddha's teachings. Even when they are preached to us directly, we cannot hear them unless we have the urge to seek them. Otherwise, even if we hear them, they will not sink deeply into our minds. The endeavor to seek the teaching must be made by ourselves—this is one of the main points that Sakyamuni Buddha taught us. This will be discussed further in the Parable of the Physician's Sons later in this chapter.

In the words "cherish a longing and a thirst for him," "a thirst for him" means to admire and respect the virtue of a buddha, just as a thirsty man yearns for water. This phrase has sometimes been interpreted as meaning having deep faith. But here we interpret these words according to their original meaning. First, applying the teaching of this paragraph to ourselves, we should reflect deeply on ourselves before worrying about the meaning of this teaching.

Although we speak of the Buddha easily, when we quietly think of him, his appearance is a rare occurrence for us in this age of degeneration, the *mappō* period. We must realize it is very hard to see the Buddha in this fearful world, where people deceive, fight, and kill one another. Realizing this, we cannot help raising the desire to see the Buddha and to be close to him. Our minds are strongly attracted by his compassion, just as we long to drink water when we feel thirsty or yearn for sunlight after a long spell of rain or snow. This kind of situation is expressed by the words "cherish a longing and a thirst for him."

If we have such a desire, we can surely purify our minds. No defilement or impurity can be harbored in a heart that desires to be close to the Buddha. The more we purify our minds, the more we can deepen our yearning to seek the Buddha's teachings and to practice them. Thus we come naturally to do good deeds for the benefit of others as well as ourselves. This is what makes a religion worthy of the name, and here lies the highest reach of Buddhism. The condition in which we cherish a longing and a thirst for the Buddha is a mental state beyond reason. We cannot be apart from the Buddha; we cannot forget him; we desire to be held by him, just as a baby innocently sucks its mother's breast. When we can attain such a mental state, we can be said to have true faith.

Then the Buddha preached as follows: "Therefore the Tathāgata, though he does not in reality become extinct, yet announces his extinction. Again, good sons! The method of all buddha-*tathāgatas* is always like this, in order to save all the living, and it is altogether real and not false."

The true worth of the Buddha's expedient means is fully shown in the words "it is altogether real and not false." The word "real" means not "fact" but "truth." It is a fact that the Buddha is the existence of non-beginning and non-end. But he does not reveal this to people of little virtue, instead announcing his extinction. Though his announcement seems to be a lie because it is not factual in the world of form, it is factual in the world of spirit. It is a reality in the mind of the Buddha for the sake of saving all living beings, and is not a lie. The word "false" here includes the meanings "empty" and "fruitless" in addition to "lie." A proverb says, "Lies are sometimes expedient," but this saying often leads to misunderstanding. We must not confuse "lie" with "expedient means."

To give an example explaining the true meaning of "expedient means," suppose that Mr. A boards a ship at Yokohama together with a young boy, saying, "I will take you to the United States to put you into school there." The boy expects the ship to sail east, but instead it sails west. The ship calls at several ports, including Manila, Singapore, and Calcutta. The boy feels discontented and restless. He wonders why Mr. A did not take him directly to America by plane. He begins to be suspicious of Mr. A's motive in taking a slow ship sailing in the opposite direction from his final destination.

Meanwhile, the ship enters the Mediterranean and finally docks at Marseilles. Mr. A disembarks there with the boy and then takes the boy to Paris. While the boy wonders about Mr. A more and more, they leave for England. After the boy has spent several days there, finally he flies with Mr. A to America, his original destination.

Why did Mr. A treat the boy in this way? The boy does not speak English well and he is not accustomed to the manners and customs of foreign countries. If he had flown to America directly and had been suddenly put into school there, he would have been unable to understand his lessons or his classmates. Therefore, Mr. A took the boy on a long sea trip in order gradually to accustom the boy to new things, people, and places. During the long sea trip, the boy became used to eating Western food, learned foreign manners and customs through contact with foreign people, and had a chance to use English in practical situations. After Mr. A made the boy gain self-confidence in studying abroad, he took him to his destination.

In this case, it is not a lie that Mr. A made the boy embark in the opposite direction in spite of his declaration that he would take the boy to America. And it is not fruitless for the boy to have taken such a roundabout route. Mr. A's thoughtful consideration for the boy is a fact and is an effective means of guiding the boy. Expedient means should be like this: both a "fact" and an "effective means" of guiding people, motivated by compassion.

In order to help people understand the true meaning of his expedient and tactful means in leading them, Sakyamuni Buddha preached this in further detail through the Parable of the Physician's Sons, the last of the seven parables in the Lotus Sutra.

THE PARABLE OF THE PHYSICIAN'S SONS. "Suppose, for instance, a good physician who is wise and perspicacious, conversant with medical art, and skillful in healing all sorts of diseases. He has many sons, say ten, twenty, even up to a hundred. Because of some matter he goes abroad to a distant country. After his departure, his sons drink his other poisonous medicines, which send them into a delirium, and they lie rolling on the ground. At this moment their father comes back to his home. Of the sons who drank the poison, some have lost their senses, others are still sensible, but on seeing their father approaching in the distance they are all greatly delighted, and kneeling, salute him, asking: 'How good it is that you are returned in safety! We, in our foolishness, have mistakenly dosed ourselves with poison. We beg that you will heal us and give us back our lives.'

"The father, seeing his sons in such distress, in accordance with his prescriptions seeks for good herbs altogether perfect in color, scent, and fine flavor, and then pounds, sifts, and mixes them and gives them to his sons to take, speaking thus: 'This excellent medicine with color, scent, and fine flavor altogether perfect, you may now take, and it will at once rid you of your distress so that you will have no more suffering.'

"Those amongst the sons who are sensible, seeing this excellent medicine with color and scent both good, take it immediately and are totally delivered from their illness. The others, who have lost their senses, seeing their father come, though they are also delighted, salute him, and ask him to heal their illness, yet when he offers them the medicine, they are unwilling to take it. Wherefore? Because the poison has entered deeply, they have lost their senses, and even in regard to this medicine of excellent color and scent they acknowledge that it is not good.

"The father reflected thus: 'Alas for these sons, afflicted by this poison, and their minds all overbalanced. Though they are glad to see me and implore to be healed, yet they are unwilling to take such excellent medicine as this. Now I must arrange an expedient plan so that they will take this medicine.' Then he says to them: 'You should know that I am worn out with old age and the time of my death has now arrived. This excellent medicine I now leave here. You may take it and have no fear of not being better.' After thus admonishing them, he departs again for another country and sends a messenger back to inform them: 'Your father is dead.' "

The words "their minds all overbalanced" mean to view things through illusion and thus misjudge them. Ordinary people are said to have the following four illusions (*shi-tendō*): *nitya-viparyāsa* (*jō-tendō*), the illusion of considering the impermanent as the permanent, that is, of regarding the changeable as the unchangeable; *sukha-viparyāsa* (*raku-tendō*), the illusion of considering suffering as pleasure; *śuci-viparyāsa* (*jō-tendō*), the illusion of considering a superficial appearance of the impure as the pure; and *ātma-viparyāsa* (*ga-tendō*), the illusion that there exists a real ego although nothing has an ego and all things exist in interdependence with one another.

There are various other illusions, including the reverse of these four. The sons in this parable were deluded through regarding that of supreme value as valueless. The parable continues:

"And now, when those sons hear that their father is dead, their minds are greatly distressed and they thus reflect: 'If our father were alive he would have pity on us, and we should be saved and preserved. But now he has left us and died in a distant country. Now we feel we are orphans and have no one to rely on.' Continuous grief brings them to their senses; they recognize the color, scent, and excellent flavor of the medicine, and thereupon take it, their poisoning being entirely relieved. The father, hearing that the sons are all recovered, seeks an opportunity and returns so that they all see him."

In the Parable of the Physician's Sons, the physician is the Buddha and the sons represent all living beings. The gist of the parable is that living beings cannot understand how much they owe to the Buddha as long as he abides in this world, but they conceive the desire to seek his teachings earnestly when he becomes extinct. For this reason, he temporarily enters nirvana through his tactful means.

The Buddha teaches us several important lessons in this parable. The first significant point is that the sons drink poisonous medicines while their father is away in a distant country. The poisonous medicines are illusions produced by the five desires. If people come in contact with the Buddha's teachings daily, they will not suffer from these five desires disturbing their minds. However, when they avoid the Buddha's teachings, they are apt to become obsessed by the five desires.

The next important point is that all the sons who drank the poison, even those who have lost their senses, to say nothing of the others who are still in their right minds, are delighted on seeing their father return home. The parable thus shows that even a madman can tell his father from other people. In the same way, even those with illusions who have lost their senses, for example, even a thoroughgoing materialist who boasts, "I don't believe in God or the Buddha," in the depths of his mind feels an unrest and loneliness that he cannot quite satisfy by material things. He seeks mental calm and satisfaction, though he is unaware of it. Therefore, if he encounters a teaching giving him spiritual peace and enlightenment, he is sure to be delighted with it. This is the same thing as the sons who have lost their senses being glad to see their father approaching in the distance.

The Buddha, seeing all living beings as sons in distress, seeks for good herbs altogether perfect in color, scent, and flavor, and then pounds, sifts, and mixes them. Good herbs with color, scent, and flavor altogether perfect indicate that in order to cure men's mental distress, various prescriptions of the Buddha are necessary, including a medicine for removing illusions from their minds, a medicine for making them gain true wisdom, and a medicine for making them raise the spirit of rendering service to others. To pound such good herbs means to enable an ordinary person to take them easily, that is, to enable him to understand the Buddha's teachings easily. To sift such good herbs means to remove impurities, namely, to be pure and unsullied from a religious point of view.

The Buddha's teachings are supreme, and those who believe in and receive them can be saved from their sufferings immediately. But there are some who have no desire to receive the supreme teachings of the Buddha. These people ought to receive such teachings, just as the sons in the parable were very glad to see their father. But people whose spirit is sickened by the poison of illusions do not receive the teachings voluntarily, though they do have a dim perception of their goodness.

Even a madman wandering about in the street recognizes his mother who comes to take him home, and he smiles at her tentatively. But he does not necessarily obey her and go home with her. He may resist her strongly or run away from her. On the same principle, not all living beings understand the Buddha's compassion, although they recognize him as their father.

As the wise physician with his sons, the Buddha as the father of all living beings does not become angry or reject them. On the contrary, he says, "Alas for these sons." We should be grateful for this great compassion of the Buddha. He is compassionate even toward living beings who turn their backs on his teachings, saying, "Ah, poor sons!" He never ignores them but acts kindly toward them, trying every means available that they may come to believe in and receive his teachings. It is one of the Buddha's tactful means to announce his entering the real nirvana while in the unreal nirvana. This should be recognized as a tactful means replete with compassion.

It is most important for us to do things for ourselves. Especially is this necessary in the case of faith. It is all right for us to adopt a faith at others' suggestion, but we cannot be real believers if we neglect to seek the Way seriously with our own minds. "If a friend repeatedly urges me to go to hear someone preach, I'll go out of a sense of obligation, though I do not really want to"—such a feeling cannot develop into real faith.

One's wife or servant serves food at the dining table, but one must eat it oneself without the help of others. One who cannot eat by himself is a sick person. However, a sick person must still chew and swallow his food himself, even if someone else carries it to his mouth. One cannot truly enjoy a meal eaten with the help of others.

The Buddha never tries to force open our mouths and cram his excellent medicine down our throats. It is a sacred task for us to take it in our hands and put it into our mouths ourselves. The Buddha uses various means so tactfully that we quickly feel inclined to do so. That is, he indicates himself or indicates others, indicates his own affairs or the affairs of others. Of these indications, the greatest and the most urgent is that he himself has become extinct. Realizing that, those who have felt complacently that they can hear his teachings whenever they like or lazy people who have become tired of the teachings cannot help suddenly becoming serious. This is the most important reason that the Buddha's extinction is a tactful means full of his great compassion.

The last important point of the parable is that the father seeks an opportunity to return home when he hears that the sons are all recovered. This suggests that all living beings can see a buddha as soon as they believe in the Buddha's teachings and remove illusions from their minds. In brief, the Buddha, whom they have missed, is recalled to their minds and they can continually abide close to him. In the words "to see a buddha," "to see" has a different meaning from the phrase "to observe something," which indicates the idea of looking at it with the desire to do so. "To see something" has the connotation of being able to see it spontaneously, without such an intention. If we have strong faith in the Buddha, we can spontaneously see a buddha. We cannot see the form of a buddha but can be aware that the Buddha abides with us in this world.

The relationship between the Buddha and human beings is not a cold one like that between ruler and ruled but is like that between father and son. The two are joined by warm affection. For this reason, if we rightly believe in and receive the Buddha's teachings even when we have missed him once, instantly he returns to our minds. Like a real father, he eternally lives with us and protects us in this world. We fully realize the Buddha's indescribable compassion in the Parable of the Physician's Sons.

After finishing this parable, the World-honored One asked the bodhisattvas and all the great assembly: "All my good sons! What is your opinion? Are there any who could say that this good physician had committed the sin of falsehood?" They answered with one voice, "No, World-honored One!" Then the Buddha said: "I also am like this. Since I became Buddha, infinite boundless hundred thousand myriad *koṭis* of *nayutas* of *asaṃkhyeya kalpas* ago, for the sake of all living beings, by my tactful power, I have declared that I must enter nirvana, yet there is none who can lawfully accuse me of the error of falsehood."

THE MOST IMPORTANT VERSE OF THE LOTUS SUTRA. Then the World-honored One spoke in verse concerning the infinite lifetime of the Original Buddha and the extinction of the appearing Buddha. The following passage, beginning with the words, "Since I attained buddhahood," is regarded as the most important of the many verses of the Lotus Sutra.

"Since I attained buddhahood,
The *kalpas* through which I have passed
Are infinite thousands of myriads
Of *koṭis* of *asaṃkhyeya* years.
Ceaselessly preached I the Law and taught
Countless *koṭis* of creatures
To enter the Way of the Buddha;
Since then are unmeasured *kalpas*.
In order to save all creatures,
By tactful methods I reveal nirvana,
Yet truly I am not yet extinct,
But forever here preaching the Law.
I forever remain in this world,
Using all my spiritual powers
So that all perverted creatures,
Though I am near, yet fail to see me."

In this passage, "nirvana" means not the state of enlightenment attained by Sakyamuni but the state of his extinction or annihilation. The words "all perverted creatures" mean all living beings, whose minds are all distorted by illusion.

"All looking on me as extinct
Everywhere worship my relics,

All cherishing longing desires,
And beget thirsting hearts of hope."

The words "cherishing longing desires" and "thirsting hearts of hope" have been explained on page 242. From the words "my relics," we can judge that Sakyamuni is referring to himself as the appearing Buddha.

"When all creatures have believed and obeyed,
In character upright, in mind gentle,
Wholeheartedly wishing to see the Buddha,
Not caring for their own lives . . ."

When all living beings cherish a longing and a thirst for the Buddha, they voluntarily begin to study deeply the teachings preached by him during his lifetime and to believe in them. Then they become upright in character. This character leads them to wish wholeheartedly to see the Buddha, with righteous minds harboring no secret desire. They also come to be gentle in mind.

The words "in mind gentle" express a major characteristic of Buddhism and Buddhists. To be gentle does not mean to be limp or flaccid but to be flexible and mild. If an athlete's body is not flexible, he cannot improve in technique, develop true stamina, or become stronger. In the same way, to be gentle in mind means to have a mind that has no ego and that readily accepts truth and right.

Buddhism itself is a gentle teaching. This teaching is of course "right," but it is not "self-righteous" in the sense of being opinionated and obstinate. As stated in the explanation of the Middle Path, the teaching of Buddhism is always in perfect accord with the truth, and its expression has the flexibility of perfect freedom. Therefore, a true Buddhist should not be obstinate or bigoted but should be flexible in accordance with the truth. Such an attitude is that of being gentle in mind.

Accordingly, those who believe and obey the teachings of the Buddha wish wholeheartedly to see him with their upright, selfless, and gentle minds. They attain the mental state of not being attached to their own lives. The words "wishing to see the Buddha" mean that we become conscious of abiding with him. When we realize clearly that we are definitely in the Buddha's arms and are caused to live by him, we are in the mental state of having seen him. This realization constitutes our great peace of mind. We are ready for anything. In attaining such a state of mind it is natural that one will come not to desire money, social status, or fame, and will not be attached even to his own life.

"Then I with all the Saṃgha
Appear together on the Divine Vulture Peak.
And then I tell all creatures
That I exist forever in this world,
By the power of tactful methods
Revealing myself extinct and not extinct.
If in other regions there are beings
Reverent and with faith aspiring,
Again I am in their midst
To preach the supreme Law.
You, not hearing of this,
Only say I am extinct."

The words "I with all the Saṃgha" mean that the Buddha appears with the people who help him to preach his teachings. Formerly, the Saṃgha referred to a Buddhist community of monks or nuns, but broadly speaking it includes laymen and laywomen who believe in and practice the Buddha's teachings. That the Buddha appears in this world not alone but together with his many disciples and believers has a very profound meaning, revealing to us that a righteous and important teaching is accompanied by those who believe, obey, and protect it.

The Buddha said, "Appear together on the Divine Vulture Peak," only because the place where he was preaching at the time was the Divine Vulture Peak. In other words, it means this world. Any place where we hear the righteous Law is the Divine Vulture Peak, whether it is in Japan or in America, in the streets or in a building, such as a Buddhist temple or training hall.

"I behold all living creatures
Sunk in the sea of suffering,
Hence I do not reveal myself
But set them all aspiring,
Till, when their hearts are longing,
I appear to preach the Law.
In such supernaturally pervading power,
Throughout *asaṃkhyeya kalpas*

I am always on the Divine Vulture Peak
And in every other dwelling place."

The words "sunk in the sea of suffering" mean literally that all living beings who do not know the Buddha's teachings are sunk in the sea of suffering. Some of them do not realize this, but even these people will feel an inexpressible unrest and loneliness and at times will desire to have something to depend on. They will sometimes feel that they cannot keep going without some absolute power to depend upon. Their minds, desiring to depend upon something and seeking earnestly for an absolute power, correspond to the mind of longing for the Buddha.

"When all the living see, at the *kalpa*'s end,
The conflagration when it is burning,
Tranquil is this realm of mine,
Ever filled with heavenly beings,
Parks, and many palaces
With every kind of gem adorned,
Precious trees full of blossoms and fruits,
Where all creatures take their pleasure;
All the gods strike the heavenly drums
And evermore make music,
Showering *mandārava* flowers
On the Buddha and his great assembly."

In this case, *kalpa* does not indicate the idea of a unit of time but the idea of a period. In ancient India, it was believed that at the end of a *kalpa* all creatures would be completely destroyed. This situation is expressed in the words "at the *kalpa*'s end."

Even though the time of the *kalpa*'s end will come to all creatures, the Buddha's world is never destroyed. On the contrary, the realm of the Buddha is always beautiful and tranquil. This means that however much the visible, phenomenal world may change, the world of the real state of all things is imperishable and eternal. The state of the Pure Land described here is equivalent to the mental state of one purified by faith, because one who has completely purified his mind by true faith can abide in the world of the real state of things while remaining in this *sahā*-world.

The human body is a material thing and is destined to change. Even in the case of such a great man as Sakyamuni Buddha, his body disappeared from this world when his life of eighty years ended. Our daily necessities, including money and other material things, are also material matters. All of them are impermanent and always changing. No one knows when they may disappear, even though he thinks they exist now. Social status and fame are also impermanent. However, if we purify our minds through religion, we can maintain a peaceful and happy mental state however much the outside world (the world of material things) changes. The mental state of religious exaltation is here compared to the description of the world of paradise.

"My Pure Land will never be destroyed,
Yet all view it as being burned up,
And grief and horror and distress
Fill them all like this.
All those sinful creatures,
By reason of their evil karma,
Throughout *asaṃkhyeya kalpas*
Hear not the name of the Precious Three."

The words "all those sinful creatures" do not necessarily mean "those who have done wrong." As explained on page 31, "sin" in the Buddha's teachings means stopping or reversing the upward advance of human life. Stopping the upward advance of human life means neglecting to endeavor to the utmost to purify our minds and to benefit others in society. This is a negative sin and evil. To reverse the advance of human life means to worry others, entrap them, seize their property, or enter into conflict with them and cause them to kill each other. Needless to say, such a deed is a great sin, a positive sin and evil.

As long as we accumulate either negative or positive sins, that is, evil karma, we cannot obtain good results because we do not produce good causes. However much time may pass, we cannot meet the Buddha, nor hear his teachings, nor join the ranks of his disciples. This situation is expressed in the words "hear not the name of the Precious Three."

The Precious Three are the three basic elements that Sakyamuni Buddha taught his disciples as the spiritual foundation of Buddhism soon after he began his missionary work: the Buddha, the Law, and the Saṃgha. Because of their supreme value, they are also called the Three Treasures.

Mention of this spiritual foundation immediately reminds us of the teaching "Make the self your light, make the Law your light." These are most reassuring words and a great encouragement to us. But here the Buddha does not refer to the self that is filled with illusions but the self that lives in the Law. We must burn with the fire of the Law and cast its light over society. Though we must live through our own efforts, our way of life should always be in accordance with the Law.

The Law is the truth, or universal law, whose true state is very hard for ordinary people to grasp. Therefore they feel insecure in depending upon it for their mental attitude and actions in their daily lives. For this reason Sakyamuni Buddha explained the Law in terms of the following three principles so that ordinary people could understand it. The first of the three principles is the Buddha. The second is the Law, meaning the Buddha's teachings. The third is the Saṃgha, whose meaning has been greatly misunderstood since ancient times. It is usually interpreted as meaning the community of Buddhist monks and nuns. But as in the case of the words "I with all the Saṃgha" (page 251), this term often indicates the idea of a believers in a broad sense, although originally it meant a religious order or community of believers. The Sanskrit word *saṃgha* means "an intimate and faithful group consisting of many believers." Sakyamuni Buddha gave the name of Saṃgha to the community of fellow believers who seek the same teachings as his disciples.

Ordinary people find it difficult to seek the Law and to practice it in complete isolation. They are apt to become lazy and fall into evil ways. But if they form a community with other believers in the same faith, they can steadily advance by teaching, admonishing, and encouraging each other. So Sakyamuni Buddha taught us to regard the Saṃgha as one of our mental foundations.

The things on which we must depend spiritually are the Three Treasures: the Buddha, the Law, and the Saṃgha. If we depend spiritually upon the Buddha, his teachings, and the community of believers, we can faithfully practice the Righteous Law in our daily lives. Therefore Buddhists always take refuge in the Three Treasures.

Those who accumulate evil karma do not know the Three Treasures. They cannot come in contact with the Buddha's teachings or be led to join the community of believers, much less meet the Buddha.

"But all who perform virtuous deeds
And are gentle and of upright nature,
These all see that I exist
And am here expounding the Law.

At times for all this throng
I preach the Buddha's life is eternal;
To those who at length see the Buddha
I preach that a buddha is rarely met.
My intelligence-power is such,
My wisdom-light shines infinitely,
My life is of countless *kalpas,*
From long-cultivated karma obtained.
You who have intelligence,
Do not in regard to this beget doubt
But bring it forever to an end,
For the Buddha's words are true, not false."

In the words "My life is of countless *kalpas,*" "my life" does not mean the life of the Eternal Original Buddha but means that Sakyamuni's life, which he obtained through the accumulation of his long practice of the bodhisattva-way in this world, is also eternal.

"Like the physician who with clever device,
In order to cure his demented sons,
Though indeed alive announces his own death,
Yet cannot be charged with falsehood,
I, too, being father of this world,
Who heals all misery and affliction,
For the sake of the perverted people,
Though truly alive, say I am extinct;
Lest, because always seeing me,
They should beget arrogant minds,
Be dissolute and set in their five desires,
And fall into evil paths.
I, ever knowing all beings,
Those who walk or walk not in the Way,
According to the right principles of salvation
Expound their every Law,
Ever making this my thought:
'How shall I cause all the living
To enter the Way supreme
And speedily accomplish their buddhahood?' "

The Buddha's deep compassion is shown most clearly here, especially in the closing words, "Ever making this my thought: / 'How shall I cause all the living / To enter the Way supreme / And speedily accomplish their buddhahood?' " This is indeed the vow and the long-cherished desire of the Buddha.

Chapter 16 ends with this verse. From this chapter, we understand clearly that we are caused to live by the great life of the Eternal Original Buddha, and we can establish this principle in our minds as the basis of our lives. If we always maintain this realization, our lives will become bright, secure, and full of courage and positive energy.

CHAPTER 17

Discrimination of Merits

THE MERITS OF RELIGIOUS PRACTICE. The previous chapter has taught us clearly that the Buddha exists together with us at all times. Understanding this, our mental state will spontaneously change for the better. Before we have attained true faith, we tend to feel insecure and are unable to maintain a truly unshakable hope and self-confidence. Of course, it cannot be said that we have never felt happiness, hope, or self-confidence. Some of us do enjoy a mental state full of hope and self-confidence. However, such happiness, hope, and self-confidence are so fragile that they are shattered as soon as any great misfortune befalls us.

People who have a superficial view of things and do not live for any purpose may be able to afford to indulge in the idle thought that today is today and tomorrow is tomorrow, so do not worry about the future but live for the moment. Most such people lack a sense of responsibility toward society, their own families, and even themselves. They are considered happy, but actually they are living counter to the truth "Nothing has an ego," absorbed in their own happiness. Such people do not accumulate good karma in this world but lead worthless dream lives.

The mental happiness, hope, and self-confidence of those who have attained true faith are not frothy and superficial but deep and firm-rooted in their minds. These people have calm, steadfast minds not agitated by anything—fire, water, or sword—because they maintain a mental attitude of great assurance, realizing, "I am always protected by the Buddha as an absolute existence; I am caused to live by the Buddha."

It is natural that life should change dramatically as soon as we attain such a mental state. It is impossible for our life *not* to change when our attitude changes. Our mental state changes because of faith, and through the change in our mind, our life changes at the same time. These are the merits of religious practice. Therefore faith is naturally associated with merits.

The merits of religious practice appear not only in man's mind but also in his body and his material life. Because his mind, his body, and the material things around him are composed of the same void (energy), it stands to reason that his body should change according to changes in his mind, and at the same time that the material things around him should change. It is irrational and unscientific to admit mental merits but deny physical and material ones.

Medicine has made remarkable progress in the study of the relation between the human mind and body. Psychosomatic medicine has established the fact that various illnesses, such as eye diseases, skin complaints, heart trouble, hypertension, hives, asthma, morning sickness, and irregular menstruation, can be caused by a person's mental state. Psychosomatic medicine has proved that stomach and intestinal disorders in particular are strongly affected by one's mind. For example, gastric ulcers are more often caused by feelings of anxiety and irritation than by overindulgence in liquor or tobacco. Physicians have compiled statistics showing that students often suffer from appendicitis when their mental tension is suddenly relaxed, such as after an examination or a sport event. It is no wonder that man can recover from disease by changing his mental attitude, since his body is inseparable from his mind. I myself know of many such examples, including the case of a person who had lost the use of his legs and who was able to stand up and walk home after receiving a few words of religious instruction. We do not consider such a thing miraculous but a natural occurrence.

It is also not strange that one should become blessed with money and material things owing to a change in mental attitude after entering into a religious life. A person's changed mental attitude leads him inevitably to change his attitude toward his work and life, and accordingly directs him to the improvement of his life in general. This is not limited to changes in one's own life. If one earnestly takes refuge in a true faith, he will elicit a different response from other people. He begins to have feelings of optimism, confidence in life, and a positive attitude toward everything. Such feelings will naturally show in his face, speech, and conduct. Because of this change, those around him will be drawn to him because they feel buoyed up and strengthened by him. Accordingly, it is quite natural that his work should progress smoothly and that as a result he should come to be blessed with material wealth.

These merits are the result of religious practice, and when they appear, we should receive them with gratitude and frankness. We need not be tied to the idea that because faith is concerned with the problem of the mind we do not need any merits other than mental ones lest our religious life be tainted by something impure. Such an idea itself reflects an impure, distorted, and prejudiced attitude.

However, people of this type are relatively rare. Many more people belong to another type, "believers with a biased view." These people do not interpret divine favors in this world as the result of their religious practice but practice in the hope of receiving such benefits from the beginning. Almost all people who enter a religious faith have some form of suffering. It is natural for them to want to free themselves from such sufferings, and they are not to be blamed for this. But when they are concerned only with the desire to recover from illness or to be blessed with money, they are merely attaching themselves to the idea of "disease" or "poverty." Though they wish to rid themselves of these problems, instead they become their victims because their minds grasp the idea of illness or poverty so tightly that they cannot let go.

People who believe in religion only in order to receive divine favors in this world easily retrogress from their stage of development in that faith. This is because they cannot truly understand the eternity of the Buddha's life, and at the same time the eternity of man's life. They think only of the present and begin to doubt the teaching or grow tired of it unless clear material merits are manifested. But there are some people who cannot receive such merits in this world because of deep and inextinguishable unfavorable karma from their former lives, even if they have faith in a true religion, purify their minds, and devote themselves to the bodhisattva practice for the benefit of others in society.

Nevertheless, people who can believe in the immortality of the Buddha's life can also feel confident of their own eternal life. Therefore they can live with self-confidence, realizing, "If we only continue this way, we are sure to extinguish our former karma eventually and will approach the mental state of the Buddha step by step." Even if they do not immediately recover from illness or become suddenly blessed with tangible wealth, their minds will be composed. Even if they seem to outsiders to be suffering, their minds are free of suffering. This is the attitude adopted by a real believer.

In considering the merits of religious practice, we must place great importance on being upright in character and gentle in mind, as taught in chapter 16. We should focus our gaze on the Buddha alone, not worrying ourselves about divine favors in this world. We should be united with the Buddha and act obediently according to his guidance. If our actual life should consequently change for the better, that is a natural phenomenon produced because our minds and actions have been set in the direction of the truth. We should receive such phenomena gratefully and frankly

The merits of religious practice are preached in three chapters of the latter half of the Lotus Sutra: chapter 17, "Discrimination of Merits"; chapter 18, "The Merits of Joyful Acceptance"; and chapter 19, "The Merits of the Preacher." We should read these chapters bearing in mind the basic significance of merits as discussed above.

The chapter "Discrimination of Merits" states in twelve stages the merits that we can obtain from believing firmly in the eternal life of the Buddha and at the same time teaches us the ideal religious life. This chapter preaches not the so-called divine favors in this world but mainly the mental merits that a believer can receive. Though those who are not familiar with the Buddha's Law may not understand what religious merits mean, readers who have studied the Lotus Sutra up through chapter 16 will appreciate the value of religious merits. Let us now proceed to the main subject of the chapter.

Countless living beings obtained a great benefit when they learned from the Buddha's preaching in chapter 16 that the length of his life is limitless and that he had been constantly instructing all people everywhere in this world. This great benefit was the following: the living beings gained the conviction that they were caused to live and were protected and instructed by the Buddha, and thus they were able to realize a deep mental joy.

Then to the Bodhisattva Maitreya as the representative of the great congregation the World-honored One preached the merits of those who believe in the eternity of the Buddha's life, dividing these merits into twelve stages according to the believers' degree of faith and discernment.

The first stage of these merits is that "six million, eight hundred thousand *koṭis* of *nayutas* of living beings, numerous as the sands of the

Ganges, have attained the assurance of their nonrebirth." The meaning of these words can be amplified as follows: those who have become able to believe in the eternity of the Buddha's life are neither glad nor sad at any change in their environment or social circumstances. They can advance from an insecure state of mind to a firm belief in life that is not agitated by external changes. Moreover, this great conviction is not temporary but will continue for their whole life.

The second stage of merits is that "again a thousand times more bodhisattva-*mahāsattvas* have attained the *dhāraṇī*-power of hearing and keeping the Law."[1] Here the words "a thousand times" is used to convey the concept of a very great number, like the expressions appearing later, such as "numerous as the atoms of a world," "numerous as the atoms of a three-thousand-great-thousandfold world," "numerous as the atoms of a middle-two-thousandfold domain," "numerous as the atoms of a small-thousandfold domain," "numerous as the atoms of four four-continental worlds,"[2] "numerous as the atoms of three four-continental worlds," "numerous as the atoms of two four-continental worlds," "numerous as the atoms of one four-continental world," and "numerous as the atoms of eight worlds." We need not take such numbers literally. The word *dhāraṇī* means the mystical power to stop all evil and to encourage all good. The words "have attained the *dhāraṇī*-power of hearing and keeping the Law" mean that by hearing and keeping the Buddha's teachings a man can obtain the mystical power to stop all evil and to encourage all good. This power of course greatly influences those around him as well as himself. This feature distinguishes the bodhisattvas from other living beings.

The next stage of merits is that "again, bodhisattva-*mahāsattvas* numerous as the atoms of a world have attained the faculty of eloquent and unembarrassed discussion." Here "eloquent" means to preach the Buddha's teachings voluntarily, not reluctantly on the orders of another person or out of a sense of duty. It means not to preach with the secret desire of appearing better than others or from selfish motives but to preach voluntarily because to do so gives one joy. This is the ideal state of mind that the preacher should maintain.

1. Literally, the door or method of hearing and keeping *dhāraṇī* (by means of which one hears and keeps the Law). This is the first of the four fearlessnesses of a bodhisattva.

2. A world of four continents surrounding a central mountain, Sumeru. The four continents are Pūrvavideha in the east, Avaragodānīya in the west, Jambudvīpa in the south, and Uttarakuru in the north.

The word "unembarrassed" means that nothing hinders the preacher from spreading the teachings. It means to preach and spread them without being discouraged even if one is laughed and sneered at, thought ill of, or persecuted by others. Such hindrances can come not only from outside but also from within oneself. Some people are zealous in their missionary work when they are well off or at leisure, but they do not care about others when they have no time or money to spare. This is caused by hindrances in both their circumstances and their minds. On the other hand, those who have attained a deep faith can devote themselves to the bodhisattva practice and widely spread the Lotus Sutra without hindrance even if they lead a hand-to-mouth existence or have personal worries.

In addition to meaning that the preacher yields to neither external nor internal hindrances, "unembarrassed" also means to possess the power of breaking down the mental resistance of the hearers of the preaching. In preaching to those who do not even try to believe in the Buddha's teachings, who take them lightly from the start, or who listen to them earnestly but cannot understand them at all, the ideal preacher is one who has the power of persuasion to make them listen to reason, make them understand, and lead them to believe sincerely without their being aware of it. Such persuasive power is called the faculty of unembarrassed discussion.

Taken all together, the meaning of "have attained the faculty of eloquent and unembarrassed discussion" can be restated as follows: a person has attained the faculty of always preaching the righteous Law to others with pleasure, yielding to neither external nor internal hindrances, and has the ability to persuade any kind of person.

The next stage of merits is as follows: "again, bodhisattva-*mahāsattvas* numerous as the atoms of a world have attained hundreds of thousands of myriad *koṭis* of the *dhāraṇī* of infinite revolutions."[3] The merits in this stage are that one can obtain the mystical power (*dhāraṇī*) to stop all evil and to encourage all good, that is, the fundamental power extending from one person to another without end. These merits are very great because numerous bodhisattvas can thus become the driving force of missionary activities that spread limitlessly.

The next stage of merits is: "again, bodhisattva-*mahāsattvas* numerous

3. The *dhāraṇī* of infinite revolutions or evolutions is the power to discriminate manifold phenomena without error. By this discrimination a bodhisattva destroys all his perplexities and exhibits many Buddha-laws.

as the atoms of a three-thousand-great-thousandfold world have been enabled to roll forward the never-retreating Law-wheel." As explained earlier, to roll the Law-wheel means to propagate the Buddha's teachings as endlessly as a wheel rolls. Therefore the words "to roll forward the never-retreating Law-wheel" indicate the idea that one must never take a single step backward no matter what obstacles or difficulties he may encounter, but continually preach and spread the teachings.

The next stage of merits is: "again, bodhisattva-*mahāsattvas* numerous as the atoms of a middle-two-thousandfold domain have been enabled to roll forward the pure Law-wheel." The merits of this stage mean that one becomes able to carry out the pure practices of the bodhisattvas in preaching the Law for its own sake, seeking no recompense. Ordinary people have difficulty in carrying out these practices, but a person who has reached the ideal perfection of faith can perform them.

The merits of the next stage are: "again, bodhisattva-*mahāsattvas* numerous as the atoms of a small-thousandfold domain after eight rebirths will attain Perfect Enlightenment." The merits here are that a person practices various religious disciplines for eight more lives, as a result of which he can attain Perfect Enlightenment.

The next stage of merits is that the bodhisattva-*mahāsattvas* will attain Perfect Enlightenment, according to the virtue each has accumulated, after four more births, three more births, two more births, or one more birth.

The next stage is that numerous living beings, hearing of the immortality of the Buddha, will all aspire to Perfect Enlightenment.

These are the twelve merits that a believer can obtain by holding an unshakable belief in the Buddha's infinite life. In brief, the Buddha teaches us that if we establish the basic idea of faith, we can infinitely generate the power both to deepen our own faith and to extend it to others. He also teaches us that we can expect to surely gain the supreme merit of attaining Perfect Enlightenment in the future if we thoroughly devote ourselves to deepening our own faith.

It is, of course, very difficult to attain Perfect Enlightenment. As preached in this chapter, some bodhisattvas cannot attain it unless they practice religious disciplines for eight more lives. How much less can we know how many years and how much effort it will cost ordinary people.

What great hope it gives us to know that we will surely attain Perfect Enlightenment at some time if we only believe in a righteous faith and endeavor to practice it. As long as we have this hope, life is happy and worth living. A person earns or loses money; he falls in love or is disappointed in love; he rises to a higher position in time or he loses his job because of a trifling mistake; he brings up his child successfully or loses it. If we pass through life in this way with no purpose, merely repeating vain feelings of joy and sorrow, even though each moment seems to be substantial and important, we will have an inexpressible sense of emptiness upon looking back over our life. But if our life has the strong backbone of a righteous faith running through it, and if we have a firm belief that we can advance to Perfect Enlightenment step by step even though life has its apparent ups and downs, its various joys and sorrows, we will be able to pass easily through whatever hardships may come, however long life's journey may be and however many rebirths it may entail.

Man's life is not limited to this world but continues eternally in each world to come. However, if we could foresee the repetition of the various occurrences of our daily lives in each and every world to come, we would be discouraged and would reject such a bleak prospect. Most people repeat the same suffering without any repentance in world after world because they cannot foresee this repetition. On the other hand, those who have been able to gain a true faith do not tire of and feel no objection to the journey of human life, however long it may be, because they know they can approach Perfect Enlightenment step by step. They can live rich lives filled with hope. This can be said to be the very greatest merit, which only believers in Buddhism can obtain.

A true believer should strive not only for the goal of his own ascent to the world of the buddhas but also for the aim of making as many other people as possible his companions there. The more true believers increase in number, the more the whole of mankind develops and the nearer this world approaches the ideal Land of Eternal Tranquil Light. Taken all together, the various merits preached in the sutras boil down to this.

When the Buddha had told of the bodhisattva-*mahāsattvas* obtaining great benefits of the Law by having a firm belief in his infinite life, from the sky there rained down *mandārava* and *mahā-mandārava* flowers, scattering over the innumerable buddhas seated on lion thrones below the jewel trees, over Sakyamuni Buddha and the long-extinct Tathāgata Abundant Treasures seated on the lion throne in the Stupa of the Precious Seven, and also over all the great bodhisattvas and the host of the four groups (*bhikshus, bhikshuṇīs, upāsakas,* and *upāsikās*).

Scattering flowers over someone in this way is an expression of gratitude; this custom still holds in India today. The raining down of flowers from the sky thus symbolizes the heavenly beings expressing their gratitude for the Buddha's teachings. The scattering of flowers over all the great bodhisattvas and the host of the four groups as well as the Buddha indicates that the disciples who hear the Buddha's teachings, as well as the Buddha himself who preaches them, are equally to be honored. When we listen to the Buddha's teachings and practice them wholeheartedly, we should imagine that beautiful *mandārava* and *mahā-mandārava* flowers rain down on us from the sky, even if these flowers are invisible to us.

The sky also rained incense of fine sandalwood, aloes, and other substances. In the sky heavenly drums resounded of themselves, with an exquisite deep resonance. This image represents extolling the Buddha's teachings. Thousands of kinds of celestial garments also rained down, and in every direction various kinds of necklaces hung down. Jeweled censers, burning priceless incense, moved everywhere of their own accord to pay homage to the great congregation. As already explained, in Buddhist terms to pay homage to someone is an action representing one's gratitude to the Buddha and his teachings.

Over each buddha the bodhisattvas held canopies, one above another, right up to the Brahma heaven. All these bodhisattvas with exquisite voices sang countless hymns extolling the buddhas. The expression "Over each buddha, bodhisattvas held canopies, one above another, right up to the Brahma heaven" symbolizes that the Buddha's teachings are omnipresent in this universe and that all living beings are saved by them.

Thereupon Maitreya Bodhisattva rose from his seat and humbly bared his right shoulder, folded his hands toward the Buddha, and spoke thus in verse:

"The Buddha has preached the rare Law
Never heard by us before.
Great is the power of the World-honored One
And his lifetime beyond estimation.
Numberless Buddha-sons,
Hearing the World-honored One in detail
Tell of those who obtained the Law-benefit,
Have been filled with joy."

With this preface, Maitreya Bodhisattva continued to speak in verse, repeating the merits preached by the Buddha. These verses can be easily understood if we have understood the preceding prose portion. Only words with different meanings will be explained below.

The words "some are steadfast in the never-retreating stage" mean that some abide in a stage of attainment from which they never slide back, whatever may happen. It has the same meaning as the expression "have attained the assurance of nonrebirth."

"To controlling myriads of *koṭis* of revolutions" has the same meaning as the expression "have attained to hundreds of thousands of myriad *koṭis* of the *dhāraṇī* of infinite revolutions."

In the words "bodhisattvas . . . who after one more birth / Will accomplish perfect knowledge," the words "perfect knowledge" mean the Buddha's wisdom. This passage refers to those bodhisattvas who after one more birth will attain the same mental stage as the Buddha.

"Have all aspired to the supreme truth" means having the aspiration to attain the supreme Way (the Buddha's enlightenment); this has the same meaning as the expression "have all aspired to Perfect Enlightenment."

The verse also says: "Śakras and Brahmas numerous as sands of the Ganges / From countless buddha-lands have come." These lines mean that the heavenly gods, including Śakras and Brahmas, have gathered from countless lands in the universe to pay homage to the Buddha.

In the lines "Before each one of the buddhas / Jeweled streamers hang fluttering," the word "streamers" refers to the victory banners that Brahman monks used to raise at the gates of their temples when they had defeated their opponents in religious dispute. This custom was common in India in ancient times, and consequently this expression appears in Buddhist sutras.

Man's belief in the eternity of the Buddha's life is the basic idea of Buddhists from which springs all teachings. Therefore, when the World-honored One preached the eternity of his life, jeweled streamers hung fluttering before each buddha who came to the great congregation as proof that the teachings preached by the Buddha are supreme.

Maitreya Bodhisattva, having repeated the Buddha's preaching in verse, ended with the following words:

"Hearing the Buddha's lifetime is infinite,
All beings are gladdened.

The Buddha's fame throughout the universe
Widely refreshes the roots of goodness
Of all living beings,
Aiding their desire for supreme truth."

It is not too much to say that the core of the first half of chapter 17 can be summed up in these words. From this verse portion we realize clearly Maitreya Bodhisattva's understanding of the Law and his faculty for expressing his understanding.

Since ancient times, the latter half of chapter 15, all of chapter 16, and the first half of chapter 17, the so-called one chapter and two halves, have been defined as the main part of the Law of Origin. The "one chapter and two halves" are thought to be not only the main part of the Law of Origin but also the core of the whole Lotus Sutra. Nichiren admired them as the soul of all of the Buddhist scriptures.

The reason that the "one chapter and two halves" are regarded as so important is that what the Buddhist should believe—the greatest and most basic of the major points of the Buddhist faith—are here thoroughly investigated, and the object of our faith is definitively established. This has already been discussed in some detail in the discussion of chapter 16.

In the first half of chapter 17 the Buddha teaches us how important and reassuring it is for us to have established the object of faith in our religious lives. The latter half of this chapter and the eleven remaining chapters of the sutra are defined as the "concluding part" of the Law of Origin, which answer two major questions: "What results will be produced by our having righteous faith?" and "What mental attitude is needed in order to have righteous faith?" It is in the concluding part of the sutra that the World-honored One gives his commission to us to preach and spread this righteous faith to posterity.

The merits preached in the first half of chapter 17 are those of faith. In the latter half of chapter 17 and the former half of chapter 18 the same merits are preached. However, beginning with the latter half of chapter 18, the merits preached are those that appear in our personal affairs or in our daily lives.

Some people may think, "We need not pay attention to such merits. If we thoroughly study the 'one chapter and two halves' as the core of the Lotus Sutra, understand them truly, and believe deeply in the eternity of the Buddha's life, we can do without the rest." That would be quite an acceptable attitude if indeed they could practice as perfectly as they think. If so, their faith would be perfect. However, is there such a person in ten thousand or even a hundred thousand? In actuality it is very hard to practice perfectly what we think.

For ordinary people, the ideal state of mind seems infinitely far from their present situation and quite alien to their actual lives when they first hear it taught. But when this ideal is expounded in a way that is based on familiar problems in their daily lives, they will feel the teaching vividly. Here lies the first important function of the concluding part of the Lotus Sutra.

The minds of ordinary people are liable to become lazy. Even being fully aware of the value of the teaching, they will soon become negligent if they understand the virtues of the teaching in theory alone. However, if they continually read and recite the sutra, which teaches that one improves himself when he both holds and practices righteous faith, they can renew their resolve whenever it slackens. This is the second function of the concluding part of the sutra.

The Buddha tells us to preach and spread the Law. This is something for which we should be grateful to him. We are heartened and inspired with courage whenever we receive his words and enter into his feelings. Here lies the third function of the concluding part of the sutra.

The concluding portion of the Lotus Sutra is indispensable to ordinary people, which means most of us. Understanding this well, we must study the concluding part of the Law of Origin as eagerly as its main part, with humility rather than arrogance.

Thereupon the Buddha addressed Maitreya Bodhisattva-Mahāsattva: "Ajita! Those living beings who have heard that the lifetime of the Buddha is of such long duration and have been able to receive but one thought of faith and discernment—the merits they will obtain are beyond limit and measure. Suppose there be any good son or good daughter who, for the sake of Perfect Enlightenment, during eight hundred thousand *koṭis* of *nayutas* of *kalpas* practices the five *pāramitās*: *dāna-pāramitā, sīla-pāramitā, kshānti-pāramitā, vīrya-pāramitā,* and *dhyāna-pāramitā, prajñā-pāramitā* being excepted;[4] these merits compared with the above-mentioned merits are not equal to even the hundredth part, the thousandth part, or one part of a hundred thousand myriad *koṭis* of it; indeed,

4. The five *pāramitās* or perfections are *dāna,* or donation; *sīla,* or keeping the precepts; *kshānti,* or perseverance; *vīrya,* or assiduity; and *dhyāna,* or meditation. The sixth *pāramitā* is *prajñā,* or wisdom.

neither numbers nor comparisons can make it known. If any good son or good daughter possesses such merits as this, there is no such thing as failing to obtain Perfect Enlightenment."

We risk misunderstanding the above words if we read them carelessly. It seems contradictory that although the Lotus Sutra strongly emphasizes the bodhisattva practice, people will obtain many more merits in having but one thought of faith and discernment concerning the eternity of the Buddha's life than in practicing the five *pāramitās* for eight hundred thousand *koṭis* of *nayutas* of *kalpas*. But in reading carefully the Buddha's words to Maitreya Bodhisattva, we can gather the difference in the values of the merits from the expression "neither numbers nor comparisons can make it known." This expression means that there is no comparison between the merits because their basic value is different. For example, we can compare ten thousand pounds or dollars or marks and one pound or dollar or mark because each is a sum of money. But the sum of ten thousand pounds cannot be compared with, say, learning because the two are originally dissimilar in kind.

To be sure, it is good for us to practice the five perfections—donation, keeping the precepts, perseverance, assiduity, and meditation—but these perfections, the practice of wisdom (*prajñā-pāramitā*) excepted, fall into the category of ordinary morality and philosophical meditation. By means of these practices alone we cannot be saved from the illusion in our deepest subconscious mind; that is, we cannot attain nirvana. Wisdom here refers to the wisdom of the Buddha, not that of ordinary people. If we practice the five *pāramitās* based on the Buddha's wisdom, such practices are perfect, are religious activities, and are a sure way to nirvana. That is why the Buddha in his words to Maitreya Bodhisattva clearly noted that he was excepting *prajñā-pāramitā*, perfect wisdom.

We cannot attain perfect nirvana even if we practice ordinary moral deeds and philosophical meditation for decades or even centuries. On the other hand, if we have but one thought of faith and discernment concerning the eternity of the Buddha's life, this mental attitude leads us to be convinced of the eternity of our own life and to realize that we are caused to live by the Buddha as the great life of the universe. The moment we realize this, we can enter the realm of great peace of mind.

The former method is the endeavor of one apart from religion, while the latter is the mental state of enlightenment from a religious point of view. The two are originally different in value, and there is no way of comparing them. If we comprehend what the Buddha really means here, we will see that it is no exaggeration to say that the merits obtained by the practice of the five *pāramitās* are not equal to one part of a hundred thousand myriad *koṭis* of the merits received through but one thought of faith and discernment.

FOUR FAITHS AND FIVE CATEGORIES. Since ancient times, the essential points of this chapter have been considered to be the "four faiths" (*shi-shin*) and "five categories" (*go-hon*). This division was first made in China by Chih-i in order to make the chapter more easily understood.

The concept of the four faiths to be followed during the Buddha's lifetime came from the idea that the ideal way of faith while the Buddha lived was to be divided into the following four stages: (1) receiving but one thought of faith and discernment concerning the eternity of the Buddha's life, (2) apprehending its meaning, (3) devotion to preaching the Lotus Sutra abroad to others, and (4) beholding and perfecting profound faith and discernment.

The five categories of faith to be pursued after the Buddha's extinction are derived from the idea that the ideal way of faith in the age of degeneration is divided into the following five categories: (1) first rejoicing over the Lotus Sutra, (2) reading and reciting it, (3) preaching it to others, (4) concurrently practicing the six *pāramitās,* and (5) intensively practicing the six *pāramitās.*

The first of the four faiths is to receive but one thought of faith and discernment concerning the eternity of the Buddha's life. This is the first stage of faith, but the merits obtained by this practice are beyond limit or measure.

Thereupon the World-honored One, desiring to proclaim the meaning of his preaching again, spoke thus in verse:

"Though a man, seeking the Buddha-wisdom,
During eighty myriad *koṭis*
Of *nayutas* of *kalpas*
Were to perform the five *pāramitās,*
And during those *kalpas*
Give alms and offerings to buddhas,
Pratyekabuddhas, and disciples,
As well as to bodhisattvas—

Rare and precious food and drink,
Superior clothing and bed furniture,
Monasteries built of sandalwood and
Adorned with gardens and groves,
Such alms as these,
Wonderful in variety—
Were he to maintain them through all those *kalpas*
As meritorious gifts to the Buddha-way;
Moreover, though he were to keep the commandments
Purely, without flaw or fault,
And seek the Supreme Way
Which all buddhas praise;
Or were he patiently to endure insult,
Stand firm in the stage of gentleness,
And though evils came upon him,
Keep his mind undisturbed;
Were he by other believers
Filled with utmost arrogance
To be scorned and distressed,
Yet able to bear even this;
Or were he to be diligent and zealous,
Ever strong in will and memory,
And during measureless *koṭis* of *kalpas*
With all his mind continue unremitting,
And during numberless *kalpas*
Dwell in secluded places,
Whether resident or vagrant,
Avoiding sleep and ever concentrating his mind;
Were he, by this means,
To be able to beget meditations
And for eighty myriad *koṭis* of *kalpas*
Calmly remain in them with unperturbed mind;
Were he, maintaining this single-minded happiness,
Willingly to seek the supreme Way, saying:
'I will attain all knowledge
And go on to the utmost point of meditation':
Were such a man for hundreds of thousands of
Myriads of *koṭis* of *kalpas*

To perform such deeds of merits
As those above expounded;
Yet any good son or daughter
Who, hearing me declare my eternal life,
Believes it with but a single thought,
This one's reward surpasses his.
If anyone be entirely free
From all doubts and misgivings
And in his deepest heart believes it but a moment,
Such shall be his reward.
If there be bodhisattvas
Who have followed good ways for innumerable *kalpas*
And hear of my announcement of my eternal life,
They will be able to receive it in faith;
Such men as these
Will bow their heads in receiving this sutra
And say: 'May we in the future
Have long life to save all the living;
And just as the present World-honored One
Who, King of the Śākyas,
On his wisdom terrace raises the lion's roar,
Preaching the Law without fear,
So may we in future ages,
Honored and revered by all,
When sitting on the wisdom terrace,
In like manner tell of the duration of life!'
If there be any of profound spirit,
Pure and upright,
Learned and able to uphold the truth,
Who understand the meaning of the Buddha's word,
Such men as these
Will have no doubts about this teaching."

This verse includes some very important words that should here be explained. In the words "As meritorious gifts to the Buddha-way," "meritorious gifts" means "merit transference" (*ekō*), the idea of transferring one's own merit to others for their attainment of buddhahood. For instance, by reading and reciting the sutras the Buddha's teachings become deeply rooted in one's mind, which in this way is purified. From this standpoint, sutra reciting is originally a religious practice for one's own attainment of buddhahood. When we recite the sutras in a memorial service for the spirits of our ancestors, we transfer the merits that we should receive to our ancestors so that they may attain enlightenment in the spiritual world. For this reason, sutra reciting in the memorial service for the spirits of the dead is called "merit transference" (*ekō*).

However, merit transference is not to be performed only for the sake of the dead. In accordance with its original meaning, it should be applicable to living people, as well. In fact, such transference is much more meaningful for the living than for the dead. If we recite the sutras while thinking of the happiness of the whole of mankind, we transfer the merits that we should receive to the whole of mankind. Thus, merit transference is the donation of the merit of the Law, which one should regard as one's most important treasure, to others. This is a much more self-sacrificing and sacred deed than to give monetary or other material offerings to others. Merit transference is the supreme act of donation.

If we give a monetary or other material offering to others with the secret expectation of its returning any merit to us, such an offering is the lowest of its kind. When we make an offering to others so that it may increase their happiness a little, this offering is based on ordinary moral standards. However, when we make an offering to others with the thought, "May this donation arouse the Buddha-mind of the receiver and lead eventually to making all people accomplish the Buddha-way in this world," such an offering is the very best of its kind. This is why the verse says: "As meritorious gifts to the Buddha-way."

Here two points must be added to the explanation of merit transference. One is that although merit transference should be performed wholly for the sake of others, the merit that results from such an act unfailingly returns to the performer of the deed. For example, a sutra-reciting service for the spirits of one's ancestors helps them to attain enlightenment in the spiritual world. At the same time, the merit that results from the service returns to the performer of the service because the more often he holds such a service, the more his evil karma can be extinguished.

The other point is that the greatest merit transference to the spirit of the ancestors is to purify and to elevate one's own self. Nothing is more joyful and reassuring to the spirits of one's ancestors than one's own improvement. Therefore we must not limit ourselves to reciting the sutras and uttering the sacred title but must endeavor to purify and elevate ourselves in our deeds and mental attitudes.

Then the World-honored One continued: "Again, Ajita! If anyone hears of the duration of the Buddha's lifetime and apprehends its meaning, the merit obtained by this man will be beyond limit and he will advance the supreme wisdom of *tathāgatas.*"

This is a mental stage beyond that of receiving but one thought of faith and discernment concerning the eternity of the Buddha's life. This stage means not only to believe and discern the eternity of the Buddha's life with a single thought but to apprehend its great meaning. We are caused to live by the Buddha as the great life of the universe, and at the same time we are united with him. The eternity of the Buddha's life means the eternity of our own life. Although our existence seems quite different from that of the Buddha because we are covered with the clouds of illusion, we will surely become buddhas eventually if we try to remove the clouds of illusion from our minds one by one. We cannot attain buddhahood after only one or two lives, but once we have realized the immortality of our own life, we can tread the path of advancement with hope and courage. If all people had the same feeling and proceeded hand in hand toward this goal, a truly peaceful and ideal society would be realized on this earth.

When we understand the profound meaning of the eternity of the Buddha's life, the teaching of which seems so simple, this marks a further step toward the wisdom of the Buddha. This mental stage, which we can attain by deepening our faith, was called by Chih-i the stage of apprehending the meaning of the eternity of the Buddha's life.

"How much more will this be the case with the one who is devoted to hearing this sutra, or causes others to hear it, or himself keeps it, or causes others to keep it, or himself copies it, or causes others to copy it, or with flowers, incense, garlands, banners, flags, silk canopies, and lamps of fragrant oil and ghee pays homage to the sutra; this man's merit will be infinite and boundless and able to bring forth perfect knowledge."

This stage is that of the believer who has gone a step further than the stage of apprehending the meaning of the eternity of the Buddha's life. In the third stage, we not only understand the true meaning of the eternity of the Buddha's life but devote ourselves to hearing his teachings and do not forget them, as they have taken root in our minds; and we devote ourselves to religious practices, including copying the sutras.

Besides such practices, we must urge and cause others to practice. This is the stage of devoting oneself to preaching the Lotus Sutra abroad to others.

At the same time, this stage teaches us to pay homage to the Lotus Sutra through various ways of revering it. Paying homage to the sutra is a way of expressing our heartfelt thanks for the Buddha's teachings. The names of the beautiful offerings and ornaments that are mentioned here symbolize the deep sense of gratitude to the Buddha shown by presenting these things to the sutra. If we have a deep sense of gratitude to the Buddha, it is natural that we try to express our appreciation. It is quite proper for believers to adorn their altars with various offerings.

"Ajita! If any good son or good daughter, hearing of my declaration of the duration of my lifetime, believes and discerns it in his inmost heart, such a one will see the Buddha always on Mount Gṛdhrakūṭa surrounded by a host of great bodhisattvas and *śrāvakas,* and preaching the Law. And he will see this *sahā*-world whose land is lapis lazuli, plain and level, its eight roads marked off with *jambūnada* gold, lined with jewel trees; it has towers, halls, and galleries all made of jewels, in which dwell together its bodhisattva host. If anyone is able so to behold, you may know that this is the sign of profound faith and discernment."

These words teach us the mental state that we attain when we believe and discern the eternity of the Buddha's life in our inmost hearts. The expression "such a one will see the Buddha always on Mount Gṛdhrakūṭa surrounded by a host of great bodhisattva and *śrāvakas,* and preaching the Law" indicates our conviction that the Buddha always dwells wherever we are. At the same time, through this expression we truly realize that the Buddha's teachings are always being preached around us.

The depiction of the *sahā*-world as a beautiful land indicates the idea that the *sahā*-world is identical with the Pure Land in essence, if we can only deepen our faith enough to perceive it. The actual world of the present will be transformed into a pure and joyous one if our minds are always filled with religious exaltation through the Buddha's teachings. In this state of mind, any place we see appears beautiful and any person whom we see looks like a bodhisattva. We can pierce the superficial ugliness of a person and see through to the inherent buddha-nature in the depths of his mind.

This, the highest state of mind that believers can attain, is called the stage of beholding and perfecting profound faith and discernment. If from the bottom of our hearts we believe and discern the Buddha as actual being and the eternity of his life, we can view life and the world according to his teachings and can dwell continuously in the world of religious exaltation. As a result, we can see the *sahā*-world as identical in essence with the Land of Eternally Tranquil Light.

FIVE CATEGORIES OF MERITS. "And again, if anyone, after the extinction of the Tathāgata, hears this sutra, and does not defame but rejoices over it, you may know that he has had the sign of deep faith and discernment."

With these words the Buddha begins to preach the ideal way of the believer following the Buddha's extinction and the five categories of merits to be obtained by the believer after the Buddha's extinction.

We cannot say we have faith so long as we only understand the Buddha's teachings in theory or acquiesce in them intellectually. We cannot enter the mental state of faith until we feel spiritual rejoicing in the teaching. When we first rejoice over the teaching, this mental state is called "first rejoicing over the teaching," the first of the five categories. This state of mind is so important that its merits will be discussed in detail in chapter 18, "The Merits of Joyful Acceptance."

"How much more the one who reads and recites, receives and keeps it—this man carries the Tathāgata on his head.[5] Ajita! Such a good son or good daughter need no more erect stupas, temples, or monasteries for me, nor make offerings of the four requisites to the monks.[6] Wherefore? Because this good son or good daughter who receives and keeps, reads and recites this sutra has already erected stupas, built monasteries, and made offerings to the monks, that is to say, has erected, for the Buddha's relics, stupas of the precious seven, high and broad, and tapering up to the Brahma heaven, hung with flags and canopies and precious bells, and with flowers, perfumes, garlands, sandal powder, unguents, incense, drums, instruments, pipes, flutes, harps, all kinds of dances and plays—singing and lauding with wondrous notes—he has already made these offerings for innumerable thousands of myriads of *koṭis* of *kalpas*."

In this mental stage, in which the believer advances a step beyond that of first rejoicing over the teaching, he firmly receives and keeps the teaching and repeatedly reads and recites it. Reading and reciting a sutra means not only to recite it from memory but also to study it by repeating it to oneself with conscious care and thought. This stage of faith is called the category of "reading and reciting the sutras."

5. That is, "holds the Tathāgata in high esteem."
6. Garments, food and drink, bed furnishings, and medicaments.

"Ajita! If anyone, after my extinction, hears this sutra and is able either to receive and keep, or himself copy or cause others to copy it, he has already erected monasteries and built red sandalwood temples of thirty-two shrines, tall as eight *tāla* trees, lofty, spacious, splendid, in which abide hundreds, thousands of *bhikshus;* adorned also with gardens, groves, and bathing pools, promenades and meditation cells; with clothing, victuals, bedding, medicaments, and all aids to pleasure provided to the full therein. Such monasteries and such numbers of temples, hundreds of thousands of myriads of *koṭis,* countless in their number, he has here in my presence offered to me and to my *bhikshus.* Therefore I say if anyone after the extinction of the Tathāgata receives and keeps, reads and recites it, preaches it to others, either himself copies it or causes others to copy it, and pays homage to the sutra, he need no longer erect stupas and temples or build monasteries and make offerings to the monks."

In this stage we come to feel that we cannot help preaching the Buddha's teachings to others as we receive and keep, read and recite the sutras, and gradually we realize their value. Here we are not necessarily limited to preaching the Buddha's teachings through speech. We can inform others of his teachings in writing, and we can publicize them in newspapers or magazines. And even a poor speaker or writer can show the value of the Buddha's teachings to others through his religious practice of silence. All these practices are included in the words "preaching the Buddha's teachings to others."

The category of preaching the Buddha's teachings to others is the mental stage in which we go further than elevating ourselves and being saved as individuals, advancing to the bodhisattva practice of benefiting and saving others. Therefore, it is natural that the merits one obtains in this category are far greater than those in the category of reading and reciting the sutras.

A few more words of clarification concerning this category are needed. In both this and the previous categories, the Buddha says that a good son or good daughter need no more erect stupas of the precious seven for his relics, nor build monasteries, nor make offerings to the monks, repeating what he has already said in chapter 10, "A Teacher of the Law."

Through this the Buddha teaches us that sincere moral offerings that a person makes to him are far more worthy than formal material offerings. He also admonishes us that the greatest offering that one can make to the Buddha is to believe and receive the Buddha's teachings, practice them, and preach and spread them. First, we must keep this in mind. Next, we must not think that we need no longer have temples or monasteries simply because the Buddha declared that his whole body is contained in his teachings and that we do not have to enshrine his relics. A person who accepts the sutras from merely an academic point of view is apt to interpret the Buddha's words literally. He does not have a sense of gratitude toward and reverence for the Buddha. Such a person merely acquiesces in the Buddha's teachings in theory and forgets to believe in them.

Needless to say, according to the Buddha's teachings believers should make the greatest effort to believe and receive the teachings, practice them, and preach them for the sake of society as a whole. At the same time, we cannot but make material offerings to the Great Beneficent Teacher who leads us to the supreme Way, and to the many bodhisattvas who have helped him through all ages.

As has been often repeated in this book, the more we are affected by the Buddha's teachings, the more we are driven to expressing our feelings in some outward way. This is why Buddhists always adorn their altars with various offerings, worship at their altars every morning and evening, extol the Buddha, and pay homage to him by practicing religious acts.

"How much less he who is able to keep this sutra and add thereto almsgiving, morality, forbearance, zeal, concentration, and wisdom. His merit will be most excellent, infinite, and boundless; even as space which east, west, south, and north, the four intermediate directions, the zenith and nadir, is infinite and boundless, so also the merit of this man will be infinite and boundless, and he will speedily reach perfect knowledge."

Here is taught the category that we can attain by further accumulation of religious practices, the category of concurrently practicing the six *pāramitās*. This means to receive and keep the Buddha's teachings, to read and recite them, and to preach them to others, and concurrently to practice the six *pāramitās*. However, at this stage it is almost impossible to practice all six of the *pāramitās* perfectly. Therefore the Buddha teaches us to begin their practice from wherever we can, according to our situation and circumstances. Sakyamuni Buddha never urges us to do the impossible. He teaches us to build our practices by degrees, beginning at whatever stage we can. In chapter 2, "Tactfulness," he preaches that all living beings can enter the Buddha-way from anywhere, even from the fact that in their play children gather sand to make a buddha's stupa. In chapter 17, the Buddha shows us the logical order in which to deepen our faith step by step.

It is important that we note that the five *pāramitās* seemed to be belittled in order to emphasize the merits obtained in the stage of receiving but one thought of faith and discernment concerning the eternity of the Buddha's life. But in the present category, the six *pāramitās,* not just the five, are emphasized as necessities of faith. Sakyamuni Buddha was endowed with perfect wisdom and was a great leader; the disciples who were directly instructed by him during his lifetime could enter into deep faith through only believing and discerning the Buddha's teachings by listening to them and appreciating them. In their practice of the five *pāramitās,* the Buddha's disciples were able to advance greatly in their practice because the Buddha directly instructed them with his perfect wisdom. To oversimplify somewhat, they were given wisdom by the Buddha and, based on this wisdom, they had only to practice intently the five other *pāramitās*—donation, keeping the precepts, perseverance, assiduity, and meditation. It can readily be imagined that they could constantly practice these *pāramitās* with deep emotion and religious exaltation because they did so in the presence of the Buddha, their model as a man of great character and a supreme leader.

However, we must study and practice his teachings through our own power in the age of degeneration, without the physical presence of Sakyamuni Buddha as our great leader and teacher. We must seek wisdom in the teachings he has left to us and must realize it for ourselves. Compared with the period when he lived, now indeed is the time when the practice of all six *pāramitās,* including wisdom, must be regarded as most important. This is why the Buddha strongly urges us in this category to practice all six *pāramitās.*

Believers who belong to the mental stage of this category practice the six *pāramitās* in different ways, each according to his circumstances. Sometimes one is in a situation in which he is unable to practice certain of the *pāramitās* and must practice them concurrently with the category of receiving and keeping the Buddha's teachings, reading and reciting them, and preaching them to other people. This is why the category is called "concurrently practicing the six *pāramitās.*"

However, in the fifth and final category believers can practice the six *pāramitās* intensively and perfectly. Next the Buddha preaches the merits they will obtain by such practice: "If anyone reads and recites, receives and keeps this sutra, preaches it to other people, or himself copies it, or causes others to copy it; moreover, is able to erect *caityas* and build monasteries, and to serve and extol the *śrāvaka*-monks, and also, with hundreds of thousands of myriads of *koṭis* of ways of extolling, extols the merits of the bodhisattvas; also if he to other people, with various reasonings according to its meaning, expounds this Law-Flower Sutra; again if he is able to keep the commandments in purity, amicably to dwell with the gentle, to endure insult without anger, to be firm in will and thought, ever to value meditation, to attain profound concentration, zealously and boldly to support the good, to be clever and wise in ably answering difficult questionings; Ajita, again, if after my extinction there be good sons and good daughters who receive and keep, read and recite this sutra, who possess such excellent merits as these, you should know that those people have proceeded toward the wisdom terrace and are near Perfect Enlightenment, sitting under the tree of enlightenment."

This category is called "intensively practicing the six *pāramitās*," meaning their perfect practice. As the Buddha has declared, if one attains this mental stage he is near Perfect Enlightenment. So the Buddha said: "Ajita! Wherever those good sons or good daughters sit or stand or walk, in that place you should erect a *caitya;* all gods and men should pay homage to it as a stupa of the relics of the Buddha."

In the fourth category the Buddha said that one need no longer erect stupas for him, whereas in the final category he proclaims that wherever one practices intensively the six *pāramitās* a *caitya* should be erected and should be paid homage to as a stupa of the Buddha's relics. Here the Buddha emphasizes the great importance of practicing his teachings and of preaching and spreading them to others in the age of degeneration. We should feel grateful for these words from the Buddha.

Next the Buddha repeated his teaching in verse. We should be able to understand these verses if we have understood the meaning of the prose section, because the verse portion includes almost exactly the same contents. The last four lines of the verse section should be regarded as most sacred words of the Buddha:

> "When a Buddha-son dwells in such a place,
> It means that the Buddha himself uses it
> And ever abides in it,
> Walking, or sitting, or lying down."

The Buddha regards anyone who believes and discerns his teachings wholeheartedly as his son and calls him a Buddha-son. He also says that wherever a Buddha-son dwells is the Buddha's abode: "It means that the Buddha himself uses it." He declares that he continually abides in such a place, walking, sitting, and lying down there.

If we have deep and thorough faith, the Buddha himself comes to wherever we may dwell and abides there together with us. For a believer nothing is more joyful or desirable. The day begins and ends with religious exaltation. We get up together with the Buddha in the morning and go to bed together with him at night. This is the perfection of man's religious life.

CHAPTER 18

The Merits of Joyful Acceptance

THIS CHAPTER PREACHES in further detail the merits of first rejoicing over the Buddha's teachings. The reason such merits are repeatedly preached is that our joyful acceptance of the Buddha's teachings, our deep feeling of gratitude for them, is indispensable to faith. Even if we have read many sutras and have memorized all Buddhist doctrines, so long as we do not accept the Buddha's teachings with heartfelt joy this means merely that we are knowledgeable in Buddhism; it does not indicate that we believe in the Buddha. To have a sense of joyful acceptance of the Buddha's teachings is to have faith in them. Therefore the merits that we obtain by the joyful acceptance of his teachings are preached repeatedly in this chapter.

Faith is often said to multiply: the object of faith is multiplied by the mind of faith. However, even if the object of faith is the most perfect in the world, its effect cannot appear in a person if he assumes the wrong attitude in believing and has a low degree of faith. Let us suppose that the Buddha's teachings are equivalent to the figure one hundred. If a person's joyful acceptance of the Buddha's teachings is zero, a hundred multiplied by zero equals zero. At the same time, however strong a person's religious feeling may be, the result will be of no value to him if the object of his faith is empty, because zero multiplied by a hundred equals zero. However earnestly one may believe in an empty object, the result will be nil. If he has faith in a wrong teaching, it stands to reason that this will lead to an evil or unhappy result. If the teaching itself is an evil religion equivalent to a negative value of minus one, supposing a man's religious mind to be equivalent to one hundred, minus one multiplied by a hundred equals minus one hundred. Thus a highly negative effect will appear in the believer because the teaching itself is originally of a negative value. From this simple multiplication, we can easily understand what a terrible effect blind belief in an evil religion will have.

The teaching of the Lotus Sutra can be compared to an infinite positive number. Suppose that the sutra is equivalent to the figure one hundred. If one deeply believes in the sutra with a single thought, at the same time feeling gratitude toward it, and if his single thought of the sutra is assumed to be equivalent to the figure one, a highly positive effect will appear in him because one multiplied by one hundred makes one hundred.

If first rejoicing over the Buddha's teachings is important for a believer, how immeasurable will be the merits as his religious feeling increases to the value of two, five, ten, and a hundred.

At that time Maitreya Bodhisattva-Mahāsattva spoke to the Buddha, saying: "World-honoerd One! If there be a good son or good daughter who, hearing this Law-Flower Sutra, accepts it with joy, how much happiness will he obtain?"

To be sure, Maitreya Bodhisattva had already understood how much happiness a person obtains from accepting the Lotus Sutra with joy. But as might be expected of one who is the idealization of the Buddha's compassion, he asked this question with the intention of making all living beings deepen their faith still further; he requested the Buddha to preach the merits of joyful acceptance in further detail for those who had a low level of understanding.

Then the Buddha addressed Maitreya Bodhisattva: "Ajita! If, after the extinction of the Tathāgata, any *bhikshu, bhikshuṇī, upāsaka, upāsikā,* or other wise person, whether old or young, on hearing this sutra has accepted it with joy, and coming out of the assembly goes elsewhere to dwell either in a monastery or solitary place, or in a city, street, hamlet, or village, to expound what he has heard, according to his ability, to his father, mother, kindred, good friends, and acquaintances; and all these people, having heard it, accept it with joy and again go on to transmit the teaching; these others, having heard it, also accepting it with joy, and transmitting the teaching, and so on in turn to the fiftieth person—Ajita! I will now tell you about the merit of that fiftieth good son or good daughter, who joyfully receives the truth. Do you hearken well!"

THREE IMPORTANT POINTS. These words of the Buddha include three important points. The first is the words "As he has heard." For an initiate, having heard the teaching, it is most important to transmit it to others just as he has heard it. If he neglects to do so, there is the danger of his misinforming others of the vital point of the teaching. To transmit the teaching correctly would seem to be a simple thing, but it is more difficult than one may think, as shown by the following experiment conducted by sociologists. A number of people are lined up in a row. The one at the head of the row whispers a very short story into the ear of the next person, and in this way it is transmitted from one to another to the end of the row. For example, suppose that the short story is as follows: "Mary happened to pass by just when John and Jim were arguing with each other. John appeared to her to be defeating Jim because the latter, his face all aglow, glared at the former, whose face was pale." Even such a brief story changes amazingly while it is being transmitted among only ten people. If the story changes a little in what each transmitter says about certain points, it does not matter too much. But in many cases, the story becomes quite different, with Jim defeating John or John's face all aglow, not Jim's.

Why is even such a short story changed in being transmitted by word of mouth among even a small group? This is because one person mishears the story, another remembers it incorrectly and misses its point while retelling it, and others inject into it their own interpretations, so departs further and further from its original form. Subjective ideas are indeed an encumbrance that often cause mishearing and slips of memory. For instance, if we have the preconceived notion that a man who is confounded by his opponent must have a pale face, we are apt to mishear "Jim had a pale face" and to mistakenly remember the story this way.

If the Buddha's teachings were transmitted with mistakes like this, it would bring serious consequences to many people. Therefore the Buddha warns us, saying, "As he has heard." A person who has grasped the essentials of the teaching should be allowed to preach it in various tactful ways—indeed, it is natural for him to change his way of preaching according to his hearers' ability. But a beginner must not forget the Buddha's warning.

It may be remarked here that the Buddha's disciples paid very close attention to the matter of faithful transmission of the teachings. His five hundred leading disciples gathered at Rājagṛha in Magadha four months after Sakyamuni Buddha's death. There they first verified the Buddha's teachings that they had heard from one another, and after ascertaining the Buddha's correct words, they endeavored to fix them firmly in their memories. Such a conference for compiling the Buddhist sutras was called *saṃgīti* (*ketsujū*), namely, a Buddhist council to decide orthodoxy.

It is said that the disciples proceeded in this council in the following way: when Ānanda, who was considered the man who had heard the Buddha's sermons most often, was chosen to recite a teaching, Mahā-Kāśyapa, who presided over the council, asked him one question after another concerning the teaching—when, where, to whom, and on what occasion the Buddha had preached it, and what its contents were. Ānanda answered each question that Kāśyapa asked. The rest of the disciples listened calmly to these questions and answers. If they found no difference in Ānanda's answer from their own memory of the teaching, they agreed with each other on the accuracy of their recall of the Buddha's teachings. Whenever one of them had an objection, it was thoroughly discussed. The disciples approved a teaching only when they unanimously agreed on it, since they were extremely aware of the sacred work of ascertaining the orthodoxy of the Buddha's teachings to be left for posterity.

When they had unanimously approved a teaching, saying, "It is exactly what we have heard directly from the Buddha," they recited it together and memorized it. This is why many Buddhist sutras begin with the words "Thus have I heard."

Repetition of exactly the same contents is found frequently in such sutras of early Buddhism as the *Āgama-sūtras* because the disciples had memorized the questions and answers in the Buddhist councils. In the Mahāyāna sutras, including the Lotus Sutra, such repetition has been edited to a great extent, but repetition has been used in portions where it is necessary to deepen the impression of the readers.

The second important point is the words "according to his ability." These words have two meanings: one indicates the idea "suited to one's power" and the other expresses the ideal "to make one put forth all one's strength."

It is hardly possible for a person who has heard the teaching for the first time to preach it as well as a high or learned priest. If a beginner discusses a teaching falteringly and is a poor speaker, that is only natural. If he is a talented writer, he ought to transmit the teaching to others through writing. At all events, one should transmit the teaching according to one's ability and one's experience. This is the first meaning of the words "according to his ability."

However, if a poor speaker earnestly endeavors to transmit the teaching to others to the very best of his ability, his enthusiasm inevitably makes an impression on the hearer. In short, sincerity is important. This is the second meaning of the words "according to his ability."

The third point is the reason that here is preached the merit of the fiftieth person who has heard with joy the teaching, which then is transmitted in turn to fifty more people. This expresses strongly the greatness of the teachings of the Lotus Sutra.

The first person, who attends a sermon, has been able to hear the teaching directly from someone who is accomplished in the Law and has persuasive power. Therefore he has been deeply moved by the sermon. This first person, having heard the teaching, then transmits it to others. He does not have an extensive knowledge of the Law or deep faith in it or long experience in preaching it. Even if he can transmit the teaching to others exactly as he has heard it, the joy that the hearer feels will gradually lessen in direct proportion to his distance from the original speaker. Thus, when the teaching is transmitted to the fiftieth person, in most cases it will not give any joy to the hearer and he will not exert himself, only dismissing it with the words, "Oh, really?"

The Lotus Sutra differs from other teachings in this regard. So long as the contents of the sutra are correctly transmitted from person to person, even the fiftieth person cannot help accepting them with joy because they are so great. Of course, the joy the fiftieth person feels will inevitably be less than that of the first person. But even this degree of joy produces a great merit. We must realize the deep meaning included in the words, "the merits of the fiftieth person who in turn hears the Lotus Sutra and accepts it with joy."

Then the Buddha speaks of the merits of the fiftieth person who joyfully receives the truth. We must note carefully here the following point: various merits are expressed in the sutra in a highly symbolic way, with abstract points represented in concrete form. We must not take such words and phrases literally but must grasp the true spirit hidden in their depth, otherwise we will be in danger of falling into a stupid misunderstanding of the Buddha's teachings. We can say the same thing of the following chapters of the sutra.

"It is as the number of all the living creatures in the six states of existence, in four hundred myriad *koṭis* of *asaṃkhyeyas* of worlds, born in the four ways, egg-born, womb-born, humidity-born, or born by metamorphosis, whether they are formed or formless, whether conscious or unconscious, or neither conscious nor unconscious; footless, two-footed, four-footed, or many-footed—it is as the sum of all these living creatures. Suppose someone, seeking their happiness, provides them with every article of pleasure they may desire, giving each creature the whole of a Jambudvīpa,[1] gold, silver, lapis lazuli, moonstone, agate, coral, amber, and all sorts of wonderful jewels, with elephants, horses, carriages, and palaces and towers built of the precious seven, and so forth. This great master of gifts thus bestows gifts for full eighty years and then reflects thus: 'I have bestowed on all these beings articles of pleasure according to their desires, but now they have all grown old and worn, over eighty years of age, with hair gray and faces wrinkled, and death is not far off—I ought to instruct and guide them in the Buddha-law.' Thereupon, gathering together those beings, he proclaims to them the Law's instruction; and by his revealing, teaching, benefiting, and rejoicing, they all in a moment become *srota-āpannas, sakṛdāgāmins, anāgāmins,* and *arhats,* free from all imperfections, having all acquired mastery of profound meditation and completed the eighty emancipations."

The six states mean the six realms or worlds in which the minds of living beings transmigrate. Born in the four ways means the following four categories of living creatures: egg-born (beings produced from eggs), womb-born (viviparous creatures), humidity-born (worms and other creatures living in damp ground), and born by metamorphosis (beings whose origin is unknown, for instance, heavenly beings). In short, the expression "born in the four ways" means all kinds of living creatures.

In the words "whether conscious or unconscious," "conscious" means one with a discriminating mind and "unconscious" means one without such a mind. In the words "neither conscious nor unconscious," "neither conscious" indicates one who has realized that he cannot see the real state of all things with the discriminating mind, and "nor unconscious" indicates one who transcends both the discriminating and the nondiscriminating mind. All together, these words indicate the possessors of all kinds of minds. We need not be rigidly bound by the various words

1. Jambudvīpa, the southern of the four continents surrounding Mount Sumeru, is the world in which we live.

used here but may regard them as referring to all kinds of living creatures. The expression "by his revealing, teaching, benefiting, and rejoicing" has already been discussed on page 117.

The categories beginning with *srota-āpannas* are the four degrees attained by a Hīnayāna Buddhist: (1) *srota-āpanna,* literally, "entrance into the stream" (leading to nirvana), is the first stage to be attained by a Hīnayāna disciple; (2) *sakṛdāgāmin,* literally, "returning," or being reborn only once more, is the second stage, in which one has avoided defilements but still has the potential of defilement; (3) *anāgāmin,* literally, "not returning," or no more rebirth, is the third stage, in which one has avoided all defilements; and (4) *arhat,* literally, "man of worth" or "honorable man," is the last stage, in which one has freed himself from all defilements and has obtained perfect knowledge and a pure mind.

In their practice the followers of Hīnayāna Buddhism endeavor to rise gradually through each of these four degrees to attain enlightenment. However, the Buddha mentions here that they have instantaneously attained the four degrees.

The words "eight emancipations" mean eight kinds of meditation to free one from attachments. A detailed explanation of the eight emancipations is not necessary here because they belong to a specialized study of Buddhist doctrines.

Then the World-honored One asked Maitreya Bodhisattva: "What is your opinion? May the merits obtained by this great master of gifts be considered many or not?"

Maitreya said to the Buddha: "World-honored One! The merits of this man are very many, infinite and boundless. Even though this master of giving had only made gifts of all those articles of pleasure to those creatures, his merits would be infinite; how much more when he causes them to attain arhatship?"

Then said the Buddha to Maitreya in a firmer voice: "I will now speak clearly to you. The merits attained by this man in bestowing those means of happiness to all beings in the six states of existence of four hundred myriad *koṭis* of *asaṃkhyeyas* of worlds, and causing them to attain arhatship do not compare with the merits of that fiftieth person who, hearing a single verse of the Law-Flower Sutra, receives it with joy; they are not equal to one hundredth, or one thousandth, or one fraction of a hundred thousand myriad *koṭis;* the power of figures or comparisons cannot express it."

There are two reasons that the power of figures or comparisons cannot express the merits of that fiftieth person. The first is that material donations differ fundamentally from the donation of the Law. To donate material things to others is certainly a good deed. But the benefits of such actions are limited and relative. For example, suppose that we give some money to destitute people. A relatively small sum may lead one person to find his feet again. But another person may lead a more comfortable life with that sum of money while he has it, and when he has spent it he may be no better off than before. On the contrary, the money may even have a harmful effect on a person, encouraging him in idle or luxury-loving habits. Thus, though a material donation is indeed good, it is a limited and relative good.

When we donate money and goods to others, if we can teach them how to start their lives anew by using these things effectively, this kind of donation will help them. This kind of teaching should be included within the donation of the Law; material donations become more effective when the donation of the Law is added to them. The ideal would be for social security to be enforced thus. But even this kind of donation is still limited and relative because its benefits will end with one's life. The donation that is truly sacred and is eternally effective is that of the Law, meaning that we give the Buddha's teachings to others. This kind of donation is not limited to one's life but extends to posterity. Therefore, nothing is so important as the merits obtained through this donation.

In the Buddha's words to Maitreya Bodhisattva, he points out that a person bestows material donations to all beings in the universe and also gives them the donation of the Law by preaching the Buddha's teachings, causing them to attain arhatship. But the merits obtained by this man do not compare with the merits of that fiftieth person who, hearing a single verse of the Lotus Sutra, receives it with joy. This may seem strange at first, but it has the following meaning.

To attain arhatship, that is, to reach the mental stage of having avoided all defilements, is the pinnacle of the Hīnayāna teaching. But if such a person isolates himself in the mountains, the merits attained by him stop at that stage. The Buddha's teachings are very valuable, but their value cannot be displayed fully unless the person preaches them, elevating his hearers and giving them power and courage, and thus improving the whole world. So long as Buddhist monks are confined to their temples after their own enlightenment and devote themselves to performing funeral and memorial services, they do not put the Buddha's true spirit to practical use.

The teaching of the Lotus Sutra is not limited to saving oneself from suffering; its aim is the bodhisattva practice of saving many others from their sufferings. When a person hears a single verse of the Lotus Sutra and receives it with joy, his feeling of joyful acceptance is sure to develop into the power of saving other people.

Suppose that arhatship is equivalent to the figure one hundred because this mental stage indicates one's own enlightenment. On the other hand, the joy one feels on first hearing a single verse of the Lotus Sutra may be worth only one mark as to his own enlightenment. However, there is a great difference in value between the figure one hundred indicating Hīnayāna enlightenment and the figure one indicating the Mahāyāna teaching. This is because the figure one in the Mahāyāna teaching expands limitlessly and has the potential of increasing eventually to one thousand or ten thousand.

For example, a person's own enlightenment can be compared to one hundred *koku*[2] of rice in a warehouse. He can live on such a large amount of rice all his life, but that is all that he can do. The rice may be eaten by weevils or grawed by rats or may rot without his realizing it. On the other hand, the sense of joy one first feels in receiving the Lotus Sutra is like one *sho*[3] of rice seed sown in a field. These seeds have the possibility of growing and increasing to hundreds or thousands of *koku* of rice. Here lies the reason that the merits of a person who, hearing a single verse of the Lotus Sutra, receives it with joy are far more than those gained in the practice of giving the greatest material donations or even of bestowing the donation of the Law, causing others to attain arhatship. Thus we realize that while the merits obtained by giving something to others are great, the merits of its receivers are also great.

So far we have been discussing the merits of the fiftieth person who hears the Lotus Sutra and accepts it with joy. What about the merits of the first hearers in the assembly? The Buddha expounded their merits as follows: "Ajita! If the merits of such a fiftieth person who in turn hears the Law-Flower Sutra and accepts it with joy are indeed so infinite, boundless, and numberless, how much more is the happiness of him who among the first hearers in the assembly receives it joyfully, surpassing happiness still more infinite, boundless, and beyond number or compare."

As explained before, because of the immeasurable value of the teach-

2. A unit of measure used for rice in Japan; one *koku* is equivalent to 4.9629 bushels.
3. One-hundredth *koku*.

ing itself, the hearer can accept with joy even the teaching that has been transmitted in turn to the fiftieth person, who is a beginner. How much greater is the joy of a person who has heard the teaching directly from a preacher who has already attained enlightenment. Such joyful acceptance will bring about a great change in his life and will have a boundless influence upon society.

THE OPPORTUNITY TO ENCOUNTER THE TEACHING. This chapter also states that even a person who is so unenlightened that when he comes in contact with the teaching he is not deeply moved by it will obtain very great merits. This teaches us how important it is to have the opportunity to encounter the teaching. We all surely have the buddha-nature, but we cannot attain salvation unless we awaken to the existence of our buddha-nature through such an opportunity. To come in contact with the teaching is a prior condition for salvation, and the opportunity to encounter it must be said to be very sacred indeed. Accordingly, our giving such an opportunity to others is also a very sacred deed.

Then the Buddha preached the merits of a person who hears and receives the Lotus Sutra even for a moment and persuades or causes others to do so: "Again, Ajita! If anyone, for the sake of this sutra, goes to a monastery and, either sitting or standing, hears and receives it even for a moment, by reason of that merit in his next bodily rebirth he will acquire the most excellent kind of elephants, horses and carriages, jeweled palanquins and litters, and ride in celestial cars. If again there be anyone who sits down in the place where this Law is preached, and when others come persuades them to sit down and hear it, or shares his seat with others, that person's merit, on his bodily rebirth, will give him a Śakra's seat, or a Brahma's, or the seat of a sacred wheel-rolling king. Ajita! If, moreover, anyone says to another: 'There is a sutra named the Flower of the Law; let us go together and listen to it,' and if he who is persuaded hears it but for a moment, that person's merit, after his bodily rebirth, will cause him to be born in the same place with bodhisattvas who have attained *dhāraṇī*."

Śakra and Brahma are the supreme guardian gods of the Buddha's teachings. A sacred wheel-rolling king, or *cakravartin,* is a great king who rules this world correctly and peacefully on the basis of the Buddha's teachings. Bodhisattvas who have attained *dhāraṇī* are those who instruct people to cause them to avoid all evil and who persuade them to do all good. People who give others the chance of encountering the Lotus

Sutra should be regarded as being just as holy as such benevolent gods, a sacred wheel-rolling king, or bodhisattvas. The next bodily rebirth of these people in the place where bodhisattvas live means that they will be reborn spiritually in this world, namely, that their lives will be completely changed and renewed.

This chapter also states that these people will be reborn not only spiritually but also physically in this world, and their sign of humanity will be perfect. Here we need not inquire into each condition of their rebirth. It is enough for us to realize that a person's spiritual rebirth shows in his features, demonstrating the truth that man's spirit influences his body. However, such a bodily change appears very slowly, and his countenance does not change greatly in the present world. In this case, human change means not one's physical beauty or ugliness but the shining loftiness of one's spirit. The more one accumulates religious practices, the more brilliantly will one's spirit shine.

When we see the portraits and images of learned or noted priests, sages, and saints preserved from ancient times, among them we find few endowed with physical beauty in the usual sense. In the depictions of the ten great disciples of the Buddha, no one could call any of them handsome except Ānanda and Rāhula. Most of them have unprepossessing faces, which has led to the saying, "A person with a face like an *arhat*." Nevertheless, each of the ten great disciples is depicted as a person who has a mild and compassionate face and also a holy sign representing the depth of his wisdom. If these great disciples accumulate the bodhisattva practice whenever they are reborn, their spiritual elevation increasingly influences their countenances and finally leads them to be the possessors of the signs of a buddha, becoming perfect in the thirty-two signs and the eighty kinds of excellence of a buddha. We too can become the possessors of such holy signs of a buddha.

The influence of man's spiritual rebirth is not limited to his mental aspect but also affects his bodily aspect. This latter change takes place very slowly, but it is sure to occur. This is how we should interpret this part of the Lotus Sutra.

CHAPTER 19

The Merits of the Preacher

THE PREVIOUS CHAPTER DETAILS the merits of a beginner, one who has just entered the teaching. The present chapter expounds the merits of a preacher who has moved to a higher level. "Preacher" does not necessarily mean monk or nun but means any person—including Buddhist monks, nuns, laymen, and laywomen—who receives and keeps the Buddha's teachings and endeavors to spread them. The practices of a preacher are of five kinds *(goshu hosshi)*: receiving and keeping the sutra (*juji*), reading it (*doku*) and reciting it (*ju*), expounding it (*gesetsu*), and copying it (*shosha*). A full explanation of these five kinds of practices has already been given in chapter 10, "A Teacher of the Law." In each of these five practices, the state of our gradually deepening faith is clearly shown.

If we believe and discern the teaching after hearing it, and if we raise the mind of joyful acceptance of it, we proceed first to keep it firmly, then, reading and reciting the sutra, to inscribe it on our memory. As a personal discipline, this practice is done to establish the foundation of our faith. When our faith reaches this stage,we cannot help transmitting the teaching to others. As a result, we expound the sutra (the teaching) and copy it. We cannot say we have attained true faith until we go through each process of the five kinds of practices of the preacher.

Then the Buddha addressed the Bodhisattva-Mahāsattva Ever Zealous: "If any good son or good daughter receives and keeps this Law-Flower Sutra, or reads, or recites, or expounds, or copies it, that person will obtain eight hundred merits of the eye, twelve hundred merits of the ears, eight hundred merits of the nose, twelve hundred merits of the tongue, eight hundred merits of the body, and twelve hundred merits of the mind; with these merits he will dignify his six organs, making them all serene."

The figures eight hundred and twelve hundred indicate the idea of obtaining the merits perfectly. We do not have to take these numbers literally.

THE MERITS OF THE EYE. What merits of the eye can the good son or good daughter obtain? Concerning these merits, the Buddha preaches as follows: "That good son or good daughter, with the natural pure eyes received at birth from his parents, will see whatever exists within and without the three-thousand-great-thousandfold world, mountains, forests, rivers, and seas, down to the Avīci hell and up to the Summit of Existence, and also see all the living beings in it, as well as see and know in detail all their karma-causes and rebirth states of retribution."

Thereupon the World-honored One, desiring to proclaim this teaching over again, spoke in verse, concluding with the following words: "Though not yet having attained divine vision, / His eyes of flesh have powers like these."

The expression "Though not yet having attained divine vision" indicates the opposite of the expression "with the natural pure eyes received at birth from his parents." The last line of the verse means that even though living beings do not yet possess the divine vision of heavenly beings, capable of discerning the real state of all things, they can receive the power to do so while living in the *sahā*-world because they have pure eyes unclouded with mental illusion. To put it more plainly, they can do so because their minds become so pure that they are devoid of selfishness, so that they view things unswayed by prejudice or subjectivity. They can see things correctly, as they truly are, because they always maintain calm minds and are not swayed by impulse.

The Buddha preaches in a certain sutra as follows: "A thing is not reflected as it is in water boiling over a fire. A thing is not mirrored as it is on the surface of water hidden by plants. A thing is not reflected as it is on the surface of water running in waves stirred up the wind." The Buddha teaches us here that we cannot view the real state of things until we are free from the mental illusion caused by selfishness and passion. We should interpret the merits of the eye in this way.

THE FOUR FEARLESSNESSES OF A BODHISATTVA. The Buddha began to speak in verse with the following words: "If one, in the great assembly,/ With fearless mind,/Preaches this Law-Flower Sutra . . ." The phrase "with fearless mind" means that one says what he believes in a dignified manner, without fear or reserve. In explaining such a fearless mind, the expression "the four fearlessnesses of a bodhisattva" has been used since ancient times. One can preach the Law with a fearless mind if he always maintains the following four fearlessnesses.

The first is *sōji-fumō:* a bodhisattva has no fear of preaching the Law, through remembering to observe all the requirements. This means that a bodhisattva has nothing to fear in preaching the Law to anybody if he learns by heart all the teachings he has heard and he does not forget them. This seems simple enough, but it is not so easy to put into practice. Whenever a person receives the teaching he listens to it with his whole heart, and whenever he has questions about it he does not hesitate to ask the preacher until he has understood it to his satisfaction. Moreover, he endeavors to remember the teaching by reading and reciting it repeatedly morning and evening. He cannot reach such a mental stage unless he perseveres in this endeavor tirelessly.

The second fearlessness is *jinchi-hōyaku:* the bodhisattva has no fear of preaching the Law, by thoroughly knowing the medicine of the Law and also the capacities, inclinations, natures, and minds of all living beings. This means that just as a physician can make up a prescription according to the nature and stage of any disease, a bodhisattva can preach the Law with no uneasiness in accordance with the differences in capacity, inclination, nature, and mind of each person. A person who is worthy to be called a bodhisattva not only remembers the teaching well but also fosters the ability to preach it freely by using tactful means.

The third fearlessness is *zennō-mondō:* the bodhisattva has no fear of preaching the Law in good and sufficient questions and answers. If it were sufficient just to speak of the Law on the spur of the moment, one could prepare for it with hastily acquired and undigested knowledge. Anyone who has a general knowledge of the Law can do so. A true preacher, however, must have enough power to answer clearly any question on his preaching and to argue logically against opposing opinions. His answers and arguments must not be deceptive or farfetched but must be in accord with the Buddha's teachings. The word "good" means that his answers are good in that they accord with the Buddha's teachings. However correct his answer may be in content, he cannot be said to be a good preacher unless he knows how to preach the Law so tactfully that he can make his hearers both understand it easily and realize completely their mistaken ideas. The word "sufficient" refers to his persuasive power. In short, one who can answer any question and any opposing opinion so explicitly and satisfactorily as to accord completely with the Buddha's teachings will preach the Law with no fear.

The fourth fearlessness is *nōdan-motsugi:* the bodhisattva has no fear of preaching the Law through sufficiently resolving doubts. Many questions arise regarding the interpretation of the Buddha's teachings because they are so profound, vast, and boundless. Every person has a different interpretation of matters, thus the saying, "As many Buddhist priests as there are interpretations of the Law." A person must be very clear-headed and decisive in his interpretation of the Law, but above all he must surpass others in virtue and must have the utmost compassion. This is because in considering such difficult problems as varying interpretations of teachings, one cannot grasp the true intention of the Buddha from theoretical knowledge alone. Only a person who has reached the mental stage of directly entering into the great compassion of the Buddha can make decisions that conform to the Buddha's intention in elucidating the delicate nuances of doubts. A bodhisattva who can sufficiently resolve doubts in this way will preach the Law without any fear.

In considering the four fearlessnesses of a bodhisattva, some people may be daunted at the thought of the difficulty of preaching the Law to others. However, we must not be afraid. These four categories describe the ideal preacher, and if one attains such a stage, then indeed one will have become a great bodhisattva. No great bodhisattva becomes so without effort; he reaches such a stage only after a long practice of severe discipline.

We, who train ourselves in the bodhisattva practice, must always preach the Law by bearing in mind the four ideals of the bodhisattva and by taking these four ideals as our yardstick. When we meet with a difficult problem or are asked questions that we do not know how to answer, we should say so frankly: "As this question is beyond me, I will ask somebody for instruction and then I will answer you." We must not dream up an answer just to make it through the occasion somehow. To say "I am not sure" does not lower us in the estimation of others as preachers but results in increasing the confidence of our listeners.

The Merits of Ear, Nose, Tongue, Body, and Thought. Then the Buddha preached the merits of the ear. He teaches that any good son or good daughter who has improved in the five practices of the preacher will be able to hear all words and sounds with his natural ears.

Things make a sound whenever they move. A person who has attained a serene mind through deepening his faith can grasp the subtle shifting of things through their sounds. Among the various sounds mentioned in this passage, those of fire, water, and wind refer to natural things. With a serene ear, one can grasp distinctly the movements of nature just by hearing the sounds of crackling fire, of murmuring water, and of whistling wind. When such a person hears the sounds of nature, he can enjoy them as much as if he were listening to beautiful music. When he hears any unusual sound of nature, he can judge its true cause and thus can save many other people as well as himself from the dangers of blizzards, typhoons or hurricanes, tidal waves, floods, and other natural disasters. Still more, he can easily recognize the movement of men's minds from the sounds of conchs, of drums, of gongs, and of bells.

A skilled mechanical engineer knows what parts of which machines are worn out or maladjusted when he enters a factory and listens to the noises that the many machines make. Among more than a hundred musicians in a symphony orchestra, an outstanding conductor can ascertain the delicate differences in their performances by listening: which instrumentalists perform with too low or too high a pitch; which do not create the right mood in their performance; which overperform. A preacher as a leader in human life is able naturally to recognize the feelings of living creatures from their words and other sounds.

Needless to say, the sounds of creatures are generated by their movements. They are produced not only by the vibrations of their vocal cords but also by the movements of their feelings and will. There are sounds of comfort, of lamentation, of suffering, and of speech. One who has developed sufficient faith can hear the true meaning of all those sounds: the sounds of the hells, of animals, of hungry spirits, and of *asuras*. He can also recognize the sounds of holy men, of *bhikshus*, of *bhikshuṇīs*, and of bodhisattvas. He can understand what teaching is preached in what place and what value its content has. Finally, he will attain the ability described in the following lines:

"The buddhas, great and holy honored ones,

Transformers of all living beings,
Who, in their great assemblies,
Proclaim the mystic Law—
He who keeps this Law-Flower
Hears in every detail."

It is natural that because the whole body of the Tathāgata is contained in the Lotus Sutra, one who keeps the sutra can hear the Buddha's preaching of the Law.

We find the following two important expressions in the verse portion in which the Buddha speaks of the merits of the ear: "He can listen without being under their control" and "He will hear without harm to his organ of hearing." The former expression means that even if he hears the sounds of beautiful music he is not attached to them. He may be charmed by music for a short time, but he has no permanent attachment to it, nor is lulled into forgetting important matters. This is a good example for us in regard to our attachment to amusements. The latter expression means that his hearing will not be impaired even if he hears all the sounds in the three-thousand-great-thousandfold world. This indicates that he will not become confused by hearing all the various kinds of sounds in the world. If an ordinary person hears the sounds of worry, of suffering, and of grief on one side and the sounds of disputes and quarrels on the other, he will be thrown into confusion. However, a person who has deepened his faith sufficiently will not be overwhelmed; he will dwell calmly amid the noise and will be able to hear these sounds with serenity.

The Buddha also discussed the merits of the nose. Among the five sense organs of men, the nose is said to be the most animallike. For this reason it is said that the art of smell has not been developed to the same extent as the arts of the eye (painting, sculpture, and so on) and of the ear (music). For this very reason, the nose has much direct influence upon human emotions. When one smells an unpleasant odor, he may lose his appetite or develop a headache, while he can be completely fascinated by a delightful perfume. The sense of smell is very difficult to pin down, but if any good son or good daughter improves in the five kinds of practices of the preacher, he will freely discern things by smell. This means that he will grasp the true state of all things.

Next, the Buddha declared the merits of the tongue. These merits are of two kinds: the first is that whatever one tastes will have the finest flavor, and the second is that when one preaches, one will send forth so profound and beautiful a voice as to give all people pleasure and joy. Concerning the first merit, it is natural for whatever one eats to taste good when one has reached this high a degree of faith and mental calm. No explanation of the second merit is needed.

Next, the Buddha preached the merits of the body. If any good son or good daughter practices the five kinds of practices of the preacher, he will obtain a body as pure as clear crystal, which all the living delight to see, and the real state of all things will be manifested in his body. A person who wholeheartedly carries out the bodhisattva practice is free from the idea of self. Because of having such a pure body, all forms and images in this world will be seen in his body just as they are, with no distortion or obscurity. Therefore, as indicated by the expression "all the living delight to see," all living beings will respect him as a leading teacher and feel joy in seeing him.

The Buddha then preached the merits of thought in the following way: "If any good son or good daughter, after the extinction of the Tathāgata, receives and keeps this sutra, or reads, or recites, or expounds, or copies it, he will obtain twelve hundred merits of thought. With this pure organ of thought, on hearing even a single verse or sentence he will penetrate its infinite and boundless meanings. Having discerned those meanings, he will be able to preach on that single sentence or verse for a month, four months, even a year. And that which he preaches, according to its several meanings, will not be contrary to the truth."

Because of having a pure organ of thought, such a person can understand the infinite and boundless meanings of the teaching when he hears even a single verse or sentence of it. Having entirely understood those meanings, he will be able to preach on that single sentence or verse for a month, four months, or even a year. In brief, having completely grasped the teaching, he can preach it from all angles, in various ways, in whatever manner and for whatever length of time he desires. Here is shown the vastness and boundlessness of the teachings of the Buddha and the deep wisdom of one who has penetrated them.

The Buddha then says: "If he refers to popular classics, maxims for ruling the world, means of livelihood, and so forth, all will coincide with the True Law." These words have a very important meaning for our daily lives today. The term "popular classics" means books to guide human life other than religious works, such as works on ethics or philosophy. Indeed, this phrase is not limited to books but also includes the

Buddha's teachings as preached through speech. The phrase "maxims for ruling the world" means teaching concerning such matters as politics, economics, and law. The phrase "means of livelihood" means discussing with and guide others in industry, such as agriculture, manufacturing, and commerce.

The ideas of a person who has attained deep faith will naturally coincide with the True Law even when he discusses such practical matters. For people of religion, this is the right way to deal with spiritual problems and the mental world, but it is not good to touch directly on political issues and the foreign policy of a nation. However, they have the very important duty to preach the principles of the correct mental attitude to whomever it may concern. Sakyamuni Buddha taught people concerning their work, economy, and other practical matters, to say nothing of the proper mental attitude for men engaged in government.

Even during the Buddha's lifetime, most believers in the Lotus Sutra must have been but lay devotees, not Buddhist monks or nuns. Therefore, sometimes the Buddha preached to believers in their homes on "popular classics," and sometimes he stated "maxims for ruling the world." How much more must it have been necessary for him to speak daily of "means of livelihood."

Discussion of people's daily lives is closely related to their common interests. For this reason what one says is apt to be greatly influenced by his ego. We tend to view things shortsightedly and to want to have things our own way, and often we do not take the broader view of things necessary to benefit others as well as ourselves. On the other hand, a person who has gained true faith can approach the viewpoint of the Buddha, that of benefiting everyone, so that naturally what he says coincides with the Buddha's teachings. This is a quality most essential in modern society.

In order to explain this teaching in more detail, the Buddha said: "The beings in the six destinies of the three-thousand-great-thousandfold world, whatever is passing in their minds, whatever are the movements of their minds, whatever arguments are diverting their minds—he knows them all. Though such a one has not yet obtained faultless wisdom, yet his organ of thought will be pure like this. Whatever he ponders, estimates, and speaks, all will be the Buddha-law, nothing but truth, and also that which former buddhas have taught in the sutra."

The living beings throughout the three-thousand-great-thousandfold world, whatever may be occupying their minds, whatever may be their mental processes, and whatever useless arguments may be distorting their minds—a person of a higher stage of faith can know them all because, though he is not yet perfectly free from illusions and has not yet obtained the wisdom to be able to penetrate the real state of all things just as they are, his organ of thought is pure enough for him to gain such a supernatural power. Whatever he ponders, estimates, and says will be in accord with the Buddha's teachings, and will also coincide with that which former buddhas have preached in the sutra.

"Former buddhas" indicates the many buddhas before the appearance of Sakyamuni Buddha in this world. This expression signifies that truth never changes and that whatever a person who has attained enough depth of faith preaches will coincide with the truth, which applies to the three temporal worlds of the past, the present, and the future.

In this way the Buddha teaches us that with the merits of the five kinds of practices of preachers any good son or good daughter can purify his or her six senses—vision, hearing, smell, taste, touch, and thought.

Finally, the major theme of the Buddha's preaching in this chapter includes two points. The first is the Buddha's encouragement to man to devote himself to his practice because if he practices the Lotus Sutra wholeheartedly he can improve both mentally and physically. The second is the Buddha's admonition that because a true believer in the Lotus Sutra must fulfill the important duty of spreading the Buddha's teachings, he should naturally possess the power to discern all things. That a person has not yet attained such a mental state is proof of the inadequacy of his personal practice. Therefore he must constantly examine himself so as not to lapse into complacency and conceit.

CHAPTER 20

The Bodhisattva Never Despise

IT IS NOT SUPPOSED that all the disciples who listened to the Buddha's preaching in chapter 19 completely understood the true meaning of his encouragement and the admonition included therein. Some of them may have become discouraged, thinking, "We cannot possibly practice all the teachings of the Lotus Sutra perfectly." Others may have been complacent, thinking, "We can obtain merit somehow or other if we just do the five kinds of practices of preachers according to form." Still others may have momentarily felt conceited, flattering themselves: "Unlike the disciples of the two vehicles, *śrāvakas* and *pratyekabuddhas,* we bodhisattvas are possessed of this kind of supernatural power. We are quite different from them."

On all occasions, the Buddha's sermons were perfect and left nothing to be desired. Whenever he perceived the slightest doubt in the minds of his disciples, he gave them enough instruction to lead them to Perfect Enlightenment. It can easily be imagined that probably he did the same in his preaching of chapter 19.

At that time, in an altered tone, the Buddha addressed the Bodhisattva-Mahāsattva Great Power Obtained: "Now you should know that if *bhikshus, bhikshuṇīs, upāsakas,* and *upāsikās* keep the Law-Flower Sutra, and if anyone curses, abuses, and slanders them, he will receive such great punishment as before announced; but those who attain the merits such as those previously announced, their eyes, ears, noses, tongues, bodies, and thoughts will be clear and pure." Then the Buddha told the story of the Bodhisattva Never Despise as an example of what he meant.

THE STORY OF THE BODHISATTVA NEVER DESPISE. "Great Power Obtained! In a past period of olden times, infinite, boundless, inconceivable, and *asaṃkhyeya kalpas* ago, there was a buddha named King of Majestic Voice Tathāgata, Worshipful, All Wise, Perfectly Enlightened in Conduct, Well Departed, Understander of the World, Peerless Leader, Controller, Teacher of Gods and Men, Buddha, World-honored One, whose *kalpa* was named Free from Decline and his domain All Complete. That buddha, King of Majestic Voice, in that world preached to gods, men, and *asuras*. To those who sought to be *śrāvakas* he preached response to the Law of the Four Noble Truths for escape from birth, old age, disease, and death, leading finally to nirvana; to those who sought to be *pratyekabuddhas* he preached response to the Law of the Twelve Causes; to bodhisattvas he by means of Perfect Enlightenment preached response to the Six *Pāramitās* for the perfecting of Buddha-wisdom. Great Power Obtained! The lifetime of this Buddha, King of Majestic Voice, was forty myriad *koṭis* of *nayutas* of *kalpas*, as many as the sands of the Ganges. The number of *kalpas* during which the Righteous Law remained in the world was equal to the atoms in a Jambudvīpa; and the number of *kalpas* during which the Counterfeit Law remained was equal to the atoms in four continents. After that buddha had abundantly benefited all living beings, he became extinct. After the Righteous Law and Counterfeit Law had entirely disappeared, in that domain there again appeared a buddha. He was also entitled King of Majestic Voice Tathāgata, Worshipful, All Wise, Perfectly Enlightened in Conduct, Well Departed, Understander of the World, Peerless Leader, Controller, Teacher of Gods and Men, Buddha, World-honored One. Thus in succession there were twenty thousand *koṭis* of buddhas who all had the same title. After the extinction of the first Tathāgata King of Majestic Voice and after the end of the Righteous Law, during the period of the Counterfeit Law *bhikshus* of utmost arrogance obtained the chief power. At that period there was a bodhisattva-*bhikshu* named Never Despise. Great Power Obtained! For what reason was he named Never Despise? Because that *bhikshu* paid respect to and commended everybody whom he saw, *bhikshu, bhikshuṇī, upāsaka,* and *upāsikā,* speaking thus: 'I deeply revere you. I dare not slight and contemn you. Wherefore? Because you all walk in the bodhisattva-way and are to become buddhas.' And that *bhikshu* did not devote himself to reading and reciting the sutras but only to paying respect, so that when he saw afar off a member of the four groups, he would especially go and pay respect to them, commending them, saying: 'I dare not slight you, because you are all to become buddhas.' Amongst the four groups, there were those who, irritated and angry and muddy-minded, reviled and abused him, saying: 'Where did this ignorant *bhikshu* come from, who takes it on himself to say, "I do not slight you," and who predicts us as destined to become buddhas? We need no such false prediction.' Thus he passed many years, constantly reviled but never irritated or angry, always saying, 'You are to become buddhas.' Whenever he spoke thus, the people beat him with clubs, sticks, potsherds, or stones. But, while escaping to a distance, he still cried aloud, 'I dare not slight you. You are all to become buddhas.' And because he always spoke thus, the haughty *bhikshus, bhikshuṇīs, upāsakas,* and *upāsikās* styled him Never Despise.

"When this *bhikshu* was drawing near his end, from the sky he heard and was entirely able to receive and retain twenty thousand myriad *koṭis* of verses of the Law-Flower Sutra, which the Buddha King of Majestic Voice had formerly preached. Whereupon he obtained as above clearness and purity of the eye-organ and of the organs of ear, nose, tongue, body, and thought. Having obtained the purity of these six organs, he further prolonged his life for two hundred myriad *koṭis* of *nayutas* of years, and widely preached this Law-Flower Sutra to the people. Then the haughty four orders of *bhikshus, bhikshuṇīs, upāsakas,* and *upāsikās* who had slighted and contemned this man, and given him the nickname Never Despise, seeing him possessed of great transcendent powers, of power of eloquent discourse, and of power of excellent meditation, and having heard his preaching, all believed in and followed him. This bodhisattva again converted thousands of myriads of *koṭis* of beings to Perfect Enlightenment.

"After the end of his lifetime, he met two thousand *koṭis* of buddhas who were all entitled Sun Moon Light, and under their Law he preached this Law-Flower Sutra. Because of this, he again met two thousand *koṭis* of buddhas, all equally entitled Sovereign Light King of the Clouds. Because under the Law of those buddhas he received, kept, read, recited, and preached this sutra to all the four groups, he obtained clearness and purity of the common eye and of the organs of ear, nose, tongue, body, and thought, and among the four groups preached the Law fearlessly.

"Great Power Obtained! This Bodhisattva-Mahāsattva Never Despise paid homage to such numerous buddhas as these, revering, honoring, and extolling them; and after cultivating the roots of goodness, again he met thousands of myriads of *koṭis* of buddhas and also under the Law of those buddhas preached this sutra; his merits being complete, he then became a buddha. Great Power Obtained! What is your opinion? Can it be that the Bodhisattva Never Despise was at that time somebody else? He was really I myself. If I in my former lives had not received and kept, read and recited this sutra, and preached it to others, I should not have been able so soon to attain Perfect Enlightenment. Because, under former buddhas, I received and kept, read and recited this sutra, and preached it to others, I so soon attained Perfect Enlightenment.

"Great Power Obtained! At that time the four groups, *bhikshus, bhikshuṇīs, upāsakas,* and *upāsikās,* with angry minds slighted and contemned me, therefore for two hundred *koṭis* of *kalpas* they never met a buddha, never heard the Law, never saw a *saṃgha,* and for a thousand *kalpas* underwent great sufferings in the Avīci hell. After their sin was brought to an end, they again met the Bodhisattva Never Despise, who taught and converted them to Perfect Enlightenment. Great Power Obtained! What is your opinion? Those four groups at that time, who constantly slighted that bodhisattva—can they indeed be somebody else? They are now in this assembly—the five hundred bodhisattvas Bhadrapāla and the others, the five hundred *bhikshuṇīs* Lion Moon and the others, the five hundred *upāsakas* Thinking of Buddha and the others, who all never retreat from Perfect Enlightenment. Know, Great Power Obtained! This Law-Flower Sutra greatly benefits all bodhisattva-*mahāsattvas* and enables them to reach Perfect Enlightenment. Therefore all bodhisattva-*mahāsattvas,* after the extinction of the Tathāgata, should ever receive and keep, read and recite, expound and copy this sutra."

Then the Buddha, desiring to proclaim this teaching over again, repeated it in verse, thus ending his preaching of this chapter.

Having read this far, readers will notice that this chapter is very different from the previous chapters of the Lotus Sutra. The chapters so far have presented us with scenes of many lands as that are beautiful and dreamlike but quite unlike this world, as well as dreadful scenes of hell. Most personages, including the buddhas, have been introduced as superhuman and ideal beings. But this chapter is strongly characterized by the human touch. The setting of the Bodhisattva Never Despise makes us think of an ordinary town today, although no description of any particular place is given. The characters appearing in the story are ordinary people such as may be met with anywhere. The words "*bhikshus, bhikshuṇīs, upāsakas,* and *upāsikās*" do not necessarily mean Buddhist monks, nuns, and lay devotees, but include people of all kinds and classes: foppish minor officials, raffish young men, middle-aged merchants posing as seasoned men of mature judgment, good-natured but strong-willed women; mingling with such people, we also imagine learned priests who boast of having a complete knowledge of Buddhism, middle-aged monks who are proud of keeping the precepts, and old priests who come to town to beg for alms but do not preach any sermons, only standing silently on a street corner with an aloof and superior air. The Bodhisattva Never Despise conjures up the image of a young monk who has the air of an earnest, serious-minded man with something unusual and refined about him.

All the chapters of the Lotus Sutra can be said to be literary in style; but chapter 20 comes closest to the feeling of modern literature. It gives us a strong sense of humanity and of things familiar to us. This is quite natural because it states vividly how, by practicing only the virtue of paying respect to others, an ordinary man realizes his faith and finally attains the perfection of his character.

In the previous chapter, the Buddha preached the five kinds of practices of preachers and referred to the vast and boundless merits that can be obtained from such practices. But the ordinary person will naturally be discouraged by the personal discipline required, thinking, "I cannot possibly fulfill the five kinds of practices of preachers." perhaps he will opportunistically think, "Well, I will try to do the five kinds of practices for form's sake." Unfortunately, ordinary people's minds operate at this level.

Sakyamuni Buddha could completely perceive the minds of those who listened to his teachings. Therefore, we can guess why he completely changed his preaching method in chapter 20. While telling of his own past life, he wished to make people realize again three important teachings. The first is that to practice thoroughly even only a single kind of good deed is indeed sacred, and to do so is the first step toward salvation. The second is that however many formalities we may learn and practice, there is no essential worth in such learning or practice; the creation of a valid human life consists in our practice of even only a single kind of good deed with devotion and earnest perseverance. The third is that the bodhisattva practice originates with revering others, that is, with our recognizing the buddha-nature of all people. If we try to save others without recognizing their buddha-nature, we only perform empty and formal deeds. True salvation lies in our disclosing of and respect for the buddha-nature innate in others.

The Buddha illustrated these three important teachings in the story of the humanistic *bhikshu* Never Despise. Moreover, he declared that Never Despise was the Buddha himself in a former existence. His declaration causes us to feel that the Buddha, who seemed far distant from us, has suddenly approached us. At the same time, we can sense that if we follow the path taken by the Bodhisattva Never Despise, we can surely attain the perfection of our own characters. The Buddha had seemed to exist somewhere above the clouds, far separated from us. However, when he shows us the Bodhisattva Never Despise as himself in a former life, a man who was friendly and humanistic, we feel as if we have found a ladder by which we can climb up to the Buddha's abode above the clouds. Thus the Buddha gives us great encouragement. We are heartened and can say to ourselves, "There is nothing impossible about the bodhisattva practice. We just begin with following the example of the Bodhisattva Never Despise." In this sense, chapter 20 has a special place in the concluding part of the Law of Origin—indeed, in the Lotus Sutra as a whole. Many important teachings are included in the story of the Bodhisattva Never Despise. Let us consider them one by one.

DISCLOSING AND REVERING OTHERS' BUDDHA-NATURE. It was in the period of the Counterfeit Law that the *bhikshu* Never Despise appeared in this world. The period of the Counterfeit Law is the time when the truth preached by the Buddha still exists but is learned and practiced as a matter of formality, and there is no longer any enlightenment. In this period, Buddhist monks devote themselves to gaining a thorough knowledge of Buddhist doctrines and formalities and are proud of themselves for being learned. Some of them only keep the precepts and practice them with indifference to others, and lead religious lives aloof from the world. The rest are weak followers. In such a period, Buddhist monks have lost touch with the true life and soul of Buddhism.

What is the true life and soul of Buddhism? It is nothing other than our realizing wholeheartedly the meaning of the saying, "All sentient beings have the buddha-nature innately." Our entire religious life starts with this realization. To become aware of one's own buddha-nature, bringing it to light from the depths of the mind, nurturing it, and developing it vigorously is the first step of one's religious life; this is the mental state of the *śrāvaka* and *pratyekabuddha.*

If one has the buddha-nature himself, others must also have it. If one can realize with his whole heart that he has the buddha-nature, he comes spontaneously to recognize that others equally possess it. Anyone who cannot recognize this has not truly realized his own buddha-nature.

There are many bad people around us. We cannot help thinking of some of them as wicked even when we try to see them in the most favorable light possible. We cannot bring ourselves to sympathize with those who kill people in order to rob them, or who cheat others out of their property. However, we judge these people as evil only by their criminal acts that are reported in the newspapers or otherwise publicized. If we were able to learn all the circumstances of their lives, we would find that there is no one who is so lost that he is without some human feeling.

A murderer may play with his baby, tossing it in his arms, when he is at home. A blackmailer may treat his dog as kindly as his own child. A gangster who extorts money from honest citizens may have a favorite follower for whom he feels as much affection as if he were his blood brother. For all that, we must not consider their crimes lightly or idealize them like movie heroes. But when we view evil people with calm and unprejudiced eyes, not with sentimental sympathy, we cannot help recognizing a bit of human nature in them, which they show when they innocently try to please their babies or treat their dogs as kindly as their own children or feel true affection for favorite followers.

A bit of human nature—this is the seed of the buddha-nature. A speck of the buddha-nature gleams forth from the mind even of a person whose mind is encrusted and stained with the evil of his crimes. It is like a tiny loophole in the wall of a dark prison. Everyone, without exception, has such a loophole in his mind, that is, a speck of buddha-nature.

We try to find the loophole in others' minds; we respect it as far as possible; and by doing so, we make others become aware of it themselves. A person who realizes the existence of the loophole in his own mind will open it wider for himself because he desires to let more light enter the depths of his mind. This is the meaning of disclosing and respecting others' buddha-nature and at the same time discovering one's own buddha-nature. To discover and respect others' buddha-nature is indeed the primary object of the bodhisattva practice, and living Buddhism consists of this.

In this context, we must not forget the words "and that *bhikshu* did not devote himself to reading and reciting the sutras, but only to paying respect." This does not mean that he did not need to read and recite the sutras but indicates that reading and reciting the sutras as merely a formality were of no value in the period of the Counterfeit Law. Therefore, the Buddha emphasized that for a *bhikshu,* it is more important to disclose and pay respect to others' buddha-nature than to read and recite the sutras, having degenerated into formalism. This point is the life and soul of Buddhism.

The Bodhisattva Never Despise paid respect to and commended everybody he saw, saying, "I deeply revere you, because you are all to become buddhas." This deed of the bodhisattva is the disclosing of and paying respect to others' buddha-nature. His words, "You are all to become buddhas," indicate that he has discovered others' buddha-nature, has paid respect to it, and has commended it.

There are two ways to make man discover his own buddha-nature. One is the way of "enlightenment in direct order"; this is the way of indicating "his own affairs" (*ko-ji*), which has been explained in chapter 16. Another is the way of "enlightenment in reverse order," that is, the way of indicating "the affairs of others" (*ta-ji*), which has also been explained in that chapter. Enlightenment in direct order means to make others realize their own buddha-nature by our discovering and commending it. This is the way taken by the Bodhisattva Never Despise. Enlightenment in reverse order means to awaken others from their ignorance by criticizing them. This is the way followed in calling someone to task and startling him with harsh words: "What do you mean by that ugly and selfish way of life? If you continue to live that way, can you imagine how you will feel when you are about to die?" This way is very effective for some people.

Enlightenment in direct order can be compared to the way in which, through an agreeable-tasting medicine, one gently melts the wall of illusion covering his buddha-nature. On the other hand, enlightenment in reverse order is like drastic surgery. If a person can bear this drastic method, he will completely change his human life through it. How ever, enlightenment in direct order is more effective in most cases because, as shown by the word "direct," this way follows the natural course of man's enlightenment and applies to the normal working of human psychology. Praise does not come amiss to anybody. A happy feeling naturally makes a person open the window of his mind, so that a warm light streams in. Then the buddha-nature in his mind begins to be active.

In prewar Japan, children were educated through scolding, the education of enlightenment in reverse order. But after World War II, education changed to teaching by praise, that is, the education of enlightenment in direct order. This is because it became understood that praise is more effective than punishment in developing children's character and drawing out their special abilities. On the other hand, a tendency has developed to rear children indulgently, which is overdoing the education of enlightenment in direct order. It is also necessary for children sometimes to train their minds through the education of enlightenment in reverse order.

Everybody feels pleased at being praised, but adults who have lost their mental purity tend at first to feel uncomfortable when praised, as if they were being flattered. This misunderstanding may be dispelled if the praise truly comes from the heart of the person who commends them. Such genuine praise will gradually open the window of one's mind, however tightly shut it may have been.

The same thing may be said of those who were paid respect and commended by the Bodhisattva Never Despise. Among them were some who became angry at the bodhisattva's words, reviled and abused him, or beat and stoned him. But he never became angry at their violence but persevered for many years, constantly repeating the same thing. His earnest attitude gradually softened the hearts of those who scorned him.

Evidence of this is seen in the fact that his enemies gave him the nickname Never Despise. If they had not had some friendly feeling for him, they would not have given him a nickname. At first, the arrogant people were angry at him, saying, "He insults us," or "He meddles in our affairs." But little by little they changed their attitude toward Never Despise and came to regard him merely as peculiar, thinking, "He is never irritated or angry even if stoned or beaten. He constantly pays respect to us and commends us, saying, 'I dare not slight you.' He is indeed an odd fellow." They had become accustomed to him, and at the same time they began to become vaguely aware of the greatness of Never Despise, admitting grudgingly, "There is something superior about this monk." The perseverance of Never Despise finally caused them to begin to feel awe and respect.

A very important teaching is shown through this bodhisattva's deed.

When a person repeats such a strange act as paying respect to everybody whom he sees, just as a fool tries to judge everything by the one thing he knows, and if he performs such an act wholeheartedly and patiently repeats it without flinching from whatever persecution he may suffer, in the end his act cannot help moving others and giving rise to awe and respect in their hearts. Because the arrogant people began to feel awe and respect for Never Despise, when he had realized the teaching of the Lotus Sutra for himself and preached it to them they all believed in and followed him.

A Japanese Buddhist monk, Zenkai, in about 1750 finished singlehandedly digging a tunnel approximately 185 meters long through a rocky hill at Yabakei Gorge, Kyūshū, after thirty years of endeavor. He had begun the project so that the local villagers could cross the gorge safely. At first he was treated as a madman and was persecuted in various ways. Nevertheless, he paid no attention but doggedly continued excavating the tunnel through the rocky hill. His attitude of working earnestly and persistently finally made such a profound impression on the villagers that they helped him voluntarily.

There have been many instances in which men who have made roads, reclaimed wasteland, or dug irrigation ditches for the benefit of other people have gone through the same kind of experience. These examples teach us a valuable lesson as to what great results come from doing a good deed wholeheartedly and with an indomitable perseverance in the face of all obstacles.

TWO IMPORTANT LESSONS. The next important teaching in the story of the Bodhisattva Never Despise is expressed in the following two sentences: "Whenever he spoke thus, the people beat him with clubs, sticks, potsherds, or stones. But, while escaping to a distance, he still cried aloud: 'I dare not slight you. You are all to become buddhas.' " We can learn two lessons from this short passage. The first is that Never Despise escaped to a distance from his attackers when they used violence against him. "Never Despise never moved, even when he was beaten so severely with sticks that his arm was broken or his forehead was cut open by a stone." Such an attitude may appeal more to some people. If so, the reason may come from their misunderstanding of the meaning of the Buddhist term *fushaku shimmyō,* which means "not to grudge one's life for the sake of the Law" or "to preach the Buddhist doctrine at the risk of one's life."

If we understand the true meaning of *fushaku shimmyō,* we know it means that we ought to devote ourselves to the Law above all else. When we devote ourselves to the Law, first of all we consider keeping the Law, developing it, and spreading it by every possible means. Therefore we drive out the petty idea that we must be ashamed of running away. If we make the decision, "I will live as long as possible and I will persevere in preaching the Law forever," we will try to escape immediately when we are exposed to danger.

This is an especially important lesson for the Japanese people. They seem to lack respect for human life. They have a tendency to take their lives lightly. In World War II many soldiers' lives were lost in vain because of the ideas of "no surrender" and "death for honor," as in the suicide attacks of kamikaze airmen. This regrettable waste came from the biased idea of the Japanese army and navy of regarding escape as ignoble and surrender as the greatest possible shame. The war leaders of Japan did not have the flexibility to realize that the man who wins in the long run is the true victor even if he has had to run away once; instead they forced the soldiers to dash at the enemy in a daredevil manner. The war leaders are to be blamed for this.

In contrast, General Douglas MacArthur, supreme commander of the American Army in the Philippines at the outbreak of the World War II, withdrew his troops from Manila to Bataan Peninsula when he was defeated by the Japanese army. When Corregidor fell, he escaped by torpedo boat to the northern part of Mindanao Island, and from there he flew to Darwin, Australia. Precisely because of his escape from the Philippines he was able eventually to take the offensive against the Japanese army, and finally occupied Japan proper.

In ancient times, however, the Japanese people seem to have had no such preconceived idea of the virtue of no surrender. For instance, when Kusunoki Masashige, a great fourteenth-century warrior, entrenched himself with his army at Akasaka Castle and was surrounded by the large force of Ashikaga Takauji, an enemy warrior, Kusunoki made a quick escape from the castle with the idea of making another attempt at fighting. He may have grasped the idea of the importance of flexibility from Buddhism because he had a strong belief in the Buddha's teachings. Because of his escape from Akasaka Castle, he was able to harass the enemy force in other battles.

The feudal lord Shimazu Yoshihiro, realizing the inevitability of defeat in the Battle of Sekigahara between the rival Toyotomi and

Tokugawa clans in 1600, broke through the enemy lines and escaped to his domain, Satsuma province in Kyūshū. Because of his escape, his clan became so strong that later the Tokugawa shogunate acknowledged its superiority, and it produced the driving force leading to success in the Meiji Restoration of 1868, which overthrew the Tokugawa regime. Shimazu Yoshihiro was also a devout believer in Buddhism.

Strangely enough, none of the Japanese people despise Kusunoki Masashige or Shimazu Yoshihiro as cowards. Everyone regards their escaping instead of dying in vain as good. When and why did the Japanese people lose their flexibility in thinking and acting? Has this rigidity been influenced by Confucianism, which was introduced into Japan from China later than Buddhism? Confucianism, however, teaches us respect for human life, as shown in the saying, "The sage never courts danger." If not, is the idea of slighting human life peculiar to the Japanese people? The historical evidence does not permit us to jump to such a conclusion. We must conclude that such a trait was implanted at some time by a certain philosophy of government, though exactly when is not clear. Scholarly investigation of this problem would be very helpful in explaining this characteristic of the Japanese people. This is a very important matter. A marked tendency to promote political and economic struggles through recourse to violence has been seen in recent years, and demonstrations and strikes by labor unions have taken a turn for the worse. In the final analysis, such a tendency comes from a lack of mental flexibility.

The willow bends to the wind and is not broken, even though the tree looks fragile. An oak branch, on the other hand, may break in a storm despite the tree's apparent sturdiness. Is it not of the first importance for the Japanese people—as for all people everywhere—to foster mental flexibility in order to build a greater nation? A true understanding of Buddhism is the shortest and best way to achieve this, I believe. This is because Buddhism teaches clearly the principle of flexibility of mind, and accordingly its believers without exception develop flexible minds. The life of the Bodhisattva Never Despise illustrates the ideal person living in this way.

Another important point in the story of Never Despise is that although he escaped from physical persecution, the bodhisattva held fast to his belief and never renounced the truth. Here lies the difference between mental weakness and flexibility. A weak-minded person will easily discard his belief when he is subjected to a little outside pressure. But a real believer maintains his belief and continually observes the truth, whatever may happen. The purpose of having a flexible mind is nothing other than to adhere to the truth to the last. The Bodhisattva Never Despise never ceased the bodhisattva practice of disclosing others' buddha-nature by paying respect to it, though escaping when physically abused. In the end, he led his persecutors to disclose their own buddha-nature. Such a man can be called truly brave.

The Bodhisattva Never Despise attained a very high spiritual state through the single practice of disclosing others' buddha-nature by paying respect to it. Therefore when he was approaching death, from the sky he heard the Lotus Sutra, which the Buddha King of Majestic Voice had formerly preached. The expression "from the sky he heard" means that he heard the Buddha's voice sounding in his mind; in other words, he realized the truth for himself. To say that he realized the truth for himself may sound mystical or mysterious, but actually the truth can be discovered by anyone.

The truth must have existed from the eternal past if it is really the truth. In the past, various outstanding people must have discovered the truth. Chapter 20 of the Lotus Sutra states that the Tathāgata King of Majestic Voice had formerly realized the truth and preached it, but the truth did not exist as a teaching in this world at the time that the Bodhisattva Never Despise lived. However, because the truth is eternal and imperishable, when an outstanding person appears in this world he can rediscover the truth. The Bodhisattva Never Despise was such a man.

Some may think that this story is meaningless for our time, when means of communication are so sophisticated. But such an idea is based on a shortsighted point of view. During the history of the universe from time immemorial, something like our present human culture must have appeared and disappeared more often than we can imagine. If a nuclear war should occur, our present culture would be destroyed along with everything else. A new and different life would be generated eventually, perhaps after hundreds of thousands or hundreds of millions of years, and in time would develop its own culture.

Thus viewing universal life from time immemorial, it is no wonder that many Tathāgatas King of Majestic Voice had preached the truth and that the Bodhisattva Never Despise realized it for himself when he was nearing death.

PATIENT REPETITION OF LEARNING AND PREACHING. How was the Bodhisattva Never Despise enabled to prolong his life although he was approaching death? Herein lies a great lesson for us. The Bodhisattva Never Despise realized for himself the teaching of the Lotus Sutra. As a result of believing in it wholeheartedly, he prolonged his life for two hundred myriad *koṭis* of *nayutas* of years. During this long period he preached the Lotus Sutra widely. He not only performed the basic bodhisattva practice of paying respect to others but also preached the Buddha's teachings in detail. In this way he advanced several stages in the bodhisattva practice. Then he enlightened all the arrogant people who had formerly scorned him. After the end of his natural lifetime, he met two thousand *koṭis* of buddhas. He worshiped, revered, honored, and extolled these buddhas and under them preached the Lotus Sutra. Because of this, he again met two thousand *koṭis* of buddhas, and under these buddhas also he preached the sutra. Because of this, he obtained clearness and purity of eye, ear, nose, tongue, body, and thought, and preached the Law fearlessly among the four groups—that is, among all kinds of people.

After cultivating the roots of goodness thus, he again met a large number of buddhas and also under these buddhas preached the Lotus Sutra; because of these merits, he again met a large number of buddhas and also received instruction from them. In this way, he repeated innumerable times practicing the Buddha's teachings himself and letting others practice them. His merits being completed, he then became a buddha.

The greatness of the religious life of the Bodhisattva Never Despise lies in the courageous spirit through which he never retrogressed but persevered until he had completely accomplished his original intention. His spirit was not reckless and rough but thorough and persistent. He trod the path to the attainment of buddhahood by learning and doing, doing and learning, for his constant improvement, that is, through the repetition of practicing the Buddha's teachings himself and letting others practice them.

We should follow his course step by step. It is quite acceptable for us to enter the way to buddhahood by performing one bodhisattva practice. If we perform one practice wholeheartedly, we can realize many truths derived from this one truth. And we do not limit our realization to ourselves but preach it to all people. By thus preaching it, we obtain its merits and also deepen our understanding of it more and more. In other words, we meet numberless buddhas in succession. Whenever we meet new buddhas (truths), we pay homage to their teachings, revering, honoring, and extolling them, and also preach their teachings to all people. Because of this, we again meet many more buddhas (truths). Through this kind of repetition, we can approach the mental stage of a buddha step by step. Sakyamuni Buddha himself bore witness to this by setting an example. He revealed this when he said, "Can it be that the Bodhisattva Never Despise was at that time somebody else? He was really I myself." By revealing this, he showed that living in the way of the Bodhisattva Never Despise is the right way to become a buddha.

As mentioned at the beginning of the chapter, this revelation should greatly encourage those who have become discouraged in their religious life. Some people may feel, "I can't possibly preach the Law to others because I haven't perfectly understood it myself." But if they only understand the principle of religious life—we have only to preach the Law as we have learned it to the best of our ability; the more often we preach it, the more we can deepen our understanding of it; we can proceed on our way to the perfection of our character step by step through patient repetition of learning and preaching—then they will be greatly encouraged.

Let us not forget the important words at the beginning of this chapter: "When he saw afar off a member of the four groups, he would specially go and pay respect to them, commending them. . . ." This is the spirit we need when we preach the Law to others. We must not adopt the passive attitude that we will teach the Law to others when they come to us to hear it or when we happen to meet. On the contrary, we must have such a positive attitude that we actively reach out to others and preach the Law to them. This is the attitude of a bodhisattva, who desires to truly save people from their sufferings. The Bodhisattva Never Despise dared to carry out such a bodhisattva practice. At first he was a nuisance to all the arrogant people because of his patient practice and aroused their anger, but they finally acknowledged his sincerity. We can learn much from the bodhisattva's positive attitude in his missionary work.

We should also pay careful attention to the following sentence: "At that time the four groups, *bhikshus, bhikshuṇīs, upāsakas,* and *upāsikās,* with angry minds slighted and contemned me, therefore for two hundred *koṭis* of *kalpas* they never met a buddha, never heard the Law, never saw a *saṃgha,* and for a thousand *kalpas* underwent great sufferings in the Avīci hell." From this we understand what the punishment for denying the Buddha's teachings is. However, we should note that this passage does not state that a god or a buddha will inflict any punishment on men. It says the following: when arrogant people with angry minds slight and contemn a person who pursues a sacred bodhisattva practice in order to disclose others' buddha-nature, for two hundred *koṭis* of *kalpas* they can never meet a buddha, never hear the Law, and never see a believer of the Buddha's teachings. Such punishment is not inflicted by anybody; these people never meet a buddha because the eyes of their minds are closed, and never hear the Law because their ears are covered. Because of this, they cannot put out the fire of illusion burning in their minds and for a thousand *kalpas* they undergo the sufferings of the Avīci hell. The Buddha never imposes any punishment on people but always saves them with this great compassion. If they do not desire to see the Buddha or a person who transmits the Buddha's teachings, he never forces them to be saved but calmly waits till the right moment, the time of extinguishing their karma, shall come.

Whatever a person's evil karma may be, if he undergoes great sufferings for a long time because of its evil retribution, such karma will disappear in compensation for his great sufferings. The eye of his mind will surely open the moment his evil karma disappears. This is because he has long been troubled by sufferings and has earnestly begun to seek real salvation, and because he cherishes a longing to reply upon something absolute and begets a thirsting heart of hope for it. In short, he awakens to hsi own buddha-nature. This is shown in the following sentence: "After their sin was brought to an end, they again met the Bodhisattva Never Despise, who taught and converted them to Perfect Enlightenment." In this way, when once a person comes into contact with the Buddha's teachings, he is sure to be saved from his suffering eventually.

In a previous existence, the arrogant people were taught the existence of their buddha-nature by the Bodhisattva Never Despise. But because they did not receive his teaching obediently, they underwent a long period of suffering. After this, they awakened to the existence of the buddha-nature in their minds. As a result, they were able at last to enter the way of salvation. If they had not been tormerly taught the existence of their buddha-nature by the Bodhisattva Never Despise, what would have become of them? They would have been eternally unable to free themselves of their sufferings.

We must not forget that whatever kind of person another may be, respecting his buddha-nature and teaching him its existence will give him a great merit and will lead him to salvation in the future. This is the most important teaching of this chapter.

In the last part of the chapter, the Buddha repeated his teaching in verse. This closing verse section is so important that we should recite it from memory, if possible. Readers will understand the meaning of the verse portion if they have firmly grasped the contents of the prose section. Here only a few phrases with special meanings will be explained. "Leader of all creatures" means that a buddha styled King of Majestic Voice will lead all living beings. "At that time the four groups / Were devoted to material things" mean that the four groups adhered to the analytical study of the Law, that is, they neglected to learn the spirit of the Law but were devoted to formality. This has the same meaning as the phrase "The groups formerly devoted to things." "Of pure believers, men and women" indicates the idea of men and women lay devotees.

CHAPTER 21

The Divine Power of the Tathāgata

THIS CHAPTER IS VERY IMPORTANT because two teachings, the Law of Appearance and the Law of Origin, are brought to their culmination herein. It also teaches us that these two teachings are not separate but, even though they seem different, are one in essence.

In the Law of Appearance, Sakyamuni Buddha revealed the aim and the content of the teachings that he had preached since his attainment of buddhahood. This is a philosophical and ethical teaching emphasizing the formation of this world, human beings as they ought to be, the right way to live, and ideal human relationships.

In the Law of Origin, Sakyamuni revealed that the Buddha is not limited to Sakyamuni himself, who appeared in this world and lived a mortal life, but is the Original Being with the great life of non-beginning and non-end. In this Law, the Buddha teaches us that in order to be finally saved and to establish true peace in our world, we must be united with the Original Buddha, that is, must take refuge in him wholeheartedly.

We can distinguish between the Law of Appearance and the Law of Origin in the following way: the former is the teaching preached by Sakyamuni, who appeared as a man in this world, while the latter is the teaching declared by the Original Buddha, who exists from the infinite past to the eternal future. Because wisdom is more necessary than anything else in order to live correctly, the former is the teaching of wisdom, while the latter is the teaching of compassion, which preaches absolute salvation. It is indeed necessary for us to distinguish these two

Laws when we go deeply into the study of the teaching of the Lotus Sutra.

Analysis is important when we study anything in depth. To analyze means to divide a thing into portions and examine its structure, its elements, its meaning, and its function. But if we conclude our study with only the analysis of a thing, we have only studied it halfway. After completing the analysis of anything, we must complete our study from a holistic point of view. Then we can ascertain the truth that applies to the whole. This is called synthesis. In every study we can obtain valid results only if analysis and synthesis go hand in hand.

This also applies to the study of the Lotus Sutra. Up to this point we have studied the Buddha's teachings by analyzing them in order to understand them correctly. If we stop with analysis, however, the teaching remains split into parts and thus tends to be jumbled in our minds. At this point we have not yet really understood it.

We should not study the Lotus Sutra for the sake of learning alone. It is not enough to have understood the sutra intellectually. We cannot be saved in the true sense, nor save the whole of society, until we proceed from understanding to faith and reach the mental state of complete union of understanding and faith.

In chapter 21 the Buddha taught that putting all his sermons in the previous twenty chapters together, the truth penetrating all these chapters is one and one alone. From this chapter, we clearly realize that the teaching shown in the Law of Appearance is entirely united with the teaching shown in the Law of Origin; understanding this, we can deepen our devotion to these two Laws.

Reading through this chapter, it may seem that no important teaching is stated in it, only the mysterious and wonderful divine power of the Tathāgata. That is what makes the chapter hard to understand. The absolute power of the Tathāgata is symbolized by his mysterious phenomena, and each such phenomenon includes the meaning of forming a complete union between the Law of Appearance and the Law of Origin.

The meaning of the ten divine powers of the Tathāgata described in this chapter will be explained according to the interpretation accepted by many Buddhist scholars since ancient times. For this reason, the discussion will become rather specialized and difficult Buddhist terms may appear. But we should not be put off by this. Such terms are tactful means to help us in understanding the explanation, and needless to say, our real goal is to realize firmly the spirit preached in this chapter.

In the final verse section of chapter 20, the World-honored One spoke as follows:

> "Therefore let his followers,
> After the Buddha's extinction,
> On hearing such a sutra as this,
> Not conceive doubt or perplexity.
> But let them wholeheartedly
> Publish abroad this sutra,
> And age by age meeting buddhas,
> They will speedily accomplish the Buddha-way."

At that time the bodhisattva-*mahāsattvas,* equal to the atoms of a great-thousandfold world, who had sprung up from the earth, all before the Buddha with one mind folded their hands, looked up into his noble countenance, and spoke to the Buddha, saying: "World-honored One! After the extinction of the Buddha, in whatever lands the transformed body of the World-honored One exists, wherever he is extinct, we will widely preach this sutra. Wherefore? Because we also ourselves wish to obtain this truly pure Great Law in order to receive and keep, read and recite, explain, copy, and make offerings to it."

The bodhisattvas who had sprung up from the earth were introduced in chapter 15, and it was noted that they were regarded as having greater virtues than the Bodhisattva Mañjuśrī and the Bodhisattva Maitreya. Now the bodhisattvas from the earth vowed to preach the Buddha's teachings widely. They told the Buddha why they would preach his teachings widely, a reason that includes a very profound meaning: because they have obtained this Great Law, they wish to receive and keep, read and recite, explain, copy, and make offerings to it.

To make offerings to the Buddha or the Law means to express one's sense of gratitude and make restitution for one's indebtedness to the Buddha or the Law. When the bodhisattvas widely preach the Buddha's teachings, this repays their debt for the teachings they have received from the Buddha. This is why the bodhisattvas who had sprung up from the earth are the great bodhisattvas. People at a lower spiritual stage would consider only themselves: "I myself can be saved by doing this practice." These bodhisattvas, however, rise above self.

We naturally receive merit by bestowing merits on others, and to refuse to accept such merits is to be overscrupulous. The Buddha's teachings are not narrow and bigoted. Therefore, in the previous chapters, the Buddha has taught repeatedly the merits we should give to others by preaching the Lotus Sutra and, at the same time, the merits we would receive from such practices. However, with this chapter, we see that the great bodhisattvas, who have many more virtues than other bodhisattvas, are perfectly free from the idea of self. This chapter teaches us the ideal state of the mind of the believer.

Another important teaching here is that even these great bodhisattvas do not neglect such practices as receiving and keeping, reading and reciting, explaining and copying the Buddha's teachings. Because they are great bodhisattvas, their understanding of the Law must be perfect. But even the great bodhisattvas endeavor to receive and keep the Buddha's teachings, deepen their understanding by reading and reciting them repeatedly, and devote themselves to the practice of keeping the teachings in memory by explaining and copying them. Such practices are most sacred and are a very important to us because we are apt to become arrogant when our understanding of the Law improves even a little.

Divine Powers Revealed by the Tathāgata. The World-honored One, on hearing the vow made by the bodhisattvas who had sprung up from the earth, nodded to himself. He said nothing to them. Then before the Bodhisattva Mañjuśrī and the other countless hundred thousand myriad *koṭis* of bodhisattva-*mahāsattvas,* as well as the *bhikshus, bhikshuṇīs, upāsakās, upāsikās,* gods, dragons, *yakshas,* and other spirits, and human and nonhuman beings—before all these creatures the World-honored One revealed his great divine powers.

He first showed the following divine power: he put forth "his broad and far-stretched tongue till it reached upward to the Brahma world." This expression may strike us today as strange, but it comes from an old Indian custom. In ancient India, to put one's tongue out was an action showing the truth of what one said. Through his first divine power, the Buddha revealed that all the teachings that he had preached were true and would be so eternally. To use a common expression, he showed that he was never two-tongued in what he preached. Through his divine power he expressed the following: the teachings that he has preached so far seem to be divided into two forms, the teaching of the appearing

Buddha and the teaching of the Original Buddha. But ultimately these two teachings are united into one.

Buddhist scholars in later ages expounded that the teaching that "the two Laws are essentially identical in faith" (*nimon-shin'itsu*) is manifested in the Buddha's mysterious phenomenon of putting forth his broad and far-stretched tongue. The "two Laws" are the Law of Appearance and the Law of Origin. At first, the Buddha as a dweller in the *sahā*-world taught the actual way to live a good life to the people there. However, later he declared that he is the Original Buddha, the being of non-beginning and non-end. He also caused us to realize that true salvation comes from our obtaining the consciousness of being caused to live by the Original Buddha of non-beginning and non-end. There seems to be a great difference between the teaching of the Buddha who appeared in this world and that of the Original Buddha. How should we consider the difference between these two teachings?

Sakyamuni should be considered as the Buddha appearing in this world, who emanated from the Eternal Original Buddha through his great compassion for all living beings. Therefore we cannot separate Sakyamuni Buddha and the Original Buddha. If Sakyamuni had not appeared in this world, we would have been unable to know the real existence of the Original Buddha. We cannot judge which is higher or lower, the appearing Buddha or the Original Buddha. The conclusion is that the Original Buddha and the appearing Buddha are ultimately united in one and that our faith should be reduced to one object. This is the teaching of "the two Laws are essentially identical in faith." The mysterious phenomenon of the Buddha putting forth his broad and far-stretched tongue till it reached upward to the Brahma world thus has a very profound meaning.

Next the Buddha revealed the following divine power: every pore radiated a "light of infinite and numberless colors, all shining everywhere throughout all the directions of the universe. Under all the jewel trees the buddhas, each seated on a lion throne, also in like manner put forth their broad and far-stretched tongues radiating infinite light. While Sakyamuni Buddha and all the other buddhas under the jewel trees were revealing their divine powers, hundreds of thousands of years had fully passed."

Sakyamuni Buddha revealed his divine power by radiating a beautiful light from his whole body, shining everywhere throughout all directions of the universe. This mysterious phenomenon signifies that the truth is the light that dispels the darkness of illusion. As has been mentioned before, darkness does not exist as a real entity. Darkness is only a nonlighted state and will disappear when light shines. The same thing can be said of illusion. Only the truth has real existence; illusion is unreal. Illusion is born from the state in which our minds do not yet realize the truth. Illusion will disappear from our minds when we realize the truth.

In the doctrine of causation, the Buddha taught that people must not be troubled by such a trivial matter as illusion. They have only to realize the truth. This is the only way to banish illusion. The Buddha taught the principle of this doctrine in the Law of Appearance. Then in the Law of Origin he taught what the absolute truth is. He taught the truth of the Buddha's real existence and his immortality, that is, the teaching that all beings are caused to live by the Buddha.

The Law of Appearance and the Law of Origin are ultimately based on the same theory. This teaching is called *nimon-ri'itsu,* "the two Laws are essentially identical in theory." This profound teaching is indicated by the fact that the light radiated from the entire body of the Buddha caused the darkness to vanish everywhere throughout the universe. In the same way as Sakyamuni Buddha, the other buddhas also put forth their broad and far-stretched tongues, radiating infinite light. This image symbolizes that the truth is one and that all the buddhas have realized the same truth, however countless in number they may be.

Truth attracts truth. They blend together and become one. The moment Sakyamuni Buddha radiated the sacred light from his body, the other buddhas also in like manner radiated infinite light, which melted into one great light that shone everywhere throughout the universe. This is an image of the ideal state at which the believers in the Lotus Sutra ultimately aim. It describes the state in which all people become buddhas and the *sahā*-world is identical in essence with the Pure Land of Tranquil Light. When we reread with understanding this short passage describing the Buddha's divine power, we can keenly feel the sacredness of its content.

Next, the following action of the buddhas is expressed: "After that they drew back their tongues, coughed simultaneously, and snapped their fingers in unison." The phrase "coughed simultaneously" means that all the teachings are united into one, and the voices raised in a cough signify the preaching of the teaching.

At first Sakyamuni Buddha preached the tactful teaching. Nevertheless, because the truth is one, it is not an inferior teaching. The tactful teaching was preached only in order to lead people finally to the absolute truth. But the Law of Appearance and the Law of Origin both express important truths and are sacred teachings. If the latter can be compared to multiplication, the former can be likened to addition. Children cannot understand multiplication if they are first taught that two multiplied by three equals six. They must learn addition first. When they understand that two plus two plus two equal six, they can clearly grasp the idea that to multiply two by three is equivalent to adding two three times. Even if they learn the multiplication tables by heart and so "know" that two multiplied by three equals six, they cannot be said to have really grasped multiplication unless they understand addition.

In faith, as in arithmetic both addition and multiplication are true; both the Law of Appearance and the Law of Origin are the truth. Though faith can be compared to multiplication, it will not become real unless faith as addition is thoroughly understood.

In chapter 18, faith was shown as multiplication: the object of faith multiplied by the mind of faith equals the result of faith. But if we declare at the start, "The object of faith must be the Buddha of non-beginning and non-end," people will be confused and unable to believe. How much more serious are the consequences of a mistaken object of faith.

In the Law of Appearance, the Buddha taught fully the formation of this world, what human beings ought to be, the right way to live, and ideal human relationships. Through this Law, we can learn the right way of life: to follow the truth permeating everything, that is, to realize the Seal of the Three Laws and the Law of the Twelve Causes, and, based on these teachings, to practice the Four Noble Truths, the Eightfold Path, and the Six Perfections. This is the mental stage of faith by addition.

For those who have understood these doctrines, the Buddha revealed that all beings are caused to live by the universal truth, that is, by the Eternal Budbha as the being of non-beginning and non-end. Then the believer realizes, "If we are united with the Buddha, we will come naturally to live according to the truth. That state is our real salvation." The tactful teaching of the first half of the Lotus Sutra and the true (in the sense of absolute) teaching revealed in the second half of the sutra are both the same truth and lead to the same salvation. This is the teaching of *nimon-kyōitsu*, "the two Laws are essentially identical in teaching." The phrase "coughed simultaneously" represents this teaching.

The last phrase, "snapped their fingers in unison," has a special meaning. This action also came from an Indian custom. The buddhas' snapping their fingers in unison represents their assurance, "I give my word," or "I promise to do it." The description of all the buddhas snapping their fingers in unison therefore signifies their solemn promise to spread the Law, in other words, their vow to perform the bodhisattva practice.

The fundamental spirit of the bodhisattva practice is union between oneself and others. To wish to save a person out of sympathy for his pitiable condition is, so to speak, an entrance to the bodhisattva practice. When we reach the mental state in which we cannot help giving a helping hand to someone who is suffering, we can say that we have attained the true mind of the bodhisattva.

A baby cries for its mother's breast. She takes it in her arms and gives her breast to it. At this time the mother's mind transcends compassion for her baby. She can perceive the baby's hunger as keenly as if she herself were hungry. Therefore she lifts the crying baby in her arms, with no idea of self, and puts it to her breast. The baby innocently takes the mother's breast and the mother contentedly watches it. There is perfect union between mother and baby, and the mother has no feeling of bestowing something on the baby. This is the pure state of the bodhisattva's mind. It is the ideal mental state between a preacher of the teaching and his listeners We can imagine that there must have been such a harmonious relationship between Sakyamuni Buddha and his disciples. As is written in a sutra, "The diseases of all the living are those of the Buddha," the ideal state of mind in carrying out the bodhisattva practice is union between oneself and others. Having studied the teachings in the Lotus Sutra so far, we know that all amount to union between oneself and others.

We seem to remove illusion from our minds and elevate our personalities according to the doctrines of the Law of the Twelve Causes, the Four Noble Truths, and the Eightfold Path for our own sake. The fact is, however, that our own elevation in turn has a good influence upon those around us. Practicing the teaching ourselves is identical with letting others practice it. To practice the teaching thoroughly is sounder and more effective than to preach it weakly. As the doctrine of the Six Perfections is the standard of the bodhisattva practice, our practice of the teaching is the practice of union between ourselves and others.

Entering into the teaching of the Law of Origin, we finally understand the theory of the union between ourselves and others. We realize that all of us are originally united with the great life of the universe. This realization means that we know that even if people seem to be separate from one another, they are originally united. Disputes and troubles often arise because people do not realize this fact. If all people truly realized it and attained the mental state of union between themselves and others, this world would soon be transformed into the Pure Land.

Thus the entire teaching of the Lotus Sutra is ultimately resolved into the spirit of union between oneself and others. This fact is called the teaching of *nimon-nin'itsu,* "the two Laws are essentially identical in person." All the buddhas snapping their fingers in unison signifies their promise to spread widely the spirit of union between oneself and others.

The next display of the buddhas' divine powers is expressed as follows: "These two sounds reached through every direction of buddha-worlds, all their lands being shaken in six ways." As often explained in previous chapters, the expression "all their lands being shaken in six ways" means that all things in the universe were strongly moved by the display of the buddhas' divine powers. "These two sounds" refer to those made when all the buddhas coughed simultaneously and snapped their fingers in unison. They snapped their fingers in unison to indicate their declaration that the truth preached in the Lotus Sutra is one and to indicate their solemn promise to establish in this world the spirit of union between oneself and others as the ideal of the bodhisattva practice. The sound of their fingers snapping in unison reverberated in every direction and produced such a profound emotion in all things in the universe that they shook.

Nobody can avoid being prompted to the practice of the teaching if he is so greatly affected by it that he feels shaken. So long as he only understands the teaching in theory and stores it in his mind as mere knowledge, he cannot proceed to its practice. But if he should feel such profound emotion at the teaching that he is shaken both mentally and physically, he will naturally begin to practice it.

What is it that he should practice? It is the bodhisattva practice because all the teachings of the Lotus Sutra are manifested therein. In the Law of Appearance, the Buddha ultimately urges people to perform the bodhisattva practice through the Six Perfections. In the Law of Origin, he teaches them that their realization of union between themselves and the Buddha leads them to their realization of union between themselves and other people, and that this realization is naturally manifested in their bodhisattva practice of saving others. Moreover, their realization develops into the great practice of the bodhisattva—the attainment of world peace and the transformation of the *sahā*-world into the Pure Land of Tranquil Light. This is the teaching of *nimon-gyōitsu,* "the two Laws are essentially identical in practice." This profound teaching is expressed in the words "all their lands being shaken in six ways."

The five divine powers of the Tathāgata mentioned so far are the manifestation of the realization, the teaching, and the vow that the Tathāgata Sakyamuni and all other buddhas have made. When these five divine powers extend to all living beings in the universe, what will be the result? The next five divine powers describe their influence upon all living beings.

The sixth divine power of the Tathāgata is stated as follows: "In the midst of these worlds all living beings, gods, dragons, *yakshas, gandharvas, asuras, garuḍas, kiṃnaras, mahoragas,* human and nonhuman beings, and the other creatures, by reason of the divine power of the Buddha, all saw in this *sahā*-world the infinite, boundless, hundred thousand myriad *koṭis* of buddhas, seated on the lion thrones under all the jewel trees, and saw Sakyamuni Buddha, together with the Tathāgata Abundant Treasures, seated on lion thrones in the midst of the stupa, and also saw the infinite, boundless, hundred thousand myriad *koṭis* of bodhisattva-*mahāsattvas,* and the four groups who reverently surround Sakyamuni Buddha. After beholding this they were all greatly delighted, obtaining that which they had never experienced before."

All creatures, both human and nonhuman beings, were enabled to see the great assembly of Sakyamuni Buddha, together with the Tathāgata Abundant Treasures and many other buddhas. In Buddhist terms, this state is called *fugen-daie,* "all creatures universally see the great assembly of the Buddha surrounded by many other buddhas." This expression signifies that all creatures can equally realize the Buddha's teachings. At present, all people are different in their capacity to understand the teachings of Buddhism. Some can grasp them easily, while others find it very difficult to do so. Tactful means to enlighten people are to be used in various ways according to their differing capacities. This is the present state of human beings, but from the standpoint of the eternal future, all of them will be able to attain enlightenment.

There are indeed many different speeds in the process of the attainment of enlightenment. The difference in people's capacity to understand the Buddha's teachings exists only in the area encompassed by "this shore" (*shigan*), the world of birth and death. But people become buddhas equally when they reach "that shore" (*higan*), the realm of nirvana. Therefore, there is no essential difference in their capacity to understand the Buddha's teachings. This is the teaching of *mirai-ki'itsu,* "man's capacity to understand the Buddha's teachings is one in the future." The Buddhist term *fugen-daie,* "all creatures universally see the great assembly of the Buddha surrounded by many other buddhas," indicates the idea that the Buddha has the divine power to lead all living beings equally to the realm of nirvana in the future.

Next the following state is described: "At the same time all the gods in the sky sang with exalted voices: 'Beyond these infinite, boundless, hundreds of thousands of myriads of *koṭis* of *asaṃkhyeya* worlds, there is a realm named *sahā*. In its midst is a Buddha, whose name is Sakyamuni. Now, for the sake of all bodhisattva-*mahāsattvas,* he preaches the Great-vehicle Sutra called the Lotus Flower of the Wonderful Law, the Law by which bodhisattvas are instructed and which the buddhas watch over and keep in mind. You should with all your utmost heart joyfully follow it and should pay homage and make offerings to Sakyamuni Buddha.' "

The expression "all the gods in the sky sang with exalted voices" means that all living beings in the *sahā*-world received inspiration from all the gods. Such an expression is not limited to Buddhism. The phrase "a voice was heard from heaven" appears in Christian writings, and the words "I hear heaven's voice" are often used in the teachings of Confucius and Mencius. These words imply that people receive revelations from heaven, that is, that they perceive the truth of faith as if an inspiration had flashed across their minds.

What did all the living beings in the *sahā*-world receive by inspiration from the exalted voices of all the gods in the sky? They realized that in the *sahā*-world, Sakyamuni Buddha preached the teaching called the Lotus Flower of the Wonderful Law, the Law by which bodhisattvas are instructed and which the buddhas watch over and keep in mind. This is a true and peerless teaching, which causes all beings in the universe to live, bestows harmony on them, and brings about their peace of mind. This realization means that although the *sahā*-world is now a realm of suffering, it will surely become the most sacred land of the universe in the future, when all teaching and learning will be united into one in the Buddha's teachings. Teaching and learning should improve humankind, but they now tend to lead to opposition and unhappiness instead. They cause antagonism among people in the fields of religion and politics, for example. To give an example in science, nuclear physics is now leading mankind to the greatest unhappiness rather than promoting human welfare.

If teaching and learning followed the ideas of respect for humanity and universal harmony taught by Sakyamuni Buddha, the Pure Land would be realized in the *sahā*-world, and this world with its remarkably advanced material civilization would become the center of the universe. This is the teaching of *mirai-kyōitsu,* "all the teachings are united into one, the Buddha's teachings, in the future."

As with the course of nature, so next is the state of all living beings expressed: "All those living beings, after hearing the voice in the sky, folded their hands toward the *sahā*-world and thus exclaimed: '*Namaḥ* Sakyamuni Buddha! *Namaḥ* Sakyamuni Buddha!' " This description represents a prediction concerning the future of humankind. Some people do not know the Buddha's teachings at present. Others do not desire to study the teachings deeply even if they have had a chance to come into contact with them. One is infatuated with a mistaken idea, while another does not think at all but merely works like a slave. Again, some do evil, violating morality and the law. But though there are many kinds and classes of people in society, the time will surely come when they will all wholeheartedly take refuge in the Buddha. Then there will be no evil or foolish person because all people will have perfected their characters. This state of mind is called *mirai-nin'itsu,* "all people equally attain the perfection of their characters in the future." This is the significance of the words, "All those living beings . . . thus exclaimed: '*Namaḥ* Sakyamuni Buddha! *Namaḥ* Sakyamuni Buddha!' "

Following this, another mysterious phenomenon is described: "Then with various flowers, incense, garlands, canopies, as well as personal ornaments, gems, and wonderful things, they all from afar strewed the *sahā*-world. The things so strewn from every quarter were like gathering clouds, transforming into a jeweled canopy, covering all the place above the buddhas." This phenomenon means that in the future the practice of all people will make equal offerings to the Buddha. The greatest offering to the Buddha is to make all one's daily practices accord with the Buddha's mind. Though there is a wide variety of daily practices, all are equal when they are in accord with the Buddha's mind. This is metaphorically expressed in the following words: "The things so strewn from every quarter are like gathering clouds, transforming into a jeweled canopy, covering all the place above the buddhas." This is the teaching of *mirai-gyōitsu,* meaning that though people's practices are now right or wrong in various ways, in the future all their practices will be united in that they will accord with the Buddha's mind.

To make all our practices accord with the Buddha's mind is an important standard for our daily lives. We must have some knowledge of laws and morals. But in society there are many acts that are not specified as good or bad by either laws or morals. Moreover, laws and morals change according to place and time. We cannot feel truly secure unless we can depend on practices that do not change according to time and place. If we adopt the standard of making our practices accord with the Buddha's mind, we can act with assurance peace of mind at all times and will never be diverted to evil or dishonest acts. Because the Buddha is the universal truth, to make our practices match his mind means to act in accordance with the universal truth. By doing so we can prevent mistakes in all our practices.

The next mysterious phenomenon is described as follows: "Thereupon the worlds of the universe were united without barrier as one buddha-land." The *sahā*-world is said to be the realm of illusion, while the Pure Land is said to be a beautiful land with no suffering and hell to be a world of great suffering. But if all living beings live perfectly for the sake of the truth by means of the Buddha's teachings, this universe will be united into one buddha-land with no distinction between the world of heaven, the *sahā*-world, and the world of hell. Because the truth is one, all things will tend toward the truth sometime in the future and will contribute to creating a world of perfect harmony. This mysterious phenomenon represents the teaching of *mirai-ri'itsu,* "all things in the universe are united into one truth in the future."

The various mysterious phenomena known as the ten divine powers of the Tathāgata are described here because this chapter contains the concluding teaching of the entire Lotus Sutra and because it shows the ultimate ideal. The Buddhist terms associated with each of the Tathāgata's ten divine powers have been explained, but readers need not worry about remembering such specialized Buddhist terms; it is quite sufficient to understand the spirit of what is taught here.

Having read this far, we will have realized that the teachings of the

Lotus Sutra are a perfect and exhaustive preparation for leading all living beings to the attainment of buddhahood, and we will feel inexpressible gratitude to the Buddha. At the same time, we will surely feel keenly that life is worth living, being aware of the possibility of approaching even a step or two toward the ideal state of mind by practicing the Buddha's teachings even though the realization of the ideal itself may be still far distant.

Nothing is more salutary than to have a firm goal in life. When a person has two or three goals at a time, his mind will be always agitated, not calm and stable. However, when he lives aiming at only the most sacred goal of advancing to the mental state of the Buddha, he is not diverted from the right direction because his life is penetrated by that great purpose at work, at home, in the company of his friends, in his reading, and in his recreation.

It is, of course, inevitable that ordinary people will sometimes have evil thoughts, be lazy or careless, commit faults, worry about personal trifles, indulge in worthless pleasures, and incessantly fall victim to various illusions. But they will not retrogress much from their purpose if they are conscious of proceeding step by step toward the mental state of the Buddha, even when they are swayed by illusions. This is because their awareness always acts as a mental support.

The ideal mental state mentioned here may seem too elevated for ordinary people, and some may regard it as a dream far removed from their real lives. They should not feel this ideal state to be something vague and abstract but should have a vivid, actual awareness of it. Moreover, they must make this mental state a living goal, and it must lead their daily lives.

At that time the Buddha addressed Eminent Conduct and the host of other bodhisattvas: "The divine powers of buddhas are so infinite and boundless that they are beyond thought and expression. Even if I, by these divine powers, through infinite, boundless hundred thousand myriad *koṭis* of *asaṃkhyeya kalpas,* for the sake of entailing it, were to declare the merits of this sutra, I should still be unable to reach the end of those merits."

The words "for the sake of entailing it" include the following meaning: "Though it may entail great effort to spread abroad this teaching, I trust you to perform your task." Hearing these words of the Buddha, we cannot help making a fresh determination to carry out the Buddha's mission.

ESSENTIAL POINTS OF THE MERITS OF THE LOTUS SUTRA. The Buddha said that he would be unable to reach the end of the merits of the Lotus Sutra even if he were to declare them by his divine powers through infinite, boundless hundred thousand myriad *koṭis* of *asaṃkhyeya kalpas.* He spoke of the essential points of those merits as follows: "Essentially speaking, all the laws belonging to the Tathāgata, all the sovereign, divine powers of the Tathāgata, all the mysterious, essential treasuries of the Tathāgata, and the very profound conditions of the Tathāgata, all are proclaimed, displayed, revealed, and expounded in this sutra." These words contain the most profound essence of the merits of the Lotus Sutra.

In the phrase "all the laws belonging to the Tathāgata," the laws are all the truths that the Tathāgata realized and showed in the Lotus Sutra. The truths realized by the Tathāgata have also been preached in other sutras, though they have not been completely stated but have been revealed as tactful teachings according to each person's capacity to understand them. A great truth applicable to every part of the universe is preached in the Lotus Sutra, one that includes all other truths and teachings. That is why this sutra is said to be the culmination of all the teachings that Sakyamuni Buddha preached in his lifetime. All the truths realized by the Tathāgata are exhaustively expressed in this sutra.

When the absolute truth realized by the Tathāgata appears as the work of saving all living beings, none is left omitted from his salvation. This is the meaning of the phrase "all the sovereign, divine powers of the Tathāgata." All these divine powers of the Tathāgata are included in the Lotus Sutra. When we read the sutra, we can be saved even by reading a single verse or a single word of it because the truth is contained in every part of it. If we realize perfectly the great truth applicable to the whole of the Lotus Sutra and practice it thoroughly, we can eventually attain the same state of the mind as the Buddha. Therefore, all the sovereign, divine powers of the Tathāgata, which are capable of saving all living beings, are contained in the Lotus Sutra.

The phrase "all the mysterious, essential treasuries of the Tathāgata" indicates the infinity of the Tathāgata's teaching. He penetrates the real state of all things and discerns the capacity of all living beings to understand his teaching. Therefore, he can preach a teaching suited to each occasion from the infinite treasury of the teaching in his heart. This infinite treasury is revealed in the Lotus Sutra.

In the phrase "the very profound conditions of the Tathāgata," the word "conditions" means "practices." If we do not proceed from theory to practice in believing the teaching, we cannot perfactly accomplish the teaching. Theory and practice must always go together. In the Lotus Sutra, the Buddha does not just preach his teachings theoretically but shows the practices that he has performed, the process through which he attained enlightenment, and the method of leading his disciples and all living beings. Moreover, he discusses not only events that occurred after he appeared in this world but also various bodhisattva practices that he carried out in his innumerable previous existences. His inmost thoughts during his period of asceticism in this world and his practices in former lives are so profound that ordinary people cannot possibly imagine them. This is the meaning of the phrase "the very profound conditions of the Tathāgata."

In this chapter, as the concluding teaching of the Lotus Sutra, the Buddha succinctly restates the point of the sutra to the following effect: "Essentially speaking, all the truths realized by the Tathāgata, all their work of saving all the living, all the teachings that have appeared as their working, and all the practices of saving all the living that the Tathāgata has showed in the past, all of these are proclaimed, displayed, revealed, and expounded in this sutra." The supreme value of the Lotus Sutra and its absolute perfection are again affirmed by the words of the Buddha himself.

The Buddha then declares the mental attitude that people must maintain after the extinction of the Tathāgata: "Therefore you should, after the extinction of the Tathāgata, wholeheartedly receive and keep, read and recite, explain and copy, cultivate and practice it [the Lotus Sutra] as the teaching. In whatever land, whether it be received and kept, read and recited, explained and copied, cultivated and practiced as the teaching; whether in a place where a volume of the sutra is kept, or in a temple, or in a grove, or under a tree, or in a monastery, or in a lay devotee's house, in a palace or a mountain, in a valley or in the wilderness, in all these places you must erect a *caitya* and make offerings. Wherefore? You should know that all these spots are the thrones of enlightenment. On these spots the buddhas attain Perfect Enlightenment; on these spots the buddhas roll the wheel of the Law; on these spots the buddhas enter *parinirvāṇa*."

The Buddha emphasizes here the holiness of his teachings themselves, and he clearly teaches that the right way to maintain faith is to receive, keep, cultivate, and practice the teachings. Accordingly, "a place where a volume of the sutra is kept" should be regarded not as a place where the sutra as an object is kept but as a place where the teaching remains or is correctly practiced and maintained. To interpret the sutra as meaning just a material object—a book or scroll—is mistaken, as we can see from the spirit permeating the passage quoted above.

Why must we be so exacting about the interpretation of the meaning of a single word? This is because we are liable to regard something *symbolizing* the teaching as supreme and sovereign rather than the teaching itself, and by devoting ourselves to the symbol, we are inclined to indulge in a mistaken faith. Something symbolizing the teaching is holy indeed. But if we devote ourselves to it alone, regarding it as supreme, or if we pay homage to it for the sake of our salvation, we lower the holy teaching of the Buddha to the level of folk religion. Such a deed is a great slandering of the Buddha's Law. Holiness consists in the Buddha's teachings themselves, as he has revealed here. A righteous faith exists in whatever place we receive, keep, cultivate, and practice the holy teaching. We must inscribe this on our memories because it is so important that it forms the foundation of our daily lives.

Next, the Buddha repeated his teaching in verse. Though the verses have substantially the same meaning as the preceding prose section, brief explanations will be given of the verses in which the Buddha used words differing in meaning from those in the equivalent prose passages.

Of the merits of those who receive, keep, cultivate, and practice this sutra, the Buddha said:

> "He who can keep this sutra
> Is one who already beholds me
> And also the Buddha Abundant Treasures,
> And all buddhas emanated from me,
> And sees besides the bodhisattvas
> Whom I have instructed until now."

As the Buddha says here, a person who wholeheartedly receives, keeps, cultivates, and practices this sutra can see the Buddha. As explained earlier, to see the Buddha means to realize surely the real existence of the Buddha. Through this realization we attain peace of mind.

Next the Buddha said:

> "He who can keep this sutra
> Will cause me and the buddhas emanated from me,

And the Buddha Abundant Treasures in nirvana,
All of us entirely to rejoice;
And the buddhas now in the universe,
And those of the past and the future,
He shall also see and serve
And cause to rejoice."

Briefly, this means that a person who receives, keeps, cultivates, and practices this sutra will cause all the buddhas to rejoice. This is because his deeds accord with the minds of all the buddhas and are the equivalent of great offerings to them.

Then the Buddha said:

"The mysterious laws that have been attained
By the buddhas each on his wisdom throne,
He who can keep this sutra
Must surely gain ere long."

This means that a person who receives, keeps, cultivates, and practices this sutra must surely gain before long the deep enlightenment that has been attained by the buddhas on their wisdom thrones. However, the words, "ere long" must not be interpreted in terms of the idea of time in this world. Ordinary people must practice the Buddha's teachings for the very long period of four or even eight rebirths. But even such a long period is a very short time from the viewpoint of eternal life.

The Buddha continued:

"He who can keep this sutra
Shall the meaning of the laws,
With their terms and expressions,
Delightedly expound without end,
Like the wind in the sky,
Which never has impediment."

This means that a person who wholeheartedly receives, keeps, cultivates, and practices this sutra will obtain the power to expound all the laws freely to others.

The Buddha concluded with the following words:

"After the Tathāgata is extinct such a one,
Knowing this sutra that the Buddha has taught,
Together with its reasoning and process,

Shall expound it according to its true meaning.
Just as the light of the sun and moon
Can dispel the darkness,
So this man, working in the world,
Can disperse the gloom of the living
And cause numberless bodhisattvas
Finally to abide in the One-vehicle.
Therefore he who has wisdom,
Hearing the benefits of this merit,
After I am extinct,
Should receive and keep this sutra.
This man shall in the Way of the Buddha
Be fixed and have no doubts."

This means that if after the extinction of the Tathāgata a person knows why, to whom, and where the Buddha has preached his teachings, together with their reasoning and process, and correctly expounds them according to their true meaning, he can disperse the gloom of others just as the light of the sun and moon can dispel the darkness. And this person can also cause numberless believers to enter into the Way of the One-vehicle. Therefore, when a person who thinks deeply about his life—a person who has wisdom—hears the benefits of this merit, after the Buddha's extinction, he should receive and keep this sutra. He who thinks deeply about life will arrive at this sutra. There is no doubt that he will surely attain the Way of the Buddha.

This concluding verse, as the concluding teaching of the Lotus Sutra, is most profound and sacred. It is regarded as one of the most important verses of the entire sutra. We should grasp its meaning well and should be able to recite it from memory.

CHAPTER 22

The Final Commission

HAVING FINISHED PREACHING chapter 21, Sakyamuni Buddha rose from his Law seat and, through his supernatural power, laid his right hand on the heads of the innumerable bodhisattva-*mahāsattvas* and spoke thus: "I, for incalculable hundreds of thousands of myriads of *koṭis* of *asaṃkhyeyas* of *kalpas*, have practiced this rare Law of Perfect Enlightenment. Now I entrust it to you. Do you wholeheartedly promulgate this Law and make it increase and prosper far and wide."

To lay one's hand on another's head or to pat someone on the head is to praise him, according to Japanese custom. In the West it is usually a gesture of affection. In India, however, such an action means to put one's trust in another, as if to say, "I leave it to you. Do your best." It is said that Sūryasoma, who taught the Lotus Sutra to his favorite disciple, Kumārajīva, laid his hand on Kumārajīva's head and said to him, "Reverently propagate this sutra." The Buddha's action of laying his right hand on the heads of the innumerable bodhisattvas through his supernatural power represents his placing deep trust in them. They must have been deeply moved by the Buddha's action.

The Buddha not only perceived that he would become extinct before long but also predicted it to his disciples. A profound emotion must have filled the minds of both the Buddha and his disciples. In the face of his approaching extinction, he taught nothing but the Law. Every Buddhist must bow before the pure, lofty, and beneficent mind of the Buddha.

Three times the Buddha laid his hand upon the heads of the bodhisattva-*mahāsattvas* and repeated the following words. From this repetition we can easily judge how important was his declaration: "I, for incalculable hundreds of thousands of myriads of *koṭis* of *asaṃkhyeyas* of *kalpas,* have practiced this rare Law of Perfect Enlightenment. Now I entrust it to you. Do you receive and keep, read and recite, and proclaim this Law abroad that all living beings universally may hear and know it. Wherefore? The Tathāgata is most benevolent and compassionate, not mean and stingy, and is able fearlessly to give the Buddha-wisdom, the Tathāgata-wisdom, and the Self-existent wisdom to all living beings."

This is an extremely important passage. The words "rare Law" and "not mean and stingy" call for deep consideration in order to understand their true meaning. We cannot attain the Buddha's enlightenment without undergoing extraordinary difficulties. Leaving aside his long period of practice in former lives, the Buddha repeatedly underwent many sufferings in this world and finally attained enlightenment. He also openly taught his rare Law of Perfect Enlightenment to all living beings without the slightest trace of a mean and stingy mind. Moreover, he used various tactful means with thoughtful consideration so that all living beings might be able to attain Perfect Enlightenment as quickly as possible and without being sidetracked.

When we compare this attitude with the common way of the world, we must acknowledge how much we owe to the Buddha. When experienced people teach knowledge and techniques to their juniors, there are very few who take the trouble to lead their juniors so successfully that they can master the learning and techniques in half the time that it took the teacher to acquire them. Most seasoned veterans take the attitude that it is beneath their dignity to initiate their juniors into the secrets of their learning and techniques, or else they force their juniors to experience as many difficulties in learning as they themselves did. Such an attitude comes from a mean and stingy mind, which is a great impediment to social progress.

The Buddha strictly admonished us against having mean and stingy minds. A person should not only generously and unstintingly teach others what he has realized but also help the learners through various methods to master it faster than he himself did. This is the true benevolent and compassionate mind. A veteran should maintain this attitude toward his juniors in teaching secular learning and techniques, to say nothing of instructing them in the Law and enlightenment. We should wholeheartedly adopt such an attitude.

The word "fearlessly" means not to be afraid of anything, not to be mentally affected by anything. One must preach the Law without a mean and stingy mind, being afraid of nothing and mentally swayed by nothing. To be afraid of something implies that one is afraid that he will be disliked or be spoken ill of by others if he preaches the Law to them. To be mentally swayed by something implies that he desires to receive some reward from others or to be thought highly of by them when he preaches the Law to them.

THREE WISDOMS OF THE TATHĀGATA. The Tathāgata is most benevolent and compassionate in preaching the Law, and he preaches it perfectly and calmly, with not the slightest mean and stingy mind, not fearful of anything or swayed by anything. We must try as hard as possible to approach the mental state of the Tathāgata. He can fearlessly give the Buddha-wisdom, the Tathāgata-wisdom, and the Self-existent wisdom to all living beings. These three wisdoms of the Tathāgata summarize the truths taught in the Lotus Sutra. However, these three wisdoms have been misunderstood by many people.

"Buddha" means the Enlightened One, or the Knower, that is, one who has realized the truth of all things in the universe. Accordingly, the Buddha-wisdom indicates the wisdom by which the Buddha has realized the universal truth and can discern the real state of all things. It is the wisdom of the truth.

"Tathāgata" means one who has come from the world of truth. There is profound significance in the fact that the Tathāgata not only has realized the truth but also has come from the world of truth. The place to which he has come is the world of living beings, this *sahā*-world of suffering and illusion. The reason that he has come to this world is his benevolent and compassionate mind, which causes all living beings to realize the truth for their salvation. Therefore, the Tathāgata-wisdom means the wisdom of benevolence and compassion.

Self-existent wisdom is the most difficult to understand of the three wisdoms. "Self-existent" means self-born, namely, a faith that is self-born in man's mind. Accordingly, Self-existent wisdom indicates the wisdom of faith.

We require all three wsidoms: the wisdoms of the truth, of benevolence and compassion, and of faith. The Tathāgata can bestow these three wisdoms upon us, for the Tathāgata is the great lord of giving to all living beings. None is a greater lord of giving than the Tathāgata, because he can give all three of these wisdoms to all living beings. All the teachings preached in the Lotus Sutra resolve themselves into these three wisdoms of the Tathāgata.

The Buddha admonished the bodhisattva-*mahāsattvas* as follows: "Do you also follow and learn the Tathāgata's example, not being mean and stingy. If good sons or good daughters in ages to come believe in the Tathāgata-wisdom, do you proclaim this Law-Flower Sutra to them that they may hear and know it, in order that they may obtain the Buddha-wisdom. If there be living beings who do not believe in it, do you show, teach, benefit, and rejoice them with the other tactful profound laws of the Tathāgata. If you are able thus to act, then you will have repaid the grace of the buddhas."

The Buddha's words, "Do you also follow and learn the Tathāgata's example," mean: "Do you well understand my spirit and follow the same way that I once took." The way is this: "You are not to be mean and stingy. If any believe in the Tathāgata-wisdom, do you proclaim this Lotus Sutra to them for the sake of causing them to obtain the Buddha-wisdom."

How do the bodhisattvas deal with people who do not believe in the sutra? The Buddha instructed the bodhisattvas: "Do you show, teach, benefit, and rejoice them with the other tactful profound laws of the Tathāgata."

As already explained, to show, teach, benefit, and rejoice someone with the teaching indicates the order that we must follow in leading people to the teaching. First we show them the general meaning of the teaching. Then, seeing that they have been affected by it, we teach them its deep meaning. Next, realizing that they appear to understand it, we lead them to practice it and to obtain its benefit. Finally, we so act toward them as to gladden them in keeping the teaching.

The Buddha's teachings are said to number eighty-four thousand, and among them there is not one that is useless. All his teachings are sacred. The Buddha freely preached the Law according to the occasion and the mental and spiritual capacities of his listeners. It may safely be said that within his teachings there are ways of preaching suitable for all kinds of people.

The Buddha taught the bodhisattvas: "If there are people who do not believe in the Lotus Sutra when you preach directly to them, you may choose any of my teachings, not limiting yourselves to the sutra." Indeed, the Lotus Sutra is the culmination of all the Buddha's teachings and therefore supreme among the many Buddhist sutras. But we must not become exclusive and rigid in our adherence to the Lotus Sutra. Nichiren did not hold only to this sutra but, in order to commend it, freely used quotations from many other sutras. We need to do so still more in the present world. If we exert every effort to lead others thus to the Righteous Law, we shall have repaid the grace of the buddhas. This is our greatest return for the buddhas' grace.

Thereupon all the bodhisattva-*mahāsattvas,* having heard the Buddha give this address, were filled with great joy and paid him added reverence, bowing, bending their heads, and with folded hands saluting the Buddha and crying in unison: "We will do all as the World-honored One has commended. Yea, World-honored One! Have no anxiety." Three times did all the host of bodhisattva-*mahāsattvas* repeat these words. This threefold repetition in unison represents the sincerity of the bodhisattvas' firm vow to do all that the Buddha had commanded. They could not have made such a promise if they had not had great resolution and confidence. From their affirmative words, we can easily judge their excellence as bodhisattvas. Scholars of old made a distinction between the rank of the bodhisattvas who were entrusted to receive, keep, and promulgate the Law in chapter 21 and those who were entrusted with the Law in chapter 22. However, our interpretation is that the Buddha entrusted the Law equally to all the bodhisattvas.

Having heard the firm vow of the bodhisattvas, the Buddha nodded. Thereupon he caused all the emanated buddhas, who had come from all directions, to return to their own lands, saying: "Buddhas! Peace be unto you. Let the stupa of the Buddha Abundant Treasures be restored as before." Having discerned that the teachings of the Lotus Sutra would be received, kept, and promulgated in future ages, he thus addressed the Buddha Abundant Treasures and all the emanated buddhas, who had come from all directions to bear witness to the truth of the teachings of the Lotus Sutra and to its infinite value.

The chapter closes with the following words: "As these words were spoken, the innumerable emanated buddhas from all directions, who were seated on lion thrones under the jewel trees, as well as the Buddha Abundant Treasures, the host of infinite *asaṃkhyeyas* of bodhisattvas, Eminent Conduct and others, also the four groups of hearers, Śāriputra and others, and all the worlds, gods, men, *asuras,* and so on, hearing the preaching of the Buddha, rejoiced greatly."

"The preaching of the Buddha" here means the conclusion of his teaching that the *sahā*-world will become the Pure Land of Tranquil Light by means of the Lotus Sutra. With chapter 22, we have completed the first stage of the Buddha's preaching in the Lotus Sutra.

CHAPTER 23

The Story of the Bodhisattva Medicine King

WITH CHAPTER 22, "The Final Commission," we have completed the first stage of the Buddha's teachings in the Lotus Sutra. It may be more appropriate to say that with chapter 22 we have come to the end of the study of the outline of the Lotus Sutra. We may well wonder why, then, the Buddha preached six more chapters.

With chapter 22, we have indeed been able to understand the basic ideas of the Buddha's teachings, to confirm our belief in them, and to gain the resolution to practice them. It is easy for ordinary people to talk about the Buddha's teachings, but very difficult to practice them. We have established a basic attitude toward practice. But when we come to actual practice of the teachings, we need to confirm our attitude once more. How should we do this? We must seek the strength to be encouraged and inspired so that we will never lose heart or forget our basic attitude toward practice. To put it briefly, we need something to serve as an effective impetus to our practice.

What is the most effective impetus? We can find a very good impetus in past examples of practice. There is nothing more inspiring than past examples of those who practiced the path of the Buddha's teachings in particular ways and thereby obtained specific merits. We can say the same thing of moral deeds in our daily lives. For example, when someone teaches his children in theory why one should be kind to old people, it is questionable whether they will translate the theory into practice. But if the parent gives a concrete example to the children—saying, for example, "Today in the bus I saw a boy giving up his seat to an old woman. His kindness and consideration really made me feel good"—the children will take an interest and will want to follow the boy's example.

Ordinary people need actual models to help them practice what is good. Whom should they take as their model in their practice of the path of the Buddha's teaching? It goes without saying that they should follow the model of Sakyamuni Buddha himself. The first thing they must do is tread the path that the Buddha has shown them. But they have no idea how to begin to emulate the Buddha because he is perfect and faultless and has accomplished all virtues. Ordinary people can much more easily aim at emulating a virtue possessed by a bodhisattva or a deed practiced by a bodhisattva. The closing chapters of the Lotus Sutra provide us with a series of such bodhisattva-models. In these chapters, each virtue of the bodhisattva is described as the highest, ideal state of mind; by describing such virtues and urging us to attain such an ideal state, the Buddha admonishes us, who are apt to be arrogant. Our religious life is a continual process of trial and error, of taking two steps forward and one back. Whenever we read the last six chapters of the Lotus Sutra, we are encouraged and inspired anew not to be neglectful or arrogant. Here lies the importance of these chapters. For this reason, we must not slight the study of the last chapters simply because we have already completed the outline of the Lotus Sutra with chapter 22.

There is one point about which we must be very careful: the many miraculous statements in these chapters in comparison to the preceding part of the sutra. We should not misunderstand these statements. We should pay special attention to the following points. In the first place, we must grasp the spirit of these miraculous statements and realize what they really mean. For example, chapter 23 states that the Bodhisattva Loveliness set fire to his arms and burned them. In ancient India there were many ascetics who actually did such things. In China and Japan, too, not to mention Vietnam, there have been instances of Buddhist monks setting fire to themselves and dying seated calmly in the raging flames. Such practices, however, go against the teaching of the Middle Path preached by the Buddha, and the practices themselves do not deserve to be extolled. Why then is the Bodhisattva Loveliness extolled for such a practice in chapter 23? It is because we today must follow the model of his spirit of zeal as shown in his practice. To burn one's arms symbolizes one's indomitable spirit in practicing the teaching. More accurately, it is the manifestation of one's spirit in practicing the Law at the risk of one's life. We should assimilate the deep meaning of such expressions as burning one's arms and not be misled by the surface meanings of the words.

In the second place, we are very wrong in our judgment if we interpret the form of salvation superficially. For example, it is stated in chapter 25, "The All-Sidedness of the Bodhisattva Regarder of the Cries of the World," that anyone who keeps in mind the Bodhisattva Regarder of the Cries of the World will be delivered from various sufferings. If we interpret this statement literally, it seems to mean that we do not have to work hard at practicing the Buddha's teachings; but with such an attitude, none of the teachings of the Lotus Sutra will bear fruit. Anyone can easily understand that in the last six chapters the Buddha cannot have been so illogical and contradictory as to deny fundamentally all of the teachings preached up through chapter 22. It is surprising to find that for centuries many people have put a shallow interpretation on something that should be so easily understood and have turned to an easy, lazy faith that they thought would allow them to become free of suffering merely by keeping in mind the Bodhisattva Regarder of the Cries of the World.

When we read chapter 25 carefully and in depth, we understand that the supernatural powers of this bodhisattva are essentially identical with the power of the Law preached by the Tathāgata Sakyamuni. We also realize that we must depend spiritually upon the Law to the last, but that in cultivating and practicing it we should take the model of the Bodhisattva Regarder of the Cries of the World as our immediate goal. It is most regrettable that misunderstanding and simplistic interpretations of Buddhist sutras have sunk deeply into the minds of the general public over a period of many centuries, vitiating the true spirit of Buddhism. It is earnestly hoped that readers of this book will not make the same mistake.

Let us proceed to the content of chapter 23.

When all rejoiced greatly at having heard the Buddha's preaching in chapter 22, "The Final Commission," the Bodhisattva Star Constellation King Flower addressed the Buddha, saying: "World-honored One! Why does the Medicine King Bodhisattva wander in the *sahā*-world? World-honored One! What hundreds of thousands of myriads of *koṭis* of *nayutas* of distresses the Bodhisattva Medicine King has to suffer! Excellent will it be, World-honored One, if you will be pleased to explain a little, so that the gods, dragon spirits, *yakshas, gandharvas, asuras, garuḍas, kiṃnaras, mahoragas,* human and nonhuman beings, and the bodhisattvas who have come from other lands, as well as these *śrāvakas,* hearing it will all rejoice." (The phrase "wander in the *sahā*-world" means that the Bodhisattva Medicine King appears freely anywhere in the *sahā*-world to enlighten and save all the living beings there.)

Thereupon the Buddha addressed the Bodhisattva Star Constellation King Flower: "Of yore, in the past, *kalpas* ago incalculable as the sands of the Ganges River, there was a buddha entitled Sun Moon Brilliance Tathāgata, Worshipful, All Wise, Perfectly Enlightened in Conduct, Well Departed, Understander of the World, Peerless Leader, Controller, Teacher of Gods and Men, Buddha, World-honored One. That buddha had eighty *koṭis* of great bodhisattva-*mahāsattvas* and a great assembly of *śrāvakas* numerous as the sands of seventy-two Ganges rivers. The lifetime of that buddha was forty-two thousand *kalpas,* and the lifetime of his bodhisattvas was the same. His domain had no women, no hells, no hungry ghosts, no animals, no *asuras,* and no disasters; its land was level as one's palm and made of lapis lazuli; it was adorned with jewel trees, covered with jewel curtains, hung with flags of jewel flowers, and jeweled vases and censers were seen everywhere in the country. Terraces were there of the precious seven, with trees for each terrace, the trees distant from it a full arrow's flight. Under all these jewel trees bodhisattvas and *śrāvakas* were seated. Above each of these platforms were a hundred *koṭis* of gods performing celestial music and singing praises to the buddha in homage to him."

As already explained in the discussion of chapter 12, "Devadatta," the reason that women are mentioned here together with hells, hungry ghosts, animals, and *asuras* comes from the idea generally accepted in ancient India that women were the incarnation of sin and an obstacle to men's practicing religious disciplines. Therefore, we should not take literally the mention of women in such a context. We must not forget that the Buddha's teachings broke down this generally accepted idea of the India of his day.

"Then that buddha preached the Law-Flower Sutra to the Bodhisattva Loveliness and all the bodhisattvas and host of *śrāvakas.* This Bodhisattva Loveliness had rejoiced to follow the course of suffering and in the Law of the Buddha Sun Moon Brilliance had made zealous progress, wandering about single-mindedly seeking the Buddha for fully twelve thousand years, after which he attained the contemplation of revelation of all forms."

The contemplation of revelation of all forms is the contemplation by which a bodhisattva freely appears in a suitable body or form and gives suitable instruction to lead people to the teaching. If they are people who can be led gently, the bodhisattva assumes a gentle expression and uses soft words. If they are people who need to be instructed strictly, he adopts a threatening expression like Fudō Myō-ō[1] and utters harsh words. The bodhisattva can make such changes with perfect freedom and without fail. A person who has not yet attained the mental state of this contemplation is prone to misjudge others' capacity to understand the teaching and therefore to fail in leading them to it. This is a very important warning to us believers in the Lotus Sutra who practice it in the age of degeneration.

"Having attained this contemplation the Bodhisattva Loveliness was very joyful and reflected thus, saying: 'My attainment of the contemplation of revelation of all forms is entirely due to the power resulting from hearing the Law-Flower Sutra. Let me now pay homage to the Buddha Sun Moon Brilliance and the Law-Flower Sutra.' No sooner did he enter into this contemplation than he rained from the sky *mandārava* flowers, *mahā-mandārava* flowers, and fine dust of hard and black sandalwood, which filled the sky and descended like a cloud; he raised also incense of inner-sea-shore sandalwood;[2] six *karshas*[3] of this incense are worth a *sahā*-world. All this he did in homage to the Buddha.

"Having made this offering, the Bodhisattva Loveliness arose from contemplation and reflected within himself, thus saying: 'Though I by my supernatural power have paid homage to the Buddha, it is not as good as offering my body.' Thereupon he partook of many kinds of incense—sandalwood, *kunduruka*,[4] *turushka*,[5] *pṛikkā*,[6] aloes, and resin incense,[7] and drank the essential oil of *campaka* and other flowers. After fully twelve hundred years, he anointed his body with perfumed un-

1. *Acala* in Sanskrit, literally meaning "the Immobile One." He is one of the few fearsome deities of the Buddhist pantheon.

2. Literally, sandalwood of "this [south] shore of the [inner] sea [of Mount Sumeru]," where this spice was believed to be found.

3. One *karsha* is 176 or 280 grains troy.

4. A milky, resinous incense; literally, "western incense."

5. A thyme-mixture incense.

6. Cloves.

7. A kind of gum; white-gum incense.

guents, and in the presence of the Buddha Sun Moon Brilliance wrapped himself in a celestial precious garment, bathed in perfumed oil, and by his transcendent vow burned his own body. Its brightness universally illuminated worlds fully numerous as the sands of eighty *koṭis* of Ganges rivers."

To partake of many kinds of incense and to drink the essential oil of flowers symbolizes purifying one's body. This symbolic deed teaches us that we must first purify our conduct before paying homage to the Buddha. In the expression "by his transcendent vow burned his own body," the words "his transcendent vow" mean his supernatural power, power exercised not for his own sake but for the purpose of propagating the Buddha's teachings. To obtain such supernatural power and freely to proclaim and spread the teachings of the Buddha are the greatest homage to the Buddha.

"The buddhas simultaneously extolled him, saying: 'Good, good! Good son! This is true zeal. It is called the True Law Homage to the Tathāgata. Offerings of flowers, scents, necklaces, incense, sandal power, unguents, flags and canopies of celestial silk, and incense of inner-sea-shore sandalwood, offerings of such various things as these cannot match it, nor can the giving of alms, countries, cities, wives, and children match it. My good son! This is called the supreme gift, the most honored and sublime of gifts, because it is the Law homage to the tathāgatas.' After making this statement they all became silent.

"His body continued burning for twelve hundred years, after which his body came to an end."

THE SUPREME GIFT. Here the Buddha teaches emphatically that true homage to the Tathāgata and a true gift are to practice the Law oneself. To burn one's own body means to devote oneself to the Law, whatever trouble and self-sacrifice may be entailed.

"The Bodhisattva Loveliness, after making such a Law offering as this, on his death was again born in the domain of the Buddha Sun Moon Brilliance, being suddenly metamorphosed, sitting cross-legged, in the house of the King Pure Virtue, to whom as his father he forthwith spoke thus in verse:

'Know, O great king!
Sojourning in that other abode,
I instantly attained the contemplation of

The revelation of all forms,
And devotedly performed a deed of great zeal
By sacrificing the body I loved.'

"After uttering this verse, he spoke to his father, saying: 'The Buddha Sun Moon Brilliance is still existing as of yore. Having first paid homage to that buddha, I obtained the *dhāraṇī* of interpreting the utterances of all the living, and moreover heard this Law-Flower Sutra in eight hundred thousand myriad *koṭis* of *nayutas, kaṅkaras, bimbaras, akshobhyas*[8] of verses. Great King! I ought now to return and pay homage to that buddha.' Having said this, he thereupon took his seat on a tower of the precious seven, arose in the sky as high as seven *tāla* trees, and on reaching that buddha, bowed down to his feet, and folding his ten fingers, extolled the buddha in verse:

'Countenance most wonderful,
Radiance illuminating the universe:
Formerly I paid homage to thee,
Now again I return to behold.'

"Then the Bodhisattva Loveliness, having uttered this verse, spoke to that buddha, saying: 'World-honored One! The World-honored One is still present in the world' "

These brief words uttered by the Bodhisattva Loveliness show clearly the Buddha's disciples' longing and thirst for him. This is a religious exaltation in which the disciples' longing for the Buddha and the Buddha's compassion toward them are perfectly blended. We should be ready to speak the same words as the Bodhisattva Loveliness whenever we see the Buddha.

"Thereupon the Buddha Sun Moon Brilliance addressed the Bodhisattva Loveliness: 'My good son! The time of my nirvana has come. The time of my extinction has arrived. You may arrange my bed. Tonight I shall enter *parinirvāṇa*.' Again he commanded the Bodhisattva Loveliness: 'My good son! I commit the Buddha-law to you. And I deliver to you all my bodhisattvas and chief disciples, my Law of Perfect Enlightenment, also my three-thousand-great-thousandfold world made of the precious seven, its jewel trees and jewel towers, and my celestial attendants. I also entrust to you whatever relics may remain

8. A *kaṅkara* is one trillion, a *bimbara* one hundred *kaṅkaras,* and an *akshobhya* one hundred *bimbaras.*

after my extinction. Let them be distributed and paid homage to far and wide. Let some thousands of stupas be erected.' "

Why was the Bodhisattva Loveliness entrusted so by the buddha? It is simply because this bodhisattva wholeheartedly practiced the Law himself and because the buddha discerned his practice. Here, we see clearly that our practice of the Law is the most important thing for us as believers in Buddhism.

THE MEANING OF ERECTING STUPAS. The Buddha Sun Moon Brilliance told the Bodhisattva Loveliness to let his relics be distributed and paid homage to far and wide. But he meant not only to let his relics themselves be paid homage to but also, through this homage, to cause all living beings to raise the mind of cherishing a longing and thirst for the Buddha. The Buddha Sun Moon Brilliance also told the bodhisattva to let thousands of stupas be erected. By this the buddha meant to cause all living beings to root the teaching in their minds through the erection of such stupas. The stupas were to be erected for the purpose of extolling the Buddha's virtues. If we erect a stupa with concern only for its form and appearance and forget the spirit of establishing the teaching in our minds, our minds cannot become attuned to the Buddha's mind. What he wishes is not appearance but substance, not empty theory but practice.

"The Buddha Sun Moon Brilliance, having thus commanded the Bodhisattva Loveliness, in the last division of the night entered into nirvana.

"Thereupon the Bodhisattva Loveliness, seeing the buddha was extinct, mourned, was deeply moved and distressed, and ardently longed for him. Then piling up a pyre of inner-sea-shore sandalwood, he paid homage to the body of that buddha and burned it. After the fire died out he gathered the relics, made eighty-four thousand precious urns, and erected eighty-four thousand stupas."

As it is said that Sakyamuni Buddha preached eighty-four thousand sermons, the expression "After the fire died out he gathered the relics, made eighty-four thousand precious urns, and erected eighty-four thousand stupas" symbolizes that the Bodhisattva Loveliness endeavored to maintain all the Buddha's teachings forever, and memorized and extolled them.

"Then the Bodhisattva Loveliness again reflected within himself, saying: 'Though I have paid this homage, my mind is not yet satisfied. Let me pay still further homage to the relics.' Thereupon he addressed the bodhisattvas and chief disciples, as well as gods, dragons, *yakshas,* and all the host, saying: 'Pay attention with all your mind, for I am now about to pay homage to the relics of the Buddha Sun Moon Brilliance.' Having said this, he thereupon before the eighty-four thousand stupas burned his arms, with their hundred felicitous signs, for seventy-two thousand years in homage to the buddha, and led a numberless host of seekers after śrāvakaship and countless *asaṃkhyeyas* of people to set their mind on Perfect Enlightenment, causing them all to abide in the contemplation of revelation of all forms."

PAYING HOMAGE TO THE BUDDHA. The greatest homage of the Bodhisattva Loveliness to the Buddha was to endeavor to maintain the Buddha's teachings forever and to memorize and extol them. However, as a believer who practiced the Lotus Sutra, he was not satisfied with such practices because he realized that the greatest homage to the Buddha is to practice his teachings oneself. Therefore the Bodhisattva Loveliness burned his arms. In other words, he devoted himself to the practice of the Law with no concern for whatever trouble, pain, or difficulty it might entail. His practices themselves became a great light that led all the people to dispel the darkness in their minds, causing them to seek the Way voluntarily. From this description, we can understand what great merit our practice of the Law will bring to us.

"Then all those bodhisattvas, gods, men, *asuras,* and others, seeing him without arms, were sorrowful and distressed and lamented, saying: 'This Bodhisattva Loveliness is indeed our teacher and instructor, but now his arms are burned off and his body is deformed.' Thereupon the Bodhisattva Loveliness in the great assembly made this vow, saying: 'Having given up both my arms, I shall yet assuredly obtain a buddha's golden body. If this assurance be true and not false, let both my arms be restored as they were before.' As soon as he had made this vow, his arms were of themselves restored, all brought to pass through the excellence of this bodhisattva's felicitous virtue and wisdom. At that moment the three-thousand-great-thousandfold world was shaken in the six ways, the sky rained various flowers, and gods and men all attained that which they had never before experienced."

The restoration of the arms of the Bodhisattva Loveliness symbolizes the ideal state of mind which those who practice the bodhisattva practice must maintain. The act of burning off both one's arms must be felt by others to be unbearably painful. Such an action, however, is not felt to be painful by a person who has attained the mental state of a great bodhisattva. However much he may sacrifice himself for the sake of the Law, he does not feel suffering. The sutra describes this mental state as follows: "The bodhisattva ever delights / And is at ease in preaching the Law." As often mentioned in this book, this is our ideal state of mind.

The Buddha then addressed the Bodhisattva Star Constellation King Flower: "In your opinion what say you, was the Bodhisattva Loveliness some other person? It was indeed the present Medicine King Bodhisattva. His self-sacrifice and gifts were of such countless hundred thousand myriad *koṭis* of *nayutas* in number as these. Star Constellation King Flower! If anyone with his mind set on and aiming at Perfect Enlightenment is able to burn the fingers of his hand or even a toe of his foot in homage to a buddha's stupa he will surpass him who pays homage with domains, cities, wives, children, and his three-thousand-great-thousandfold land with its mountains, forests, rivers, pools, and all its precious things.

"Again, if anyone offers a three-thousand-great-thousandfold world full of the seven precious things in homage to buddhas, great bodhisattvas, *pratyekabuddhas,* and *arhats,* the merit this man gains is not equal to the surpassing happiness of him who receives and keeps but a single fourfold verse of this Law-Flower Sutra."

TEN SIMILES PRAISING THE LOTUS SUTRA. The Buddha continued: "Star Constellation King Flower! Suppose just as, amongst all brooks, streams, rivers, canals, and all other waters the sea is the supreme, so is it also with this Law-Flower Sutra; amongst all the sutras preached by *tathāgatas* it is the profoundest and greatest. And just as amongst all mountains—the earth mountains, the Black Mountains, the Small Iron Circle Mountains, the Great Iron Circle Mountains, the ten precious mountains, and all other mountains—it is Mount Sumeru which is the supreme, so is it also with this Law-Flower Sutra; amongst all sutras it is the highest. Again, just as amongst all stars the princely moon is the supreme, so is it also with this Law-Flower Sutra; amongst thousands of myriads of *koṭis* of kinds of sutra-law it is the most illuminating. Further, just as the princely sun is able to disperse all darkness, so is it also with this sutra; it is able to dispel all unholy darkness. Again, just as amongst all minor kings the holy wheel-rolling king is the supreme, so is it also with this sutra; amongst all the sutras it is the most honorable.

Again, just as what Śakra is amongst the gods of the thirty-three heavens, so is it also with this sutra; it is the king of all sutras. Again, just as the Great Brahma Heavenly King is the father of all living beings, so is it also with this sutra; it is the father of all the wise and holy men, of those training and the trained, and of the bodhisattva-minded. Again, just as amongst all the common people *srota-āpanna, sakṛdāgāmin, anāgāmin, arhat,* and *pratyekabuddha* are the foremost, so is it also with this sutra; amongst all the sutras preached by *tathāgatas,* preached by bodhisattvas, or preached by *śrāvakas,* it is the supreme. So is it also with those who are able to receive and keep this sutra—among all the living they are supreme. Amongst all *śrāvakas* and *pratyekabuddhas,* bodhisattvas are supreme; so is it also with this sutra; amongst all the sutras, it is the supreme. Just as the buddha is king of the laws, so is it also with this sutra; it is king amongst the sutras."

In the above ten similes praising the Lotus Sutra, this sutra is repeatedly stated to be the supreme and the most sublime of all sutras. This illustrates the Buddha's intention to cause us to write indelibly on our hearts that our practice of the Law is the first essential for the accomplishment of the way to buddhahood.

Noteworthy among these similes is the following: "Just as the Great Brahma Heavenly King is the father of all living beings, so is it also with this sutra; it is the father of all the wise and holy men, of those training and the trained, and of the bodhisattva-minded." In India, for a long time before Sakyamuni Buddha appeared in this world, people believed that the Great Brahma Heavenly King is the father of all living beings and that this heavenly king governs all creatures. In the simile mentioned above the Buddha does not say specifically that this is a mistaken idea, but preaches: "Just as all living beings regard the Great Brahma Heavenly King as their father, so this sutra is the father of them all." It is a characteristic of Buddhism to lead ordinary people to the path of the truth in the gentle way shown here by the Buddha. He preaches, gently but firmly, "The truth is the father of all living beings."

The Buddha continued: "Star Constellation King Flower! This sutra is that which can save all the living; this sutra can deliver all the living from pains and sufferings; this sutra is able greatly to benefit all the living and fulfill their desires."

The Buddha preaches here in more detail that the Lotus Sutra itself enables all living beings to be saved, be delivered from pain and suffering, be benefited, and be fulfilled in their desires. The word "desires" does not mean immediate desires for material satisfactions or a comfortable life. It indicates the ideal that is the real goal of one's life. Although every person has his own specific desire, or goal, it should always be one that benefits others. For Buddhists this is of crucial importance. Misinterpretation of the Lotus Sutra arises when people misunderstand the word "desires" as meaning immediate desires based on man's greed. There is nothing so dangerous and terrible as to misinterpret the Law. We must take great care to understand it correctly.

TWELVE SIMILES OF DIVINE FAVOR BROUGHT ABOUT BY THE LOTUS SUTRA. The Buddha continued: "Just as a clear, cool pool is able to satisfy all those who are thirsty, as the cold who obtain a fire are satisfied, as the naked who find clothing, as a caravan of merchants who find a leader, as children who find their mother, as at a ferry one who catches the boat, as a sick man who finds a doctor, as in the darkness one who obtains a lamp, as a poor man who finds a jewel, as people who find a king, as merchant venturers who gain the sea, and as a torch which dispels the darkness, so is it also with this Law-Flower Sutra; it is able to deliver all the living from all sufferings and all diseases, and is able to unloose all the bonds of mortal life."

Here the Buddha mentions twelve similes of divine favor brought about by the Lotus Sutra. When we carefully examine each one, we realize that it is not merely extolling the divine favor of the sutra. The last phrase, "is able to unloose all the bonds of mortal life," has a very important meaning. "The bonds of mortal life" means the state of mind in which we are astonished or dismayed by immediate changes in our circumstances and feel insecure. Why can we not feel secure? This is because we are shaken and influenced by immediate changes in our circumstances. When we realize the three essentials of Buddhism—all things are impermanent, nothing has an ego, and nirvana is quiescence—we can become free from all the bonds of mortal life and can attain true peace of mind, not agitated by whatever changes may occur around us.

Then the Buddha said: "If anyone, hearing this Law-Flower Sutra, either himself copies or causes others to copy it, the limits of the sum of merit to be obtained cannot be calculated even by the Buddha-wisdom. If anyone copies this sutra and pays homage to it with flowers, scents, necklaces, incense, sandal power, unguents, flags, canopies, garments, and various kinds of lamps, ghee lamps, oil lamps, lamps of scented oil, lamps of *campaka* oil, lamps of *sumana* oil, lamps of *pāṭala* oil, lamps of *vārshika* oil, and lamps of *navamālikā* oil, the merit to be obtained by him is equally inestimable."

To pay homage to the sutra with a material offering is to express one's gratitude to it. It has been frequently mentioned in this book that when one expresses one's appreciation for the Law, first of all one must practice, proclaim, and spread the Law abroad. Here paying homage to the sutra with flowers, scents, incense, and various kinds of lamps represents paying homage to the Law with various bodhisattva practices.

The first part of this chapter has commented on the Lotus Sutra as a whole; following this it refers to the merits specifically discussed in this chapter—that is, the merits of the deed of the Medicine King Bodhisattva. The reason that this chapter first emphasizes the merits of receiving and keeping the Lotus Sutra is that the Law cannot be brought to life until it is practiced, and this chapter extols primarily the holiness that one displays in one's personal practice of the Lotus Sutra. Therefore, we should on no account interpret the chapter as urging us to receive and keep this chapter alone. Such a shallow interpretation produces a religion of a low standard. We cannot make such a mistake if we read the sutra carefully and deeply.

For example, the buddhas utter the following words: "Excellent, excellent! Good son! You have been able to receive and keep, read and recite, and ponder this sutra in the Law of Sakyamuni Buddha and to expound it to others."

The buddhas call our special attention to the importance of receiving and keeping, reading and reciting, and pondering this sutra of the Law of Sakyamuni Buddha and of expounding it to others. What we must receive and keep is always the whole of the Lotus Sutra. It is especially necessary for us to remember this point when reading chapter 25, "The All-Sidedness of the Bodhisattva Regarder of the Cries of the World."

THE FIVE PERIODS OF FIVE HUNDRED YEARS. First, a preliminary caution concerning the rest of this chapter. As mentioned before, readers should not take literally seemingly disparaging statements about women, such as the following: "She, after the end of her present woman's body, will not again receive one" and "If there be any woman who hears this sutra and acts according to its teaching . . ."

Next, concerning the phrase "after the extinction of the Buddha, in the last five hundred years," we must be sure to understand correctly the words "five hundred years." Sakyamuni Buddha foresaw that after his decease, Buddhism would pass through five periods, each five hundred years in duration. According to the *Mahāsaṃnipāta-sūtra,* after the Buddha's entry into nirvana there would be five periods of five hundred years each. In the first period, people's minds are fixed on and devoted to salvation, while in the second, they are devoted to meditation. These two are the periods in which the Righteous Law (*shōbō*) is maintained in its purity. The third period is characterized by devotion to reading and chanting, or the letter of the Law, and the fourth period to erecting stupas and temples, that is, memorials to teachers and prophets. These two are the periods of the Counterfeit Law (*zōbō*). The fifth period, that of the disappearance of the White or True Law and of devotion to strife and division, being the final five hundred years, is also the beginning of the period of the Decay of the Law (*mappō*).

The first five-hundred-year period is said to be one in which the people will practice the Buddha's teachings firmly and will be free from the bonds of illusion and suffering. During this time the great character of the Buddha will remain firm in people's minds, influencing them for the better, and they will lead good and peaceful lives spiritually if they only practice the teachings. This is an easy period in which people need not attain enlightenment by themselves but merely practice the teachings as they have received them. People are indebted to the personal virtue of the Buddha for their easy practice in this period. This period will come to an end after five hundred years, although the Buddha's teachings remain forever.

The second five-hundred-year period will be one in which those who receive and keep the Buddha's teachings will devote themselves to meditation and will ponder the application of the teachings in a new age. Society will change greatly at the end of the first five hundred years following the Buddha's decease. People will have to ponder how they should interpret the teachings and how they should apply them to society in order to make the right use of them. This period is one in which they will have more difficulty in practicing the teachings than in the previous period, though the teachings remain undistorted. Therefore, in the second period meditation will flourish.

The third five-hundred-year period will be one in which the study of the Law will continue to flourish. In this period, when a thousand years have passed since the Buddha's decease, the people will come to regard the Buddha as a great historical figure rather than a leader in actual human life. He will be far removed from people's everyday life, and consequently they will revere him but will have less longing and thirst for him. At the same time, as material civilization advances and society becomes more complex, Buddhism, which has heretofore been a living teaching in people's daily lives, will come to be something studied from a scholarly point of view.

The fourth five-hundred-year period will be one in which the erection of temples and stupas will continue to flourish. In this period, people will belittle the study of the Law, and will wish to receive divine favors from the Buddha by merely building stupas and temples. In this period Buddhism will continue to flourish in form, but its spirit will be entirely lost. Noble and influential men will believe that their construction of gorgeous temples will ensure the prosperity of their families. Buddhist monks will live luxurious lives under the protection of such noble and influential men, and the mass of people will fall into thinking that they will be saved by merely visiting temples and folding their hands before the images of buddhas.

The fifth five-hundred-year period will be one in which the Buddhist order will be torn apart by strife and heresy will flourish. In this period, even purely formal religion will be largely disregarded. People will become selfish and will pursue profit for themselves and their own family, group, country, or social class. As a result, they will compete for profit and will constantly quarrel. They will be antagonistic to one another in their mutual self-assertion, which will finally lead to great strife and bloodshed. Even under normal conditions, there will be a successive occurrence of greater or lesser conflicts in society, and people will be unable to lead peaceful lives. The present time is equivalent to this period.

Among the five periods of five hundred years, the first thousand years are said to constitute the period of the Righteous Law because the Buddha's teachings will be maintained and practiced correctly during this time. The next thousand years are said to be the period of the Counterfeit Law because the teachings will still exist, but in form only. The last period is said to be that of the Decay of the Law because the teachings will disappear. In this period, people will lose the teachings, which themselves are imperishable and eternal. This is the very period when the Buddha's teachings are most needed. That is why the Buddha preached again and again the holiness of those who receive, keep, practice, proclaim, and spread the Lotus Sutra in the period of the Decay of the Law.

Next, the Buddha said: "If, after the extinction of the Buddha, in the last five hundred years, there be any woman who hears this sutra and acts according to its teaching, at the close of this life she will go to the Happy World, where Amita Buddha dwells, encompassed by his host of great bodhisattvas, and will there be born in the middle of a lotus flower upon a jeweled throne."

About five hundred years after the Buddha's extinction, a belief centering on Amita Buddha (also called Amitābha and Amitāyus) began to spread from western India. Its believers sought rebirth in the Pure Land, the paradise of Amita, by relying completely on the power of this buddha. Although this buddha is regarded as having great compassion and the power to bring all living beings to the Pure Land, this faith is incomplete so long as it suggests the idea of salvation through relying absolutely on his power. It is impossible for living beings to achieve rebirth in the Land of Amita Buddha unless they realize the universal truth and endeavor actually to live according to it. The salvation of this buddha will be realized when people seek wisdom and practice the way leading to the perfection of their character. So that all living beings might not misunderstand this or fall into depending completely on the power of Amita Buddha, Sakyamuni Buddha added the conditional phrase, "If there be any woman who hears this sutra and acts according to its teachings." The faith of Amita Buddha will display its true power by virtue of the truth taught in the Lotus Sutra.

THE THREE POISONS. The Buddha continued: "Never again will he [the transformed woman] be harassed by desire, nor be harassed by anger and foolishness. . . ." The three defilements of desire, anger, and foolishness are considered the original poisons that lead ordinary people to degeneration. If they could remove these three poisons from their minds, they would receive great merits. Because of the three poisons in their minds, they are harassed by pride, envy, and uncleanliness. The fault of uncleanliness is common to both men and women but should be especially watched for by women. This is shown by the phrase "If there be any woman who . . ."

Next the Buddha said: "If there be anyone who, hearing this chapter of the former deeds of the Medicine King Bodhisattva, is able joyfully to receive and applaud it, that man during his present life will ever breathe out the fragrance of the blue lotus flower, and from the pores of his body will ever emit the fragrance of ox-head sandalwood." These words mean that a person who hears the chapter of the former deeds of Medicine King Bodhisattva and joyfully receives and applauds it will exert a good influence upon those around him. His fragrance not only will remain on his clothes but will be transmitted to those who touch his garments. The phrase "breathe out the fragrance of the blue lotus flower" means that the words spoken by one who joyfully receives and applauds the Lotus Sutra will spontaneously make the minds of those around him beautiful. The phrase "emit the fragrance of ox-head sandalwood from the pores of his body" indicates that those around him will naturally be influenced by his good acts. This is an ideal state of mind, which those practicing the Buddha's teachings must attain for themselves.

The Buddha continued: "Star Constellation King Flower! Guard and protect this sutra by your transcendent powers. Wherefore? Because this sutra is good medicine for the diseases of the Jambudvīpa people." The word "diseases" indicates the mental distortions of all living beings. As explained earlier, it is natural that as one recovers from a mental disorder he is also cured of physical illnesses. To interpret "diseases" as meaning simply physical diseases will cause misunderstanding. We must be most careful about this.

In the next words of the Buddha, "he will deliver all living beings from the sea of old age, disease, and death," the words "old age, disease, and death" mean man's mortal life. These words stand for the major changes of human life. If man can unloose all the bonds of mortal life, he will not be surprised at the various changes of human life, nor will he be confused by them.

As shown by his name, the Bodhisattva Medicine King gives good medicine to all living beings to make them recover from their mental disorders. When their mental diseases are entirely cured by this bodhisattva, then their physical ones will be ameliorated. This bodhisattva obtained his transcendent power to heal through his having made the offering of burning his arms when he was the Bodhisattva Loveliness in a former life. In other words, it was due to his personal practice of the Lotus Sutra. Because the Bodhisattva Loveliness practiced the Lotus Sutra himself, he was reborn as the Bodhisattva Medicine King, who had the transcendent power to cure the mental diseases of all living beings. His healing of mental diseases greatly ameliorates physical ones. Therefore, we come to this conclusion: our wholeheartedly receiving, keeping, and practicing the Lotus Sutra becomes a driving force in our healing the various kinds of mental distortions of others. Chapter 23 teaches us this principle and encourages us to spread it abroad.

CHAPTER 24

The Bodhisattva Wonder Sound

This chapter relates the story of the Bodhisattva Wonder Sound, who has come to the *sahā*-world from an ideal world. Important points in the story will be explained as needed. Let us proceed then to the story.

The Ray of Light from the White Hair-Circle. When Sakyamuni Buddha finished preaching the story of the Bodhisattva Medicine King, he "emitted a ray of light from the protuberance on his cranium,[1] the sign of a great man, and emitted a ray of light from the white hair-circle sign between his eyebrows, everywhere illuminating eastward a hundred and eight myriad *koṭis* of *nayutas* of buddha-worlds, equal to the sands of the Ganges. Beyond those numbers of worlds is a world named Adorned with Pure Radiance. In that domain there is a buddha styled King Wisdom of the Pure Flower Constellation Tathāgata, Worshipful, All Wise, Perfectly Enlightened in Conduct, Well Departed, Understander of the World, Peerless Leader, Controller, Teacher of Gods and Men, Buddha, World-honored One."

The ray of light emitted from the white hair-circle between the eyebrows of Sakyamuni Buddha shone throughout the domain of the buddhas. This means that although the Original Buddha exists everywhere, living beings can first know of his existence only through the teachings of Sakyamuni. The ray of light from the white hair-circle of Sakyamuni

1. A protuberance on a buddha's cranium forming a hairtuft; the first of the thirty-two signs of a buddha.

Buddha is the symbol of his Buddha-wisdom, which has revealed the universal truth. This fact has been expressed continually since chapter 1 of the Lotus Sutra, but it is especially important for us to be reawakened to its significance in this chapter. That is why the story begins with the mention of the Buddha's emitting from the white hair-circle a ray of light that shines throughout the domain of the buddhas. Unless we realize the significance of this, we are liable to have only a shallow understanding of the story or, worse, to misunderstand it altogether.

THE CONTEMPLATION OF THE LAW-FLOWER. The Buddha said: "At that time in the domain Adorned With All Pure Radiance there was a bodhisattva whose name was Wonder Sound, who for long had cultivated many roots of virtue, paid homage to and courted innumerable hundred thousand myriad *koṭis* of buddhas, and perfectly acquired profound wisdom. He had attained the contemplation of the wonderful banner sign, the contemplation of the Law-Flower, the contemplation of pure virtue, the contemplation of the Constellation King's sport, the contemplation of causelessness, the contemplation of the knowledge seal, the contemplation of interpreting the utterances of all beings, the contemplation of collection of all merits, the contemplation of purity, the contemplation of supernatural sport, the contemplation of wisdom torch, the contemplation of the king of adornment, the contemplation of pure luster, the contemplation of the pure treasury, the contemplation of the unique, and the contemplation of sun revolution; such hundreds of thousands of myriads of *koṭis* of great contemplations as these had he acquired, equal to the sands of the Ganges."

Contemplation, *samādhi* in Sanskrit, means to concentrate one's mind on a single object, not distracted by anything. Here are mentioned sixteen kinds of contemplations, each of which has a particular meaning. The contemplation of the wonderful banner sign means to believe firmly and unshakably that the Lotus Sutra is the core of all the teachings of the Buddha. The contemplation of the Law-Flower means to believe deeply in the teachings of the Lotus Sutra, practicing them oneself, and not to be distracted by anything. This contemplation is representative of all sixteen contemplations; the remaining fifteen can be said to be derived from the contemplation of the Law-Flower. The contemplation of pure virtue means one's mental state of possessing pure virtue but not being conscious of it. A person who enters this contemplation is not arrogant or selfish, and his speech and conduct naturally influence those around him for the better. The contemplation of the Constellation King's sport means to keep one's mind upon desiring to be a buddha or a great bodhisattva who has been endowed with fine virtue from former lives and has the power to lead others freely by means of his virtue, and also to have a firm determination in one's own desire for buddhahood.

The contemplation of causelessness means to devote oneself to the spirit of saving not only those related to oneself but also those unrelated to one. The contemplation of the knowledge seal means to concentrate one's mind on abiding in such a mental state that one's deep knowledge will exert a strong favorable influence upon the minds of others close to one. The contemplation of interpreting the utterances of all beings means being in the mental state of discerning the desires of all living beings and of meditating on preaching teachings suitable to them. The contemplation of collection of all merits means to concentrate one's mind on the idea that the merits of all the teachings amount to only one merit, that both oneself and others will become buddhas. The contemplation of purity means to devote one's heart and soul to a single object, by which one removes all illusions from one's mind and keeps one's body pure. The contemplation of supernatural sport means to endeavor so wholeheartedly as to maintain the mental state of being free from all circumstances.

The contemplation of wisdom torch means to devote oneself to the desire to direct the light of one's wisdom into one's surroundings, just as a torch throws its light afar. The contemplation of the king of adornment means to keep one's mind upon desiring to be a person who has such virtue as to influence others. The contemplation of pure luster means to desire to purify one's surroundings by emitting a spotless luster from one's body. The contemplation of the pure treasury means to keep one's mind upon the desire to fill one's mind with purity. The contemplation of the unique means to have the firm ideal of attaining the same mental state as the Buddha and to practice the teachings toward that ideal. The contemplation of sun revolution means not to have a distracted mind but to desire to attain such a mental state as to cause all things to live, just as the life-giving sun shines incessantly on all things.

No sooner had the ray from Sakyamuni Buddha shone upon the Bodhisattva Wonder Sound than he said to the Buddha King Wisdom of the Pure Flower Constellation: "World-honored One! I should go to visit the *sahā*-world to salute, approach, and pay homage to Sakyamuni Buddha, as well as to see the Bodhisattva Mañjuśrī, son of the Law-king, the Bodhisattva Medicine King, the Bodhisattva Courageous Giver, the Bodhisattva Star Constellation King Flower, the Bodhisattva Mind for Higher Deeds, the Bodhisattva King of Adornment, and the Bodhisattva Medicine Lord."

Then the Buddha King Wisdom of the Pure Flower Constellation addressed the Bodhisattva Wonder Sound: "Do not look lightly on that domain or conceive a low opinion of it. Good son! That *sahā*-world with its high and low places is uneven, and full of earth, stones, hills, and filth; the body of the Buddha is short and small, and all the bodhisattvas are small of stature, whereas your body is forty-two thousand *yojanas* high and my body six million, eight hundred thousand *yojanas*. Your body is of the finest order, blessed with hundreds of thousands of myriads of felicities, and of a wonderful brightness. Therefore on resorting there do not look lightly on that domain, nor conceive a low opinion of the Buddha, nor of the bodhisattvas nor of their country."

The Bodhisattva Wonder Sound replied to the buddha: "World-honored One! That I now go to visit the *sahā*-world is all due to the Tathāgata's power, the Tathāgata's magic play, and the Tathāgata's adornment of merit and wisdom."

THE GAP BETWEEN IDEAL AND ACTUALITY. What is meant by the statement that in comparison with the Buddha King Wisdom of the Pure Flower Constellation and the Bodhisattva Wonder Sound, the body of Sakyamuni Buddha is short and small and all the bodhisattvas are small of stature, not emitting rays of light from their bodies? This figure of speech points out the gulf between ideal and actuality. The domain where the Buddha King Wisdom of the Pure Flower Constellation dwells is an ideal world situated in the heavens. For this reason the bodies of the buddhas and the bodhisattvas in that domain are extraordinarily large and of a wonderful brightness.

On the other hand, what is the actuality? There is nothing impressive about it when compared with the ideal. The actuality appears to be far smaller, lower, and plainer than the ideal. A person who has perfected his character in such an actual world is far more sacred than an ideal form in the heavens, even if his body is small and has no apparent brightness. There is nothing more sacred than the attainment of the mental state of the Buddha in the actual world, where obstructions are often thrown up by evil-minded people. The Buddha King Wisdom of the Pure Flower Constellation preached this earnestly to the Bodhisattva Wonder Sound.

Thereupon the Bodhisattva Wonder Sound, without rising from his seat and without stirring his body, entered into contemplation. By the power of his contemplation, on Mount Gṛdhrakūṭa, not far distant from the Law seat, there appeared in transformation eighty-four thousand precious lotus flowers with stalks of *jambūnada* gold, leaves of white silver, stamens of diamond, and cups of *kimśuka* gems.

Thereupon Mañjuśrī, son of the Law-king, seeing those lotus flowers, said to the Buddha: "World-honored One! For what reason does this auspicious sign first appear? There are some thousands and myriads of lotus flowers with stalks of *jambūnada* gold, leaves of white silver, stamens of diamond, and cups of *kimśuka* gems."[2]

Then Sakyamuni Buddha informed Mañjuśrī: "It is the Bodhisattva-Mahāsattva Wonder Sound who desires to come from the domain of the Buddha King Wisdom of the Pure Flower Constellation, with his company of eighty-four thousand bodhisattvas, to this *sahā*-world in order to pay homage to, draw nigh to, and salute me, and who also desires to pay homage to the Law-Flower Sutra."

Mañjuśrī said to the Buddha: "World-honored One! What roots of goodness has that bodhisattva planted, what merits has he cultivated, that he should be able to have such great transcendent power? What contemplation does he practice? Be pleased to tell us the name of this contemplation; we also desire diligently to practice it, for by practicing this contemplation, we may be able to see that bodhisattva—his color, form, and size, his dignity and behavior. Be pleased, World-honored One, by thy transcendent power, to let us see the coming of that bodhisattva."

Sakyamuni Buddha told Mañjuśrī: "The Tathāgata Abundant Treasures, so long extinct, shall display to you the sign." Instantly the Buddha Abundant Treasures addressed that bodhisattva: "Come, good son! Mañjuśrī, son of the Law-king, wishes to see you."

Thereupon the Bodhisattva Wonder Sound disappeared from that domain and started out along with eighty-four thousand bodhisattvas. The countries through which they passed were shaken in the six ways, lotus flowers of the precious seven rained everywhere, and hundreds of thousands of heavenly instruments resounded of themselves. That bodhisattva's eyes were like the broad leaves of the blue lotus. His august countenance surpassed the combined glory of hundreds of thousands of myriads of moons. His body was of pure gold color, adorned with infi-

2. The *kimśuka* is a tree with red flowers, called the "red gem" or "macaw gem" because its flowers are as red as a macaw's beak.

nite hundreds of thousands of meritorious signs; he was of glowing majesty, radiant and shining, marked with the perfect signs, and of a body strong as Nārāyaṇa's.[3] Entering a seven-jeweled tower, he mounted the sky seven *tāla* trees above the earth and, worshiped and surrounded by a host of bodhisattvas, came to Mount Gṛdhrakūṭa in this *sahā*-world. Arrived, he alighted from his seven-jeweled tower and, taking a necklace worth hundreds of thousands, went to Sakyamuni Buddha, at whose feet he made obeisance and to whom he presented the necklace, saying to the Buddha: "World-honored One! The Buddha King Wisdom of the Pure Flower Constellation inquires after the World-honored One: 'Hast thou few ailments and few worries? Art thou getting on at ease and in comfort? Are thy four component parts[4] in harmony? Are thy worldly affairs tolerable? Are thy creatures easy to save? Are they not overcovetous, angry, foolish, envious, arrogant; not unfilial to parents or irreverent to *śramaṇas;* not having perverted views or being of bad mind, unrestrained in their five passions? World-honored One! Are thy creatures able to overcome the Māra-enemies? Does the Tathāgata Abundant Treasures, so long extinct, still abide in the Stupa of the Precious Seven and come to listen to the Law?' King Wisdom also inquires of the Tathāgata Abundant Treasures: 'Art thou at ease and of few worries? Wilt thou be content to remain long?' World-honored One! We now would see the body of the Buddha Abundant Treasures. Be pleased, World-honored One, to show and let us see him."

Then Sakyamuni Buddha said to the Buddha Abundant Treasures: "This Bodhisattva Wonder Sound desires to see you." Instantly the Buddha Abundant Treasures addressed Wonder Sound: "Excellent, excellent, that you have been able to come here to pay homage to Sakyamuni Buddha, to hear the Law-Flower Sutra, and to see Mañjuśrī and the others."

The words spoken by the Buddha Abundant Treasures contain an important meaning. As a witness to the truth, the Buddha Abundant Treasures declared clearly in his praise of the Bodhisattva Wonder Sound that the first requisite for everybody is always to do the following three things: to pay homage to Sakyamuni Buddha, who preached the truth; to hear the teaching of the truth, namely, the Lotus Sutra; and to follow the pattern of the virtuous bodhisattvas who practice the teaching.

Then the Bodhisattva Flower Virtue said to the Buddha: "World-

3. Nārāyaṇa, "firm and solid" or "original man"; a title of Brahma as creator.
4. The four elements, earth, water, fire, and wind, of which every body is composed.

honored One! This Bodhisattva Wonder Sound—what roots of goodness has he planted, what merits has he cultivated, that he possesses such transcendent powers?" The Buddha answered Flower Virtue Bodhisattva: "In the past there was a buddha named King of Cloud Thundering Tathāgata, Arhat, Samyaksaṃbodhi, whose domain was named Display of All Worlds and whose *kalpa* named Joyful Sight. The Bodhisattva Wonder Sound, for twelve thousand years, with a hundred thousand kinds of music, paid homage to the Buddha King of Cloud Thundering and offered up eighty-four thousand vessels of the precious seven. Being rewarded for this reason, he has now been born in the domain of the Buddha King Wisdom of the Pure Flower Constellation and possesses such transcendent powers. Flower Virtue! What is your opinion? The Bodhisattva Wonder Sound who at that time paid homage to the Buddha King of Cloud Thundering with music and offerings of precious vessels—was it some other person? It was indeed the present Bodhisattva-Mahāsattva Wonder Sound. Flower Virtue! This Bodhisattva Wonder Sound had before paid homage to and been close to innumerable buddhas, for long had cultivated roots of virtue, and had met hundreds of thousands of myriads of *koṭis* of *nayutas* of buddhas, numerous as the sands of the Ganges."

To pay homage to the Buddha with music means to extol his virtue. This should be interpreted as praising the Buddha with words rather than as actually playing music.

THE POWER OF WORDS. Buddhism places great importance on words. Smiles and kind words are regarded as one way of leading people to emancipation. In esoteric Buddhism, secret and mystic words are believed to have the power of counteracting all evils and curses. In chapter 26 of the Lotus Sutra, *dhāraṇīs,* formulas of mystic syllables that maintain the religious life of the reciter, are supposed to contain a mystic power.

The same thing can be found in Christianity. The Gospel of John opens with these words: "In the beginning was the Word, and the Word was with God, and the Word was God." Modern science points out that thoughts are born from words. When we think of something, we formulate it in words in our mind. We cannot think of anything without using words.

When we think deeply of why the Bodhisattva Wonder Sound was called by that name, we realize that the name of this bodhisattva must be derived from an expression meaning "the words of the truth." The

Buddha is not delighted by people's merely paying homage to him with music, however beautiful it may be. His mind is truly satisfied by people's extolling him with words of truth.

Considering this, we can understand the phrase "paid homage to the Buddha King of Cloud Thundering and offered up eighty-four thousand vessels of the precious seven." Offering many beautiful vessels to the Buddha would not in itself please him. In Buddhism, the term "eighty-four thousand" is used to indicate a limitless number of sutras. The phrase "offered up eighty-four thousand vessels of the precious seven" therefore means that the Bodhisattva Wonder Sound preached the Buddha's teachings to many people in return for having received the Buddha's grace.

The Buddha continued to preach to the following effect: "Flower Virtue! You merely see here one body of the Bodhisattva Wonder Sound. But this bodhisattva appears in many kinds of bodies everywhere preaching this sutra to the living. Sometimes he appears as Brahma, or appears as Śakra, or appears as Īśvara, or appears as Maheśvara, or appears as a divine general, or appears as the divine king Vaiśravaṇa, or appears as a holy wheel-rolling king, or appears as one of the ordinary kings, or appears as an elder, or appears as a citizen, or appears as a minister, or appears as a Brahman, or appears as *bhikshu, bhikshuṇī, upāsaka,* or *upāsikā,* or appears as the wife of an elder or a citizen, or appears as the wife of a minister, or appears as the wife of a Brahman, or appears as a youth or maiden, or appears as a god, dragon, *yaksha, gandharva, asura, garuḍa, kiṃnara, mahoraga,* human or nonhuman being, and so on, and preaches this sutra."

Here the Buddha mentions thirty-four kinds of bodies in which the Bodhisattva Wonder Sound appears. This means that the bodhisattva transforms himself and appears in various ways according to time and circumstance, not limited to these thirty-four kinds of bodies. In the *sahā*-world and in all realms, he leads all living beings by his various tactful means according to various beings' character and capacity.

Then the Bodhisattva Flower Virtue said to the Buddha: "World-honored One! This Bodhisattva Wonder Sound has indeed deeply planted his roots of goodness. World-honored One! In what contemplation does this bodhisattva abide, that he is able thus to transform and manifest himself according to circumstances, to save the living?" The Buddha answered Flower Virtue Bodhisattva: "Good son! That contemplation is named revelation of all forms. The Bodhisattva Wonder Sound, abiding in this contemplation, is able thus to benefit countless beings."

While this chapter of the Bodhisattva Wonder Sound was preached the eighty-four thousand who had come with the Bodhisattva Wonder Sound all attained the contemplation of revelation of all forms, and countless bodhisattvas in this *sahā*-world also attained this contemplation and *dhāraṇī*.

Then the Bodhisattva-Mahāsattva Wonder Sound, having paid homage to Sakyamuni Buddha and to the stupa of the Buddha Abundant Treasures, returned to his own land. The countries through which he passed were agitated in the six different ways, raining precious lotus flowers and performing hundreds of thousands of myriads of *koṭis* of kinds of music. Having arrived at his own domain, he, with the eighty-four thousand bodhisattvas around him, went to the Buddha King Wisdom of the Pure Flower Constellation and said to him: "World-honored One! I have been to the *sahā*-world, done good to its living beings, seen Sakyamuni Buddha, also seen the stupa of the Buddha Abundant Treasures, and worshiped and paid homage to them; I have also seen the Bodhisattva Mañjuśrī, son of the Law-king, as well as the Bodhisattva Medicine King, the Bodhisattva Attainer of Earnestness and Zeal, the Bodhisattva Courageous Giver, and others, and caused those eighty-four thousand bodhisattvas to attain the contemplation of revelation of all forms."

The chapter concludes: "While this chapter on the going and coming of the Bodhisattva Wonder Sound was preached, the forty-two thousand heavenly sons attained the assurance of no rebirth, and the Bodhisattva Flower Virtue attained the contemplation termed Law-Flower."

When we read the closing portion of this chapter we may wonder if the Bodhisattva Wonder Sound is identical with the Eternal Original Buddha. It is mentioned that the Bodhisattva Wonder Sound can transform himself and appear in various forms anywhere. It is even written, "To those whom he must save in the form of a buddha, he then appears in the form of a buddha and preaches the Law."

However, the Bodhisattva Wonder Sound is not identical with the Eternal Original Buddha but is a bodhisattva who acts as his messenger. This bodhisattva is far inferior to the Tathāgata Sakyamuni as the appearing Buddha in his power of enlightening all living beings.

As mentioned earlier, the Bodhisattva Wonder Sound is the symbol of an ideal; he is a bodhisattva who in various ways teaches people an ideal state of mind. He teaches the supreme virtue at which each person must aim—the ideal state of mind for statesmen, for businessmen, for scholars, and for housewives. The teaching of an ideal state of mind is holy indeed, but it does not show its worth so long as it lies idle in one's mind. The true worth of the ideal teaching is appreciated only when and where people realize it little by little in their daily lives.

This is clearly displayed through the actions of the Bodhisattva Wonder Sound: this Bodhisattva (or ideal), with a bright golden body of infinite size, went to Sakyamuni Buddha, who had perfected the thirty-two signs and the eighty distinctive bodily marks of a buddha but had assumed the form of an ordinary man, and the bodhisattva made obeisance at the Buddha's feet and presented a precious necklace to him. The Bodhisattva Wonder Sound, as the symbol of an ideal, praised Sakyamuni Buddha, who appeared in this world as a perfected man, saying, "You are the one indeed who has realized our ideal." The Bodhisattva Wonder Sound came to the actual world from an ideal realm for the purpose of praising and proving how great and holy a thing it is for people to endeavor to establish the Righteous Law and to build an ideal society in this *sahā*-world, filled as it is with defilements and evils.

The true spirit of chapter 24 is that an ideal is not truly holy until it is actually realized by people little by little. Although the buddhas dwelling in ideal worlds, such as the Tathāgata Mahāvairocana and the Tathāgata Amita, are surely very holy, the Eternal Original Buddha, whom people can revere through the Tathāgata Sakyamuni as the personified ideal thereof, should be the object of worship for those living in this world.

CHAPTER 25

The All-Sidedness of the Bodhisattva Regarder of the Cries of the World

Of the twenty-eight chapters of the Lotus Sutra, there is none that has been more misinterpreted than this one. Having been interpreted superficially and literally, it has been regarded as teaching an easygoing faith: anyone who calls upon the Bodhisattva Regarder of the Cries of the World will be delivered instantly from all his sufferings.

To be sure, the first half of this chapter deals for the most part with the supernatural power of this bodhisattva, declaring that if living beings keep in mind and revere the Bodhisattva Regarder of the Cries of the World, they will be freed from the seven dangers of fire, water, wind, sword, demon, torture, and robbery. If they continue to revere the bodhisattva, they will be delivered from the four human sufferings of birth, old age, sickness, and death. If they revere the bodhisattva still more, they will be emancipated from the three poisons of desire, anger, and foolishness, and they will be able to obtain the kind of children they desire. When ordinary people read chapter 25 with a shallow understanding, it is only to be expected that they will fall into an easygoing faith. Such a misinterpretation of this chapter comes from their insufficient understanding of the teachings preached in the rest of the Lotus Sutra. If they could truly understand at least chapter 16, "Revelation of the [Eternal] Life of the Tathāgata," they could not misunderstand chapter 25 in this way.

The causes of their misunderstanding are basically two. The first is their superficial idea of salvation, which they seek in something outside themselves. As has already been explained in chapter 16, salvation lies in our awareness of the existence of the Eternal Buddha, who is omnipresent both within and outside us, and in our earnest and heartfelt realization that we are caused to live by the Buddha.

Such a firm realization leads us to true peace of mind. At the same time, our speech and conduct come naturally to be in accord with the Buddha and will produce harmony in our surroundings. The Land of Eternally Tranquil Light, namely, an ideal society, will be formed when a harmonious world gradually spreads in all directions.

True salvation comes about in this way. Misunderstanding salvation is caused by our mistakenly regarding it as meaning freedom from pain and distress through the help of some outside agency. This is just like a person who suffers from a headache caused by constipation and takes aspirin for the headache. He will temporarily feel relief from his headache because of the medicine, but he will not recover completely so long as he is not cured of his constipation, the root cause. In the same way, to rely completely on power outside oneself will not cause one to be truly saved from suffering, even though he may be relieved of an immediate problem.

Secondly, there is a great misunderstanding of the status of bodhisattvas. True salvation is realized only through the Buddha; this should be clear from the principle of salvation discussed above. Salvation comes from our realization of the existence of the truth, and there is only one truth. A bodhisattva is one who has a great will to save others, and he can certainly save all living beings suffering from illusion and suffering on specific occasions. Fundamental salvation, however, is not brought about except by our realization of the existence of the Buddha. How does a bodhisattva manifest his salvation to living beings? This is, of course, a salvation revealed by him to save them from their illusions and suffering on specific occasions. A much more important working of his salvation, however, is to transmit the Buddha's teachings as his messenger and to provide us with a good example of religious life. The true salvation of the bodhisattva lies in leading us to salvation through his good example.

The great bodhisattvas have perfected their virtues, and each is possessed of special virtues peculiar to him. For example, the Bodhisattva Never Despise is characterized by his practice of paying respect to others and disclosing their buddha-nature. The Bodhisattva Medicine King displays his distinctive character in his practice of repaying the Buddha's grace through his personal practice of the teachings. The Bodhisattva

Wonder Sound is characterized by his practice of having a great regard for the realization of an ideal. We can model ourselves after the special virtues of one or another of the various bodhisattvas.

The Bodhisattva Regarder of the Cries of the World is not a buddha but a bodhisattva. He is one whom we regard as a model, but he should not be the object of our prayers for salvation. In this chapter, the Buddha declares the supernatural power of the Bodhisattva Regarder of the Cries of the World as a model in order to cause us to wish to be as splendid as this bodhisattva and to try all the harder to practice the teachings of the Lotus Sutra.

To keep in mind and revere the Bodhisattva Regarder of the Cries of the World is to think about this bodhisattva and to feel a longing for him as an ideal model. To keep in mind this bodhisattva, with deep longing for him, will help improve our character. However, since ancient times most people have not interpreted the meaning of keeping in mind the Bodhisattva Regarder of the Cries of the World in this way but have revered the bodhisattva in order to be set free from actual suffering through the bodhisattva's supernatural power. This cannot be said to be true faith; true faith is much more profound.

Let us study chapter 25 with these basic points in mind. This chapter includes a few difficult or puzzling terms, but it will be enough for us to understand its general teaching and the meaning of the important points.

WHAT IS AVALOKITEŚVARA? The chapter begins with the following question that the Bodhisattva Infinite Thought asked the Buddha: "World-honored One! For what reason is the Bodhisattva Avalokiteśvara named Regarder of the Cries of the World?" The Buddha answered that if there are countless living beings suffering from pain and distress who call upon the name of the Bodhisattva Regarder of the Cries of the World, the bodhisattva will instantly regard their cries and all of them will be delivered, and for this reason he is named Regarder of the Cries of the World.

Kanzeon or Kannon is the name in Japanese of Avalokiteśvara, the bodhisattva of great compassion, mercy, and love. *Kan* means to behold something, and *zeon* indicates the idea of the cries of the people. These cries are not limited to people crying out aloud but include their earnest desires and aspirations. The Bodhisattva Kanzeon may be considered as the bodhisattva who, by virtue of his supernatural power, is capable of regarding or taking notice of the cries of the people whether these represent either suffering or desire, letting them be delivered from their suffering by preaching the teaching suitable to each one, leading them to their desire, and appearing in the forms suited to those to be led.

These are absolutely indispensable conditions for those who are in a position of leading others. The parents in a family must always watch over their children's health and their state of mind in order to bring them up correctly. When the parents regard the cry of each child—this child needs a certain food, or that child seeks something—they prepare suitable meals, give the children sound training, and advise them on their problems. The parents lead their children in the way conducive to their health and suited to their desires. All parents worthy of the name make sacrifices for the happiness of their children. Such people are ideal parents and are also a manifestation of the spirit of the Bodhisattva Regarder of the Cries of the World.

At work, managers and supervisors must discern in each person who works under them what his character is, how much ability he has, what he is dissatisfied with, what he is worried about, and what hope or ambition he cherishes, and they must guide and manage each employee in the way best suited to him. Through such discernment, guidance, and management, they can supervise a large number of people and can cultivate each one's ability. Managers can then efficiently accomplish the work in their charge. The need of such a spirit and ability is even greater in the case of high executives and presidents of companies, teachers responsible for the education of many students, politicians, and government ministers. All leaders need accurate insight into human nature and the spirit of great compassion that makes one willing to undergo any self-sacrifice for the sake of others, as with the Bodhisattva Regarder of the Cries of the World.

A believer in the Lotus Sutra, who has the earnest wish to spread the Buddha's teachings abroad, to lead all people to the way of the perfection of their character, and to establish an ideal society in this world based on the spirit of great benevolence and compassion shown by the Bodhisattva Regarder of the Cries of the World, must clearly discern the worries, sufferings, and desires of those around him. He must also be able to lead those people freely with the tactful means best suited to each one. Then he can effectively carry out the practices of the bodhisattvas.

By virtue of his supernatural power, the Bodhisattva Regarder of the Cries of the World can save all living beings from the seven dangers and three poisons, give them what they desire, and preach the Law freely by appearing in whichever of his thirty-three incarnations suits the nature of the follower. The supernatural power displayed by this bodhisattva is the goal that a believer in the Lotus Sutra must endeavor to reach by following the example of the bodhisattva, and it is also the ideal required of a leader, who must set an example for others through his position.

THE COMPASSION OF AVALOKITEŚVARA. Since ancient times, statues and paintings of the Bodhisattva Regarder of the Cries of the World have featured a very compassionate and peaceful facial expression. Buddhist sculptors and painters have traditionally depicted this bodhisattva as an ideal leader characterized by gentleness, tolerance, and compassion. Our minds are naturally mellowed by worshiping a sculpture or painted image of this bodhisattva.

Dr. Hideki Yukawa, a theoretical physicist and winner of the Nobel Prize for physics in 1951, had a photograph of the Eleven-faced Kannon with a Thousand Arms made the frontispiece of his book *Man and Science*. He appended the following commentary: "Although this image of Kannon has eleven faces and a thousand arms, it seems to lose nothing of the harmony of the whole body and radiates mental peace. It may not suit the taste of modern people, and its perfect features may instead dissatisfy them somewhat. People today possess many faces and arms as a result of the remarkable progress of science and technology. They now have new eyes for their work, such as the microscope and periscope. They have produced magic hands in order to avoid the danger of radioactivity. Electronic computers have replaced men's brains. These all aid the advance of human beings through science. People today, however, live in a world surrounded by machinery, and have gradually become angular and nervy. They seem to be in the process of discovering a fresher, sharper, more streamlined beauty. A peaceful and compassionate expression like that of Kannon is not to be seen in today's people. There is a certain danger in the tendency to believe that a person who is not somewhat neurotic is abnormal. But is it not true that the more marked this tendency becomes, the more deeply and keenly do they seek mental peace and world peace?"

How can we attain the self-sacrificing spirit, the supreme discerning power and leadership of the Bodhisattva Regarder of the Cries of the World? We can do this only by receiving, keeping, cultivating, and practicing the teachings preached by Sakyamuni Buddha. This bodhisattva has also obtained his supernatural power by means of the truth preached by the Buddha. This is clearly expressed in the sutra as follows: "The Bodhisattva Infinite Thought said to the Buddha: 'World-honored One! Let me now make an offering to the Bodhisattva Regarder of the Cries of the World.' "

"Thereupon he unloosed from his neck a necklace of pearls worth a hundred thousand pieces of gold and presented it to him, making this remark: 'Good sir! Accept this pious gift of a pearl necklace.' But the Bodhisattva Regarder of the Cries of the World would not accept it.

"Again the Bodhisattva Infinite Thought addressed the Bodhisattva Regarder of the Cries of the World: 'Good sir! Out of compassion for us, accept this necklace.' Then the Buddha said to the Bodhisattva Regarder of the Cries of the World: 'Out of compassion for this Bodhisattva Infinite Thought and the four groups, and for the gods, dragons, *yakshas, gandharvas, asuras, garuḍas, kiṃnaras, mohoragas,* human and nonhuman beings, and others, accept this necklace.' Then the Bodhisattva Regarder of the Cries of the World, having compassion for all the four groups and the gods, dragons, human and nonhuman beings, and others, accepted the necklace, and dividing it into two parts, offered one part to Sakyamuni Buddha and offered the other to the stupa of the Buddha Abundant Treasures."

The division of the necklace into two by the Bodhisattva Regarder of the Cries of the World indicates the following: "I owe my supernatural power to the Tathāgata Sakyamuni, who taught me the truth, and to the Tathāgata Abundant Treasures, who bore witness to the truth." The bodhisattva revealed here that he had obtained his transcendent power as the result of realizing and practicing the truth taught by the Tathāgata Sakyamuni. Since many people have lost sight of this important point, they entertain the superstitious and simplistic belief that they will be saved from their sufferings by merely keeping in mind and revering the Bodhisattva Regarder of the Cries of the World. Modern people must reject such a mistaken belief entirely.

THE VOW OF AVALOKITEŚVARA. We can understand this clearly through the following verse spoken by the Buddha in answer to the inquiry of the Bodhisattva Infinite Thought as to why this bodhisattva was named Regarder of the Cries of the World.

"Listen to the deeds of the Cry Regarder,
Who well responds to every quarter;
His vast vow is deep as the sea,
Inconceivable in its eons.
Serving many thousands of *koṭis* of buddhas,
He has vowed a great pure vow."

To paraphrase: Listen first to all the deeds that the Bodhisattva Regarder of the Cries of the World has accumulated. This bodhisattva made a vow to help all people out of difficulties in the way suited to each one. His vast vow is as deep as the sea and inconceivable by ordinary people for eons. With such a vast vow, he has served countless buddhas and has vowed a great pure vow.

From the above verse, we see that all the supernatural powers of the Bodhisattva Regarder of the Cries of the World are based on his vow to save all living beings by means of his powers, and that he obtained such powers as the result of his having made this vow and having practiced the Buddha's teachings for a very long time. The prose portion of the chapter indicates the effect of the bodhisattva's supernatural power and the verse portion its cause—the great vow itself. Through both portions of this chapter, the Buddha teaches us that if we make vows to benefit others and vows of compassion, and practice with a steadfast mind, we will surely attain the same stage as the Bodhisattva Regarder of the Cries of the World.

The verse portion of this chapter is one of the famous in the Lotus Sutra. In the first part the Buddha mentions various difficulties and calamities that beset living beings. Then, summarizing, he preaches as follows:

"The living, crushed and harassed,
Oppressed by countless pains:
The Cry Regarder with his mystic wisdom
Can save such a suffering world.
Perfect in supernatural powers,
Widely practiced in wisdom and tact,
In the lands of the universe there is no place
Where he does not manifest himself.
All the evil states of existence,
Hells, ghosts, and animals,

Sorrows of birth, age, disease, death,
All by degrees are ended by him."

The mystic wisdom of the Cry Regarder is one through whose power he can discern people's minds and can give them the teaching of salvation suited to them. The Cry Regarder desires to be perfect in such supernatural powers as can save a suffering world. He wishes to practice wisdom and tact extensively and to manifest himself to save people throughout the universe. He aspires to save those who have fallen into the evil states of existence, including the realms of the hells, ghosts, and animals. He is also anxious to gradually remove the sorrows of birth, age, disease, and death from people's minds, and finally to lead them to extinguish all sorrows. This is the great vow taken by the Cry Regarder.

According to the extant Sanskrit text of the sutra, the above verse is followed by the sentences: "Hearing from the Buddha this, / Infinite Thought with joy and satisfaction / Spoke thus in verse." When this verse portion from the Sanskrit is inserted, the continuity becomes clearer and harmonizes with the whole of the Lotus Sutra. The next portion should be considered as the verses with which the Bodhisattva Infinite Thought, moved by the verses spoken by the Buddha concerning the various vows of compassion of the Cry Regarder, answered commending the Bodhisattva Regarder of the Cries of the World.

"True regard, serene regard,
Far-reaching wise regard,
Regard of pity, compassionate regard,
Ever longed for, ever looked for!
Pure and serene in radiance,
Wisdom's sun destroying darkness,
Subduer of woes of storm and fire,
Who illumines all the world!
Law of pity, thunder quivering,
Compassion wondrous as a great cloud,
Pouring spiritual rain like nectar,
Quenching the flames of distress!
In disputes before a magistrate,
Or in fear in battle's array,
If he thinks of the Cry Regarder's power
All his enemies will be routed.
His is the wondrous voice, voice of the world-regarder,

Brahma-voice, voice of the rolling tide,
Voice all world-surpassing,
Therefore ever to be kept in mind,
With never a doubting thought.
Regarder of the World's Cries, pure and holy,
In pain, distress, death, calamity,
Able to be a sure reliance,
Perfect in all merit,
With compassionate eyes beholding all,
Boundless ocean of blessings!
Prostrate let us revere him."

True regard signifies the bodhisattva's ability to penetrate the truth, serene regard his freedom from illusions, far-reaching wise regard his perfected wisdom of saving all living beings, regard of pity his pity for all suffering living beings and his determination to save them from such a state, and compassionate regard the compassion by which he leads them to happiness. These regards imply admiration of the eyes with which the Bodhisattva Regarder of the Cries of the World is endowed. To admire the eyes of the bodhisattva, of course, indicates admiration of his mind.

The phrase "ever longed for, ever looked for" means that we desire to have eyes (a mind) like the Bodhisattva Regarder of the Cries of the World and to take the bodhisattva as our model.

Because of his compassionate mind, the bodhisattva radiates a ray of pure and serene light and illuminates everything around him. This is the ray of light emitted by his warm character, and it naturally brightens the minds of those around him. The phrase "pure and serene in radiance" includes this very holy meaning. His wisdom's sun destroys darkness. As often mentioned in this book, darkness disappears as soon as true wisdom's sun shines upon it, because darkness comes from the state in which the real existence of all things is covered with illusion. When illusion vanishes, various calamities will disappear and the whole of society will become bright. This state is expressed in the lines, "Subduer of woes of storm and fire, / Who illumines all the world!"

The words "law of pity, thunder quivering" commend the great power of the precepts kept by the bodhisattva. The worth of the precepts depends on the fundamental spirit of the person who establishes and keeps them. The value of rules, laws, and ordinances depends on the spirit of those who establish and issue them. The more selfishness their spirit contains, the lower the value of such rules, laws, and ordinances becomes. It is not good to ignore the general public, forcing people to observe difficult laws or rules simply because the formulaters of such laws have themselves already reached a high state of mind; laws or rules based on such a self-centered and self-satisfied premise are inferior.

On the other hand, the precepts of the Bodhisattva Regarder of the Cries of the World arise from his compassionate mind, through which he feels pity for all living beings and desires to remove their sufferings. His precepts, based on his compassionate mind, have as great a power as the roll of thunder. Here is the model for those who are in positions of leadership.

A profound meaning is included in the following lines: "Compassion wondrous as a great cloud, / Pouring spiritual rain like nectar, / Quenching the flames of distress!" Compassion indicates the spirit of the Bodhisattva Regarder of the Cries of the World, who desires to make all living beings happy. His compassionate mind is as infinite as a great cloud covering the sky. With this spirit, he pours the rain of the Law on living beings and quenches the flames of their distress, just as the rain of dew reinvigorates withered plants.

The supernatural power of this bodhisattva is described in the following lines: "In disputes before a magistrate, / Or in fear in battle's array, / If he thinks of the Cry Regarder's power / All his enemies will be routed." Here we must read between the lines. All disputes, large or small, originate in the conflict of egos. They come from man's merciless mind, which does not care what becomes of others, and his intolerant mind, which cannot forgive others. At such times, we must keep in mind the name of the Bodhisattva Regarder of the Cries of the World and must think of his power. The bodhisattva has made a great vow to regard the cries of people's minds and to remove their sufferings. We must remember his gentle mind, his self-sacrificing spirit, and his compassionate face, full of warmth. Then there will be responsive communion between his mind and ours.

RESPONSIVE COMMUNION. If we think of the Bodhisattva Regarder of the Cries of the World, our mind is spontaneously led to the same mental stage as his. As a result, we will generate feelings of warmth and tolerance. We can rid ourselves of disputatiousness caused by egoism and attain a peaceful state of mind. We will feel easy even in conflicts and disputes, and accordingly these will be brought to a peaceful settlement. This is the true meaning of responsive communion between the bodhisattva and ordinary people.

The following lines also contain heartening words: "His is the wondrous voice, voice of the world-regarder, / Brahma-voice, voice of the rolling tide, / Voice all world-surpassing, / Therefore ever to be kept in mind." As mentioned before, "the wondrous voice" means the word of the truth. The words "voice of the world-regarder" have already been explained. The words "Brahma-voice" express the idea of the teaching preached with a pure mind. The words "voice of the rolling tide" indicate that the teaching affects the depth of listeners' minds, just as the voice of the rolling tide reverberates within one even at a long distance. The words "voice all world-surpassing" mean the teaching with the supernatural power that enables it to overcome any illusion and suffering in the world. Therefore, all living beings should ever keep in mind the Bodhisattva Regarder of the Cries of the World, who preaches the teaching that is supreme in every respect, and should desire to be like this bodhisattva.

The verse section ends with the following lines:

"With never a doubting thought.
Regarder of the World's Cries, pure and holy,
In pain, distress, death, calamity,
Able to be a sure reliance,
Perfect in all merit,
With compassionate eyes beholding all,
Boundless ocean of blessings!
Prostrate let us revere him."

We must not keep in mind the Bodhisattva Regarder of the Cries of the World doubting whether our desire will be accomplished or not. We can always rely upon this bodhisattva in the face of pain, distress, death, and calamity. He is perfect in all merits and beholds all living beings with his compassionate eyes. All blessings can be bestowed on us by virtue of his power of compassion. For this reason we must prostrate ourselves before him, revering him and following his practices.

Chapter 25 ends with the following words: "Thereupon the Bodhisattva Stage Holder rose from his seat, and went before and said to the Buddha: 'World-honored One! If any living being hears of the sovereign work and the all-sided transcendent powers shown in this chapter of the Bodhisattva Regarder of the Cries of the World, it should be known that the merits of this man are not a few.'

"While the Buddha preached this chapter of the All-sided One, the eighty-four thousand living beings in the assembly all set their minds upon Perfect Enlightenment, with which nothing can compare."

Summarizing the teachings of this chapter, the following three points may be mentioned:

The first teaching is: If a person is in a position of leadership, he must regard the wishes of all the people and with a perfect mind of compassion sacrifice himself for the suffering people, and he must help them in their suffering and distress. The second teaching is: When a person is confronted by a crushing or harassing problem or any conflict, or feels the urge to indulge in any evil, he should call to mind the Bodhisattva Regarder of the Cries of the World, who is gentle, peaceful, and tolerant. Then he will be able to open his mind and cope calmly with any problem, however crushing or harassing. He will also become free of disputatiousness and all evil impulses. The third teaching is: A person should aim at reaching the mental stage of the Bodhisattva Regarder of the Cries of the World, who possesses excellent virtue and supernatural power. For this purpose, he must follow the teaching of the truth taught by the Tathāgata Sakyamuni and practice the disciplines without retrogression.

From these three teachings, we can well understand the true intention of the Buddha in this chapter.

CHAPTER 26

Dhāraṇīs

THIS CHAPTER DECLARES how with mystic syllables nonhuman beings representing the spiritual world, who are deeply moved by the teachings of the Lotus Sutra, vow to protect the teachings and their preachers.

First two bodhisattvas, Medicine King and Courageous Giver, vow to guard and protect the preachers of the Lotus Sutra. Their vows are only to be expected, for these two bodhisattvas are the disciples and messengers of the Buddha. Next two Brahma heavenly kings, the Divine King Vaiśravaṇa and the Divine King Domain Holder, vow to protect the sutra. The vows of these two non-Buddhist divine kings signify that the Buddha's teachings comprehend all other teachings and infuse religious life into them.

Following this, ten female *rākshasas* and the Mother of Demon Sons[1] vow to protect the Lotus Sutra. These female demons with one voice declared before the Buddha that if anyone harassed the preachers of the sutra, they would protect the preachers an rid them of such persecution. Their declaration bears witness to the fact that the Buddha-mind is found even in these demons. Conversely, the teachings of the Lotus Sutra can be said to have the power to enable even these demons to become buddhas.

1. Also called "Joyful Mother" or "Mother Who Loves Her Children." She is a *rākshasī*, or female *rākshasa*, who devoured the babies of others every day until her own five hundred babies were hidden by Sakyamuni Buddha and she was converted. After her conversion she vowed to protect the Buddha-law and especially to guard babies.

FIVE KINDS OF UNTRANSLATABLE WORDS. Many mystic Sanskrit words appear in this chapter. Why were these words not translated? The reason is due to the prudence of Kumārajīva, who translated the Lotus Sutra from Sanskrit into Chinese. When the Mahāyāna sutras were rendered into Chinese from Sanskrit, the translators, including Kumārajīva, left "untranslatable words" untouched. These translators defined as untranslatable the following five kinds of words:

1. Words with meanings alien to Chinese, that is, the names of animals, plants, and demons peculiar to India but foreign to China. For example: the fragrance of *tamālapattra* and of *tagara,* mentioned in chapter 19, and such beings as *garuḍas* and *kiṃnaras.*
2. Words with many meanings, that is, words that cannot be fully translated by a single word. For example: *dhāraṇī,* sometimes meaning the mystic power that enables a reciter to maintain the teaching he has heard, sometimes meaning the power of checking all evil and of encouraging all good, sometimes meaning the mystic syllables by which the reciter can escape disaster. The mystic syllables in chapter 26 belong to the last category.
3. Mystic words. For example: the *dhāraṇī* spells appearing in chapter 26. These words were left as they were because their profound meaning would be impaired if they were translated.
4. Transliterations well established by precedent. For example: *anuttara-samyak-saṃbodhi,* which can be translated as "Perfect Enlightenment" or "the unsurpassed wisdom of the Buddha."
5. Words with profound meanings, which would lose their true meaning if translated. For example: *buddha* and *bodhi.*

These five kinds of untranslatable words (*goshu-fuhon*) were invariably left untouched by any translator.

When the Buddha had finished preaching chapter 25, Medicine King Bodhisattva arose from his seat and, humbly baring his right shoulder, folded his hands toward the Buddha and spoke to the Buddha, saying: "World-honored One! If there be any good son or good daughter who is able to receive and keep the Law-Flower Sutra, either reading or reciting or studying or copying the sutra, what is the extent of the blessings obtained?"

The Buddha answered Medicine King: "Suppose any good son or good daughter pays homage to eight hundred myriad *koṭis* of *nayutas* of buddhas, equal to the sands of the Ganges, in your opinion are not the blessings so obtained rather numerous?"

"Very numerous, World-honored One!" was the reply.

The Buddha continued: "If any good son or good daughter is able, in regard to this sutra, to receive and keep but a single four-line verse, read and recite, understand its meaning, and do as it says, his merits will be still more numerous."

Thereupon Medicine King Bodhisattva said to the Buddha: "World-honored One! To the preachers of the Law I will now give *dhāraṇī* spells[2] for their guard and protection."

Then he delivered the following spell: *"Anye manye mane mamane citte carite same samitā viśānte mukte muktame same avishame samasame jaye [kshaye] akshaye akshīṇe śānte samite dhāraṇī ālokabhāshe pratyavekshaṇi nidhiru abhyantaranivishṭe abhyantarapāriśuddhi utkule mutkule araḍe paraḍe sukāṅkshī asamasame buddhavilokite dharmaparīkshite saṃghanirghoshaṇi [nirghoshaṇī] bhayābhayaviśodhani mantre mantrākshayate rute rutakauśalye akshaye akshayavanatāye [vakkule] valoḍa amanyanatāye [svāhā].*

"World-honored One! These supernatural *dhāraṇī* spells have been spoken by buddhas numerous as the sands of sixty-two *koṭis* of Ganges rivers. If anyone does violence to the teacher of this Law, then he will have done violence to these buddhas."

Then Sakyamuni Buddha extolled Medicine King Bodhisattva, saying: "Good, good, O Medicine King! Because you are compassionate and protect these teachers of the Law, you have pronounced these *dhāraṇīs,* which will abundantly benefit the living."

Thereupon the Bodhisattva Courageous Giver spoke to the Buddha, saying: "World-honored One! I, too, for the protection of these who read and recite, receive and keep the Law-Flower Sutra, will deliver *dhāraṇīs.* If these teachers of the Law possess these *dhāraṇīs,* neither *yakshas,* nor *rākshasas,* nor *pūtanas,* nor *kṛityas,* nor *kumbhāṇḍas,* nor hungry ghosts, nor others spying for their shortcomings can find a chance." Then, in the presence of the Buddha, he delivered the following spell: *"Jvale mahājvale ukke [tukku] mukku aḍe aḍāvati nṛtye nṛtyāvati iṭṭini viṭṭini ciṭṭini nṛtyeni nṛtyāvati [svāhā].*

"World-honored One! These supernatural *dhāraṇī* spells have been

2. Talismantic formulas, one of the four kinds of *dhāraṇīs.* There are four kinds of spells: (1) to heal disease, (2) to put an end to the consequences of sin, (3) to protect the sutras, and (4) for wisdom. Here the spells are for the protection of this sutra.

spoken by buddhas numerous as the sands of the Ganges, and all approved. If anyone does violence to the teachers of this Law, he will have done violence to these buddhas."

Thereupon the Divine King Vaiśravaṇa, protector of the world, spoke to the Buddha, saying: 'World-honored One! I, too, in compassion for the living and for the protection of these teachers of the Law, will deliver these *dhāraṇīs*.' Whereupon he delivered the following spell: *"Aṭṭe [taṭṭe] naṭṭe vanaṭṭe anaḍe nāḍi kunaḍi [svāhā].*

"World-honored One! By these supernatural spells I will protect the teachers of the Law. I will also myself protect those who keep this sutra, so that no corroding care shall come within a hundred *yojanas*."

Thereupon the Divine King Domain Holder, who was present in this congregation, with a host of thousands of myriads of *koṭis* of *nayutas* of *gandharvas* reverently encompassing him, went before the Buddha, and folding his hands said to the Buddha: "World-honored One! I, too, with supernatural *dhāraṇī* spells, will protect those who keep the Law-Flower Sutra." Whereupon he delivered the following spell: *"Agaṇe gaṇe gauri gandhāri caṇḍāli mātaṅgi [pukkaśi] saṃkule vrūsali sisi [svāhā].*

"World-honored One! These supernatural *dhāraṇī* spells have been spoken by forty-two *koṭis* of buddhas. If anyone does violence to these teachers of the Law, he will have done violence to these buddhas."

There were female *rākshasas*, the first named Lambā, the second named Vilambā, the third named Crooked Teeth, the fourth named Flowery Teeth, the fifth named Black Teeth, the sixth named Many Tresses, the seventh named Insatiable, the eighth named Necklace Holder, the ninth named Kuntī, and the tenth named Spirit Snatcher. These ten female *rākshasas*, together with the Mother of Demon Sons and her children and followers, all went to the Buddha and with one voice said to the Buddha: "World-honored One! We, too, would protect those who read and recite, receive and keep the Law-Flower Sutra, and rid them of corroding care. If any spy for the shortcomings of these teachers of the Law, we will prevent their obtaining any chance." Whereupon in the presence of the Buddha they delivered the following spell: *"Iti me, iti me, iti me, iti me, iti me; ni me, ni me, ni me, ni me, ni me; ruhe, ruhe, ruhe, ruhe [ruhe]; stuhe, stuhe, stuhe, stuhe, stuhe [svāhā].*

"Let troubles come on our heads, rather than on the teachers of the Law; neither *yakshas*, nor hungry ghosts, nor *pūtanas*, nor *kṛityas*, nor *vetaḍas*, nor *kashāyas*, nor *umārakas*, nor *apasmārakas*, nor *yaksha-*

kṛityas, nor man-*kṛityas,*[3] nor fevers, whether for a single day, or quotidian, or tertian, or quartan, or weekly, or unremitting fevers; whether in male form, or female form, or form of a youth, or form of a maiden, even in dreams shall ever cause distress." Then in the presence of the Buddha they spoke in verse:

"Whoever resists our spell
And troubles a preacher,
May his head be split in seven
Like an *arjaka* sprout;
May his doom be that of a parricide,
His retribution that of an oil-expresser
Or a deceiver with false measures and weights,
Or of Devadatta who brought schism into the Saṃgha;
He who offends these teachers of the Law,
Such shall be his retribution."

This is a famous verse. It is said that if one touches an *arjaka* flower its petals will open and fall into seven pieces. The lines "May his head be split in seven / Like an *arjaka* sprout" mean, "May that man's doom be that of a parricide." The words "His retribution that of an oil-expresser" refer to an Indian custom. When one grinds sesame, he puts a weight on the grinder to press down the sesame. If this weight presses only moderately on the sesame, the worms in it are not squeezed. If he puts too heavy a weight on the grinder in order to press the sesame faster, they are squeezed and the sesame will lose its flavor. Therefore, in ancient India, this was regarded as symbolizing the crime by which one takes another's life for the sake of his own self.

The same thing can be said of the crime of one who deceives with false measures and weights. Although such a crime cannot be compared with that of homicide in today's legal system, it is a heinous deed from a spiritual point of view. Therefore, such a deed was considered a great crime in ancient India.

THE CRIME OF BRINGING SCHISM INTO THE SAṂGHA. Next is the phrase, "Or of Devadatta who brought schism into the Saṃgha." Devadatta

3. A *vetaḍa* is a red demon, a *kashāya* a yellow demon, an *umāraka* a black demon, and an *apasmāraka* a blue demon; a *yaksha-kṛitya* is a *kṛitya* in the form of a *yaksha,* and a man-*kṛitya* a *kṛitya* in the form of a human being.

committed the evil of breaking the close and loyal concord in Sakyamuni's community of believers. It goes without saying that man commits a great crime when he brings schism into the community formed by the fellow believers of a faith. A person who disturbs the preachers of the Lotus Sutra is no better than a criminal, and his retribution will be such that his head will be split in seven like an *arjaka* sprout.

Reading this passage superficially, the female *rākshasas* appear to be vowing vengeance on the enemies of the Lotus Sutra. This is a mistaken interpretation, however. We should consider rather that their vigor and zeal caused them to utter passionate words because they had not accumulated such great virtues as the disciples of the Buddha and because of their demonic nature. Otherwise Sakyamuni Buddha, who preached tolerance for all living beings, could not have unconditionally extolled the female *rākshasas,* saying, "Good, good!"

The explanation of the principle of punishment in Buddhism (discussed on pages 62 and 319) fully applies here. The verse reads, "May his head be split in seven," not "May the Buddha split his head in seven." And again, we read, "Such shall be his retribution," following the list of the various dooms for offending teachers of the Law. This expression accords with the principle of the Buddhist concept of punishment, which teaches that one will be punished by his own crimes, not by some outside agency or arbitrary force.

After the female *rākshasas* had uttered this stanza, they addressed the Buddha, saying: "World-honored One! We ourselves will also protect those who receive and keep, read and recite, and practice this sutra, and give them ease of mind, freedom from corroding care and from all poisons."

The Buddha addressed the *rākshasa* women: "Good, good! Even if you are only able to protect those who receive and keep the name of the Law-Flower, your happiness will be beyond calculation; how much more if you protect those who perfectly receive, keep, and pay homage to the sutra with flowers, scents, necklaces, sandal powder, unguents, incense, flags, canopies, and music, burning various kinds of lamps—ghee lamps, oil lamps, lamps of scented oil, lamps of oil of *campaka* flowers, lamps of oil of *vārshika* flowers, and lamps of oil of *udumbara* flowers, such hundreds of thousands of kinds of offerings as these. Kuntī! You and your followers should protect such teachers of the Law as these."

The chapter concludes: "While this chapter of the *dhāraṇīs* was preached, sixty-eight thousand people attained the assurance of no rebirth."

CHAPTER 27

The Story of King Resplendent

THIS CHAPTER SEEMS TO RELATE a fantastic story from a remote world and time, but actually it teaches a lesson that applies to our daily lives. First, it concerns religion in the family, which here is presented as the problem of a father and his sons who believe in different faiths. The problem of a father who believes in a mistaken faith and his sons who have faith in a right religion, and the attitude of the mother, who must deal with both father and sons, is one common in today's society.

The story also concerns the problem of the faith that those who are in a position of leadership should hold. In today's society, freedom of religion is guaranteed to every individual, and no authority can deprive him of such freedom. The religious beliefs of those who are in positions of authority inevitably exert an influence upon many other people, even though it is a private matter of personal faith. The actions of King Resplendent suggest this problem to us. King Resplendent and his two sons renounced the world. In our time, religion and daily life are not considered to be in opposition but are regarded as compatible. If we take literally the royal sons' renunciation of the world and the king's abdication of his throne, we are liable to misinterpret this story. The renunciation of the world by the two princes, who were in easy circumstances, indicates the idea that mental peace through one's spiritual life is far more important than satisfaction in material life. The story of King Resplendent's abdicating the throne in favor of his younger brother and entering religious life expresses the idea that the spiritual kingdom established in man's mind is far more worthy than the worldly power of a king.

We should not interpret the words "renunciation of the world" literally but should take them as meaning the conversion of man's spiritual life.

Proceeding to the substance of this chapter, let us first trace the story of King Resplendent and then discuss the important words and terms.

At that time the Buddha addressed the great assembly: "Of yore, in a former eon, infinite, boundless, and inconceivable *asaṃkhyeya kalpas* ago, there was a buddha named Thunder Voice Constellation King of Wisdom, Tathāgata, Arhat, Samyaksaṃbodhi, whose domain was named Adorned with Radiance, and whose *kalpa* was named Joyful Sight. Under the spiritual rule of that buddha there was a king named Resplendent. The wife of that king was called Pure Virtue, who had two sons, one named Pure Treasury, the other named Pure-Eyed. Those two sons possessed great supernatural power, blessedness, and wisdom, and had for long devoted themselves to the ways in which bodhisattvas walk, that is to say, donation *pāramitā*, keeping the precepts *pāramitā*, perseverance *pāramitā*, assiduity *pāramitā*, meditation *pāramitā*, wisdom *pāramitā*, tactfulness *pāramitā*, benevolence, compassion, joy, indifference, and the thirty-seven kinds of aids to the Way—all these they thoroughly understood. They had also attained the bodhisattva contemplation—the pure contemplation, the sun constellation contemplation, the pure light contemplation, the pure color contemplation, the pure illumination contemplation, the ever resplendent contemplation, and the contemplation of the treasury of great dignity, in which contemplations they were thoroughly accomplished.

"Then that buddha, desiring to lead King Resplendent and having compassion for the living, preached this Law-Flower Sutra. Meanwhile the two sons, Pure Treasury and Pure-Eyed, went to their mother and, putting together their ten-fingered hands, spoke to her, saying: 'We beg you, mother, to go and visit the Buddha Thunder Voice Constellation King of Wisdom. We also would wait on, approach, serve, and worship him. Wherefore? Because that buddha among the host of gods and men is preaching the Law-Flower Sutra, and we ought to hear it.' The mother replied to her sons: 'Your father believes in the heretics and is deeply attached to the Brahman law. Do you go and speak to your father that he may go with us.' Pure Treasury and Pure-Eyed, putting together their ten-fingered hands, said to their mother: 'We are sons of the Law-king, though born in this home of heretical views.' The mother spoke to her sons, saying: 'You should have sympathy for your father, and show him some supernatural deed so that seeing it his mind will become clear and he will perhaps permit us to go to that buddha.'

"Thereupon the two sons, with a mind for their father, sprang up into the sky, seven *tāla* trees high, and displayed many kinds of supernatural deeds, walking, standing, sitting, and lying in the sky; the upper part of their bodies emitting water, the lower emitting fire, or the lower emitting water and the upper emitting fire; or enlarging themselves till they filled the sky, and again appearing small, or small and again appearing large; then vanishing from the sky and suddenly appearing on the earth, or entering into the earth as into water, or walking on water as on the earth; displaying such various supernatural deeds, they led their father, the king, to cleanse his mind to faith and discernment.

"When their father saw his sons possessed of such supernatural powers he was greatly delighted at so unprecedented an experience and with joined hands saluted his sons, saying: 'Who is your master? Whose pupils are you?' The two sons replied: 'Great king! That Buddha Thunder Voice Constellation King of Wisdom, who is now under the seven-jeweled Bodhi tree, seated on the throne of the Law, preaching abroad the Law-Flower Sutra in the midst of the world-host of gods and men—he is our master, we are his pupils.' The father then said to his sons: 'I also would now like to see your master; let us go together.'

"On this the two sons descended from the sky, went to their mother, and with folded hands said to her: 'Our father the king, has now believed and understood, and been able to set his mind on Perfect Enlightenment. We have done a buddha-deed for our father. Be pleased, mother, to permit us to leave home and under that buddha pursue the Way.'

"Then the two sons, desiring again to announce their wish, said to their mother in verse:

'Be pleased, mother, to release us
To leave home and become *śramaṇas.*
Hard it is to meet the buddhas,
And we would be followers of a buddha.
As the blossom of the *udumbara,*
Even harder is it to meet a buddha,
And hard it is to escape from hardships.
Be pleased to permit us to leave home.'

"Then the mother spoke, saying: 'I grant you permission to leave home; and why? Because a buddha is hard to meet.'

"On this the two sons said to their parents: 'Good, father and mother! We beg that you will now go to the Buddha Thunder Voice Constellation King of Wisdom, approach him, and pay him homage. Wherefore? Because a buddha is as hard to meet as an *udumbara* flower, or as the one-eyed tortoise that meets the hole in the floating log.[1] But we, richly blessed through a former lot, have met the Buddha-law in this life. Therefore, father and mother, listen to us and let us go forth from home. Wherefore? Because buddhas are hard to meet and the occasion is also hard to encounter.'

"At that juncture all the eighty-four thousand court ladies of King Resplendent became capable of receiving and keeping this Law-Flower Sutra. The Bodhisattva Pure-Eyed had for long been thorough in the Law-Flower contemplation. The Bodhisattva Pure Treasury had for infinite hundreds of thousands of myriads of *koṭis* of *kalpas* been thorough in the contemplation of free from evil paths, which sought to lead all the living away from all evil states of existence. The queen of that king had attained the contemplation of assemblage of buddhas and was able to know the secret resources of buddhas. Thus did the two sons with tact wisely convert their father, bringing his mind to believe, discern, and delight in the Buddha-law.

"Thereupon King Resplendent accompanied by his ministers and retinue, Queen Pure Virtue accompanied by her fine court ladies and retinue, and the two sons of that king, accompanied by forty-two thousand people, at once set out together to visit the buddha. Arriving and prostrating themselves at his feet, they made procession around the buddha three times and then withdrew to one side.

"Then that buddha preached to the king, showing, teaching, profiting, and rejoicing him, so that the king was greatly delighted. Then King Resplendent and his queen unloosed the necklaces of pearls worth hundreds and thousands from their necks and threw them upon the buddha, which in the sky were transformed into a four-columned jeweled tower; on the tower was a large jeweled couch spread with hundreds of thousands of myriads of celestial coverings, on which was the buddha sitting cross-legged, emitting a great ray of light. Whereupon King Resplendent reflected thus: 'Rare, dignified, extraordinary is the buddha's body, perfect in its supreme, refined coloring!'

1. According to Indian legend, in the ocean there lives a blind tortoise infinite *kalpas* old, who rises to the surface once every hundred years. In the ocean there is also a floating log with only one hole. What are the chances of their meeting?

"Then the Buddha Thunder Voice Constellation King of Wisdom addressed the four groups, saying: 'You see this King Resplendent standing before me with folded hands? This king, having become a *bhikshu* within my rule, and being zealous in observing the laws which aid the Buddha-way, shall become a buddha entitled Śālendra Tree King, whose domain will be named Great Luster, and his *kalpa* named Great High King. This Buddha Śālendra Tree King will have countless bodhisattvas and countless *śrāvakas,* and his domain will be level and straight. Such will be his merits.'

"The king at once made over his domain to his younger brother; the king together with his queen, two sons, and retinue forsook his home and followed the Way under the rule of that buddha. Having forsaken his home, for eighty-four thousand years the king was ever diligent and zealous in observing the Wonderful Law-Flower Sutra, and after these years passed attained the contemplation of adorned with all pure merits.

"Whereupon he arose in the sky to a height of seven *tāla* trees and said to that buddha: 'World-honored One! These my two sons have already done a buddha-deed by their supernatural transformations, turning my heretical mind, establishing me in the Buddha-law, and causing me to see the World-honored One. These two sons are my good friends, for out of a desire to develop the roots of goodness planted in my former lives and to benefit me, they came and were born in my home.'

"Thereupon the Buddha Thunder Voice Constellation King of Wisdom addressed King Resplendent, saying: 'So it is, so it is, it is as you say. Any good son or good daughter, by planting roots of goodness, will in every generation obtain good friends, which good friends will be able to do buddha-deeds, showing, teaching, profiting, and rejoicing him, and causing him to enter into Perfect Enlightenment. Know, great king! A good friend is the great cause whereby men are converted and led to see the buddha and aroused to Perfect Enlightenment. Great king! Do you see these two sons? These two sons have already paid homage to buddhas sixty-five times the hundreds of thousands of myriads of *koṭis* of *nayutas* of the sands of the Ganges, waiting upon and revering them; and among those buddhas received and kept the Law-Flower Sutra, having compassion for the living with their false views, and establishing them in right views.'

"King Resplendent thereupon descended from the sky and said to the buddha: 'World-honored One! Rare indeed is the sight of the *tathāgata;* by his merits and wisdom the protuberance on his head shines brilliantly; his eyes are wide open and deep blue; the tuft between his eyebrows is white as the pearly moon; his teeth are white, even, close, and ever shining; his lips are red and beautiful as *bimba* fruit.' Then, when King Resplendent had extolled that buddha's so many merits, countless hundreds of thousands of myriads of *koṭis* of them, with all his mind he folded his hands before the *tathāgata* and again addressed that buddha, saying: 'Unprecedented is the World-honored One. The Tathāgata's teaching is perfect in its inconceivable and wonderful merits. The moral precepts which he promulgates are comforting and quickening. From this day onward I will not again follow my own mind, nor beget false views, nor a haughty, angry, or any other sinful mind.' Having uttered these words, he did reverence to the buddha and went forth."

Finishing this story, the Buddha said to the great assembly: "What is your opinion? This King Resplendent—could he be any other person? He is indeed the present Bodhisattva Flower Virtue. That Queen Pure Virtue is the Bodhisattva Shining Splendor now in the presence of the Buddha, who out of compassion for King Resplendent and his people was born amongst them. These two sons are the present Medicine King Bodhisattva and Medicine Lord Bodhisattva. Those Bodhisattvas Medicine King and Medicine Lord, having perfected such great merits, under countless hundred thousand myriad *koṭis* of buddhas, planted virtuous roots and perfectly attained qualities of goodness beyond conception. If there be anyone who is acquainted with the names of these two bodhisattvas, gods and men in all the world will pay him homage."

The chapter closes with these words: "While the Buddha preached this chapter, 'The Story of King Resplendent,' the eighty-four thousand people departed from impurity and separated themselves from uncleanliness, and acquired pure spiritual eyes in regard to spiritual things.

Let us now consider the important points of this story. First, we must think of the true meaning of the two sons' showing their father many kinds of supernatural deeds. This does not mean that they became able to display supernatural deeds by means of the Buddha's teachings, nor that they stimulated their father's curiosity by showing him such deeds. Their performing various supernatural deeds means that they completely changed their character and their daily lives by studying and believing the Buddha's teachings. Their showing their father supernatural deeds thus means nothing but the fact that before their father they proved the true value of the Buddha's teachings by their deeds and led him to be aroused to the aspiration for Perfect Enlightenment.

When we lead others to the teachings of the Buddha, none will follow us only through hearing us praise the teachings. We must clearly show them the reason that the Buddha's teachings are worshipful. It is important for us to explain the content of the teachings. We must elucidate the teachings to others' satisfaction according to their level of understanding, sometimes simply, sometimes theoretically, sometimes by using parables, and sometimes in the light of modern science.

LIVING EVIDENCE IS NECESSARY TO LEAD OTHERS. The quickest and simplest way to lead others to the Buddha's teachings is to justify the teachings by our own practice of them. Our first consideration is to show others living evidence—"I have changed in this way since believing in the Buddha's teachings and practicing them." There is no more powerful and direct a way of leading others. However, we cannot show such living evidence to those whom we seldom see during the limited time we have together unless we have decisive evidence, such as recovery from disease or a favorable change in our circumstances. On the other hand, members of a family living together can sense clearly even little changes in one's everyday actions and attitudes. If sons or daughters change through believing in the Buddha's teachings, their parents will notice a great change in their speech, their attitude toward their parents, brothers, and sisters, and their attitude those outside the family. Such evidence will certainly influence each member of the family.

Conversely, in leading members of one's family to the teachings, however repeatedly we explain to them their content and however much our explanation may satisfy them intellectually, it will not lead to any practical result unless we change our attitudes in our daily lives. We can spout fine words to outsiders, but we betray our true selves in the family. When a member of our family sees us acting contrary to what we say, he stops listening to our words and criticizes us: "The teaching may be good, but I can't possibly believe it so long as you as a believer act like that."

It would seem to be easy for us to lead the members of our families to the Buddha's teachings, but in reality it is most difficult. We find it especially difficult in cases where a son leads his father to the teachings or a wife her husband. Both father and husband hold authority in the family. Unlike a young son, who has little experience in worldly affairs and is single-minded, older men have gained experience in the ways of the world and stubbornly hold to their opinions. They separate themselves from their juniors by relating their wide experience to their selfish ideas. Therefore, even if they feel the teachings to be basically good, they cannot bring themselves to believe in them, much less act on them. Although nothing of King Resplendent's character was described, he may be considered a model of the typical father.

The two royal sons regretted that their father believed in the heretics and was deeply attached to his deluded ideas. But their wise mother never told her sons to urge their father openly to visit the Buddha Thunder Voice Constellation King of Wisdom because she foresaw that such attempts would produce the opposite result. Nor did she say she would intercede between her husband and sons. This is because she did not think it permissible for her, with her lukewarm attitude, to act as an intermediary in the serious problem of faith. The wise mother suggested instead that her sons show their father concrete evidence of the results of their practice of their faith.

King Resplendent was a good father. When he saw the evidence of faith shown by his sons, he recognized it with good grace. He had a flexible mind. Most fathers, shown such impressive evidence, will criticize it on one pretext or another, will try to catch the speaker out in some trivial mistake, and will not abandon their stubborn ideas and mistaken beliefs. Although they may be inwardly impressed by striking evidence of the results of faith, they will hesitate to admit it, feeling that to do so would diminish their prestige. The attitude of King Resplendent is admirable indeed. It is only right for one to follow the truth obediently when he meets with it; that is the natural reaction, but a person who is in the position of the father of a family or the king of a country does not usually act as firmly and frankly as King Resplendent. He had no scruples about saving face as king and was not attached to the throne but respected the truth and its transmitter. This is revealed by the king's calling his two sons his good friends.

The words "good friends" include the meaning not only of friendship but also of leadership. King Resplendent, who as a king exercised power over his country and as a father had absolute authority in the family, had such a frank and open mind as to be able to call his sons good friends. We cannot help admiring his attitude of venerating only the truth. Thus the problem of faith was solved in a satisfactory way in the family of King Resplendent. All the members of the king's family joined the faith of Buddhism and entered into religious lives with joy and exaltation. His was an ideal family.

THE IDEAL STATE OF FAITH FOR LEADERS. Another important point is that the faith of King Resplendent influenced his ministers and retinue, and the people of his country. We must seriously consider to what a great extent the faith of a leader effects the people serving under him. Faith is basically an individual matter and is apt to become impure when it interferes in secular power, such as politics. Faith should be maintained through one's mental attitude, which comes from the depth of one's mind, and then power should be exercised on this foundation. This is the ideal relationship of faith and temporal power.

We must not jump to the conclusion that the great influence that the faith of a leader has on the people under him is sure to be manifested by some kind of power. Some may think that people in such a subordinate position would follow the faith of their leader in order to flatter or from obsequiousness. But this is a disingenuous way of thinking. It is quite natural that if a man is a leader who is really respected and trusted by others, his actions will exert a great influence upon many people.

All people are equal before the teachings of the Buddha. As the Buddha's disciple, a commoner is equal to a great king. In terms of potential influence, however, a commoner's resolution to attain Perfect Enlightenment cannot be compared to a king's. Therefore the Buddha Thunder Voice Constellation King of Wisdom was delighted with King Resplendent's resolution to seek Perfect Enlightenment and immediately predicted his Perfect Enlightenment.

A leader who has a large following should believe in a right faith. But he should not force it on those under him. If he can handle them with virtue and dignity based on his faith, his fine personality will surely have a good effect on them, just as perfume smells good to everyone in its vicinity.

This chapter thus touches upon many important problems of actual life. We should take the various characters in the story as models, appreciating their attitudes according to their positions. The attitude of King Resplendent is an example of that which a person engaged in politics or national leadership should take toward the truth; the deeds of the two royal sons, Pure Treasury and Pure-Eyed, show how children may open their parents' eyes to faith (this also applies to a wife's opening her husband's eyes to it); Queen Pure Virtue is a model of the attitude a mother ought to take in mediating between progressive sons and a conservative father in order to promote the truth.

CHAPTER 28

Encouragement of the Bodhisattva Universal Virtue

THE BODHISATTVA MAÑJUŚRĪ represents the Buddha's wisdom, while the Bodhisattva Universal Virtue typifies the Buddha's practice. These two bodhisattvas are regarded as a pair: the wisdom represented by Mañjuśrī symbolizes one's realization of the truth and the practice typified by Universal Virtue one's practice of the truth.

We have already studied the realization of the truth in the Law of Appearance. In the assembly of the Buddha's preaching of this Law, the Bodhisattva Mañjuśrī was the representative of the Buddha's disciples. We learned the entity of the truth in the "one chapter and two halves"—the latter half of chapter 15, all of chapter 16, and the first half of chapter 17. In this assembly, the Bodhisattva Maitreya represented the disciples. We were taught the practice of the truth through the example of the practices of various bodhisattvas in the latter half of chapter 17 and the following chapters, which are defined as the concluding part of the Law of Origin. Finally, the Bodhisattva Universal Virtue appears in the last chapter of the Lotus Sutra. There is a deep significance to his appearance at this particular point.

FOUR PRACTICES OF THE BODHISATTVA UNIVERSAL VIRTUE. As shown in this chapter and in the Sutra of Meditation on the Bodhisattva Universal Virtue, the so-called closing sutra of the Lotus Sutra, the Bodhisattva Universal Virtue is perfect in the following four practices:

1. He himself practices the teachings of the Lotus Sutra.
2. He protects the teachings from all persecutions.

3. He bears witness to the merits obtained by one who practices the teachings and to the punishments suffered by one who slanders the teachings or persecutes its followers.
4. He proves that even those who violate the teachings can be delivered from their sins if they are sincerely penitent.

The Bodhisattva Universal Virtue encourages those who have finished hearing the Lotus Sutra and are beginning a new life with these words: "I vow to do these four practices as a conclusion of the practices of the Lotus Sutra. Try to be assiduous in your practices, without anxiety."

His encouragement may be likened to the commencement address that the principal of a school delivers to the graduating students. They are now leaving school, carrying with them the truth that they have studied there. When they go out into the world, they are often puzzled as to how best to use what they have studied at school. Sometimes they have the unfortunate experience of having the truth they have studied denied by others, or even of being persecuted for it. "Whenever you have trouble, you can visit your old school. We will try to prove that the truth is not wrong. Moreover, we will teach you how you should apply the truth to each practical problem. If you fail in anything, we will show you how to overcome your failure." In this way, the principal's commencement speech guarantees the graduates the protection of their activities even after leaving school. No farewell speech of encouragement could be more inspiring than this.

Let us now proceed to the content of chapter 28.

At that time the Bodhisattva Universal Virtue, with sovereign supernatural power, majesty, and fame, accompanied by great bodhisattvas, unlimited, infinite, incalculable, came from the eastern quarter; the countries through which he passed were shaken, jeweled lotus flowers rained down, and countless hundred thousand myriad *koṭis* of kinds of music were performed. Encompassed also by a great host of countless gods, dragons, *yakshas, gandharvas, asuras, garuḍas, kiṃnaras, mahoragas,* men, nonhuman beings, and others, all displaying majestic supernatural powers, he arrived at Mount Gṛdhrakūṭa in the *sahā*-world.

Nonhuman beings, such as gods, dragons, and *yakshas,* have often been mentioned as part of the assembly listening to the Buddha's preaching since their first appearance at the beginning of the Sutra of Innumerable Meanings. However, the description in this chapter differs from those in preceding chapters. The difference lies in the expression "all displaying majestic supernatural powers." This means that their listening to the Buddha's preaching of the Lotus Sutra has caused them to attain and manifest majestic supernatural powers.

Having prostrated himself before Sakyamuni Buddha, the Bodhisattva Universal Virtue made procession around him to the right seven times and addressed the Buddha, saying: "World-honored One! I, in the domain of the Buddha Jeweled Majestic Superior King, hearing afar that the Law-Flower Sutra was being preached in this *sahā*-world, have come with this host of countless, infinite hundred thousand myriad *koṭis* of bodhisattvas to hear and receive it. Be pleased, World-honored One, to preach it to us, and tell how good sons and good daughters will be able to obtain this Law-Flower Sutra after the extinction of the Tathāgata."

The Buddha replied to the Bodhisattva Universal Virtue: "If any good son or good daughter acquires the four requisites, such a one will obtain this Law-Flower Sutra after the extinction of the Tathāgata: first, to be under the guardianship of the buddhas; second, to plant the roots of virtue; third, to enter the stage of correct concentrations; fourth, to aspire after the salvation of all the living. Any good son or good daughter who acquires such four requisites will certainly obtain this sutra after the extinction of the Tathāgata."

THE FOUR REQUISITES. The phrase "such a one will obtain this Law-Flower Sutra" means not only that one encounters the teaching but that he who has encountered it understands it sufficiently to apply it. To understand the sutra sufficiently is to obtain its true merits. The Buddha teaches us here the four requisites necessary in order to obtain the Lotus Sutra after his extinction. We must understand these well because they are essential points of faith.

The first requisite is to be under the guardianship of the buddhas. This means having an absolutely unshakable faith in being under the protection of the buddhas. In other words, it means one's establishment of faith. However thoroughly a person may understand the Lotus Sutra from a doctrinal point of view, he cannot apply it to his practical life if he does not establish faith in his mind.

The second requisite is to plant the roots of virtue. This means continually doing good deeds in one's daily life. The phrase "roots of virtue" indicates a good mind, which is the foundation of one's attaining enlightenment. To plant such a good mind means not only to sow seeds of goodness but also to nurture them by watering and fertilizing them.

By what is one's good mind fostered? To do good deeds is the first consideration. Man's practice of good deeds is caused by his good mind, and at the same time his practice of good deeds fosters his good mind. These two, man's good deeds and his good mind, form a cycle of being, reinforcing each other for constant improvement. Like the chicken and the egg, we cannot say which comes first or causes the other. The two are inseparable, each contingent on the other.

Indeed, when we practice anything good even for mere form's sake, we feel somehow pleased and refreshed. Our good mind is growing within us. One's intention does not necessarily precede one's deeds. Evidence of this is what happens when we force a smile in looking at ourselves in the mirror. If we repeat this, we come to feel light at heart. On the contrary, when we make a poor attempt at suppressing tears before a mirror, we begin to feel more melancholy. To return to the subject, to practice good deeds daily is to plant the roots of virtue in one's mind—to begin really to comprehend the teachings of the Lotus Sutra.

The third requisite is to enter the stage of correct concentration. This means entering the group of those who have decided to do good. In Buddhism, groups of people are divided into three types: those having correct, incorrect, and unsettled concentration. The first group, with correct concentration, is that of those who have decided to do good, for example, the assembly of people who believe in a correct religion. The second group, with incorrect concentration, is that of those who have decided to do evil, for instance, a gang of pickpockets or hoodlums. The third group, with unsettled concentration, is that of those who vacillate between good and evil. Most assemblies of ordinary people belong to this third group, in which they are inclined toward good but are so unstable that they may turn to evil at any moment.

We believers must join the group having correct concentration. Needless to say, this is easier and better for us if we belong to a group of people who believe in the same faith than if we seek the Law in isolation. When we are in a group with correct concentration, we can encourage each other not to retrogress from a mental state that we have attained with great effort. Even if we do not speak of encouragement or nonretrogression, we are linked mentally in a close relationship with each other just by discussing and listening to the Law together, and we can display the power of faith much more strongly than if we were alone. The third requisite, to enter the stage of correct concentration, teaches us this.

The fourth requisite is to aspire after the salvation of all the living. No explanation of this expression should be necessary at this point. The true attainment of buddhahood does not mean realization for one's own sake alone or being saved only from one's own suffering. The fundamental spirit of Mahāyāna Buddhism lies in the salvation of others as well as oneself and in the establishment of an ideal realm in this world. If we act contrary to this fundamental spirit, however assiduously we seek the Law and practice religious disciplines, such an effort will bear no fruit, nor will it lead us to the realization of the true merits of the Law.

The four requisites can be rephrased as follows:

1. Always to tell ourselves that we are caused to live by the Buddha.
2. Always to endeavor to practice good deeds.
3. Always to be part of a group of true believers.
4. Always to render service to others.

These four requisites must be regarded as most sacred teachings of the Buddha. They must also be considered as the culmination of the Buddha's teachings, revealing in plain words that although he has preached various difficult teachings heretofore, what is essential for all living beings is to devote themselves to the four requisites in their practice of the teachings. When those people who shrink from trying to fathom the profound and difficult teachings of the Lotus Sutra hear this simple explanation of the four requisites, they will surely feel encouraged.

When the Bodhisattva Universal Virtue, who represents the practice of the Lotus Sutra, was anxious as to how he should guide living beings in the age of degeneration, he was clearly taught the four requisites by the Buddha, and he must have been deeply moved by the Buddha's guidance.

Then the Bodhisattva Universal Virtue said to the Buddha: "World-honored One! In the latter five hundred years of the corrupt and evil age, whoever receives and keeps this sutra I will guard and protect, eliminate the anxiety of falling away, and give ease of mind, so that no spy shall find occasion—neither Māra, nor Māra-sons, nor Māra-daughters, nor Māra-people, nor Māra-satellites, nor *yakshas,* nor *rākshasas,* nor *kumbhāṇḍas,* nor *piśācakas,* nor *kṛityas,* nor *pūtanas,* nor *vetaḍas,* nor other afflicters of men—that none may find occasion. Wherever such a one walks or stands, reading and reciting this sutra, I will at once mount the six-tusked white elephant king and with a host of great bodhisattvas go to that place and, showing myself, will serve and protect him, comforting his mind, also thereby serving the Law-Flower Sutra."

We must take careful note of the expression, "showing myself, will serve and protect him, comforting his mind, also thereby serving the Law-Flower Sutra." Some people are apt to take it for granted that because they are believers in the Lotus Sutra, they are certain to be protected by the Buddha. No protection or merit will accrue to those who are apparently believers in the sutra but do not really practice its teachings. A good admonition is delivered in the phrase, "also thereby serving the Law-Flower Sutra."

Another expression, "I will at once mount the six-tusked white elephant king," indicates that the Bodhisattva Universal Virtue is contrasted with the Bodhisattva Mañjuśrī, who rides a lion. The lion is the symbol of realization of the truth. The lion, called the king of beasts, has control of the other animals and rouses awe in them. Therefore he can roam freely on the plain. Like the lion, the truth governs all things in the universe and is itself under the control of nothing. The truth is, so to speak, the king of the universe, and it appears freely in all phenomena.

On the other hand, the elephant represents great power of execution. Wherever this animal with his gigantic body forges ahead, nothing can check him. If there is a great tree in his path, he knocks it down. When he finds a rock in his way, he rolls it aside. When he fords a river or swamp, he walks steadily on the bottom. Therefore the elephant is the symbol of thorough practice.

The six tusks of the white elephant king that the Bodhisattva Universal Virtue rides symbolize the doctrine of the Six Perfections. This doctrine teaches us the practice of benefiting both oneself and others. The Bodhisattva Universal Virtue, who rides the six-tusked white elephant king as a messenger of the Buddha, and shows himself to all the living, is the symbol of the great man who removes all obstacles and unswervingly practices the Law.

The Bodhisattva Universal Virtue continued: "Wherever such a one sits, pondering this sutra, I will at once again mount the white elephant king and show myself to him. If such a one forgets be it but a single word or verse of the Law-Flower Sutra, I will teach it to him, read and recite it with him, and again cause him to master it."

The phrase "Wherever such a one sits, pondering this sutra" indicates the practice of meditation, one of the Six Perfections. Wherever anyone practices meditation, the Bodhisattva Universal Virtue mounts the white elephant and shows himself to the believer. This means that the bodhisattva appears in the believer's mind whenever he recalls the bodhisattva.

The words "If such a one forgets be it but a single word or verse of the Law-Flower Sutra, I will teach it to him" should be understood as meaning that if one cannot grasp the true meaning of the teaching in spite of much thought and meditation, he must first think of its practice. Then he can surely grasp the true meaning of the teaching. Since the Lotus Sutra is the teaching of the practice of the Law, if we forget its practice and only try to climb the mountain of its profound doctrine, we are sure to lose our way. If we then sit calmly and ponder the Lotus Sutra, which is after all the teaching of the practice of saving ourselves and others, we will immediately find the right way to the summit. The words of Universal Virtue quoted below then naturally follow: "Thereupon he who receives and keeps, reads and recites the Law-Flower Sutra on seeing me will greatly rejoice and renew his zeal. Through seeing me, he will thereupon acquire the contemplation and *dhāraṇīs* named the *dhāraṇī* of revolution,[1] the *dhāraṇī* of hundreds of thousands of myriads of *koṭis* of revolutions,[2] and the *dhāraṇī* of skill in Law-sounds;[3] such *dhāraṇīs* as these will he acquire.

"World-honored One! If in the latter age, in the last five hundred years of the corrupt and evil age, the *bhikshus, bhikshuṇīs, upāsakas,* and *upāsikās,* seekers, receivers and keepers, readers and reciters, or copiers desire to put in practice this Law-Flower Sutra, they must with single mind devote themselves to it for three times seven days. After the three times seven days are fulfilled, I will mount the six-tusked white elephant and, together with countless bodhisattvas surrounding me, appear before those people in the form all the living delight to see and preach to them, revealing, instructing, benefiting, and rejoicing them."

FORMING GOOD SPIRITUAL HABITS. We do not have to take literally the figure of three times seven days, but we should occasionally devote ourselves to a religious discipline for a fixed period. In today's busy world, lay devotees find it difficult to confine themselves in a mountain temple

1. This is interpreted as "revolution unhindered," meaning the contemplation of all phenomena as the void. It is the contemplation of the void.

2. This means to turn the void to phenomena, that is, to contemplate all phenomena as existing. It is the contemplation of existence.

3. This is the contemplation of the Middle Path, neither void nor existence, unifying the above two kinds of contemplation.

to practice religious discipline for an extended period. But for even a day—say, on Sunday—or for three days in succession when we can spare the time, we should try to forget all worldly affairs and positively devote ourselves to the study of the teaching, or meditation, or reciting and copying the sutra. Why is this necessary? Because, just as repeated deeds become a habit, thus we form good spiritual habits; repeated deep pondering or earnest thinking will become a habit of mind.

Let us suppose that we hear someone report, "Students marched through the streets in a demonstration, carrying banners and placards." Some people will immediately feel disapproving—"Ah, the students are demonstrating again!"—even though they do not know the reason for the demonstration. On the other hand, others may be glad: "Oh, good! Some trouble must be brewing." A teacher will worry about the education of young people when he hears of the demonstration. A stockbroker will immediately think of the potential influence of the demonstration on stock prices. All such attitudes are due to one's habit of mind.

When we try to forget worldly affairs for a fixed period of time and concentrate our mind on a single object, such a practice becomes a habit of the spirit. Suppose that a person continually thinks, "Others as well as myself are all caused to live by the Buddha," for three weeks. He will form the habit of immediately thinking on every occasion, "Wait a minute; he as well as myself is caused to live by the Buddha." The strength and persistence of such a habit differ according to how earnest our practice is, how thoroughly we maintain it, and how long we persevere. If we continuously think of something for an hour and then allow our attention to be distracted, our thinking will never become a habit. If we try to continue thinking deeply of only one thing for a day, such a mental tendency may continue for about a week. From the standpoint of forming religious habits, it is indeed enviable that people in Christian countries make a custom of going to church on Sundays.

Single-minded devotion to an object for three weeks causes us to build up a good spiritual habit (although an outstanding person may receive a great revelation from God or the Buddha, that is an exceptional case). Those who are too busy to set aside a specific period of time should try to devote themselves to the profound teachings of the Buddha for even an hour a day as often as possible. Such repetition also forms a habit of the spirit.

The purified mind and religious exaltation that we feel after devoting ourselves to religious disciplines can be compared to the feeling of seeing the Bodhisattva Universal Virtue mounted on the white elephant.

The bodhisattva continued: "Moreover I will give them *dhāraṇīs,* and obtaining these *dhāraṇīs,* no human or nonhuman beings can injure them, nor any woman beguile them. I myself also will ever protect them. Be pleased, World-honored One, to permit me to announce these *dhāraṇī* spells."

The words "no human or nonhuman beings" refers to money or material things. If these things are sought and used for the right purpose, they never become an obstacle to faith, but an excessive desire for them warps one's mind. The expression "nor any woman beguile them" reflects the male standpoint, but the converse expression applies from a female standpoint. The expression simply indicates the opposite sex. Conjugal love between husband and wife is, of course, an important factor in forming the individual home and society. However, people have a tendency to become attached to such love and to become selfish in their affections. They are apt to ignore the much larger love they should have for all human beings. Others abandon themselves to sexual love for many people and perform dishonest acts. If they always think of the practice of the Bodhisattva Universal Virtue, their minds, which are liable to be led astray by desire for the opposite sex, can return to the right way, full of a generous and pure human love.

Then in the presence of the Buddha the Bodhisattva Universal Virtue uttered the following spell: *"Adaṇḍe daṇḍapati daṇḍāvartani daṇḍakuśale daṇḍasudhāri sudhāri sudhārapati buddhapaśyane dhāraṇī āvartani saṃvartani saṃghaparīkshite saṃghanirghātani dharmaparīkshite sarvasattvarutakauśalyānugate siṃhavikrīḍite [anuvarte vartani vartāli svāhā].*

"World-honored One! If there be any bodhisattvas who hear these *dhāraṇīs,* they shall be aware of the supernatural power of Universal Virtue. If while the Law-Flower Sutra proceeds on its course through Jambudvīpa there be those who receive and keep it, let them reflect thus: 'This is all due to the majestic power of Universal Virtue.' If any receive and keep, read and recite, rightly remember it, comprehend its meaning, and practice it as preached, let it be known that these are doing the works of Universal Virtue and have deeply planted good roots under numberless countless buddhas, and that their heads will be caressed by the hands of the *tathāgatas.* If they only copy it, these when their life is ended will be born in the heaven Trāyastriṃśa; on which occasion eighty-four thousand nymphs, performing all kinds of music, will come to welcome them, and they, wearing seven-jeweled crowns, will joy and delight among those beautiful nymphs; how much more those who receive and keep, read and recite, rightly remember it, comprehend its meaning, and practice it as preached! If there be any who receive and keep, read and recite it, and comprehend its meaning, when their life is ended the hands of a thousand buddhas will be proffered, that they fear not, neither fall into any evil destiny, but go straight to Maitreya Bodhisattva in the Tushita heaven, where Maitreya Bodhisattva, possessed of the thirty-two signs, is surrounded by a host of great bodhisattvas and has hundreds of thousands of myriads of *koṭis* of nymph-followers, amongst whom they will be born."

The phrase "their heads will be caressed by the hands of the *tathāgatas*" means that the believers are praised and trusted by the Buddha. It implies their greatest joy, a life full of religious exaltation. The next phrase, "If they only copy it, these when their life is ended will be born in the heaven Trāyastriṃśa," means that they will not reach the mental stage of religious exaltation but, suffering removed from their minds, will lead happy and peaceful lives.

The phrase "go straight to Maitreya Bodhisattva" means that the believers will be possessed of compassionate minds like Maitreya Bodhisattva and will become assiduous in the daily practices of the bodhisattvas. Three bodhisattvas who represent three important points in the teachings of the Lotus Sutra have already been mentioned (see page 213): the Bodhisattva Mañjuśrī (the Buddha's wisdom), the Bodhisattva Maitreya (his compassion), and the Bodhisattva Universal Virtue (his practice). The Bodhisattva Maitreya, who typifies the compassion of the Buddha, is regarded as the successor to the Tathāgata Sakyamuni. In Japanese he is called *fusho no bosatsu,* "the bodhisattva who will succeed to (the Buddha's) position." Maitreya is believed to be living in Tushita heaven, waiting for the time when he will come down to this *sahā*-world and become the next Buddha as the result of his practice. In a sense, he can be said to be the highest bodhisattva. For this reason, he is possessed of the thirty-two signs of the Buddha. The phrase "go straight to Maitreya Bodhisattva" also means that if anyone continues the practice of compassion in the *sahā*-world, he will feel the worth of life and a great joy in life.

Universal Virtue continued: "Such are their merits and benefits. Therefore the wise should with all their mind themselves copy it, or cause others to copy it, receive and keep, read and recite, rightly remember it, and practice it as preached. World-honored One! I now by my supernatural power will guard and protect this sutra so that, after the extinction of the Tathāgata, it may spread abroad without cease in Jambudvīpa."

THE HIGHEST REACH OF RELIGIOUS EXALTATION. Then Sakyamuni Buddha extolled the bodhisattva: "It is well, it is well, Universal Virtue, that you are able to protect and assist this sutra, and bring happiness and weal to the living in many places. You have already attained inconceivable merits and profound benevolence and compassion. From a long distant past have you aspired to Perfect Enlightenment and been able to make this supernatural vow to guard and protect this sutra. And I, by my supernatural power, will guard and protect those who are able to receive and keep the name of the Bodhisattva Universal Virtue. Universal Virtue! If there be any who receive and keep, read and recite, rightly remember, practice, and copy this Law-Flower Sutra, know that such are attending on Sakyamuni Buddha as if they were hearing this sutra from the Buddha's mouth; know that such are paying homage to Sakyamuni Buddha; know that the Buddha is praising them—'Well done'; know that the heads of such are being caressed by the hands of Sakyamuni Buddha; know that such are covered by the robe of Sakyamuni Buddha."

The phrase "such are covered by the robe of Sakyamuni Buddha" refers to the mental state in which one is firmly held in the Buddha's arms; this is the highest reach of religious exaltation and peace of mind. No obstacle can harm the faith or practice of one who has reached this stage.

The Buddha continued: "Such as these will not again be eager for worldly pleasure, nor be fond of heretical scriptures and writings, nor ever again take pleasure in intimacy with such men or other evil persons, whether butchers, or herders of boars, sheep, fowl, and dogs, or hunters, or panderers. But such as these will be right-minded, have correct aims, and be auspicious."

We must take careful note of the words "Such as these will not again be eager for worldly pleasure." This means not that it is bad for people to lead happy and pleasant lives but that it is bad for them to be attached to happiness and pleasure and to crave them. It is also not bad to study the heretical scriptures and may indeed be useful in helping one to widen one's mental vision and become better able to distinguish between truth and nontruth. But one must not be attached to heretical scriptures because if he is, he will lose sight of the truth.

The word "writings" means "poetry" in the Sanskrit text, but here this word can be taken to mean secular literature in general. This means not that literature is bad for people but that it is bad for them to be engrossed in decadent and popular literature so that their minds become clouded and unable to see the truth.

We must be especially careful not to misunderstand the following words: "nor ever again take pleasure in intimacy with such men, or other evil persons, whether butchers, or herders of boars, sheep, fowl, and dogs, or hunters, or panderers." This means not that we must not associate with such people but that we should not be affected by the atmosphere they generate. If we, who desire to spread the Buddha's teachings abroad in this world, should exclude those who are engaged in such occupations, we would grossly violate the Buddha's true intention to save all living beings. We would be unable to obtain the spiritual happiness described in the words: "But such as these will be right-minded, have correct aims, and be auspicious."

The following sentence also appears: "Such will not be harassed by the three poisons, nor be harassed by envy, pride, haughtiness, and arrogance." The three poisons are desire, anger, and foolishness, which are considered to be the original poisons leading ordinary people to degeneration. "Pride" means egoism, self-pride. "Haughtiness" means false arrogance, thinking oneself correct in spite of one's wrong conduct. "Arrogance" means haughtiness and conceit due to one's illusion of having completely understood what one has hardly comprehended at all. Envy is generated by one's feeling of inferiority, while pride, haughtiness, and arrogance are born from a false sense of superiority. These kinds of pride and arrogance are caused by looking at things from a distorted, self-centered point of view. Those who have truly understood the Buddha's teachings and been able to obtain a right view of things will never succumb to such warped thinking.

The Buddha also declares: "Such will be content with few desires and able to do the works of Universal Virtue." The words "few desires" mean having little desire for worldly things. Here "desires" include not only the desire for money and material things but also the wish for status and fame. It also indicates seeking the love and service of others.

A person who has attained the mental stage of deep faith has very few desires and is indifferent to them. We must note carefully that though such a person is indifferent to worldly desires, he is very eager for the truth, that is, he has a great desire for the truth. To be indifferent to the truth is to be slothful in life. To be content with few desires means to be satisfied with little material gain, that is, not to feel discontented with one's lot and to be free from worldly cares. Nevertheless, this does not mean to be unconcerned with self-improvement but to do one's best in one's work without discontent. Such a person will never be ignored by those around him. But even if he were, he would feel quite happy because he lives like a king from a spiritual point of view.

The Buddha continued: "Universal Virtue! After the extinction of the Tathāgata, in the latter five hundred years, if anyone sees one who receives and keeps, reads and recites the Law-Flower Sutra, he must reflect thus: 'This man will ere long go to the wisdom floor, destroy the host of Māra, attain Perfect Enlightenment, and rolling onward the Law-wheel, beating the Law-drum, blowing the Law-conch, and pouring the rain of the Law, shall sit on the lion throne of the Law amid a great assembly of gods and men.' "

We can interpret this passage as describing Sakyamuni Buddha's attainment of Buddhahood under the Bodhi tree and his work of spreading the Law. We can also regard it as the Buddha's assurance that anyone who receives and keeps, reads and recites the Lotus Sutra will definitely attain buddhahood.

The Buddha then declared: "Universal Virtue! Whoever in future ages shall receive and keep, read and recite this sutra, such persons will no longer be greedily attached to clothes, bed things, drink, food, and things for the support of life; whatever they wish will never be in vain, and in the present life they will obtain their blessed reward."

The words "things for the support of life" mean the necessities of life. The words "whatever they wish will never be in vain" imply that their desire for all others to be perfectly happy will surely be fulfilled. Therefore "in the present life they will obtain their blessed reward." Not to be greedily attached to material life indicates an unselfish mind. The desire for all others to be perfectly happy comes from one's compassionate and selfless mind. Anyone with such a generous mind will surely obtain a reward in the present life because his own life will become filled with joy, mental peace, and hope.

THE SIN OF SLIGHTING AND SLANDERING BELIEVERS. The Buddha continued: "Suppose anyone slights and slanders them, saying, 'You are only madmen, pursuing this course in vain with never a thing to be gained.' The doom for such sin as this is blindness generation after generation. If anyone takes offerings to and praises them, he will obtain visible reward in the present world."

The words "The doom for such sin as this is blindness generation after generation" are a figurative expression of the depth of sin. Why is it such a great sin to slight and slander believers in the Lotus Sutra? This is because the speech and conduct of such a person hinders the turning of the wheel of the Law. Suppose a person constantly steals and swindles. It is beyond doubt that such deeds violate the five precepts of Buddhism and that such evildoing brings trouble to others. However, as evil deeds bring inevitable retribution, such a person is eventually convicted and pays the penalty for his evil deeds. Other people, seeing this, think: "Evil deeds will be discovered sooner or later. We must never do such things."

Such evil deeds have an influence in a comparatively narrow sphere. On the other hand, although speech and conduct obstructing the spread of the Righteous Law are not punishable by law, they exert a great influence on man's environment. If the Law is spread in every direction, innumerable people will obtain its merits and will abandon the life of evil through it. When a person stops others from spreading the Law, he commits a grave sin. His sin is invisible, but its influence is so inestimable that Buddhists call this "cutting off the Law-seed," a figure of speech that well expresses the gravity of slandering the Law.

The terrible recompense received as the result of slandering the Law is described figuratively as follows: "Again, if anyone sees those who receive and keep this sutra, and proclaims their errors and sins, whether true or false, such a one in the present life will be smitten with leprosy. If he ridicules them, generation after generation his teeth will be sparse and missing, his lips vile, his nose flat, his hands and feet contorted, his eyes asquint, his body stinking and filthy with evil scabs and bloody pus, dropsical and short of breath, and with every evil disease."

Then the World-honored One said: "Therefore, Universal Virtue, if one sees those who receive and keep this sutra, he should stand up and greet them from afar just as if he were paying reverence to the Buddha." With these words, the Buddha concluded his preaching of the Lotus Sutra, extending over the two places and three assemblies. He says that because the whole body of the Tathāgata is included in the teachings of the Lotus Sutra, those who believe and practice the teachings should be revered just like the Buddha. We should accept these words of the Buddha with gratitude.

Chapter 28 closes with the following words: "While this chapter of the encouragement of the Bodhisattva Universal Virtue was being preached, innumerable incalculable bodhisattvas equal to the sands of the Ganges attained to the *dhāraṇī* of the hundreds of thousands of myriads of *koṭis* of revolutions, and bodhisattvas equal to the atoms of a three-thousand-great-thousandfold world became perfect in the Way of Universal Virtue.

"When the Buddha preached this sutra, Universal Virtue and the other bodhisattvas, Śāriputra and the other *śrāvakas,* and the gods, dragons, human and nonhuman beings, and all others in the great assembly greatly rejoiced together and, taking possession of the Buddha's words, made salutation to him and withdrew."

Part Three: The Sutra of Meditation on the Bodhisattva Universal Virtue

The Sutra of Meditation on the Bodhisattva Universal Virtue

IT IS NOT KNOWN when and by whom this sutra, the so-called closing sutra of the Lotus Sutra, was first recited. The first man to do so, however, was surely a great person. This is because the Sutra of Meditation on the Bodhisattva Universal Virtue is so profound that it is considered to be the continuation of the Buddha's preaching of the Lotus Sutra, and because it teaches us how we should actually apply the Lotus Sutra in our daily lives. This method is repentance. The Sutra of Meditation on the Bodhisattva Universal Virtue teaches us the true meaning and method of repentance so thoroughly that it is commonly called "the Sutra of Repentance."

TWO MEANINGS AND METHODS OF REPENTANCE. The word "repentance" has two meanings and applications. One is repentance in a general sense, the confession of our own past physical and mental misdeeds. Our minds are purified by such repentance, and because it frees us from a sense of sin, we feel greatly refreshed. There are cases too numerous to mention of Risshō Kōsei-kai members recovering from disease or being freed from family problems just by confessing their misdeeds before fellow members in group-counseling sessions. Psychoanalysts, especially those practicing depth analysis, have applied this principle in helping many disturbed people.

Recovery from illness is, of course, dependent on our repentance, whose true value consists in disclosing our buddha-nature. Through the Lotus Sutra, we have become able to understand that all people have the buddha-nature equally. Through this sutra we are awakened to the fact that all of us possess the invaluable gem of the buddha-nature. In fact, the Lotus Sutra can be said to be the teaching of the disclosing of our buddha-nature.

Immediately after it is mined, a gemstone is covered with mud and does not display its true brilliance. It does not disclose its nature as an invaluable gem until the mud is washed off. Washing the mud from the gem is like the first stage of repentance. The surface of our buddha-nature is covered with various illusions acquired in the course of our daily lives. Through repentance we remove such illusions from our buddha-nature, just as water washes the mud from a precious stone.

Repentance toward others is the first stage of repentance. We must pass through this stage, but as our faith deepens, eventually we come to repent all our sins directly toward the Buddha. We examine ourselves as being imperfect and mistaken, study the Buddha's teachings more deeply, meditate on Buddhist doctrines, and elevate ourselves ever higher. This is the secret principle of repentance; this is true repentance.

This second stage of repentance is the practice through which we constantly polish the gem of our buddha-nature. A gem does not reveal its brilliance even after the mud has been washed from it. Its surface is coated with mineral deposits, and it cannot display its intrinsic brilliance until polishing removes such impurities from its surface. The same thing can be said of our buddha-nature. The second stage of repentance is the practice by which we polish our buddha-nature.

As stated in chapter 20 of the Lotus Sutra, "The Bodhisattva Never Despise," in order to disclose the buddha-nature of others it is important for us to revere it, that is, to pay respect to everyone. We must have a much stricter attitude toward ourselves. We must constantly cleanse and polish our buddha-nature. We feel pain when we pour cold water on our body and scrub vigorously with a wet towel in order to cleanse it. When we dare to cleanse and polish our buddha-nature despite pain, it begins to emit a brilliant light.

The Sutra of Meditation on the Bodhisattva Universal Virtue teaches concretely and thoroughly the meaning and practice of the second stage of repentance. Let us now proceed to the sutra itself.

Once, when the Buddha was staying at the two-storied assembly hall in the Great Forest Monastery at Vaiśālī, he addressed all the *bhikshus,* saying: "After three months, I shall surely enter *parinirvāṇa.*" Thereupon the honored Ānanda rose from his seat, straightened his garments, and with joined palms and folded hands he made procession around the Buddha three times and saluted him, kneeling with folded hands, and attentively gazed at the Tathāgata without turning away his eyes for a moment. The elder Mahā-Kāśyapa and the Bodhisattva-Mahāsattva Maitreya also rose from their seats, and with folded hands saluted and gazed up at his honored face. Then the three great leaders with one voice spoke to the Buddha, saying: World-honored One! After the extinction of the Tathāgata, how can living beings raise the mind of the bodhisattva, practice the sutras of Great Extent, the Great-vehicle, and ponder the world of one reality with right thought? How can they keep from losing the mind of supreme buddhahood? How, without cutting off their earthly cares and renouncing their five desires, can they also purify their organs and destroy their sins? How, with the natural pure eyes received at birth from their parents and without forsaking their five desires, can they see things without any impediment?"

The Buddha said to Ānanda: "Do you listen to me attentively! Do you listen to me attentively, ponder, and remember it! Of yore on Mount Gṛdhrakūṭa and in other places the Tathāgata had already extensively explained the way of one reality. But now in this place, to all living beings and others in the world to come who desire to practice the supreme Law of the Great-vehicle, and to those who desire to learn the works of Universal Virtue and to follow the works of Universal Virtue, I will now preach the Law that I have entertained. I will now widely make clear to you the matter of eliminating numerous sins from anyone who may happen to see or not see Universal Virtue. Ānanda! The Bodhisattva Universal Virtue was born in the eastern Pure Wonder Land, whose form I have already clearly and extensively explained in the Sutra of Miscellaneous Flowers. Now I, in this sutra, will briefly explain it again.

"Ānanda! If there be *bhikshus, bhikshuṇīs, upāsakas, upāsikās,* the eight groups of gods and dragons, and all living beings who recite the Great-vehicle, practice it, aspire to it, delight to see the form and body of the Bodhisattva Universal Virtue, have pleasure in seeing the stupa of the Buddha Abundant Treasures, take joy in seeing Sakyamuni Buddha and the buddhas who emanated from him, and rejoice to obtain the purity of the six organs, they must learn this meditation. The merits of this meditation will make them free from all hindrances and make them see the excellent forms. Even though they have not yet entered into the contemplation, just because they recite and keep the Great-vehicle they will devote themselves to practicing it, and after having kept their minds continuously on the Great-vehicle for a day or three times seven days, they will be able to see Universal Virtue; those who have a heavy impediment will see him after seven times seven days; again, those who have a heavier one will see him after one birth; again, those who have a much heavier one will see him after two births; again, those who have a still heavier one will see him after three births. Thus the retribution of their karma is various and not equal. For this reason, I preach the teaching variously."

Several important points are included in the above passage. Especially noteworthy is the following expression: "How, without cutting off their earthly cares and renouncing their five desires, can they also purify their organs and destroy their sins?"

The ideal of our practice is to cut off our earthly cares and renounce our five desires. Though such an ideal should be demanded of Buddhist monks, it is much more difficult for lay devotees to pursue because they must maintain their faith while living and working in secular society. In their circumstances, situations caused by the five desires occur continually, and they are surrounded by people and situations that cause them earthly cares. Ideally speaking, they should become free from all desires, but in actuality, to expect them to reach such a spiritual level immediately is asking too much. Nevertheless, as long as they are believers, they must aim toward their ultimate ideal. But how should they bridge the gap between their ideal and actuality? This sutra teaches the answer to this practical question, which believers face in the age of degeneration.

Running through the entire sutra is a concept expressed in the following words: "Even though they have not yet entered into the contemplation, just because they recite and keep the Great-vehicle they will devote themselves to practicing it. . . ." Only a person who has undergone considerable religious training can concentrate his mind on a single object and enter directly into the mental stage of discriminating the real state of all things. One who has not yet attained such a mental stage, by reciting and keeping the Great-vehicle wholeheartedly, will approach the practice of the Bodhisattva Universal Virtue little by little. Some will approach the practice of this bodhisattva after three times seven days, while others will do so only after three births. In either case, the assurance of approaching such a mental stage step by step is a great encouragement to us in the age of degeneration.

VIRTUES AND POWERS OF THE BODHISATTVA UNIVERSAL VIRTUE. The Buddha said: "The Bodhisattva Universal Virtue is boundless in the size of his body, boundless in the sound of his voice, and boundless in the form of his image. Desiring to come to this world, he makes use of his free transcendent powers and shrinks his statue to the small size of a human being. Because the people in Jambudvīpa have the three heavy hindrances, by his wisdom-power he appears transformed as mounted on a white elephant. The elephant has six tusks and, with its seven legs, supports its body on the ground. Under its seven legs seven lotus flowers grow. The elephant is white as snow, the most brilliant of all shades of white, so pure that even crystal and the Himalaya Mountains cannot be compared with it. The body of the elephant is four hundred and fifty *yojanas* in length and four hundred *yojanas* in height. At the ends of the six tusks there are six bathing pools. In each bathing pool grow fourteen lotus flowers exactly the size of the pools. The flowers are in full bloom as the king of celestial trees. On each of these flowers is a precious daughter whose countenance is red as crimson and whose radiance suprasses that of nymphs. In the hand of that daughter there appear, transformed of themselves, five harps, and each of them has five hundred musical instruments as accompaniment. There are five hundred birds including ducks, wild geese, and mandarin ducks, all having the color of precious things, arising among flowers and leaves. On the trunk of the elephant there is a flower, and its stalk is the color of a red pearl. That golden flower, is still a bud and has not yet blossomed. Having finished beholding this matter, if one again further repents one's sins, meditates on the Great-vehicle attentively with entire devotion, and ponders it in his mind incessantly, he will be able to see the flower instantly blossom and light up with a golden color. The cup of the lotus flower is a cup of *kimśuka* gems with wonderful Brahma jewels, and the stamens are of diamond. A transformed buddha is seen sitting on the petals of the lotus flower with a host of bodhisattvas sitting on the stamens of the lotus flower. From the eyebrows of the transformed buddha a ray of light is sent forth and enters the elephant's trunk. This ray, having the color of a red lotus flower, emanates from the elephant's trunk and enters its eyes; the ray then emanates from the elephant's eyes and enters its ears; it then emanates from the elephant's ears, illuminates its head, and changes into a golden cup. On the head of the elephant there are three transformed men: one holds a golden wheel, another a jewel, and yet another a diamond-pounder. When he raises the pounder and points it at the elephant, the latter walks a few steps immediately. The elephant does not tread on the ground but hovers in the air seven feet above the earth, yet the elephant leaves on the ground its footprints, which are altogether perfect, marking the wheel's hubs with a thousand spokes. From each mark of the wheel's hub there grows a great lotus flower, on which a transformed elephant appears. This elephant also has seven legs and walks after the great elephant. Every time the transformed elephant raises and brings down its legs, seven thousand elephants appear, all following the great elephant as its retinue. On the elephants' trunk, having the color of a red lotus flower, there is a transformed buddha who emits a ray from his eyebrows. This ray of light, as mentioned before, enters the elephant's trunk; the ray emanates from the elephant's trunk and enters its eyes; the ray then emanates from the elephant's eyes and again enters its ears; it then emanates from the elephant's ears and reaches its head. Gradually rising to the elephant's back, the ray is transformed into a golden saddle which is adorned with the precious seven. On the four sides of the saddle are pillars of the precious seven, which are decorated with precious things, forming a jewel pedestal. On this pedestal there is a lotus-flower stamen bearing the precious seven, and that stamen is also composed of a hundred jewels. The cup of that lotus flower is made of a great jewel.

"On the cup there is a bodhisattva called Universal Virtue who sits cross-legged. His body, pure as a white jewel, radiates fifty rays of fifty different colors, forming a brightness around his head. From the pores of his body he emits rays of light, and innumerable transformed buddhas are at the ends of the rays, accompanied by the transformed bodhisattvas as their retinue."

Here, in cadenced sentences, are listed the virtues and the powers possessed by the Bodhisattva Universal Virtue. Brief explanations of important words and expressions follow.

The expression "The Bodhisattva Univerrsal Virtue is boundless in the size of his body, boundless in the sound of his voice, and boundless in the form of his image" indicates the unfathomed store of virtues and powers possessed by the Bodhisattva Universal Virtue. If this bodhisattva looked completely different from the people of this *sahā*-world when he appeared to instruct them, they would feel ill at ease with him and would feel unable to follow him. Therefore he appears in human form and as such should be regarded as the personification of the "principle of half a step" discussed on page 125.

The "three hindrances" refer to the three evils of arrogance, envy, and covetousness. Because people in the *sahā*-world are burdened with these three heavy hindrances, they should be guided through practices that relate to their own environment. This is the work of the Bodhisattva Universal Virtue. For this reason he rides a white elephant, which is symbolic of Buddhist practice and represents purity. The six tusks of the elephant suggest the purity of the six sense organs: eye, ear, nose, tongue body, and mind. The elephant's seven legs suggest the absence of the seven evils of killing, stealing, committing adultery, lying, ill speaking, improper language, and a double tongue.

Next, the body of the elephant and its beauty are described in various ways. This symbolizes how beautiful and valuable it is to practice the Buddha's teachings. Then is mentioned a precious daughter appearing on each of the lotus flowers that grow from the bathing pools at the end of the elephant's tusks, along with many musical instruments and colorful birds. This means that if anyone practices the Buddha's teachings, those around him will be naturally purified.

Another description reads: "On the trunk of the elephant there is a flower, and its stalk is the color of a red pearl. That golden flower is still a bud and has not yet blossomed." This symbolizes the state in which one's faith is not perfect, like a flower bud, and in which one has not yet attained enlightenment. However, if one is aware of this state, further repents his sins, and pursues wholeheartedly the bodhisattva practice, he will be able to see the flower of faith instantly blossom and shine with a golden color. A transformed buddha is seen sitting on the petals of this lotus flower. From the eyebrows of the transformed buddha a ray of light beams forth and enters the elephant's eyes; the ray emanates from its eyes and enters its ears; the ray then emanates from the elephant's ears and illuminates its head. This indicates the idea that the Buddha's mind dwells in each action of whoever practices his teachings.

The following expression then occurs: "On the head of the elephant there are three transformed men: one holds a golden wheel, another a jewel, and yet another a diamond-pounder." The golden wheel typifies the leadership with which one can freely govern people, the jewel indicates the power of wisdom with which one can discern the real state of all things, and the diamond-pounder signifies the power of refuting erroneous views, with which power one can smite the wicked and their sins. Anyone who practices the Buddha's teachings gradually comes to be endowed with such powers.

"When he raises the pounder and points it at the elephant, the latter walks a few steps immediately." This expression means that one's practice of the teaching begins with the repentance of smiting his own evils and sins. "The elephant does not tread on the ground but hovers in the air seven feet above the earth, yet the elephant leaves on the gound its footprints, which are altogether perfect, marking the wheel's hubs with a thousand spokes." This figure of speech teaches that while one proceeds toward his ideal (the elephant that hovers in the air), he will actually receive the results of his right practice.

"From each mark of the wheel's hub there grows a great lotus flower, on which a transformed elephant appears. This elephant also has seven legs and walks after the great elephant. Every time the transformed elephant raises and brings down its legs, seven thousand elephants appear, all following the great elephant as its retinue." This means that as a person practices the Buddha's teachings, he influences many other people, causing them to believe the teachings, and these people gradually come to practice the teachings by following the example of those senior to them in the faith.

The Buddha continued: "The elephant walks quietly and slowly, and goes before the follower of the Great-vehicle, raining large jeweled lotus flowers. When this elephant opens its mouth, the precious daughters, dwelling in the bathing pools on the elephant's tusks, play music whose sound is mystic and extols the way of one reality in the Great-vehicle." The phrase "extols the way of one reality in the Great-vehicle" means that anyone who devotes himself to the practice of the Buddha's teachings will surely attain enlightenment.

"Having seen this wonder, the follower rejoices and reveres, again further reads and recites the profound sutras, salutes universally the innumerable buddhas in all direction, makes obeisance to the stupa of the Buddha Abundant Treasures and Sakyamuni Buddha, and salutes Universal Virtue and all the other great bodhisattvas. Then the follower makes this vow: 'Had I received some blessings through my former destinies, I could surely see Universal Virtue. Be pleased, honored Universal Fortune, to show me your form and body!" The expression "the follower makes this vow" means not only to make a vow but also to make all possible efforts to realize it.

The efforts one should make in order to realize his vow are indicated in the following words: "Having thus made his vow, the follower must salute the buddhas in all directions six times day and night, and must practice the law of repentance; he must read the Great-vehicle sutras and recite them, think of the meaning of the Great-vehicle and reflect on its practice, revere and serve those who keep it, see all people as if he were thinking of the Buddha, and treat living beings as if he were thinking of his father and mother." This teaches us that when a person makes all possible efforts to realize his vow, he will become deeply conscious of the honorable virtues and works of the Bodhisattva Universal Virtue.

"When he finishes reflecting thus, the Bodhisattva Universal Virtue will at once send forth a ray of light from the white hair-circle, the sign of a great man, between his eyebrows. When this ray is displayed, the body of the Bodhisattva Universal Virtue will be dignified as a mountain of deep gold, so well ordered and refined that it possesses all the thirty-two signs. From the pores of his body he will emit great rays of light which will illuminate the great elephant and turn it to the color of gold. All the transformed elephants will also be colored gold and all transformed bodhisattvas will be colored gold. When these rays of light shine on the innumerable worlds in the eastern quarter, they will turn them all to the color of gold. So, too, will be it in the southern, western, and northern quarters, in the four intermediate directions, in the zenith and the nadir.

"Then in each quarter of all directions there is a bodhisattva who, mounting the six-tusked white elephant king, is exactly equal to Universal Virtue. Like this, by his transcendent powers, the Bodhisattva Universal Virtue will enable all the keepers of the Great-vehicle sutras to see transformed elephants filling the infinite and boundless worlds in all directions."

This passage indicates that one good deed (a transformed elephant) produces more good deeds (more transformed elephants). Good deeds increase by geometrical progression, until finally the worlds in all directions are filled with good deeds. This idea teaches us that the believers in this sutra can gain the deep conviction of the realization of an ideal society in this *sahā*-world

"At this time the follower will rejoice in body and mind, seeing all the bodhisattvas, and will salute them and speak to them, saying: 'Great merciful and great compassionate ones! Out of compassion for me, be pleased to explain the Law to me!' When he speaks thus, all the bodhisattvas and others with one voice will each explain the pure Law of the Great-vehicle sutras and will praise him in various verses. This is called the first stage of mind, in which the follower first meditates on the Bodhisattva Universal Virtue."

SEEING UNIVERSAL VIRTUE IN A DREAM. The Buddha continued: "Thereupon, when the follower, having beheld this matter, keeps the Great-vehicle in mind without forsaking it day and night, even while sleeping, he will be able to see Universal Virtue preach the Law to him in a dream. Exactly as if the follower were awake, the Bodhisattva will console and pacify the follower's mind, speaking thus: 'In the sutras you have recited and kept, you have forgotten this word or have lost this verse.' Then the follower, hearing Universal Virtue preach the profound Law, will comprehend its meaning and keep it in his memory without forgetting it."

"To see Universal Virtue in a dream," a metaphor that appears often in this chapter, has two meanings. First, it means that though when one is awake he can try consciously to keep the Great-vehicle in mind, when asleep he cannot control his mind (the subconscious mind). Even if he wants to have a certain dream or determines not to talk in his sleep, it is impossible for him to control his mind and actions while asleep. However, if a person truly deepens his faith, he can see the Bodhisattva Universal Virtue preach the Law to him even in his dreams. This bodhisattva will appear before him in a dream and will encourage him, saying, "You will be able to attain the mental stage of a bodhisattva," and will give him careful advice, saying, "You have forgotten this word or have misunderstood this verse."

Secondly, "to see Universal Virtue in a dream" suggests the following meaning: a person who has truly deepened his faith can frequently realize the truth of the teaching by intuition. This phrase indicates the mental state of having obtained a revelation from the Buddha or of having attained enlightenment by oneself. However, the revelation that a person obtains from the Buddha by intuition is just like a dream; it is not materialized. When he examines his revelation thoroughly and is confident that it is certainly the truth when judged from every angle, it will be beneficial to him and will be a teaching worthy of transmitting to others.

The Buddha continued: "As the follower does like this day by day, his mind will gradually acquire spiritual profit. The Bodhisattva Universal Virtue will cause the follower to remember the buddhas in all directions. According to the teaching of Universal Virtue, the follower will rightly think and remember everything, and with his spiritual eyes he will gradually see the eastward buddhas, whose bodies are gold colored and very wonderful in their majesty. Having seen one buddha, he will again see another buddha. In this manner, he will gradually see all the buddhas everywhere in the eastern quarter, and because of his profitable reflection, he will universally see all the buddhas in all directions."

The words "east" and "eastward" have often appeared in preceding chapters of this book. East is the direction where the sun rises, thus implies the beginning of everything. On the other hand, west is the direction where the sun sets, and so implies the end of everything. The latter idea is associated with the belief within Buddhism that anyone who invokes the name of Amita Buddha with a sincere heart can achieve rebirth in the Pure Land in the west. In this chapter, the phrase "see the eastward buddhas" suggests the time when a person has just begun to practice a true faith.

The expression, "Having seen one buddha, he will again see another buddha," means that though the truth is one, the believer will be able to see many manifestations of the truth in succession if he realizes one truth. If a person can see all the buddhas everywhere in the eastern quarter, he will become able to reflect on himself much more profitably and will thus become able to see all the buddhas in all directions. Attaining this state of mind, his spiritual joy will deepen. The Buddha teaches us in the next sentence, however, that even though the believer can reach such a mental stage, he should not be satisfied with it but should further repent his sins. Through this we understand that the practice of true repentance must not be limited only to the confession of our sins. Repentance is not limited to washing our buddha-nature but includes polishing it.

Specifically, how should we practice repentance? The Buddha teaches us to have the following mental attitude even if we attain the higher state of mind mentioned above: "Having seen the buddhas, he [the follower] conceives joy in his heart and utters these words: 'By means of the Great-vehicle, I have been able to see the great leaders. By means of their powers, I have also been able to see the buddhas. Though I have seen these buddhas, I have yet failed to make them plain. Closing my eyes I see the buddhas, but when I open my eyes, I lose sight of them.' After speaking thus, the follower should universally make obeisance, prostrating himself down to the ground toward the buddhas in all directions. Having made obeisance to them, he should kneel with folded hands and should speak thus: 'The buddhas, the world-honored ones, possess the ten powers, the fearlessnesses, the eighteen unique characteristics, the great mercy, the great compassion, and three kinds of stability in contemplation. These buddhas, forever remaining in this world, have the finest appearance of all forms. By what sin do I fail to see these buddhas?' "

The words "closing my eyes I see the buddhas, but when I open my eyes I lose sight of them" describe an experience that every Buddhist will recognize.

THE TEN POWERS. The ten powers mean perfect comprehension in the ten fields of knowledge that belong only to the Buddha. A brief explanation of these powers will be given here because it is very important for believers in the Lotus Sutra to understand them. The ten powers attributed to the Buddha are: (1) the power to know right and wrong states, (2) the power to know the consequences of karma, (3) the power to know all meditations and contemplations, (4) the power to know the various higher and lower capabilities of living beings, (5) the power to know what living beings understand, (6) the power to know the basic nature and actions of living beings, (7) the power to know the causes and effects of living beings in all worlds, (8) the power to know the results of karmas in past lives, (9) the power to know by supernatural insight, and (10) the power of being free from all error, or infallibility in knowledge.

The eighteen unique characteristics are the eighteen merits that belong only to the Buddha. These special characteristics are: (1) faultlessness in body, (2) faultlessness in speech, (3) faultlessness in mind and thought, (4) no unsteadiness of mind, (5) impartiality, (6) perfect resignation, (7) imperishable aspiration to save all living beings, (8) unfailing zeal, (9) unfailing memory of all teachings of all buddhas past, present, and future, (10) unfailing contemplation, (11) unfailing wisdom, (12) unfailing freedom from all hindrances, (13) all bodily deeds being in accord with wisdom, (14) all deeds of speech being in accord with wisdom, (15) all deeds of thought being in accord with wisdom, (16) unhindered knowledge of the past, (17) unhindered knowledge of the future, and (18) unhindered knowledge of the present.

The three kinds of stability in contemplation mean the attitudes that the Buddha assumes toward all living beings by dividing them into three types: the first stability in contemplation (*sho-nenjo*), the second stability in contemplation (*ni-nenjo*), and the third stability in contemplation (*san-nenjo*).

When living beings praise the virtue of the Buddha, he applauds their praising him rather than the fact that he is being prasied. This attitude is the first stability in contemplation. When anyone blasphemes or curses the Buddha, the Buddha never feels sorrowful toward such a person or becomes angry with him because he is being reviled. With his deep compassion, he instead feels pity for such a person. This attitude is the second stability in contemplation. Among the many living beings, some take refuge in the Buddha's teachings, but others do not. The Buddha never discriminates between these two kinds of living beings but has compassion equally for all of them because they all possess the buddha-nature. This attitude, with which the Buddha treats all living beings without discrimination, is the third stability in contemplation. These three attitudes are attributed only to the Buddha, but we must follow the Buddha's example when we spread his teachings.

The Buddha continued: "Having spoken thus, the follower should again practice further repentance. When he has achieved the purity of his repentance, the Bodhisattva Universal Virtue will again appear before him and will not leave his side in his walking, standing, sitting, and lying, and even in his dreams will ceaselessly preach the Law to him. After awaking from his dreams, this person will take delight in the Law. In this manner, after three times seven days and nights have passed, he will thereupon acquire the *dhāraṇī* of revolution. Through acquiring the *dhāraṇī*, he will keep in his memory without losing it the wonderful Law that the buddhas and bodhisattvas have taught. In his dreams, he will also see constantly the Seven Buddhas of the past, among whom only Sakyamuni Buddha will preach the Law to him. These world-honored ones will each praise the Great-vehicle sutras. At that time the follower will again further rejoice and universally salute the buddhas in all directions. After he salutes the buddhas in all directions, the Bodhisattva Universal Virtue, abiding before him, will teach and explain to him all karmas and environments of his former lives, and will cause him to confess his black and evil sins. Turning to the world-honored ones, he should confess his sins with his own mouth."

ONLY SAKYAMUNI BUDDHA PREACHES THE LAW. A very important expression occurs in the above paragraph: "In his dreams, he will also see constantly the Seven Buddhas of the past, among whom only Sakyamuni Buddha will preach the Law to him." It is true that all the buddhas of the past are sacred, but among them only Sakyamuni Buddha preaches his teachings to us in the *sahā*-world. Through these teachings we can know the truth that has existed unchanged since the infinite past. Therefore, we have only to take refuge in Sakyamuni Buddha; through doing so we also take refuge in the other buddhas (the various manifestations of the truth).

To see the buddhas in one's dreams means that one gains a vague awareness of existing together with the buddhas. Gaining such an indistinct awareness, one feels still more spiritual joy and universally salutes the buddhas in all directions. Then the Bodhisattva Universal Virtue will appear before the believer and will teach him that he has been unable to see the buddhas because of all the karmas and environments of his former lives, and will cause him to confess his sins. This means that the believer awakens to his own sins through the Bodhisattva Universal Virtue. This is the repentance that one practices before the buddhas. The expression "he should confess his sins with his own mouth" implies the repentance that he performs mentally.

The Buddha continued: "After he finishes confessing his sins, then he will attain the contemplation of revelation of buddhas to men.[1] Having attained this contemplation, he will plainly and clearly see the Buddha Akshobhya and the kingdom of Wonderful Joy in the eastern quarter. In like manner he will plainly and clearly see the mystic lands of the buddhas in each of all directions. After he has seen the buddhas in all directions, he will have a dream: on the elephant's head is a diamond-man pointing his diamond-pounder at the six organs; after pointing it at the six organs, the Bodhisattva Universal Virtue will preach to the follower the law of repentance to obtain the purity of the six organs. In this way the follower will do repentance for a day or three times seven days. Then by the power of the contemplation of revelation of buddhas to men and by the adornment of the preaching of the Bodhisattva Uni-

1. The contemplation in which the buddhas always reveal themselves to everyone.

versal Virtue, the follower's ears will gradually hear sounds without impediment, his eyes will gradually see things without impediment, and his nose will gradually smell odors without impediment. This is as preached extensively in the Wonderful Law-Flower Sutra.[2] Having obtained the purity of the six organs, he will have joy of body and mind and freedom from evil ideas, and will devote himself to this Law so that he can conform to it. He will again further acquire a hundred thousand myriad *koṭis* of the *dhāraṇī* of revolution and will again see extensively a hundred thousand myriad *koṭis* of innumerable buddhas. These world-honored ones will all stretch out their right hands, laying them on the head of the follower, and will speak thus: 'Good! Good! You are a follower of the Great-vehicle, an aspirant to the spirit of great adornment, and one who keeps the Great-vehicle in his mind. When of old we aspired to buddhahood, we were also like you. Do you be zealous and do not lose the Great-vehicle! Because we practiced it in our former lives, we have now become the pure body of the All Wise. Do you now be diligent and not lazy! These Great-vehicle sutras are the Law-treasury of the buddhas, the eyes of the buddhas from all directions in the past, present, and future, and also the seed which produces the *tathāgatas* in the past, present, and future. He who keeps these sutras has the body of a buddha and does the work of a buddha; know that such is the apostle sent by the buddhas; such is covered by the robes of the buddhas, the world-honored ones; such is a true Law-heir of the buddhas, the *tathāgatas*. Do you practice the Great-vehicle and do not cut off the Law-seeds! Do you now attentively behold the buddhas in the eastern quarter!'

"When these words are spoken, the follower sees all the innumerable worlds in the eastern quarter, whose lands are as even as one's palm, with no mounds or hills or thorns, but with ground of lapis lazuli and with gold to bound the ways. So, too, is it in the worlds of all directions. Having finished beholding this matter, the follower will see a jewel tree which is lofty, wonderful, and five thousand *yojanas* high. This tree will always produce deep gold and white silver, and will be adorned with the precious seven; under this tree there will be a jeweled lion throne of itself; the lion throne will be two thousand *yojanas* high and from the throne will radiate the light of a hundred jewels. In like manner, from all the trees, the other jewel thrones, and each jewel throne will radiate the light of a hundred jewels. In like manner, from all the trees, the other

2. See page 296.

jewel thrones, and each jewel throne will emerge of themselves five hundred white elephants on which all the Bodhisattvas Universal Virtue mount."

The diamond-pounder was originally a kind of weapon used in ancient India. In Buddhism it is regarded as a symbol of the *bodhi*-mind because it can destroy all defilement and false views. Therefore the phrase "pointing his diamond-pounder at the six organs" indicates the believer's power to destroy the defilement of his six organs. It bears witness to the fact that his mind is moving toward repentance. The expression "the Bodhisattva Universal Virtue will preach to the follower the law of repentance to obtain the purity of the six organs" means that through his practice of repentance the believer can gain the awareness of being purified in body and mind.

Another noteworthy expression is: "When these words are spoken, the follower sees all the innumerable worlds in the eastern quarter. . . ." This indicates that if everyone deeply understands the holiness of the Buddha's teachings and the preaching of them (jewel trees and jewel thrones), and if the Buddha's teachings spread universally, all people, society, and the whole world will become beautiful.

"Thereupon the follower, making obeisance to all Universal Virtues, should speak thus: 'By what sin have I only seen jewel grounds, jewel thrones, and jewel trees, but have been unable to see the buddhas?' "

In the passage preceding this occurred the following words: "because of his profitable reflection, he will universally see all the buddhas in all directions." Readers may think that this statement conflicts with the words "By what sin have I . . . been unable to see the buddhas?" but the two are not really inconsistent. Even if one has gained a strong awareness of existing together with the buddhas, if he has not yet attained the mental stage of a bodhisattva this awareness will fade as soon as something else catches his interest and distracts him.

"When the follower finishes speaking thus, he will see that on each of the jewel thrones there is a world-honored one who is sitting on a jewel throne and very wonderful in his majesty. Having seen the buddhas, the follower will be greatly pleased and will again further recite and study the Great-vehicle sutras. By the power of the Great-vehicle, from the sky there will come a voice, praising and saying: 'Good! Good! Good son! By the cause of the merit you have acquired practicing the Great-vehicle, you have seen the buddhas. Though you have now been able to see the buddhas, the world-honored ones, you cannot yet see Sakyamuni Buddha, the buddhas who emanated from him, and the stupa of the Buddha Abundant Treasures.'

"After hearing the voice in the sky, the follower will again zealously recite and study the Great-vehicle sutras. Because he recites and studies the sutras of Great Extent, the Great-vehicle, even in his dreams he will see Sakyamuni Buddha staying on Mount Gṛdhrakūṭa with the great assembly, preaching the Law-Flower Sutra and expounding the meaning of one reality. After the teaching is preached, with repentance and a thirsting heart of hope, he will wish to see the Buddha. Then he must fold his hands, and kneeling in the direction of Mount Gṛdhrakūṭa, he must speak thus: 'Tathāgata, the world's hero forever remains in this world. Out of compassion for me, please reveal yourself to me.' "

Readers may wonder why the follower says, "Please reveal yourself to me," in spite of the declaration that "even in his dreams he will see Sakyamuni Buddha staying on Mount Gṛdhrakūṭa." This is because the follower wants to grasp the true intention of the Buddha more clearly and more deeply. When he reflects thus and pictures Mount Gṛdhrakūṭa to himself, he can see the following beautiful scene:

"After he has spoken thus, he will see Mount Gṛdhrakūṭa adorned with the precious seven and filled with countless *bhikshus*, *śrāvakas*, and a great assembly; this place is lined with jewel trees, and its jewel ground is even and smooth; there a wonderfully jeweled lion throne is spread. On it sits Sakyamuni Buddha, who sends forth from his eyebrows a ray of light, which shines everywhere throughout all directions of the universe and passes through the innumerable worlds in all directions. The buddhas emanated from Sakyamuni Buddha in all directions where this ray reaches assemble like a cloud at one time, and preach extensively the wonderful Law—as it is said in the Wonderful Law-Flower Sutra.[3] Each of these emanated buddhas, having a body of deep gold, is boundless in the size of his body and sits on his lion throne, accompanied by countless hundreds of *koṭis* of great bodhisattvas as his retinue. The practice of each bodhisattva is equal to that of Universal Virtue. So, too, is it in the retinue of the countless buddhas and bodhisattvas in all directions. When the great assembly have gathered together like a cloud, they will see Sakyamuni Buddha, who from the pores of his whole body emits rays of light in each of which a hundred *koṭis* of transformed buddhas dwell. The emanated buddhas will emit rays of light from the white hair-circles, the sign of a great man, between their eyebrows, streaming

3. See page 149.

on the head of Sakyamuni Buddha. Beholding this aspect, the emanated buddhas will also emit from all the pores of their bodies rays of light in each of which transformed buddhas, numerous as the atoms of the sands of the Ganges, abide."

The above paragraph contains four important descriptions. The first is that the buddhas emanated from Sakyamuni Buddha are seen through a ray of light emitted from his eyebrows. This means that if a person takes refuge in the Buddha's teachings, his mind will communicate with the minds of all the buddhas; in other words, if he realizes the truth taught by Sakyamuni Buddha, he will come to understand the true meaning of all the teachings. The second is that the buddhas emanated from Sakyamuni Buddha preach the same Law as preached in the Lotus Sutra. This proves that all the teachings are unified in the Lotus Sutra. The third is that the practice of each one of the countless hundreds of *koṭis* of great bodhisattvas is equal to the practice of the Bodhisattva Universal Virtue. This means that the holiness of a bodhisattva consists before all else in his practice. The fourth is that when rays of light emitted from the eyebrows of the emanated buddhas stream onto the head of Sakyamuni Buddha, the emanated buddhas emit from all the pores of their bodies rays of light in each of which innumerable transformed buddhas abide. This signifies that the Buddha's teachings spread limitlessly. The light of the truth reaches everywhere, and everything consonant with the truth shines by its reflected light. But anything that covers the truth with illusions and sins does not shine even if it receives the reflected light of the truth. Therefore, so long as a person does not remove illusions and sins from his mind by the practice of repentance, he remains spiritually base.

"Thereupon the Bodhisattva Universal Virtue will again emit the ray of light, the sign of a great man, between his eyebrows, and put it into the heart of the follower. After this ray has entered into his heart, the follower himself will remember that under the countless hundreds and thousands of buddhas in the past he received and kept, read and recited the Great-vehicle sutras, and he will himself plainly and clearly see his former lives. He will possess the very faculty of transcendent remembrance of former states of existence.[4] Immediately attaining a great enlightenment, he will acquire the *dhāraṇī* of revolution and a hundred thousand myriad *koṭis* of *dhāraṇīs*."

4. One of the six transcendent powers. These are mysterious powers of the Buddha and *arhats* that can be gained by meditation and wisdom.

"Immediately attaining a great enlightenment" does not mean that we can then end our practice of repentance. Nothing could be further from the truth. Even if we believe ourselves to have attained enlightenment, there is a great difference between the Buddha's enlightenment and ours. Therefore we must not neglect the practice of polishing our buddha-nature as long as we live.

SIX OBJECTS OF REFLECTION. The Buddha continued: "Rising from his contemplation, he will see before himself all the emanated buddhas sitting on lion thrones under all the jewel trees. He will also see the ground of lapis lazuli springing up from the lower sky like heaps of lotus flowers; between each flower there will be bodhisattvas, numerous as the atoms of the sands of the Ganges and sitting cross-legged. He will also see the bodhisattvas who emanated from Universal Virtue, extolling and expounding the Great-vehicle among their assembly.

"Then the bodhisattvas with one voice will cause the follower to purify his six organs. One bodhisattva's preaching will say: 'Do you reflect on the Buddha'; another's preaching will say: 'Do you reflect on the Law'; yet another's preaching will say: 'Do you reflect on the Saṃgha'; still another's preaching will say: 'Do you reflect on the precepts'; still another one's preaching will say: 'Do you reflect on gift-giving'; yet another's preaching will say: 'Do you reflect on the heavens.' And the preaching will further say: 'Such six laws are the aspiration to buddhahood and are the ones that beget the bodhisattvas. Before the buddhas, do you now confess your previous sins and repent them sincerely.' "

The bodhisattvas here tell the follower what to do in order to purify his six organs. This means that he examines and reflects upon his imperfections when comparing his own practices with those of the bodhisattvas as related in the Great-vehicle sutras. This should be regarded as a voice coming from the sky. The first voice orders the follower: "Do you reflect on the Buddha." This voice tells him: "You believe yourself to have taken refuge in the Buddha, but your taking refuge is not yet perfect. You will not become a really good believer unless you devote yourself much more to the worship of the Buddha." Another voice orders the follower: "Do you reflect on the Law." This voice says to him: "Do you flatter yourself that you are so assiduous that you have completely understood the Buddha's teachings? Are you not arrogant to think so? The teachings of the Buddha are very profound. Unless you study them very profoundly and have a deep understanding of them, you will not truly understand them."

Yet another voice orders the follower: "Do you reflect on the Saṃgha." This voice reproaches him: "The unity and harmony of believers are absolutely necessary for spreading the Buddha's teachings in this world. Did you strive for the realization of these two things essential to the Saṃgha? Is your endeavor sufficient? You should remove the selfishness from your mind and labor for the community of fellow believers."

Another voice asks the follower whether he keeps the precepts given by the Buddha or not; still another voice asks him whether he practices gift-giving or not; yet another voice asks him whether he has already attained the mental stage of the heavens, one perfectly free from illusion and suffering.

The voices further say that the follower will attain enlightenment when he is perfect in the six requisites—the Buddha, the Law, the Saṃgha, the precepts, gift-giving, and the heavens—and that the practice of these six requisites is the way to become a bodhisattva. Therefore the follower must confess his imperfections before the buddhas and sincerely practice repentance.

THE SINS OF ONE'S EYES. The spirit of repentance that the follower must maintain is shown clearly in the following words: "In your innumerable former lives, by reason of your organ of the eye, you have been attached to all forms. Because of your attachment to forms, you hanker after all dust.[5] Because of your hankering after dust, you receive a woman's body and you are pleasurably absorbed in all forms everywhere you are born age after age. Forms harm your eyes and you become a slave of human affections. Therefore forms cause you to wander in the triple world. Such fatigue of your wandering there makes you so blind that you can see nothing at all. You have now recited the sutras of Great Extent, the Great-vehicle. In these sutras the buddhas of all directions preach that their forms and bodies are not extinct. You have now been able to see them—is this not true? The evil of your eye-organ often does much harm to you. Obediently following my words, you must take refuge in the buddhas and Sakyamuni Buddha, and confess the sins due to your organ of the eye, saying: 'Law-water of wisdom-eye

5. This symbolizes illusions, because the illusions preventing living beings from attaining knowledge are as innumerable as atoms of dust.

possessed by the buddhas and the bodhisattvas! Be pleased, by means of it, to wash me and to let me become pure!'

"Having finished speaking thus, the follower should universally salute the buddhas in all directions, and turning to Sakyamuni Buddha and the Great-vehicle sutras, he should again speak thus: 'The heavy sins of my eye-organ of which I now repent are such an impediment and are so tainted that I am blind and can see nothing at all. May the Buddha be pleased to pity and protect me by his great mercy! The Bodhisattva Universal Virtue on board the ship of the great Law ferries the company of the countless bodhisattvas everywhere in all directions. Out of compassion for me, be pleased to permit me to hear the law of repenting the evil of my eye-organ and the impediment of my bad karma!'

"Speaking thus three times, the follower must prostrate himself down to the ground and rightly reflect on the Great-vehicle without forgetting it. This is called the law repenting the sin of the organ of the eye. If there be anyone who calls upon the names of the buddhas, burns incense, strews flowers, aspires to the Great-vehicle, hangs silks, flags, and canopies, speaks of the errors of his eyes, and repents his sins, such a one in the present world will see Sakyamuni Buddha, the buddhas who emanated from him, and countless other buddhas, and will not fall into the evil paths for *asaṃkhyeya kalpas*. Thanks to the power and to the vow of the Great-vehicle, such a one will become an attendant of the buddhas, together with all the bodhisattvas of *dhāraṇī*. Anyone who reflects thus is one who thinks rightly. If anyone reflects otherwise, such is called one who thinks falsely. This is called the sign of the first stage of the purification of the eye-organ."

Next the Buddha teaches the follower that he should not be satisfied with the purification of his eye-organ but should further practice repentance. How he should do this the Buddha shows him in the following words: "Having finished purifying the organ of the eye, the follower should again further read and recite the Great-vehicle sutras, kneel and repent six times day and night, and should speak thus: 'Why can I only see Sakyamuni Buddha and the buddhas who emanated from him, but cannot see the Buddha's relics of his whole body in the stupa of the Buddha Abundant Treasures? The stupa of the Buddha Abundant Treasures exists forever and is not extinct. I have defiled and evil eyes. For this reason, I cannot see the stupa.' After speaking thus, the follower should again practice further repentance."

As preached in chapter 11 of the Lotus Sutra, the Buddha Abundant Treasures appears in order to bear testimony that all that the Tathāgata Sakyamuni says is true. Thus, the follower should be stern toward himself and not deceive himself. If he does not have a full understanding of any of the Buddha's teachings, he must criticize himself for his imperfection and repent of it. After seven days, his repentance will be rewarded as follows: "After seven days have passed, the stupa of the Buddha Abundant Treasures will spring out of the earth. Sakyamuni Buddha with his right hand opens the door of the stupa, where the Buddha Abundant Treasures is seen deep in the contemplation of the universal revelation of forms. From each pore of his body he emits rays of light as numerous as the atoms of the sands of the Ganges. In each ray there dwells one of the hundred thousand myriad *koṭis* of transformed buddhas. When such a sign appears, the follower will rejoice and make procession around the stupa with praising verses. When he has finished making procession around it seven times, the Tathāgata Abundant Treasures with a great voice praises him, saying: 'Heir of the Law! You have truly practiced the Great-vehicle and have obediently followed Universal Virtue, repenting the sins of your eye-organ. For this reason, I will go to you and bear testimony to you.' Having spoken thus, the Tathāgata extols the Buddha, saying: 'Excellent! Excellent! Sakyamuni Buddha! Thou art able to preach the great Law, to pour the rain of the great Law, and to cause all the defiled living to accomplish their buddhahood.' Thereupon the follower, having beheld the stupa of the Buddha Abundant Treasures, again goes to the Bodhisattva Universal Virtue, and folding his hands and saluting him, speaks to him, saying: 'Great teacher! Please teach me the repentance of my errors.' "

The contemplation of the universal revelation of forms means the contemplation in which the bodies or forms of the Buddha Abundant Treasures appear everywhere. This expression teaches us that if we attain the mental stage of realizing thoroughly the absolute truth of the Buddha's teachings, we can see the Buddha Abundant Treasures at any time.

THE SINS OF ONE'S EARS. The Buddha continued: "Universal Virtue again speaks to the follower, saying: 'Through many *kalpas*, because of your ear-organ, you dangle after external sounds; your hearing of mystic sounds begets attachment to them; your hearing of evil sounds causes the harm of one hundred and eight illusions. Such retribution of your hearing evils brings about evil things and your incessant hearing of evil sounds produces various entanglements. Because of your perverted hearing, you will fall into evil paths, faraway places of false views, where the Law cannot be heard. At present you have recited and kept the Great-vehicle, the ocean-store of merits. For this reason, you have come to see the buddhas in all directions, and the stupa of the Buddha Abundant Treasures has appeared to bear testimony to you. You must yourself confess your own errors and evils and must repent all your sins.' "

Good advice for everyone is included in the above paragraph. Ordinary people have a regrettable tendency to take amiss what others say. This habit is shown at its worst in gossip. When we interpret unfavorably what others say, we become obsessed by prejudice and foster the spirit of hatred and enmity. We must be most careful to guard against such a habit in our daily lives.

"Then the follower, having heard thus, must again further fold his hands, and prostrating himself down to the ground, he must speak thus, saying: 'All Wise, World-honored One! Be pleased to reveal yourself and bear testimony to me! The sutras of Great Extent are the masters of compassion. Be pleased to look upon me and hear my words!' " The sentence "The sutras of Great Extent are the masters of compassion" is most important. It indicates the idea that the teachings of the Great-vehicle are the masters of compassion, that these teachings are the foundation of one's compassionate practice. One cannot truly raise the spirit of compassion and practice deeds of compassion until one realizes that all people equally possess the buddha-nature.

" 'Until my present life, for many *kalpas,* because of my ear-organ, I have been attached to hearing evil sounds, like glue sticking to grass; my hearing of evil sounds causes the poison of illusions which are attached to every condition and I am not able to rest even for a little while; my raising evil sounds fatigues my nerves and makes me fall into the three evil ways. Now having for the first time understood this, I confess and repent it, turning to the world-honored ones.' Having finished repenting thus, the follower will see the Buddha Abundant Treasures emitting a great ray of light which is gold-colored and universally illuminates the eastern quarter as well as the worlds in all directions, where the countless buddhas appear with their bodies of pure gold color. In the sky of the eastern quarter there comes a voice uttering thus: 'Here is a buddha, the world-honored one named Excellent Virtue, who also possesses innumerable emanated buddhas sitting cross-legged on lion thrones under jewel trees. All these world-honored ones who enter into the contemplation of universal revelation of forms speak to the follower, praising him and saying: "Good! Good! Good son! You have now read and recited the Great-vehicle sutras. That which you have recited is the mental stage of the Buddha." ' "

After repenting thus, the follower purifies his mind still more and comes to be firmly aware that he is following the way to the mental stage of a buddha. However, his repentance does not end with this stage. The Bodhisattva Universal Virtue urges the follower to practice further repentance: "After these words have been spoken, the Bodhisattva Universal Virtue will again further preach to the follower the law of repentance, saying: 'In the innumerable *kalpas* of your former lives, because of your attachment to odors, your discrimination and your perception are attached to every condition and you fall into birth and death. Do you now meditate on the cause of the Great-vehicle! The cause of the Great-vehicle is the Reality of All Existence.'

"Having heard these words, the follower should again further repent, prostrating himself down to the ground. When he has repented, he should exclaim thus: '*Namaḥ* Sakyamuni Buddha! *Namaḥ* stupa of the Buddha Abundant Treasures! *Namaḥ* all the buddhas emanated from Sakyamuni Buddha!' Having spoken thus, he should universally salute the buddhas in all directions, exclaiming: '*Namaḥ* the Buddha Excellent Virtue in the eastern quarter and the buddhas who emanated from him!' The follower should also make obeisance to each of these buddhas as wholeheartedly as if he saw them with his naked eyes, and should pay homage to them with incense and flowers. After paying homage to the buddhas, he should kneel with folded hands and extol them with various verses. After extolling them, he should speak of the ten evil karmas and repent all his sins. Having repented, he should speak thus, saying: 'During the innumerable *kalpas* of my former lives, I yearned after odors, flavors, and contacts and produced all manner of evils. For this reason, for innumerable lives I have continuously received states of evil existence including hells, hungry spirits, animals, and faraway places of false views. Now I confess such evil karmas, and taking refuge in the buddhas, the kings of the Righteous Law, I confess and repent my sins.'

"Having repented thus, the follower must again read and recite the Great-vehicle sutras without negligence of body and mind. By the power of the Great-vehicle, from the sky there comes a voice saying: 'Heir of the Law! Do you now praise and explain the Law of the Great-vehicle, turning to the buddhas in all directions, and before them do you yourself speak of your errors! The buddhas, the *tathāgatas,* are your merciful fathers.' "

The words "the buddhas, the *tathāgatas,* are your merciful fathers" are very important. Because the follower has repeatedly practiced repentance to the point of being extremely severe with himself, some people, taking a superficial view of such repentance, may feel oppressed. Other people may regard the repenting follower as a pitiable person who trembles with fear and prostrates himself before a ruler sternly scrutinizing his sins, confesses them, and begs the ruler's pardon. However, such an idea is greatly mistaken. The buddhas are our merciful fathers, who think only of the salvation of all living beings. Therefore the buddhas praise us because through our repentance we remove defilements from our mind little by little. We do not practice repentance because we fear the buddhas but rather with the hope of being extolled by the buddhas, for whom we cherish a longing desire and a thirsting heart. The expression "the buddhas, the *tathāgatas,* are your merciful fathers" has this profound significance.

THE SINS OF ONE'S TONGUE. Following is the description of the repentance of the sins of one's tongue. One's tongue, moved by evil thoughts, produces various kinds of sins. Rectifying these necessitates rectifying one's mind. Conversely, careless words often cause one to develop evil thoughts. One ought to be especially cautious of one's tongue because both mind and words can be the cause as well as the effect of evil.

"Do you yourself speak of the evils and bad karmas produced by your organ of the tongue, saying: 'This organ of the tongue, moved by the thought of evil karmas, causes me to praise false speaking, improper language, ill speaking, a double tongue, slandering, lying, and words of false views, and also causes me to utter useless words. Because of such many and various evil karmas I provoke fights and dissensions and speak of the Law as if it were not the Law. I now confess all such sins of mine.' "

"Useless words" may be regarded as not particularly harmful. However, if a person indulges in idle talk, his mind will become dulled and he will depart from the habit of thinking of and discussing meaningful things. This is why we should try to refrain from useless and meaningless talk.

"Having spoken thus before the world's heroes, the follower must universally revere the buddhas in all directions, prostrating himself down to the ground, and folding his hands and kneeling salute them, and he must speak thus, saying: 'The errors of this tongue are numberless and boundless. All the thorns of evil karmas come from the organ of the tongue. This tongue causes the cutting off of the wheel of the Righteous Law. Such an evil tongue cuts off the seeds of merits. Preaching of meaningless things is frequently forced upon others. Praising false views is like adding wood to a fire and further wounding living beings who already suffer in raging flames. It is like one who dies drinking poison without showing sores or pustules. Such reward of sins is evil, false, and bad, and causes me to fall into evil paths for a hundred or a thousand *kalpas*. Lying causes me to fall into a great hell. I now take refuge in the buddhas of the southern quarter and confess my errors and sins.'

"When the follower reflects thus, there will come a voice from the sky saying: 'In the southern quarter there is a buddha named Sandalwood Virtue who also possesses countless emanated buddhas. All these buddhas preach the Great-vehicle and extinguish sins and evils. Turning to the innumerable buddhas and the great merciful world-honored ones in all directions, you must confess such sins, false evils, and repent them with a sincere heart.' When these words have been spoken, the follower should again salute the buddhas, prostrating himself down to the ground.

"Thereupon the buddhas will send forth rays of light which illuminate the follower's body and cause him naturally to feel joy of body and mind, to raise a great mercy, and to reflect on all things extensively. At that time the buddhas will widely preach to the follower the law of great kindness, compassion, joy, and indifference, and also teach him kind words to make him practice the six ways of harmony and reverence. Then the follower, having heard this royal teaching, will greatly rejoice in his heart and will again further recite and study it without laziness."

Joy and indifference are two of the four infinite virtues. The infinite virtue of joy means enjoying the sight of those who have obtained happiness. That of indifference signifies abandoning attachment to the benefits one gives to others and even to the harm he receives from his enemies. Taken all together, the words "joy and indifference" indicate a mental attitude in which one abandons attachment to himself and thinks only of the benefit of others.

The expression "kind words" means affectionate words, one of the four virtues of the bodhisattva. The six ways of harmony and reverence are the six kinds of practices through which believers harmonize with and respect each other in the course of seeking enlightenment.

THE SINS OF ONE'S BODY AND MIND. The Buddha continued: "From the sky there again comes a mystic voice, speaking thus: 'Do you now practice the repentance of body and mind! The sins of the body are killing, stealing, and committing adultery, while the sins of the mind are entertaining thoughts of various evils. Producing the ten evil karmas and the five deadly sins is just like living as a monkey, like birdlime and glue, and the attachment to all sorts of conditions leads universally to the passions of the six sense organs of all living beings. The karmas of these six organs with their boughs, twigs, flowers, and leaves entirely fill the triple world, the twenty-five abodes of living beings, and all the places where creatures are born. Such karmas also increase ignorance, old age, death, and the twelve sufferings and infallibly reach through to the eight falsenesses and the eight circumstances. Do you now repent such evil and bad karmas!' "

The five deadly sins are killing one's father, killing one's mother, killing an *arhat,* injuring the body of a buddha, and causing disunity in the community of monks. Those who commit these five sins will fall into the Avīci hell. The twenty-five abodes of living beings are the four evil worlds (the hells, animals, hungry spirits, and *asuras*), the four continents of the world of men, the six heavens of the world of desire, the seven heavens of the world of form, and the four heavens of the formless world. The eight circumstances indicate the eight conditions in which one is unable to see the Buddha or hear the Law. These are hell, animals, hungry spirits, the heaven of long life, remote places, the state of being blind or deaf, secular prejudice, and the period of the Buddha's absence.

"Then the follower, having heard thus, asks the voice in the sky, saying: 'At which place may I practice the law of repentance?'

"Thereupon the voice in the sky will speak thus, saying: 'Sakyamuni Buddha is called Vairocana Who Pervades All Places, and his dwelling place is called Eternally Tranquil Light, the place which is composed of permanency-*pāramitā* and stabilized by self-*pāramitā,* the place where purity-*pāramitā* extinguishes the aspect of existence, where bliss-*pāramitā* does not abide in the aspect of one's body and mind, and where the aspects of all laws cannot be seen as either existing or nonexisting, the place of tranquil emancipation or *prajñā-pāramitā*. Because these forms are based on permanent law, thus you must now meditate on the buddhas in all directions.' "

The expressions "Vairocana Who Pervades All Places" and "Eternally Tranquil Light," like those that follow, signify the transcending of all limitations of time and space, based on the idea of *śūnya,* or the void (explained below). Positively, it means the absolute universality of the Buddha and the Buddha-land.

"Then the buddhas in all directions will each stretch out their right hands, laying them on the head of the follower, and will speak thus: 'Good! Good! Good son! Because you have now read and recited the Great-vehicle sutras, the buddhas in all directions will preach the law of repentance. The bodhisattva practice is not to cut off binding and driving nor to abide in the ocean of driving. In meditating on one's mind, there is no mind one can seize, except the mind that comes from one's perverted thought. The mind presenting such a form rises from one's false imagination like the wind in the sky, which has no foothold. Such a form of the law neither appears nor disappears. What is sin? What is blessedness? As one's own mind is void of itself, sin and blessedness have no existence. In like manner all the laws are neither fixed nor going toward destruction. If one repents like this, meditating on his mind, there is no mind he can seize. The law also does not dwell in the law. All the laws are emancipation, the truth of extinction, and quiescence. Such an aspect is called the great repentance, the greatly adorned repentance, the repentance of the non-sin aspect, and the destruction of discrimination. He who practices this repentance has the purity of body and mind not fixed in the law but free as flowing water. Through each reflection, he will be able to see the Bodhisattva Universal Virtue and the buddhas in all directions."

"Thereupon all the world-honored ones, sending forth the ray of light of great mercy, preach the law of nonaspect to the follower. He hears the world-honored ones preaching the Void of the first principle. When he has heard it, his mind becomes imperturbable. In due time, he will enter into the real bodhisattva standing."

"Binding and driving" is a Buddhist term denoting defilement, which binds human beings to transmigration and drives them to the world of sufferings. The bodhisattva practice is the middle way between excessive austerity and excessive indulgence. In the words "void of itself," "void," *śūnya* or *śūnyatā* in Sanskrit, means first nonsubstance, and second nonattachment. The expression "sin and blessedness have no existence" signifies the state of nonatatchment, that is, *śūnya.* When a person reaches the state of nonattachment, the problem of good and evil is eliminated.

The Buddha addressed Ānanda: "To practice in this manner is called repentance. This is the law of repentance which the buddhas and great bodhisattvas in all directions practice. After the extinction of the Buddha, if all his disciples should repent their evil and bad karmas, they must only read and recite the Great-vehicle sutras. These sutras of Great Extent are the eyes of the buddhas. By means of the sutras the buddhas have perfected the five kinds of eyes. The three kinds of the Buddha's bodies grow out of the sutras of Great Extent. This is the seal of the great Law with which the ocean of nirvana is sealed. From such an ocean are born the three kinds of pure bodies of the Buddha. These three kinds of the Buddha's bodies are the blessing-field for gods and men, and the supreme object of the worship. If there be any who recite and read the sutras of Great Extent, the Great-vehicle, know that such are endowed with the Buddha's merits, and having extinguished their longstanding evils, are born of the Buddha's wisdom."

The five kinds of eyes are (1) the eye of those who have a material body; (2) the divine eye of celestial beings in the realm of form; (3) the eye of wisdom, by which the followers of the two vehicles perceive the nonsubstantiality of things; (4) the eye of the Law, by which the bodhisattvas perceive all teachings in order to lead human beings to enlightenment; and (5) the Buddha's eye, the four kinds of eyes enumerated above existing in the Buddha's body.

Then the World-honored One repeated the gist of his teaching in verse:

"If one has evil in his eye-organ
And his eyes are impure with the impediment of karmas,
He must only recite the Great-vehicle
And reflect on the first principle.
This is called the repentance of the eye,
Ending all bad karmas.
His ear-organ hears disordered sounds
And disturbs the principle of harmony.
This produces in him a demented mind,
Like that of a foolish monkey.

He must only recite the Great-vehicle
And meditate on the void nonaspect of the Law,
Ending all the longstanding evils,
So that with the heavenly ears he may hear sounds from all directions.
His organ of smell is attached to all odors,
Causing all contacts according to lusts.
His nose thus deluded
Gives birth to all dust of illusions according to his lusts.
If one recites the Great-vehicle sutras
And meditates on the fundamental truth of the Law,
He will become free from his longstanding evil karmas,
And will not again produce them in his future lives.
His organ of the tongue causes five kinds
Of bad karmas of evil speech.
Should one wish to control them by himself,
He must zealously practice mercy,
And considering the true principle of quiescence of the Law,
He should not conceive discriminations.
His organ of thought is like that of a monkey,
Never resting even for a little while.
Should one desire to subdue this organ,
He must zealously recite the Great-vehicle,
Reflecting on the Buddha's greatly enlightened body,
The completion of his power, and his fearlessness.
The body is the master of its organs,
As wind causes dust to roll,
Wandering in its six organs,
Freely without obstacles.
If one desires to destroy these evils,
To be removed from the longstanding illusions of dust,
Ever dwelling in the city of nirvana,
And to be at ease with mind tranquil,
He should recite the Great-vehicle sutras
And reflect on the mother of bodhisattvas.[6]
Innumerable surpassing means of tactfulness
Will be obtained through one's reflection on reality.

6. This refers to the doctrine of the Great-vehicle as the mother and supporter of the bodhisattvas.

Such six laws
Are called the purification of the six sense organs.
The ocean of impediment of all karmas
Is produced from one's false imagination.
Should one wish to repent of it
Let him sit upright and meditate on the true aspect of reality.
All sins are just as frost and dew,
So wisdom's sun can disperse them.
Therefore with entire devotion
Let him repent of his six sense organs."

The essence of repentance in Buddhism is summed up in the following lines from the above verses:

"Should one wish to repent of it
Let him sit upright and meditate on the true aspect of reality.
All sins are just as frost and dew,
So wisdom's sun can disperse them."

These lines are so sacred and important that we should learn them by heart and constantly keep them in mind.

THE MERITS OF REPENTANCE. Having spoken these verses, the Buddha again addressed Ānanda: "Do you now repent of these six organs, keep the law of meditating on the Bodhisattva Universal Virtue, and discriminate and explain it widely to all the gods of the universe and men. After the extinction of the Buddha, if all his disciples receive and keep, read and recite, and expound the sutras of Great Extent, whether in a quiet place or in a graveyard, or under a tree, or in a place of the *āraṇya,* they must read and recite the sutras of Great Extent, and must think of the meaning of the Great-vehicle. By virtue of the strong power of their reflecting on the sutras, they will be able to see myself, the stupa of the Buddha Abundant Treasures, the countless emanated buddhas from all directions, the Bodhisattva Universal Virtue, the Bodhisattva Mañjuśrī, the Bodhisattva Medicine King, and the Bodhisattva Medicine Lord. By virtue of their revering the Law, these buddhas and bodhisattvas, abiding in the sky with various wonderful flowers, will extol and revere those who practice and keep the Law. By virtue of their only reciting the sutras of Great Extent, the Great-vehicle, the buddhas and bodhisattvas will day and night pay homage to those who keep the Law.

"I as well as the bodhisattvas in the Virtuous *kalpa*[7] and the buddhas in all directions, by means of our thinking of the true meaning of the Great-vehicle, have now rid ourselves of the sins of birth and death during hundreds of myriad *koṭis* of *asaṃkhyeya kalpas.* By means of this supreme and wonderful law of repentance, we have each become the buddhas in all directions. If one desires to accomplish Perfect Enlightenment rapidly and wishes in his present life to see the buddhas in all directions and the Bodhisattva Universal Virtue, he must take a bath to purify himself, wear clean robes, and burn rare incense, and must dwell in a secluded place, where he should recite and read the Great-vehicle sutras and think of the meaning of the Great-vehicle.

"If there are living beings who desire to meditate on the Bodhisattva Universal Virtue, they must meditate thus. If anyone meditates thus, such is called one who meditates rightly. If anyone meditates otherwise, such is called one who meditates falsely. After the extinction of the Buddha, if all his disciples obediently follow the Buddha's words and practice repentance, let it be known that these are doing the work of Universal Virtue. Those who do the work of Universal Virtue see neither evil aspects nor the retribution of evil karmas. If there be any living beings who salute the buddhas in all directions six times day and night, recite the Great-vehicle sutras, and consider the profound Law of the Void of the first principle, they will rid themselves of the sins of birth and death produced during hundreds of myriad *koṭis* of *asaṃkhyeya kalpas* in the short time it takes one to snap his fingers. Anyone doing this work is a real Buddha-son who is born from the buddhas. The buddhas in all directions and the bodhisattvas will become his preceptors. This is called one who is perfect in the precepts of the bodhisattvas. Without going through the ceremony of confession, he will of himself accomplish bodhisattvahood and will be revered by all the gods and men."

A preceptor is a teacher who gives the Buddhist precepts to one who is becoming a monk in a ceremony in which the latter vows to observe the precepts. Here it is confirmed that the buddhas in all directions and the bodhisattvas will become the preceptors of a real Buddha-son, one who is perfect in the precepts of the bodhisattvas.

The "ceremony of confession," called *jñapti-karman* in Sanskrit, is a ceremony in which a person confesses transgressions of the rules of discipline that the Buddha set forth for monks and nuns (see also below,

7. The present *kalpa,* also known as the *kalpa* of the sages.

page 457). Here it is said that without going through such ceremony of confession, a real Buddha-son will of himself accomplish bodhisattva-hood and will be revered by all the gods and men.

Next, the Buddha teaches the follower to practice repentance in the following way if he desires to be perfect in the precepts of the bodhisattva: "At that time, if the follower desires to be perfect in the precepts of the bodhisattva, he must fold his hands, dwell in the seclusion of the wilds, universally salute the buddhas in all directions, and repent his sins, and must himself confess his errors. After this, in a calm place, he should speak to the buddhas in all directions, saying thus: 'The buddhas, the world-honored ones, remain forever in this world. Because of the impediments of my karmas, though I believe in the sutras of Great Extent, I cannot clearly see the buddhas. I have now taken refuge in the buddhas. Be pleased, Sakyamuni Buddha, All Wise and World-honored One, to be my preceptor! Mañjuśrī, possessor of great compassion! With your wisdom, be pleased to bestow on me the laws of pure bodhisattvas! Bodhisattva Maitreya, supreme and great merciful sun! Out of your compassion for me, be pleased to permit me to receive the laws of the bodhisattvas! Buddhas in all directions! Be pleased to reveal yourselves and bear testimony to me! Great bodhisattvas! Through calling each upon your names, be pleased, supreme great leaders, to protect all living beings and to help us! At present I have received and kept the sutras of Great Extent. Even if I should lose my life, fall into hell, and receive innumerable sufferings, I would never slander the Righteous Law of the buddhas. For this reason and by the power of this merit, Sakyamuni Buddha! Be now pleased to be my preceptor! Mañjuśrī! Be pleased to be my teacher! Maitreya in the world to come! Be pleased to bestow on me the Law! Buddhas in all directions! Be pleased to bear witness to me! Bodhisattvas of great virtues! Be pleased to be my friends! I now, by means of the profound and mysterious meaning of the Great-vehicle sutras, take refuge in the Buddha, take refuge in the Law, and take refuge in the Saṃgha.' "

The Buddha tells the follower to say this three times. The faith and desires of Buddhists are summed up in this paragraph. The expressions "Be pleased to reveal yourselves and bear testimony to me" and "Be pleased to bear witness to me" mean, "I call all the buddhas to witness whether I practice my vows or not." The words "supreme great leaders" refer to the bodhisattvas.

"Even if I should lose my life, fall into hell, and receive innumerable sufferings, I would never slander the Righteous Law of the buddhas": this is the mental attitude of a true believer. When people do not obtain any apparent merit from their religious practices because of longstanding evil karmas from their former lives, they tend to slander God or the Buddha. In doing so, they let go their hold on the lifeline that can save them from suffering. No one who believes in the Righteous Law of the Buddha can fall into hell. Even if a believer in the Righteous Law should come to this, he must maintain his determination to persevere to the end. Such a person, having a pure mind devoted to his faith, will be saved naturally from his sufferings.

In the invocation "Mañjuśrī! Be pleased to be my teacher!" the word "teacher" means an eminent priest who, as the assistant of a preceptor, gives instruction to novices in the ceremony in which they receive the Buddhist precepts. "Maitreya in the world to come! Be pleased to bestow on me the Law!" indicates the follower's desire to receive the Law from the Bodhisattva Maitreya, who it is believed will appear in this *sahā*-world 5,670,000,000 years after the *parinirvāṇa* of Sakyamuni Buddha. "Be pleased to be my friends!" signifies the follower's wish for the bodhisattvas of great virtues to instruct him as his companions on the way to enlightenment. The final sentence mentions that the follower must take refuge in the Three Treasures of the Buddha, the Law, and the Saṃgha. The meaning of the Three Treasures has been discussed in detail in chapter 16.

The Buddha continued: "The follower must speak thus three times. Having taken refuge in the Three Treasures, next he must himself vow to receive the sixfold laws. Having received the sixfold laws, next he must zealously practice the unhindered brahma-conduct, raise the mind of universally saving all living beings, and receive the eightfold laws. Having made such vows, in the seclusion of the wilds, he must burn rare incense, strew flowers, pay homage to all the buddhas, the bodhisattvas, and the sutras of Great Extent, the Great-vehicle, and must speak thus, saying: 'I have now raised the aspiration to buddhahood: may this merit save all the living!'

"Having spoken thus, the follower should again further prostrate himself before all the buddhas and the bodhisattvas, and should think of the meaning of the sutras of Great Extent. During a day or three times seven days, whether he be a monk or a layman, he has no need of a preceptor, nor does he need to employ any teacher; even without attending the ceremony of the *jñapti-karman,* because of the power coming from his receiving and keeping, reading and reciting the Great-vehicle sutras and because of the works which the Bodhisattva Universal Virtue helps and inspires him to do—they are in fact the eyes of the Righteous Law of the buddhas in all directions—he will be able, through this law, to perform by himself the five kinds of Law-bodies: precepts, meditation, wisdom, emancipation, and knowledge of emancipation. All the buddhas, the *tathāgatas,* have been born of this Law and have received the prediction of their enlightenment in the Great-vehicle sutras."

The sixfold laws are the following six Buddhist precepts: not to take life, not to steal, to refrain from wrong sexual activity, not to lie, not to drink intoxicants, and not to speak of other people's faults. The eightfold laws are the preceding six precepts plus two others: not to conceal one's faults and not to emphasize other people's shortcomings rather than their good points. *Jñapti-karman* is a compound word having two meanings; *jñapti* signifies announcement or declaration, while *karman* means the proceedings at a meeting of a Buddhist assembly. This is part of the Buddhist ordination ceremony, in which the candidate confesses his past sins and vows to follow the Buddha's teachings.

THE REPENTANCE OF THE THREE MAJOR CLASSES. Next the Buddha preaches the repentance that must be practiced by each of the major classes: *śrāvakas* (monks), *upāsakas* (male lay devotees), and all people, including kings, ministers, Brahmans, citizens, elders, state officials, and so on. "Therefore, O wise man! Suppose that a *śrāvaka* breaks the threefold refuge, the five precepts, and the eight precepts, the precepts of *bhikshus,* of *bhikshuṇīs,* of *śrāmaṇeras,* of *śrāmaṇerikās,* and of *śikshamāṇās* and their dignified behavior, and also suppose that because of his foolishness, evil, and bad and false mind he infringes many precepts and the rules of dignified behavior. If he desires to rid himself of and destroy these errors, to become a *bhikshu* again and to fulfill the laws of monks, he must diligently read the sutras of Great Extent, considering the profound Law of the Void of the first principle, and must bring this wisdom of the Void to his heart; know that in each one of his thoughts such a one will gradually end the defilement of all his longstanding sins without any remainder—this is called one who is perfect in the laws and the precepts of monks and fulfills their dignified behavior. Such a one will be served by all gods and men."

The five precepts are not to take life, not to steal, to refrain from wrong sexual activity, not to lie, and not to drink intoxicants. The eight precepts are the preceding five plus three others: to avoid perfume, dancing, and the theater; not to sit or sleep in an adorned chair; and not to eat after noon. A *śrāmaṇera* is a novice who has received the ten precepts, after which he may become a *śramaṇa,* a monk or ascetic. A *śikshamāṇā* is a female novice between the ages of eighteen and twenty who practices the five general precepts and the additional one of not eating at unregulated hours.

The Buddha continued: "Suppose any *upāsaka* violates his dignified behavior and does bad things. To do bad things means, namely, to proclaim the errors and sins of the Buddha-laws, to discuss evil things perpetrated by the four groups, and not to feel shamed even in committing theft and adultery. If he desires to repent and rid himself of these sins, he must zealously read and recite the sutras of Great Extent and must think of the first principle. Suppose a king, a minister, a Brahman, a citizen, an elder, a state official, all of these persons seek greedily and untiringly after desires, commit the five deadly sins, slander the sutras of Great Extent, and perform the ten evil karmas. Their recompense for these great evils will cause them to fall into evil paths faster than the breaking of a rainstorm. They will be sure to fall into the Avīci hell. If they desire to rid themselves of and destroy these impediments of karmas, they must raise shame and repent all their sins.

"Why is it called a law of repentance of *Kshatriyas* and citizens? The law of repentance of *Kshatriyas* and citizens is that they must constantly have the right mind, not slander the Three Treasures nor hinder the monks nor persecute anyone practicing brahma-conduct; they must not forget to practice the law of the six reflections; they must again support, pay homage to, and surely salute the keeper of the Great-vehicle; they must remember the profound doctrine of sutras and the Void of the first principle. One who thinks of this law is called one who practices the first repentance of *Kshatriyas* and citizens. Their second repentance is to discharge their filial duty to their fathers and mothers and to respect their teachers and seniors—this is called one who practices the law of the second repentance. Their third repentance is to rule their countries with the Righteous Law and not to oppress their people unjustly—this is called one who practices the third repentance. Their fourth repentance is to issue within their states the ordinance of the six days of fasting and to cause their people to abstain from killing wherever their powers reach. One who practices such a law is called one who practices the fourth repentance. Their fifth repentance is to believe deeply the causes and results of things, to have faith in the way of one reality, and to know that the Buddha is never extinct—this is called one who practices the fifth repentance."

The law of the six reflections means to reflect on the six important things: the Buddha, the Law, the Saṃgha, the precepts, gift-giving, and the heavens. Here we can interpret "the heavens" as meaning to remain untainted with worldly defilements. The six days of fasting are the days of purification, on which offerings are made to the dead. The six days are the eighth, fourteenth, fifteenth, twenty-third, twenty-ninth, and thirtieth days of the month, on which laymen observe the eight precepts; in Japanese they are called the *roku sainichi,* or six days of fasting. Interpreted in modern terms, the expression "to issue within their state the ordinance of the six days of fasting and to cause their people to abstain from killing wherever their powers reach" means that all people should respect the lives of all creatures.

The phrase "the cause and result of things," found in the fifth repentance, indicates the fundamental principle that if one sows good seed, he will surely reap a good harvest; if he sows bad seed, he must inevitably reap a bad harvest. Though the results may appear quickly or slowly, everyone will be sure to receive the results that accord with their actions. Anyone who has deeply understood this principle will never do evil. In the phrase "the way of one reality," "one reality" means only one truth, namely, the immutable one existence (truth, or the Buddha) among the various changing phenomena of this world.

"The Buddha addressed Ānanda: 'If, in future worlds, there be any who practices these laws of repentance, know that such a man has put on the robes of shame, is protected and helped by the buddhas, and will attain Perfect Enlightenment before long.' As these words were spoken, ten thousand divine sons acquired pure spiritual eyes, and also the great bodhisattvas, the Bodhisattva Maitreya and others, and Ānanda, hearing the preaching of the Buddha, all rejoiced and did as the Buddha commanded."

The Sutra of Meditation on the Bodhisattva Universal Virtue ends with these words. I am afraid that some readers may have found it hard to understand fully some parts of the sutra because it is very profound and difficult in content. However, we may say in conclusion that repentance is to learn the teaching of the Great-vehicle and to practice it. Repentance means not compromising with oneself, not having a lukewarm or equivocal attitude, but polishing one's buddha-nature by gradually removing illusions and defilements from one's mind. The practice of repentance consists in the bodhisattva practice, through which one not only polishes his buddha-nature but also renders service to others. Repentance is an indispensable requisite of religious life. It is to be hoped that all people will repeatedly read and recite this sutra on repentance, realize its essence, and put it into practice in their daily lives.

Here ends the commentary on the Threefold Lotus Sutra. When you have read through the entire Threefold Lotus Sutra and have examined yourself in the light of its teachings, you may find that the actual state of your mind is so imperfect as to seem hopeless, and you may feel at a loss as to what to do. I was told that someone confessed that he found it hard to approach the Lotus Sutra again after having read it because of its extreme profundity. I can understand why he felt cowed by the profundity of the sutra. I suspect, however, that he had not read the sutra deeply enough, and that if he had read it repeatedly, he would have come to regard it as the teaching capable of leading all of us directly to salvation. We should start our practice from even one teaching in the Lotus Sutra and from even the smallest act in our daily lives. The sutra itself exhorts us not to think that its teachings are beyond our capacities.

There is an appropriate story in the Sutra of a Hundred Parables (*Hyakuyu-kyō*) with which I would like to conclude. Once there was a very stupid man. As he was parched with thirst, he roamed here and there looking for water. While walking about, he luckily arrived at the shore of the Sindh River. For some reason, however, he just stood on the riverbank instead of drinking. A friend nearby wondered at his behavior and asked him, "Why don't you drink the water in the river?" The man answered, "I am dying for a drink! But the river has so much water that I cannot possibly drink it all. So I am hesitating as to whether I should drink or not."

I sincerely hope that no one will harbor such a foolish idea toward the teaching of the Threefold Lotus Sutra.

Index